# An Introduction to the Geography of Tourism

# An Introduction to the Geography of Tourism

Velvet Nelson

ROWMAN & LITTLEFIELD PUBLISHERS, INC.
*Lanham • Boulder • New York • Toronto • Plymouth, UK*

Published by Rowman & Littlefield Publishers, Inc.
A wholly owned subsidiary of The Rowman & Littlefield Publishing Group, Inc.
4501 Forbes Boulevard, Suite 200, Lanham, Maryland 20706
www.rowman.com

10 Thornbury Road, Plymouth PL6 7PP, United Kingdom

British Library Cataloguing in Publication Information Available

**Library of Congress Cataloging-in-Publication Data**
Nelson, Velvet, 1979–
  An introduction to the geography of tourism / Velvet Nelson.
    pages cm
  Includes bibliographical references and index.
  ISBN 978-1-4422-1071-4 (cloth : alk. paper) — ISBN 978-1-4422-1072-1 (pbk. : alk. paper) —
ISBN 978-1-4422-1073-8 (electronic) 1. Tourism—Environmental aspects. 2. Geographical
perception. I. Title.
  G156.5.E58N45 2013
  338.4'791—dc23
                                                                          2012050789

∞™ The paper used in this publication meets the minimum requirements of American
National Standard for Information Sciences—Permanence of Paper for Printed Library
Materials, ANSI/NISO Z39.48-1992.

Printed in the United States of America

# Contents

# Illustrations

## Figures

# Maps

# Tables

# Boxes

# Preface

When I undertook this project I first wondered if I would have enough material to fill a textbook. However, once I started working on it, I quickly realized that this concern was misplaced. Instead, I began to wonder how I was going to fit all of the material I wanted to cover into one textbook. The possibilities for subjects to be discussed in this book are endless. Making choices about what to include was made even more difficult by the fact that every day I would read about some new product, destination, issue, or trend in tourism.

My goal for this textbook was to provide a broad overview of tourism from a geographic perspective. I wanted it to help students in geography use the foundation that they've been building to learn about a new topic and to help students in tourism look at their topic from a new perspective. I drew from the ever-growing literature on tourism in general, and tourism geography specifically, and covered a wide range of subjects and approaches. But there is much more that could be done. For example, in chapter 3, I introduce a number of tourism products. For the most part, these are products that are useful in framing the discussions in subsequent chapters, such as the economic, social, and environmental issues associated with tourism. But these are only a small sampling. New products, designed for various purposes, needs, and/or special interests, are emerging all the time, including things like medical/dental tourism, roots tourism, dark tourism, slow tourism, slum tourism, creative tourism, tourism for peace, even space tourism. Each new product has its own implications, many of which still remain to be seen.

Tourism is clearly a dynamic industry, and the geography of tourism is an exciting field of study. This book is just a place to start. I encourage students to use this introduction as an opportunity to decide what part of the topic interests them most and learn more about it. For additional secondary research, begin by checking out the sources listed at the end of each chapter. However, in my opinion, a more in-depth knowledge of tourism geography requires *primary* research. For this, I recommend the participant observation methodology—get out there and experience it yourself!

There are, of course, many people who have made invaluable contributions to this project. I must first thank Susan McEachern, editorial director at Rowman & Littlefield Publishers, for her interest in publishing a book such as this, and her support throughout the entire process, as well as Dave Kaplan for suggesting the project in the first place. Thanks to Tom Nelson for all of the time he put in serving as my sounding board and proofreader, and also to Carolyn Nelson, Matt Stewart, Ava Fujimoto-Strait, and the spring 2012 GEO 3352 class for reading chapter drafts and providing feedback. Thanks also to Gang Gong for producing some of the maps used in the case studies. In addition, I am grateful to all of the family and friends who not only shared with me the travel photos and stories that appear in this book but also patiently answered my seemingly random questions, such as "Give me an example of a place that you've always wanted to go based on a movie." (Most common answer: "That place in Thailand from *The Beach*.") I appreciate all those who played along— although I did have to promise confidentiality to the source whose answer was "The redwood forests in California because of the Ewok scene in *Return of the Jedi*." Thanks also go to Rebecca Torres for introducing me to the geography of tourism, to Brian Cooper for agreeing with me that travel is an essential part of my job, and to Barret Bailey for providing me with support and encouragement.

# Abbreviations

| | |
|---|---|
| AAG | Association of American Geographers |
| BTA | Barbados Tourism Authority |
| CTC | Canadian Tourism Commission |
| CTD | central tourism district |
| CTO | Caribbean Tourism Organization |
| GIS | geographic information system |
| IGU | International Geographical Union |
| NCGE | National Council for Geographic Education |
| NGO | nongovernmental organization |
| NGS | National Geographic Society |
| PPT | pro-poor tourism |
| RGS | Royal Geographical Society |
| SIDS | small island developing states |
| TALC | tourist area life cycle |
| TIES | The International Ecotourism Society |
| TRA | tourism resource audit |
| UNESCO | United Nations Educational, Scientific, and Cultural Organization |
| UNODC | United Nations Office on Drugs and Crime |
| UNWTO | United Nations World Tourism Organization |
| WWF | World Wildlife Federation |

# Part I

# THE GEOGRAPHY OF TOURISM

While the study of tourism has at times been dismissed as the study of fun, tourism has an undeniable social, cultural, political, economic, and environmental impact on the world today. In fact, tourism has never been more important. The value of the tourism industry continues to increase. In 2011, international tourism receipts reached US$1,030 billion. At the same time, more people are participating in tourism than ever before. In 2012, international tourism arrivals were projected to exceed one billion for the first time. This perhaps surprisingly complex global phenomenon is naturally a topic of geographic inquiry, and geography has much to contribute to our understanding of tourism.

This section establishes the framework for our examination of the geography of tourism. Chapter 1 introduces the relationship between geography and tourism and outlines the thematic approach that will be used throughout the text. Chapter 2 lays the foundation for our discussion with the basic terminology of tourism and key concepts from the perspective of both the demand side of tourism and the supply side. Chapter 3 explores the concept of tourism products and introduces several products that will be referenced in the remaining sections.

# CHAPTER 1

# Geography and Tourism

At first glance, "the geography of tourism" appears to be a statistically improbable phrase. Individually, neither "geography" nor "tourism" is remarkable. After all, most people have some idea—albeit not always an accurate one—of each. It is the combination of the two that is unexpected. Yet if we look closer, we see that there's really nothing improbable about it. Admittedly, the phrase is not likely to become part of our everyday vocabulary anytime soon. Nonetheless, as we seek to develop a greater appreciation for and understanding of tourism, we will find the geography of tourism provides a powerful approach to the astonishingly complex phenomenon.

We typically think of tourism in terms of our own experiences. Tourism is something that we *do*: the vacation we took, the site we visited, or the place we've always wanted to go. Of course, we may not want to admit that we're tourists. We are all too familiar with the highly satirized images that have appeared in everything from classic literature to popular films in which tourists are characterized as overly pale (or conversely, badly sunburned), wearing loud print shirts and black socks with sandals, wielding cameras, brandishing maps and guidebooks, talking loudly, and eating ice cream. In this respect, we may actually think of tourism as something that we do *not* want to do: visit an overcrowded place filled with . . . tourists.

Beyond our own perspective, we may also think of tourism as an enormous global industry. Nearly every country in the world is now trying to get a piece of this multibillion-dollar business. It has become so economically significant that scarcely an event occurs where we do not hear about its potential impact on tourism.

There are many aspects of tourism that we generally do not think about. However, if we are to truly understand tourism, we must consider everything from the characteristics of the places that tourists are coming from to the characteristics of the places that they are visiting, how they are getting there, what they are doing, and what effects they have. Once we start to think about all of these things—and more—we begin to appreciate that this idea of tourism is far more complicated than we ever realized.

In recognition of this complexity, tourism studies have grown exponentially in recent years. Although new departments, schools, and faculties dedicated to tourism have been developed around the world, many programs—particularly in the United States—are housed in other schools. For example, it may be a part of a business school (e.g., an emphasis on tourism as an industry) or various health, leisure, and recreation departments (e.g., an emphasis on tourism as an activity). However, there is a largely underexplored and underutilized alternative: geography. Geography can provide the framework to help us understand this often-confusing mix of aspects, activities, and perspectives that constitute tourism.

Simply put, tourism is the subject of this textbook, and geography is the approach. In the chapters that follow, we will make an in-depth examination of tourism. We will first introduce the subject and then break it down with the use of different geographic themes or topics.

## What Is Geography?

While the question "what is geography?" seems simple enough, the answer often proves surprisingly elusive. We have heard the term "geography" all our lives. It is typically part of the primary school social studies curriculum. It is inherently tied to the popular *National Geographic* media. It is even a category in *Trivial Pursuit*. Yet, ideas that come from these sources—and others—do not make it any easier to answer the question. In fact, the more you know about the topic, the harder it becomes to produce a neat, concise definition that encompasses everything geography is and geographers do.

From the literal translation of the original Greek word, *geography* means "writing about or describing the earth." People have always had a desire to know and understand the world they live in. Particularly during the ages of exploration and empire, there was a distinct need for the description of new places that people encountered. People wanted to know *where* these new places were, but they also wanted to know *what* these places were like. This included both the physical characteristics of that place and the human characteristics. They wanted to know how these new places were similar to and different from those places with which they were familiar. Therefore, the description of places—where they were and what was there—provided vast amounts of geographic data.

Thus, geography and travel have long been interconnected. The fundamental curiosity about other places, and the tradition of travel to explore these places, continued with scientific travelers of the eighteenth and nineteenth centuries. Although Charles Darwin is the most famous of these, the German Alexander von Humboldt (1769–1859) was one of the most notable geographers. Geographic historian Geoffrey Martin argues that von Humboldt was one of the figures who played an important role in the transition between the classical era of geography and what geography would become in the modern era.[1] Von Humboldt traveled extensively in Eurasia and the Americas and produced a tremendous body of work based on his observations. Through his descriptions of traveling in and experiencing new places, he generated significant interest in geography and inspired subsequent generations of travelers, including Darwin himself.

By the contemporary period, geography had outgrown the classical tradition of description. There were few places left in the world that were uncharted. Although the need for description was diminished, the need to understand the world persisted.

In fact, this need seemed greater than ever before. The world was changing. Countless new patterns were emerging, new problems had to be faced, and new connections were forged between places. Having established the where and the what, geographers turned their attention to the *why*. Today, geographers continue to seek an understanding of the patterns of the world, everything from the physical processes that shape our environment to the various patterns of human life, and all of the ways in which the two—the physical and the human—come together, interact, and shape one another. Obviously, this is an enormous undertaking that involves an incredible diversity of work by geographers on topics like the processes of chemical weathering in the Himalayas, spatial modeling of deforestation in West Africa, natural resource management in Australia, the effect of extreme weather events on Central American coffee growers, the quantification of India's urban growth through the use of remote sensing data, American immigration patterns, the geographical dimensions of global pandemics, and more.

When we look at it this way, it shouldn't be surprising that it is no easy task to craft a definition that, in a few words, summarizes all of this. Over time, geographers and geographic associations have proposed compound definitions and frameworks to provide a mechanism for organizing the field. In one example, the Joint Committee on Geographic Education of the National Council for Geographic Education (NCGE) and the Association of American Geographers (AAG) proposed the following five themes in geography: (1) location, (2) place, (3) human-environment interactions, (4) movement, and (5) regions.[2] Frameworks such as this highlight some of the important concepts in geography and provide a starting point for discussing the ways in which geographers view the world. However, there is still no one universally accepted definition or set of concepts for geography.

Taking a different approach, we can return to geography's broad mandate of understanding the world. While this is an admirable goal, it is certainly an unrealistic task for any one geographer to take on alone. Therefore, geographers must necessarily break things down to understand particular parts of the world. On one hand, we can focus on the events and patterns of specific places or regions. Both place and region are identified as key themes in geography. **Regions** have long been a fundamental concept in geography as a means of effectively organizing and communicating spatial information. Essentially, regions help us break down the world into more manageable units. We can determine those areas of the earth's surface that have some commonality—based on a specific physical or human characteristic, like climate or religion, or a combination of characteristics—that distinguishes it from other parts of the world. Regions are still very much a part of the world that we live in. Not only do we continue to conceptualize the world in regional terms (e.g., Eastern Europe or the Middle East), but we have also seen an unprecedented rise in regional organizations in recent years (e.g., the North American Free Trade Agreement or the European Union). However, the concept of regions has, to some extent, been superseded by place in geography in recent years. **Place** generally refers to parts of the earth's surface that have meaning based on the physical and human features of that location.

On the other hand, we can focus on the issues associated with specific topics in geography. For example, figure 1.1 provides a graphic illustration of the discipline of

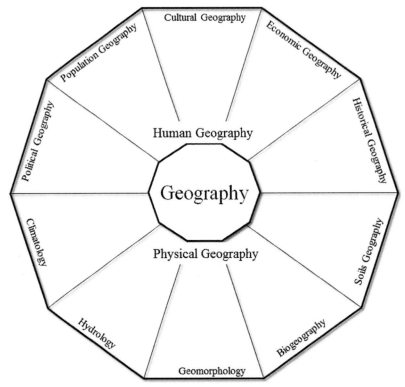

**Figure 1.1. This graphic representation of geography illustrates the topical approach in which the discipline is broken down based on various topics in human and physical geography. Topical geography allows us to understand a particular aspect of the world.**

geography. This diagram demonstrates a hierarchy of just some of the topics studied in geography. Geography as a whole is broken down into two principal subdivisions. **Human geography** is the subdivision that studies the patterns of human occupation of the earth, while **physical geography** is the subdivision that studies the earth's physical systems. These subdivisions are further broken down into the topical branches of geography. The subjects addressed by each of these topical branches, including everything from climate to culture, may be examined through the key concepts in geography.

Thus, **regional geography** studies the varied geographic characteristics of a region, while **topical geography** studies a particular geographic topic in various place or regional contexts. Both provide a means of helping us work toward the goal of understanding the world. That an understanding of the world is important should need no explanation. Yet, the widely publicized abysmal results of American eighteen-to-twenty-four-year-olds on the National Geographic-Roper Survey of Geographic Literacy in both 2002 and 2006 indicate that a knowledge of the geographic context of the world is sorely lacking.[3] This context is fundamental if we are to understand the varied and complex relationships between people and place in the ways that matter most. These may be the factors that affect our day-to-day lives or that shape the big topics of the world today, whether we are considering food security, international trade relations, the spread of AIDS, patterns of migration, global environmental change, or the massive human phenomenon we know as tourism.

# What Is Tourism?

The classic United Nations World Tourism Organization (UNWTO) definition (now also recognized by the United Nations Statistical Commission) considers **tourism** to be "the activities of persons traveling to and staying in places outside of their usual environment for not more than one consecutive year for leisure, business, and other purposes."[4] This is a broad definition that includes movement from one place to another, accommodation at the place of destination, and any activities undertaken in the process. Moreover, it accounts for different purposes. Leisure activities are most commonly associated with tourism, but this definition allows for business to be the primary motivation for travel, as well as "other purposes," which may include health, education, or visiting family and friends. While any of these may be the explicit reason for travel, there are also secondary reasons for both travel and any tourism activities undertaken at the destination.

While providing an encompassing description, this definition has limitations. It indicates that only movement that takes people away from their home environment for at least a day—and lasting a variable amount of time up to one year—would be considered tourism. As such, local and day trip activities would be classified as part of normal recreation activities undertaken in our **leisure time**, or the free time that we have left over after we have done what is necessary—from work to household chores to sleep—and during which we can do what we choose. Nevertheless, these people are often participating in the same activities that would be considered "tourism" for someone coming from farther away. Depending on one's starting location, day trips can even take place over international borders.

In addition, this definition focuses more on tourists and their activities—essentially the demand side of tourism. The concept of supply and demand has, of course, been borrowed from the field of economics. Adapted for the purpose of tourism, *demand* is defined as "the total number of persons who travel, or wish to travel, to use tourist facilities and services at places away from their places of work and residence."[5] When we think about experiences of tourism, we are thinking about the demand side of tourism. This is a fundamental component of tourism; essentially tourism would not exist without tourists and the demand for tourism experiences. *Supply* is defined as "the aggregate of all businesses that directly provide goods or services to facilitate business, pleasure, and leisure activities away from the home environment."[6] When we think about tourism as an industry, we are thinking about the supply side of tourism. Just as demand is a fundamental component of tourism, so is supply. Tourism necessarily involves the production of services and experiences. Although we are generally familiar with this side of tourism from participating in tourism in one form or another, few of us ever consider tourism beyond our own interests and experiences. In fact, the very nature of tourism often means that we don't *want* to have to think about all of the things that comprise the supply side of tourism and make our experiences possible.

Depending on our perspective, we may focus more on **tourism demand** than **tourism supply**, or vice versa. However, both are fundamental components of tourism contingent upon and shaped by each other, and therefore both must be considered if we are to understand the whole of tourism.

# How Is Tourism Geographic?

Tourism is inherently geographic. As we put together the components of tourism, we can begin to conceptualize tourism as a geographic activity. Tourism is fundamentally based on the temporary movements of people across space and interactions with place. Thus, basic concepts in geography can contribute to our understanding of tourism.

Like place, discussed earlier, space is an essential geographic concept. **Space** may be defined as locations on the earth's surface, and the related concept of **spatial distribution** refers to the organization of various phenomena on the earth's surface. To break this down further, location is one of the geographic themes. Location can refer to one of two things. Absolute location is the exact position of a place based on some type of structure or grid, such as longitudinal and latitudinal coordinates. For our purposes, however, relative location is more important. **Relative location** is the position of a place in relation to other places and how they are connected. This is related to movement, another geographic theme. Movement is, of course, a fairly self-explanatory concept that allows geographers to explore the ways in which places are connected. Thus, tourism involves clear spatial patterns, including not only where people are coming from and where they are going, but also how they are getting there.

A destination that has a good location relative to large tourist markets has a distinct advantage over one that is much farther away. However, accessibility can help equalize this factor. **Accessibility** is the relative ease with which one location may be reached from another. For example, a direct flight or a high-speed train increases the accessibility of a place. Yet, it is often the case that remote locations are harder to get to and from because of fewer transportation connections, longer travel times, and frequently higher transportation costs. As such, remote places are less likely to develop into large destinations in terms of the quantity of tourists received. Of course, that doesn't mean these locations cannot develop tourism, just that they are likely to develop in a different way than one that is more accessible. Such destinations may receive smaller numbers of tourists who stay at the destination for longer periods of time and spend more money.

Think, for example, of the difference between the Bahamas and the Seychelles. Both are small tropical island destinations with attractive beach resources, among others. Just off the coast of Florida, the Bahamas are strategically located relative to the large North American tourist market and well connected via transportation networks. As such, they have a well-developed tourism industry. With 1.6 million stay-over tourists and 3.4 million cruise ship passengers, the majority of whom are coming from the United States and Canada, the islands receive over US$2 billion in tourist spending annually. Yet, these tourists are spending, on average, less than five nights at the destination. In contrast the Seychelles, located nearly 1,000 miles off the coast of eastern

Africa in the Indian Ocean, is far from the principal tourist markets in North America, Europe, and even East Asia. Despite significant tourism resources, these islands receive only 129,000 stay-over tourists, 6,000 cruise passengers, and US$192 million in tourist spending annually. These tourists average at least seven nights.[7]

Place refers to parts of the earth's surface that have meaning based on the physical and human features of that location. Destinations are the places of tourism. The ideas and meanings attached to these places create a demand for experiences in these places. For example, we could reduce Paris to an absolute location at 48°50'N latitude and 2°20'E longitude, but it is, of course, far more than that. As a place, it is associated with the physical characteristics (e.g., the Seine, the many architectural sites) and the human characteristics of a well-known tourism destination (e.g., culture, history, an atmosphere for romance).

Tourism occurs at different geographic scales. **Scale** generally refers to the size of the area studied. Increasingly, we think of tourism in global terms. The tourism industry has become increasingly globalized with things like global airline alliances and multinational hotel chains. As a result, tourism activities have also become more global. In 2010, international tourist arrivals numbered 935 million,[8] a number that has been steadily increasing (with some temporary fluctuations) for more than half a century. Yet, this movement of people across space creates connections between places, and tourism involves distinctly local, place-based activities. These activities depend on the unique physical and/or human characteristics of that place. In fact, tourism is often used to highlight and promote unique local resources.

There has been much debate about the effect on local places of **globalization** and the increasing interconnectedness of the world. One argument maintains that places are becoming more similar with the forces of globalization, such as the diffusion of popular culture through media and the standardization of products from large multinational corporations. Yet, another argument suggests that, in light of globalization, it is more important than ever to create or reinforce a sense of distinctiveness at the local or regional scale. Tourism has been recognized as an extraordinarily important component in creating and/or promoting a sense of distinctiveness to raise awareness about that place or enhance its reputation.

Finally, tourism provides unique opportunities for interactions between tourists and the peoples and environments of the places they visit. Tourism may be considered one of the most significant ways in which people know places that are not their own. It creates connections between geographically distinct groups of people, people who otherwise might have little knowledge of or contact with one another. It also offers people the potential to explore new environments that are different from the ones with which they are familiar. At the same time, these interactions between tourists and places have specific effects for both the peoples and environments of those places. Therefore, tourism can actively play a role in shaping the world in which we live.

For example, the densely populated—not to mention well-connected—urban areas of the Northern Hemisphere, such as the North American megalopolis (i.e., the large urbanized area along the Northeast coast stretching from Boston to Washington, D.C.), constitute a significant tourist market. Although there are always exceptions, cold-climate city dwellers have an interest in environments vastly different from their own,

# Box 1.1.   Case Study: Geotourism as a Strategy for Tourism Development in Honduras

The incredible growth of the global tourism industry has been accompanied by the development of increasingly specialized tourism products to meet demands for ever more specific tourism experiences. Geotourism is one such product based on the intersection of geography and tourism. As defined by the National Geographic Society (NGS), **geotourism** is "tourism that sustains or enhances the geographical character of a place—its environment, culture, aesthetics, heritage, and the well-being of its residents."[1] As such, geotourism should highlight and enhance the human and physical characteristics of a place that make it unique. Likewise, it should be economically profitable, to contribute to the conservation of those characteristics.

In 2004, the government of Honduras announced that it would become the first nation in the world to sign the National Geographic Geotourism Charter and make geotourism its official tourism strategy. Honduras is a Central American nation that has struggled with crime and corruption, chronic unemployment, endemic poverty, high rates of emigration, and devastating natural hazards. Consequently, it has remained one of the least developed countries in the region. Based on the successful examples of other countries in the region such as Costa Rica and Belize, Honduras sought to develop tourism to create jobs, increase foreign exchange, diversify its economy, and alleviate poverty. Yet, Honduras had been unable to pinpoint a strategy to effectively and appropriately develop its tourism potential, until the discovery of geotourism.

Honduran Minister of Tourism Thierry de Pierrefeu stated that the country was "ideal" for the implementation of the then newly developed geotourism concept. Honduras has a diverse set of resources for tourism, including white sand beaches and coral reefs, mountain topography, tropical rain forest vegetation, national parks and biosphere reserves, pre-Columbian architectural ruins, Spanish colonial history, and indigenous cultures, among others. Moreover, like other countries with similar circumstances, Honduras would like to maintain these resources, raise awareness about the authenticity of such place-based characteristics among international audiences, and strengthen national identity and pride among its own citizens.

Despite the National Geographic framework, geotourism development in Honduras has been slow. One of the first steps in developing and implementing this strategy included creating a geotourism map guide to the country's primary tourist region along the Caribbean coast to highlight and protect key tourism resources. At the same time, NGS and the Honduras Institute of Tourism looked to establish a center to attract tourists who would be interested in the experience Honduras has to offer and support the tenets of geotourism. Yet, problems with political instability and social unrest continue to be key barriers to the development of tourism. In particular, many countries imposed travel alerts for Honduras after a governmental coup took place in 2009. Although these alerts have since been lifted, perceptions of insecurity can linger for years.

Honduras was only the first destination to take the initiative in developing geotourism. Since 2004, other destinations such as Guatemala, Norway, Romania, and the U.S. states of Arizona and Rhode Island have signed on to become geotourism destinations and emphasize the character of place.

*Discussion topic*: If geotourism is intended to highlight the unique geographic character of a place, do you think all tourism might be considered geotourism? Why or why not?

*Tourism on the web*: Honduras Institute of Tourism, "Honduras: The Central America you know—the country you'll love," at http://www.letsgohonduras.com

## Note

1. National Geographic Society, "The Geotourism Charter," accessed February 1, 2011, http://travel .nationalgeographic.com/travel/sustainable/pdf/geotourism_charter_template.pdf, 1.

## Source

Burnford, Angela. "Honduras, National Geographic Announce 'Geotourism' Partnership." *National Geographic News*, October 24, 2004. Accessed February 1, 2011. http://news.nationalgeographic.com/ news/2004/10/1025_041025_travelwatch.html.

such as the tropical rain forest climate and biome in places like Hawaii, Costa Rica, or Thailand. Recognizing the attractiveness of such destinations, countries possessing these environments have a clear incentive to protect these forests as parks and preserves instead of developing them in more environmentally destructive ways. Yet, as more and more tourists come to visit the park, the overcrowding overwhelms the infrastructure, paths are degraded, natural features are vandalized, waste builds up, and so on.

# What Is the Place of "the Geography of Tourism" in Geography?

As we recognize that travel has long been a part of geography and that tourism is an inherently geographic activity, "the geography of tourism" should seem less and less improbable. In recent years, the field has seen considerable growth. Major academic geographic associations now have special groups or commissions devoted to the topic, including the Recreation, Tourism and Sport specialty group of the Association of American Geographers (AAG), the Geography of Leisure and Tourism research group of the Royal Geographical Society (RGS), and the Commission on the Geography of Tourism, Leisure, and Global Change of the International Geographical Union (IGU). Research on topics in the field is published in journals across both geography and tourism studies, including the dedicated journal *Tourism Geographies*. Yet, the place of the geography of tourism within the field of geography is still not widely understood and could use some further discussion. In particular, if we return to our introduction of geography, we see that we can approach the subject regionally or topically.

## TOURISM AND REGIONAL GEOGRAPHY

The concept of regions has long been considered an effective means of organizing and communicating spatial information, especially to nongeographers. As such, regions are applied in the context of tourism in a number of ways, not the least of which is the study of tourism generally and the geography of tourism specifically. Many tourism geography textbooks use a regional approach to examine circumstances of tourism in different parts of the world.

Taken a step farther, the concept of regions may be used to explain patterns or trends in tourism. For example, **tourist-generating regions** are source areas for tourists, or where the largest numbers of tourists are coming from. We can identify characteristics of these regions that stimulate demand for tourism, such as an unfavorable climate or a high level of economic development. Likewise, we can identify characteristics of regions that would facilitate demand, such as a good relative location and a high level of accessibility. Tourist-generating regions are important in helping us understand why certain people may be more likely to travel and where. Theoretically, this information may be used to create new opportunities for people to travel. Specifically, if we understand the barriers to travel for a particular region, we can begin to develop strategies to overcome these barriers. In practical terms, tourism marketers use this information. If a destination identifies its largest potential tourist market, then it will be able to develop a promotional campaign targeted at that audience.

Conversely, **tourist-receiving regions** are destination areas for tourists, or where the largest numbers of tourists are going. We can identify characteristics of these regions that contribute to the supply of tourism. Again, a good relative location and a high level of accessibility are important, as well as the attractions of the region and a well-developed tourism infrastructure. Tourist-receiving regions are important in helping us understand why certain places have successfully developed as destinations. This information may be used as an example for other places also seeking to develop tourism.

International agencies such as the UNWTO use regions to examine trends in the global tourism industry. The UNWTO identifies Europe as both the single largest tourist-generating region and the largest receiving region. As of 2009, the European region accounted for 55 percent of international tourists and 52 percent of international tourist arrivals. This is attributed to a range of factors, including a diverse set of attractive destinations, high levels of accessibility, a well-developed tourism infrastructure, and a long tradition of travel. Yet, long-standing trends in international tourism have been changing in recent years. The importance of Europe as both a generating and a receiving region has been declining with the emergence of new tourists and new destinations. Although the economic troubles of 2009 contributed to a 4 percent decline in international tourist arrivals, the UNWTO reported that Europe posted one of the largest rates of decline among receiving regions.[9]

Finally, destinations use regions to present information to potential tourists. In some cases, a national destination will use the concept to organize smaller destination regions. This allows tourists searching for a destination to match their interests or requirements to a particular place within that country. For example, the Canadian Tourism Commission (CTC), establishes five distinct regions based on different resources and experiences: Atlantic Canada, Canada's North, Central Canada, Mountains West, and the Prairies. In other cases, several nations will work together to generate interest in and awareness of themselves as a destination region. For instance, the Caribbean

Tourism Organization (CTO) is made up of thirty-five members in the greater Caribbean basin, and the organization's stated purpose is "to increase significantly the inclusion of the Caribbean region in the set of destinations being considered by travelers."[10]

The regional approach to the geography of tourism is particularly useful for examining cases of tourism within different regional contexts. Moreover, there are distinct applications for critical regional geography in research on the geography of tourism. In particular, this research examines regional concepts and meanings and the implications this has for the development of tourism (see box 1.2). However, this approach is limited in its potential to fundamentally unpack the concept of tourism. Instead, we will be using a topical approach throughout this textbook.

## TOURISM AND TOPICAL GEOGRAPHY

If we return to the graphic depiction of geography in figure 1.1, we can see how topical branches fit together to comprise the subdivisions of human geography and physical geography, as well as geography as a whole. Yet, fitting the geography of tourism into this picture is no easy task. If pressed, most geographers would probably consider the geography of tourism to be a branch of human geography. Certainly tourism is a human phenomenon, and much of the focus in the geography of tourism is on human ideas and activities. Likewise, the majority of geographers who study the geography of tourism are, in fact, human geographers. This would suggest that we could insert a new "wedge" into the pie for tourism geography, and it would largely go unquestioned (figure 1.3).

This kind of conceptualization may be useful in showing that the geography of tourism is a topical branch that coexists with the others at the center of geography. However, it is less useful in helping us understand how to approach its study. As a new space for the geography of tourism is created, it may be tempting to come to the conclusion that the topic can stand alone. To some extent, overlap exists between the topical branches. Yet, this goes beyond mere overlap in the case of the geography of tourism. All of these other areas—cultural geography, economic geography, population geography, political geography, etc.—have much to contribute to the study of tourism through the lens of geography. Moreover, by tracing the geography of tourism through the human side, we lose some of the components in physical geography—geomorphology, climatology, hazards, etc.—that also play extraordinarily crucial roles in shaping tourism destinations and activities. Furthermore, we cannot truly separate the human and physical divisions, as much of tourism involves interactions between people and the environments of the places they visit.

Rather than thinking of the geography of tourism as part of this hierarchy of topics, it may be more productive for our purposes to think of the geography of tourism in the same way geography as a whole is conceptualized. With the geography of tourism in the center of the schematic, we can recognize that there are both human and physical components at work in tourism, and each of the topical branches can help us understand a different part of the complex phenomenon that is tourism (figure 1.4).

# Box 1.2.  In-Depth: A Critical Regional Geography of Tourism

The concept of regions has a very long tradition in geography. Throughout the classical era, regions were used to divide the world into units in which geographers could describe the physical and human characteristics of these areas. However, geography in the contemporary era moved away from this description of places to focus on explanations of geographic patterns. This shift in emphasis caused many geographers to question the role of regions in the modern study of geography. Some felt that regions were an outdated concept that had outlived its usefulness in the field. But others argued that regions still undeniably have a part to play in the world today, and, as geographers, it is our responsibility to try to understand the world. As a result, these geographers adapted the concept of regional geography to provide the means of understanding how people continue to view the world through regions. This **critical regional geography** is based on the idea that regions are "social constructions," which means that regions do not just exist in the world—people define them, create boundaries for them, and give them meanings. In addition, they are constantly evolving with the world as new events occur and new ideas are created.

In tourism, regions are frequently used to organize patterns and destinations. The UNWTO organizes data and activities based on broad regional categories (e.g., Europe, Asia and the Pacific, the Americas, the Middle East, and Africa). Similarly, popular tourism guidebooks geographically group destinations (e.g., Europe, Central America, East Africa, or the South Pacific). At the most basic level, these categories provide "containers" for information; in other words, they make it easier for people to find and process information for a particular area. Yet, these categories are also associated with meanings. Although it's probably unconsciously done, we mentally organize the world by regions, so we mentally locate a destination by the region we associate it with. This means that what we think about that region shapes what we think about that destination. In the geography of tourism, then, we might critically evaluate regional concepts to understand how these ideas might affect the development of a place as a tourism destination.

For example, dating back to the Cold War era, Europe was conceptually (and to some extent physically) divided into an East and a West. To the American audience, "Europe" meant Western Europe. In contrast, areas behind the Iron Curtain in Eastern Europe came to be seen as a separate region colored by Cold War propaganda. This type of regional categorization presents things as black-and-white, but the reality of things is hardly this clear. The Cold War has been over for more than twenty years, but ideas about regions can take a long time to change. While tourism can help change people's ideas about places through experience, it can also perpetuate patterns. In particular, widely used European guidebooks published by companies such as Rick Steves, Lonely Planet, Frommer's, or Fodor's only cover popular destinations in Western Europe in places such as England, France, and Spain. These companies also produce guides for Eastern Europe as a separate, less developed, and less distinguished destination region. As a result, Europe continues to be perceived as two distinct regions, even among the newest generation of tourists, who were born as the Cold War was ending.

This presents a challenge for the small European nation of Slovenia. It isn't widely known in the American tourist market, which means that it is dependent on regional information to help potential tourists locate and identify it in their minds. Because the country was once part of Yugoslavia—and thus considered one of those areas behind the Iron Curtain—it isn't included in the European guidebooks. Categorized as Eastern European, Slovenia is subject to the lingering negative perceptions about the region. In an effort to promote tourism to markets outside of Europe, the Slovenian Tourist Board has attempted to emphasize its Europeanness by highlighting its geographic location at the center of the European continent (map 1.1) and its attractions that are comparable to the other popular European destinations. This includes its coastal destinations on the Adriatic Sea with a Mediterranean climate and its mountain destinations in the Julian Alps near the borders with Austria and Italy (figure 1.2).

*Discussion topic*: What, if anything, comes to mind when you think about each of the following European regions: (a) Eastern Europe, (b) the Mediterranean, and (c) the Alps? How would your responses influence your decision to visit that region?

*Tourism on the web*: Slovenian Tourist Board, "I Feel Slovenia: The Official Travel Guide," at http://www.slovenia.info

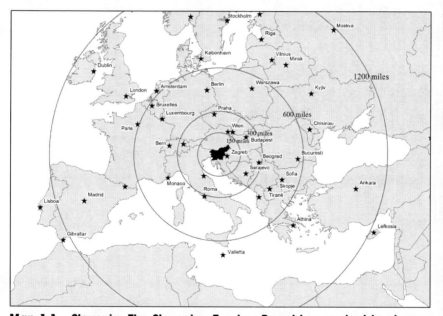

**Map 1.1.   Slovenia. The Slovenian Tourism Board has worked to change westernized perspectives of the country as located in, and associated with traditional concepts of, Eastern Europe. Maps such as this deftly re-shape perceptions of the European region to highlight Slovenia's central location. In fact, it makes popular European tourism destinations, such as Athens (Athina), Lisbon (Lisboa)—even London and Paris—seem peripheral. (Source. Gang Gong)**

*(continued)*

## Box 1.2.  (continued)

**Figure 1.2.  Slovenia's Lake Bled, surrounded by the snow-capped mountains of the Julian Alps, is one of the most popular tourism destinations in the country. Moreover, this iconic image is so widely promoted in both the country and regional tourism literature that it has come to characterize Slovenia as a destination. (Source: Tom Nelson)**

## Sources

Gilbert, Anne. "The New Regional Geography in English- and French-Speaking Countries." *Progress in Human Geography* 12 (1988): 208–28.

Nelson, Velvet. "The Construction of Slovenia as a European Tourism Destination in Guidebooks." *Geoforum* 43 (2012): 1099–1107.

Okey, Robin. "Central Europe/Eastern Europe: Behind the Definitions." *Past & Present* 137 (1992): 102–33.

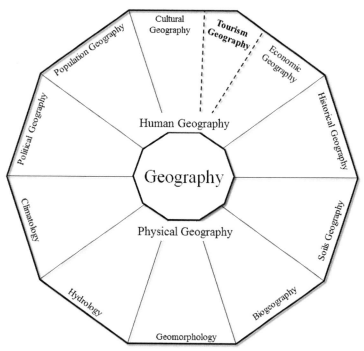

**Figure 1.3.** We can try to fit the topical branch of tourism geography into our graphic representation of the discipline. Based on what we know about tourism so far—that tourism is often seen as an activity or an industry—the argument could be made that the geography of tourism has a place between the major topical branches of cultural geography and economic geography.

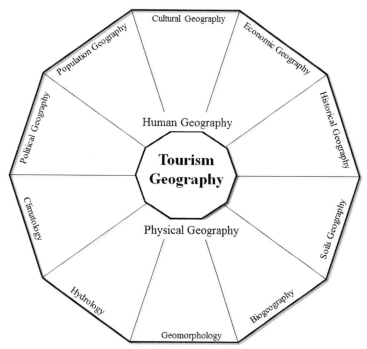

**Figure 1.4.** If we adapt the graphic representation of geography for the geography of tourism, we can begin to appreciate all the components of tourism. Likewise, we can see how the topical structure of geography will allow us to break down and investigate this complex phenomenon.

# Box 1.3. Terminology: *Affect* and *Effect*

*Affect. Effect.* The two words may sound the same when they are pronounced. There's only a difference of one letter in the spelling. It probably doesn't help that one is often used in the definition of the other. But that doesn't mean they can be used interchangeably. They do, in fact, have different meanings, and they have distinct implications for our purposes in the geography of tourism.

We will be using *affect* as a verb. To **affect** is to act on or produce a change in something. We can use the topical branches of geography—on both the human and physical sides—to understand the factors that affect the tourism industry. For example, our understanding of climatology or political geography can help us understand how climatic hazards (e.g., hurricanes and cyclones) or geopolitical events (e.g., war and terrorism) have the potential to affect the tourism industry—that is, to act on or produce a change in tourism. Any of these events have the potential to destroy the tourism infrastructure and prevent people from visiting a destination, at least for a while.

We will be using *effect* as a noun. An **effect** is something that is produced by an agency or cause; it is a result or a consequence. Again, we can use the topical branches of geography to understand what kinds of effects the tourism industry has. For example, our understanding of economic geography or environmental geography can help us understand the effects of tourism—that is, the results of tourism. The flow of income and investment into a place from the tourism industry may act as a catalyst for other types of development, or increased tourism development in fragile natural environments may cause environmental degradation.

*Discussion topic*: Pick a tourism destination and identify three factors that you think might *affect* tourism at that destination and three *effects* that you think tourism might have on that destination. What topical branches of geography would you use to examine each of these factors and effects?

For example, we can use the tools and concepts of climatology to help us understand tourism. Patterns of climate provide insight into things like tourism demand and supply and, by extension, tourist-generating and receiving regions. Winter vacations are often popular among people who live in the higher latitudes because long, cold winters generate a demand for the experience of a warm, sunny place. As such, cold climates are significant source areas for tourists, while tropical climates have long been significant destinations. Likewise, we can use the framework of political geography to provide insights into patterns of tourism. On a routine basis, politics and international relations create barriers to tourism between two places through visa requirements, complicated permits, and so on. Conversely, the removal of these barriers can create new opportunities. While geopolitical events like terrorism and armed conflicts will obviously have a direct impact on tourism for that destination, they can also have ripple effects on tourism throughout the world. After the events of September 11, 2001, there was an immediate decline in tourism to New York City and Washington, D.C., as well as a general decline in travel globally.

# Who Are Tourism Geographers?

Tourism geographers are geographers. Geography provides us with the flexibility to study an incredible diversity of topics from a variety of perspectives. Although geographers specialize both regionally and topically in order to make the task of understanding the world more manageable, many geographers shun labels. Therefore, regardless of what we study, where, or how, we are geographers above all else. Geography provides the framework, or lens, through which we can view, explore, and understand various phenomena of the world in which we live. Second, labels are often unnecessarily restrictive. As discussed above, topical areas in geography do not stand alone; there is considerable overlap between them.

For some geographers, tourism is the primary theme in their research. Yet, these researchers will draw on various perspectives from different topical branches. These geographers are just as likely to be called cultural geographers, economic geographers, environmental geographers, or any other type of geographer for that matter, as they are to be called tourism geographers. In his report on the geography of tourism, Chris Gibson compiled a bibliography of academic articles on tourism written by geographers.[11] His study found that the most common themes in these articles came from the areas of environmental geography, historical geography, and cultural geography.

For others, tourism may not be the primary theme or object of their work, but it is still a topic that has a distinct part to play. This is indicative of the fact that tourism is such a far-reaching phenomenon in today's world. These geographers may never be called tourism geographers; however, their contributions to the geography of tourism should be considered important nonetheless. Gibson's findings confirm that some of the most widely cited authors of papers on issues related to the geography of tourism do not list this as one of their topical specialties. He argues that geography is a discipline that allows researchers to work on some aspect of tourism, as it is situated within wider issues such as sustainability, poverty, changing patterns of land use, the rights of indigenous peoples, and others.

Finally, Gibson's study explores where this research is coming from. Published geographic research has been dominated by the so-called Anglo-American regions of the world and particularly the United States and the United Kingdom. Although much research in the geography of tourism does, in fact, come from these areas, the proportion is considerably smaller than for geography as a whole. In contrast, the Australasia region, including Australia, New Zealand, and Singapore, has made some of the greatest contributions to the geography of tourism. Similarly, parts of Europe have also recognized the value of this research and have made key contributions to the field.

# Box 1.4.  Experience: Business or Pleasure? Traveling as a Tourism Geographer

As a geographer, and especially as a tourism geographer, every trip I take and every place I go is work. I was working when I took a vineyard tour in Napa Valley, California. I was working when I attended the lectures of leading experts at the UNWTO's International Conference on Climate Change and Tourism held in scenic Davos, Switzerland. I was working when I wandered the streets of Paris. I was working when I conducted research at St. Vincent's botanical gardens. I was working when I spent the night at a cottage perched on the edge of the Zambezi River Gorge in Zimbabwe. I was working when I traveled to rural Guizhou Province, China, to learn about the cultures of ethnic minorities. I was working when I got hopelessly lost hiking in Slovenia. I was working when I presented my research at the International Geographical Congress in Tunis, Tunisia. I was even working when I was in Barbados. (No, really.)

Geographers rarely need an excuse to travel. For us, the world is our classroom. If we are to understand the world, we must experience it, and travel gives us that opportunity. Through travel, we build our knowledge of places other than our own, which finds its way into the classes we teach and shapes the topics we research. As geographers first, we rely on this knowledge of place to provide an important framework for understanding tourism as a place-based activity. For tourism geographers, travel has the added benefit of allowing us to explore the circumstances of tourism in other places. Tourism exists in many forms at different scales and across different parts of the world. Through travel, we gain insight into the patterns of this often complex phenomenon. Thus, there is much to be learned from every trip we take, even our own vacations.

Work though it may be, I certainly have no room to complain. Beyond the professional benefits of travel, each trip has had tremendous personal value. I got to know an old family friend as she took me to her favorite vineyards in Napa Valley. I fell in love with the Alps in Switzerland and swore to go back as soon as I could. I checked Paris off of my "bucket list" and swore to never go back. I made a friend on St. Vincent who showed me parts of the island I never would have found on my own. I watched a full moon rise over the Zambezi River from my cottage at the top of the gorge. I successfully used my rudimentary Mandarin to order at a restaurant in a small town in Guizhou where no one spoke a word of English. I never did find the ruins of the twelfth-century castle in Slovenia, but I won't soon forget the experience of looking for it. For hours. In the rain. I learned how to argue with a taxi driver in Tunis. And yes, I thoroughly enjoyed lying on one of Barbados's beautiful beaches once my work was done. Travel has given me the opportunity to meet amazing people and to have these incredible experiences that I never would have had at home. Moreover, it has given me new perspectives on my life, and I've learned a lot about myself in the process.

So is it business, or pleasure? It is, undoubtedly, both.

# Conclusion

Geography has a long tradition based on the fundamental human desire to understand the world, and the modern discipline provides us with the tools and concepts to explain the patterns and phenomena that comprise the world. Although geography and tourism may not automatically be associated with one another, the relationship is undeniable. As such, geography is particularly well suited to provide the framework for exploring the massive worldwide phenomenon of tourism. In particular, we will use a topical approach in geography to break this complicated concept down into more manageable pieces.

This textbook is intended to be precisely what it says it is: an introduction. It is not, and cannot be, comprehensive. Any one of the topics discussed in the chapters of this text could very well merit an entire text of its own. In fact, there are many excellent examples available that discuss such specific topics in much greater depth than what has been done here. At the same time, there are many other topics that could have just as easily been included. The fact that they were not is more a function of a lack of space than a lack of importance. This text is but a beginning, a starting point.

This first chapter briefly discussed each geography and tourism for the purpose of introducing this idea of a "geography of tourism." The remaining chapters in Part I continue to develop a basis in tourism that will allow us to subsequently examine key issues through the framework of geography. Specifically, chapter 2 ("Basic Concepts in Tourism") introduces some of the terminology and ideas in tourism that will provide the foundation for discussions in the remaining chapters, while chapter 3 ("Overview of Tourism Products") provides a brief overview of the types of tourism experiences (i.e., the "products" of the tourism industry) that are offered by destinations around the world.

# Key Terms

- accessibility
- affect
- critical regional geography
- effect
- geotourism
- globalization
- human geography
- leisure time
- physical geography
- place
- region
- regional geography
- relative location
- scale
- space
- spatial distribution
- topical geography
- tourism
- tourism demand
- tourism supply
- tourist-generating regions
- tourist-receiving regions

# Notes

1. Geoffrey J. Martin, *All Possible Worlds: A History of Geographical Ideas* (New York: Oxford University Press, 2005).

2. David A. Lanegran and Salvatore J. Natoli, *Guidelines for Geographic Education in the Elementary and Secondary Schools* (Washington, DC: Association of American Geographers, 1984).

3. National Geographic Education Foundation, "Survey Results: U.S. Young Adults Are Lagging," accessed August 22, 2011, http://www.nationalgeographic.com/geosurvey/highlights.html; John Roach, "Young Americans Geographically Illiterate, Survey Suggests," *National Geographic News*, May 2, 2006, accessed August 22, 2011, http://news.nationalgeographic.com/news/2006/05/0502_060502_geography.html.

4. World Tourism Organization, *Collection of Tourism Expenditure Statistics, Technical Manual No. 2* (Madrid: World Tourism Organization, 1995), accessed January 22, 2011, http://pub.unwto.org/WebRoot/Store/Shops/Infoshop/Products/1034/1034-1.pdf, 9.

5. Alister Mathieson and Geoffrey Wall, *Tourism: Economic, Physical, and Social Impacts* (London: Longman, 1982), 1.

6. Stephen L. J. Smith, "Defining Tourism: A Supply Side View," *Annals of Tourism Research* 15, no. 2 (1988): 183.

7. Jerome L. McElroy and Courtney E. Parry, "The Characteristics of Small Island Tourist Economies," *Tourism and Hospitality Research* 10, no. 4 (2010): 319–20.

8. United Nations World Tourism Organization, "International Tourism 2010: Multi-Speed Recovery," January 17, 2011, accessed January 27, 2011, http://85.62.13.114/media/news/en/press_det.php?id=7331&idioma=E.

9. United Nations World Tourism Organization, *World Tourism Barometer* 8, no. 1 (2010), accessed October 24, 2010, http://www.unwto.org/facts/eng/pdf/barometer/UNWTO_Barom10_1_en.pdf, 3.

10. Caribbean Tourism Organization, "About Us," accessed October 24, 2010, http://www.onecaribbean.org/aboutus/.

11. Chris Gibson, "Locating Geographies of Tourism," *Progress in Human Geography* 32, no. 3 (2008).

# CHAPTER 2

# Basic Concepts in Tourism

The concept of tourism means something different to all of us because we have different perspectives and experiences. For example, people in significant tourist-generating regions may think of tourism as something that they have done in the past and that they would probably like to do again sometime in the future. This is a demand-side perspective. In contrast, people in significant tourist-receiving regions may associate tourism with all of the tourists who come and go during the course of a season. This is a supply-side perspective. Both are fundamental in understanding tourism.

In this chapter, we will discuss some of the key terms and concepts from the perspective of both the demand side of tourism and the supply side. In particular, we will consider what tourism means from the demand side, who tourists are, and what geographic factors motivate them and affect their demand for travel and tourism. We will also examine what types of tourism are provided on the supply side, what characteristics of places create tourism attractions, and what constitutes the tourism industry.

---

### Box 2.1. Terminology: Tourism

In chapter 1, we discussed the classic UNWTO definition of tourism. But because tourism can be approached from different perspectives, some additional terminology is useful. **Inbound tourism** is where tourists from somewhere else, typically another country, are traveling to that destination. **Outbound tourism** is where tourists are traveling from a place to a destination, again typically in another country. This marks a distinction between **domestic tourism**, which includes those tourists traveling within their own country, and **international tourism**, which includes those tourists traveling to another country. Additional distinctions may be made between short-haul tourism and long-haul tourism. This is based on either distance or travel time by a particular mode, or type, of transport. For example, a short-haul flight is generally considered to be less than three hours, while a long-haul flight is longer than six. However, there is no standardized measure for how these categories are actually defined.

*Discussion topic*: Do you think short-haul tourism can be international tourism and long-haul tourism domestic tourism? Why or why not?

---

# The Demand Side

One approach to tourism is from the demand side, with a focus on tourists. This is, of course, a fundamental component of tourism: tourism would not exist without tourists and the demand for tourism experiences. Interestingly, however, the demand side has often been a less studied component in the geography of tourism. Instead, this approach has been seen as a topic more in the realm of psychology, sociology, or anthropology. Yet, the demand side nonetheless has distinct implications for our understanding of geographic patterns in tourism. The first half of this chapter introduces some of the theories and concepts that have been put forth to help us understand tourism from the demand side.

## TOURISM

In the last chapter, we began to consider the different ways we think of tourism. When we think about our experiences, we are thinking about the demand side of tourism. Therefore, one of the easiest ways for us to conceptualize tourism is as a process with a series of stages (figure 2.1).

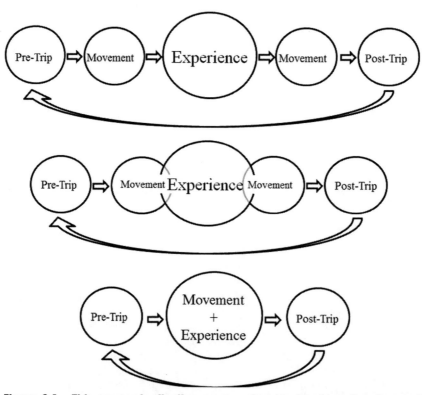

**Figure 2.1.  This conceptualization approaches tourism from the demand side and takes into consideration the stages that contribute to the overall process of tourism. These stages do not necessarily occur in a linear fashion but may overlap and influence the others.**

This process begins in the **pre-trip stage**, when we think about traveling and consider our options. We might evaluate different destinations in terms of the resources and attractions of each place, the tourism products (i.e., the type of experiences) offered there, and the level of infrastructure (e.g., accommodations or transport accessibility), and how they match up with our interests and expectations. Likewise, we will consider the overall cost of a trip to these places in relation to our budget. We have access to a tremendous amount of information to aid us in this evaluation and decision-making process. We rely on our previous experiences, input from family and friends, and the ideas and images of destinations that come from a range of media sources (e.g., news, movies, popular television shows, travel-related television shows, tourism guidebooks, travel magazines, and destination promotional literature). In particular, the Internet has become the most important source of tourism information in today's society. This includes travel booking sites like Expedia or Travelocity, review sites like TripAdvisor, destination-specific websites, and a host of professional and personal travel blogs. In general, the Internet has made this stage easier—at least in the parts of the world with widespread Internet access—in that almost all aspects of pre-trip planning may be completed online.

The next three stages comprise the trip itself. For many trips, these stages will occur one after the other. In the **movement stage**, we use some form of transportation to reach the place of destination. At the destination, the **experience stage** is the main component in the process, in which we participate in a variety of activities. Then we repeat the movement stage as we return home again. For example, the Midwestern family taking a trip to Disneyworld may fly from their nearest airport to Orlando, Florida (movement), spend a few days at the resort and/or theme parks (experience), and then fly home (movement). In this case, movement is simply a means to an end to get to the destination and the experience stage. However, these stages are not always distinct, and the act of traveling can be an integral part of the experience stage. For example, the Midwestern family on a road trip may take a scenic route and visit any number of attractions over the course of the trip. In this case, the movement stage lasts the duration of the trip, from the time they leave home to the time they return. The experience stage takes place concurrently with the movement stage.

The final stage is the **post-trip stage**, which occurs after we return from our trip. We relive our trip through memories and conversations about the trip, as well as through tangible products of the trip, like pictures and souvenirs. These memories can be positive or negative, depending on what happened during the three principal stages of the trip. This stage is typically most intense in the period immediately following the trip, and although it diminishes over time, memories can be triggered by many things for a long time afterward. The tourism process then becomes circular, when we tap into these memories and past experiences to help us make decisions when we start planning our next trip (i.e., the pre-trip stage).

One of the principal advantages of this demand side conceptualization of tourism is that it is readily understood and doesn't complicate something that should be relatively straightforward. In addition, it takes into consideration the role of pre-trip planning and the decision-making process, which are neglected in typical definitions of tourism that focus only on travel to a destination and activities undertaken there.

## TOURISTS

Based on the United Nations World Tourism Organization (UNWTO) definition of tourism quoted in chapter 1, a tourist could be defined as a person who travels to and stays in a place outside of his or her usual environment for not more than one consecutive year for leisure, business, or other purposes. While this official-sounding definition is often used to identify tourists for the purpose of record keeping and statistics, it holds relatively little practical meaning to help us conceptualize who tourists are, as it is broad enough to encompass anything from children on vacation with their parents to adults traveling for work, and from week-long spring break partiers to students spending a semester studying abroad. Instead, it is popular ideas and stereotypes that have long been more influential in shaping our ideas about tourists.

The term *tourist* came into widespread use in the nineteenth century, and even then there were clear—and not always flattering—connotations. Up to this time, explorers were recognized to be individuals who traveled to places that had not previously been extensively visited or documented by others from their society. Likewise, travelers were considered to be those who traveled for a specific purpose, such as business enterprises or official government functions. The new category of "tourists," however, was different from either of these. Unlike travelers, tourists were regarded as individuals who did not travel for any purpose other than the experience of travel itself and the pleasure they derived from that experience. Unlike explorers, tourists were often criticized for traveling to the same places and having the same experiences as all of the explorers, travelers, and even other tourists who came before them.

From this time, highly satirized representations of tourists began to appear in various media, from newspapers to novels. Today, these ideas are more widespread—and more exaggerated—than ever. Take, for example, the opening scene of the 2010 family-friendly animated comedy *Despicable Me*, in which the unruly child of the loud, overweight, brightly dressed, camera-wielding American tourists accidentally exposes the villainous theft of the Great Pyramid of Giza. It is this well-known concept of tourists as a category of people that provokes the sort of reaction expressed in the hilarious *Uncyclopedia* entry titled "Tourist—The Stereotype": "Tourists. We all have 'em. They infest every corner of the globe. Korea, with admirable common sense, arrests all tourists at the border and nukes 'em. . . . Most other nations on Earth, sadly, tolerate them."[1]

Although it has long been easy to make fun of tourists based on stereotypes, it is far more difficult to make generalizations about tourists in reality. Of course, there are always tourists who continue to fuel the stereotypes. Yet, there are also those who may be closer in spirit to the early explorers or have motivations in common with travelers (as even the official UNWTO definition explicitly includes business as well as other purposes). To accommodate the differences that exist between tourists, scholars have developed **tourist typologies** to identify categories (or types) of tourists. Typologies have used many different variables to categorize tourists, such as motivations and behavior as well as demographic characteristics, lifestyle, personality, and more. This type of framework is typically conceptualized as a spectrum or continuum of tourists, in which several important categories are identified and defined. These categories merely identify some of the characteristics of tourists at certain points on the continuum. Not all tourists can be grouped into these defined categories but instead will fall at various points along the continuum between categories.

While many different typologies have been proposed, the following simplified framework is often used as a summary of key categories from the most influential typologies. To some extent, this framework is similar to the earlier distinctions made between explorers, travelers, and tourists; it divides tourists into four broad types based on factors such as the purpose of travel and the type of experience sought.[2]

The **drifter** occupies one end of the spectrum. Drifters are tourists who likely do not consider themselves tourists. Like explorers from an earlier era, this category of tourist may be characterized as a pioneer who is the first to "discover" new and developing destinations. They seek out these destinations in an effort to avoid other tourists. Such places may have little in the way of a dedicated tourism infrastructure or tourism services. As a result, these tourists may stay in local guesthouses or private homes, use local transportation, shop at local markets, and eat at local restaurants and kitchens. Whether it is out of interest—or necessity, given the nature of these destinations—drifters immerse themselves in the local culture. For some, this is a process of education and self-exploration. For others, it is about doing something different, something not usually done.

The **explorer** bears resemblance to the earlier definition of a traveler. This category of tourist may have motivations for travel other than simply diversion, whether education, religious enlightenment, mental or physical well-being, or other specific types of experiences at the destination. These tourists look for unusual types of experiences and greater contact with the local population than just interacting with the people who hold service positions in the tourism industry, such as front desk clerks, restaurant servers, or housekeeping and maintenance staff. Explorers typically make their own travel arrangements and rely on a combination of both the tourism infrastructure and the local infrastructure. For example, these tourists may arrive at the destination by the same means as other categories of tourists, but instead of taking a tour bus or hiring a private taxi to explore the destination, they may take the local bus (figure 2.2).

In this typology, the traditional "tourist" category is divided into two different types. The next type along the continuum is the **individual mass tourist**. For these tourists, the primary motivation is typically some form of relaxation, recreation, or diversion, and they have some desire for things that are familiar and comfortable. They are generally dependent on the tourism infrastructure for getting to and staying at the destination, and they may use tourism industry services for at least part of their trip, such as taking a guided tour at the destination. However, these tourists are also interested in having experiences at the destination that would not be available to them in their home environment, and they will seek the opportunity to explore the destination, albeit in a relatively safe manner.

Finally, the **organized mass tourist** occupies the position at the opposite end of the continuum. These tourists are primarily interested in diversion and escaping the boredom or repetition of daily life. They place a high emphasis on rest and relaxation and enjoying themselves with good food and/or entertainment. These tourists are less

**Figure 2.2.  This "explorer" is waiting for Bus Éireann in Trim, Ireland. Although Trim Castle can be visited on guided traveling tours and day trips, he preferred utilizing the public transportation infrastructure and having the freedom to choose his experiences instead of a pre-packaged alternative. (Source: Carolyn Nelson)**

interested in unique experiences of place and are more likely to travel to destinations that are familiar or have characteristics that are familiar. Therefore, even if they travel to a foreign destination, they will stay in recognized brand name (i.e., multinational) resorts. These facilities are designed to provide the standard of accommodation, services, or types of food that such tourists are accustomed to at home. Organized mass tourists are highly dependent on the tourism infrastructure and services to structure their vacation. This may be a package that bundles services together at competitive prices, whether it is a comprehensive guided tour (with all transportation, accommodation, most meals, and tour services included) or a resort package (accommodation, some or all meals, and airport transfers included). As a result, little additional planning for the trip is necessary, there is little uncertainty about what will happen on the trip, and there may be little incentive to stray from the confines of the tour bus or resort complex. Thus, there is little to no interaction with the people or the place of the destination.

# Box 2.2.    In-Depth: Place-Specific Tourist Typologies

Although tourist typologies have primarily come out of tourism studies based in fields such as psychology, sociology, and anthropology, these frameworks have utility for the geography of tourism as well. Many early tourist typologies sought to explore general categories of tourists that could be applied across different types of destinations for the purpose of better understanding tourists and tourism. However, more recent typologies have recognized that these general typologies are often not particularly useful in efforts to understand tourism as a place-based phenomenon. As a result, studies in the geography of tourism have developed place-specific typologies that are geographically bound to a particular destination to provide a better understanding of its specific circumstances. This will allow **tourism stakeholders** (i.e., the various individuals or organizations that have an interest, or stake, in tourism) to better plan, manage, and market tourism at that destination.

In one example, a place-specific tourist typology developed for Cancún, Mexico, took data provided by actual tourists from visitor surveys and interviews to identify categories of tourists and to discuss the characteristics of these tourists. Tourism stakeholders can use the resulting typology to understand how the services and experiences provided at that destination match the expectations and desires of tourists and, perhaps more importantly, how it can be improved. The Cancún typology follows the model established by the generalized typology—although, given the nature of this destination, tourists were concentrated at the mass tourist end of the spectrum (table 2.1).

For example, the "Euro Off-Beat" tourist category characterized the explorer/independent mass tourist end of the continuum. This category describes European tourists in their late twenties to early forties who stay at the destination for a week or longer and are interested in experiencing the region's historical and cultural attractions. As is typical of this type of tourist, they are likely to stay in the destination's principal resorts, but they also seek to explore the destination beyond the resort. Consequently, they typically do not use all-inclusive packages but take tours and eat at restaurants outside of the hotel. In general, these tourists find it difficult to have the type of experience they desire, and the data indicate that, given current conditions, they would be unlikely to return.

In contrast, the "Sun, Sea, and Sand Family" tourist category occupies a position at the organized mass tourist end of the continuum. This category describes predominantly American families looking for a good value vacation of a week or less. They may have some interest in visiting popular tourist attractions in the region, such as the archaeological ruins at Chichén Itzá, but they will typically spend most of their time at the beach or pool, participating in resort activities, and eating at on-site restaurants. These family tourists don't like the party atmosphere that attracts the "Spring Breaker" tourists, and they consider this a detraction for the destination. However, these tourists appreciate the range of discount packages offered by the destination that gives them the opportunity to take their families on a beach vacation.

*Discussion topic*: What could the destination do to better meet the expectations and demands of the Euro Off-Beat tourists? Of the Sun, Sea, and Sand Family tourists?

*Tourism on the web*: Cancún Convention and Visitor Bureau, "Cancún Travel," at http://cancun.travel/en/

*(continued)*

## Box 2.2.   *(continued)*

**Table 2.1.   Summary of Characteristics for Each of the Categories of Tourists Identified in Cancún's Place-Specific Typology (Categories derived from data provided by tourists at the destination.)**

| Type of Tourist | Key Characteristics |
|---|---|
| "Euro Off-Beat" Tourist | • Late 20s to early 40s<br>• European, not American<br>• Not "all-inclusive" tour<br>• Longer stay<br>• Visits off-beat, historical, archaeological, and "Mundo Maya" sites |
| "Sun, Sea, and Sand Family" Tourist | • Older—early 40s to late 60s<br>• Family vacation<br>• Mostly interested in "sun and sand"<br>• Strong interest in good service and good food<br>• May visit a mass tourism archaeology site |
| "Business Breaker" Tourist | • Late 20s to late 30s<br>• Nonfamily vacation<br>• Not "all-inclusive" tour<br>• High expenditures<br>• Brief stay<br>• Mostly interested in "sun and sand"<br>• Not interested in visiting archaeological, historical, or "Mundo Maya" sites |
| "Non-Breaker Student" Tourist | • Early 20s<br>• Likely to be American<br>• Organized student package tour, but not classic "Spring Breaker"<br>• Visits off-beat, archaeological, and historical sites |

## Source

Torres, Rebecca Maria, and Velvet Nelson. "Identifying Types of Tourists for Better Planning and Development: A Case Study of Nuanced Market Segmentation in Cancún." *Applied Research in Economic Development* 5, no. 3 (2008): 12–24.

## TOURIST MOTIVATIONS

Clearly these types of tourists have different motivations for and interests in tourism experiences. In the geography of tourism, we need to know what factors cause people to temporarily leave one place for another. If we understand these factors, we can begin to explain why certain places developed as significant tourist-generating regions and why others became significant receiving regions. Likewise, it helps destinations to better know where their potential tourist markets are by matching up what they have to offer with the places where the demand for that product is greatest. However, motivations may be complicated, and it is rarely just one thing that causes people to seek tourism experiences.

The motivation that has long been most commonly associated with tourism is the pursuit of pleasure. However, implicit in this motivation is the real or perceived need for a temporary change of setting. This may be considered a geographic **push factor**, or something that impels people to temporarily leave home to travel somewhere else. We may think of this as an escape from the routine of daily life with the associated home and work issues, or boredom with familiar physical and social environments. Correspondingly, it is assumed that there is something that can be obtained at the destination that cannot be obtained at home. This may be considered a geographic **pull factor**, or something that attracts people to a particular destination. The pull may be something tangible that may be obtained at the destination, like being able to buy certain types of local products or eat authentic local cuisine. In most cases, however, it is an intangible, like having the opportunity to interact with new people, getting a week's worth of sunny 80°F weather in the middle of winter, or having access to fresh snow at a prime ski resort. For both the push and the pull, this "something" will be different for everyone.

Borrowing from one of geography's related disciplines—anthropology—we can see how these motivations have been laid out in Nelson Graburn's concept of **tourist inversions**.[3] In this theory, the experience we seek in our temporary escape is one of contrasts. Much of this involves a shift in attitudes or patterns of behavior away from the norm to a temporary opposite. One of the most common examples is the inversion from work and stress to peace and relaxation. For example, when we spend a long period of time working hard at school or at a job (or, in some cases, both simultaneously), tourism becomes our means of seeking the opposite: going on vacation for a period of rest and relaxation away from the stresses of what occupies us in our daily lives. Likewise, the shift from economy to extravagance is another common inversion that applies to many of us. We often have to budget our money in the course of our daily lives, but we will save up and splurge on a vacation. During these few days, we may spend more on food, drinks, entertainment, and other activities than we normally would.

In some cases, these inversions in behavior contribute to the generally poor reputation of tourists in many parts of the world. In particular, many inversions go from moderation to excess. Graburn suggests that overindulgence in food is the product of one tourist inversion. The same idea applies to overindulgence in alcohol and drugs. This inversion, as highlighted by MTV, is the one that gives spring break tourists—and, by extension, spring break destinations—a bad name. In the case of this inversion, students who usually go to class, study, work, party occasionally, and generally live within the norms of society travel to a spring break hotspot during the designated semester break and party to excess, with all that it entails.

There is also a geographic dimension to tourist inversions, in terms of a shift away from the tourist's home and community toward a temporary opposite. This shift is much more locally contingent, and the inversions may, in fact, work both ways. One of the most common inversions of this type involves the movement from cold climates to warm ones. People in middle and upper latitudes that experience long, cold winters may seek to escape that weather—and the associated symptoms of seasonal affective disorder—for a short time by traveling to a warm, sunny place in the lower latitudes (figures 2.3 and 2.4). At the same time, people in warm climates may travel to colder ones to be able to participate in winter sports, such as skiing. People in densely populated urban areas may seek to escape the congestion, noise, and pollution of the city for expansive natural areas such as the national parks, although people living in rural areas or small towns may seek to get away from the insularity of that life by getting lost in a big city.

## TYPES OF DEMAND

In the last chapter, our definition of demand included both those persons who travel and those who wish to travel. Consequently, we need to distinguish between different types of demand, including effective demand, suppressed demand, or no demand. **Effective demand** is the type of demand we typically think of, as it refers to those people who wish to and have the opportunity to travel. We can measure effective demand relatively easily with tourism statistics like visitation rates and participation in certain tourism activities.

**Figure 2.3. For many people who live in cold-weather climates, long winters of dealing with icy and snowy conditions, such as these occurring in the U.S. state of Ohio, can be a distinct geographic push factor for tourism. (Source: Amber Fisher)**

**Figure 2.4.    Just as a cold-weather climate can serve as a push factor, warm and sunny climates, such as that found on the Caribbean Island of Tortola, British Virgin Islands, can serve as a distinct geographic pull factor and create a demand for the winter/spring break. (Source: Tom Nelson)**

However, this does not give us a complete picture, as participation is not always reflective of desire. How many of us have wanted to travel (i.e., have had a demand for travel) at some point in our lives but have not been able to, for one reason or another? **Suppressed demand** refers to the people who wish to travel but do not. It is much more difficult to measure the number of people who simply *want* to travel. Moreover, there are many reasons why people who wish to travel do not, so we can break this category down even further. **Potential demand** is a type of suppressed demand that refers to those people who want to travel and will do so when their circumstances change. For example, students often have a potential demand for tourism. This means that they may have an interest in (or a perceived need for!) tourism experiences, but they may not have the **discretionary income** (i.e., the money that is left over after taxes and all other necessary expenses of life like rent, food, transportation, clothing, tuition, and books have been taken care of) to travel.

**Deferred demand** is a type of suppressed demand that refers to those people who want to travel but have to put off their trip, not because of their own circumstances but because of some problem or barrier in the supply environment. This could be a problem—or even a perceived problem—at the desired destination. For example, after the April 2010 explosion on the Deepwater Horizon drilling rig and the subsequent oil spill in the Gulf of Mexico, there was much speculation about the number of tourists who would cancel their summer vacations to the many Gulf Coast destinations due to

## Box 2.3.  Case Study:
## Barbados's "Perfect Weather"

It hardly seems like one would need a reason to visit the Caribbean island nation of Barbados. That it has a reputation as a tropical island paradise is usually enough to create a distinct demand for the experience of such a destination. Yet, the island does not attract visitors from all over the world. Rather, there is a distinct geographic distribution of tourists to Barbados, as 79 percent come from only two geographic regions: North America and Europe. In particular, 34 percent come from just one country: the United Kingdom. Of course, there are many variables that we would need to consider if we were to fully understand these geographic patterns, such as historical relations, modern transportation connections between tourist-generating regions and the destination, levels of development in the generating regions, the type of attractions offered by the destination, and many more. However, one of the simplest explanations is weather.

Although there is relatively little seasonal variation for Barbados, there is nonetheless a distinct tourism season from November through April. In 2009, fully two-thirds of total tourist arrivals, including over three-fourths of cruise passenger arrivals, were concentrated in this six-month time period, consisting of the most difficult winter and early spring conditions for the majority of Barbados's North American and Northern European tourists. In particular, December accounted for the largest number of arrivals, with nearly 14 percent of total arrivals. Conversely, the months that received the lowest visitor arrivals were the summer months, when these generating regions experience the most favorable weather conditions and when Barbados experiences its least favorable conditions. June saw the lowest arrivals by cruise ship, with only three percent of passengers. September, the peak of Atlantic hurricane season, saw the lowest arrivals by air, with only five percent of stay-over tourists.

Among Barbados's many unique cultural and heritage attractions—and highly developed tourism amenities—one aspect of the destination that the Barbados Tourism Authority (BTA) emphasizes most is the island's weather. In recognition of weather as a geographic push factor for their primary tourist market in Northern Hemisphere countries such as the United Kingdom, the United States, and Canada, the BTA has worked to ensure that these tourists are well aware that Barbados has the corresponding pull factor. Visit Barbados, the official website of the BTA, explicitly highlights the island's "perfect weather." On a designated page, the BTA claims, "With an average daily high temperature of 78°F/26°C, an average daily rainfall of less than ¼ inch and 3000 hours of annual sunshine, it's hard to imagine a place that enjoys weather any more perfect than in Barbados."[1] At the time of this writing—in February with overcast skies, a chance of wintery mixed precipitation, and a current local temperature of 28°F (in Texas, no less)—the page's "perfect weather" weather report showed sunny skies and temperatures ranging from 82°F to 84°F for the following four days.

*Discussion topic*: What do you consider to be the greatest geographic push factor(s) for tourism from your home environment and why? What destination(s) do you think have the corresponding pull factor?

*Tourism on the web*: Barbados Tourism Authority, "Visit Barbados," at http://www.visitbarbados.org/

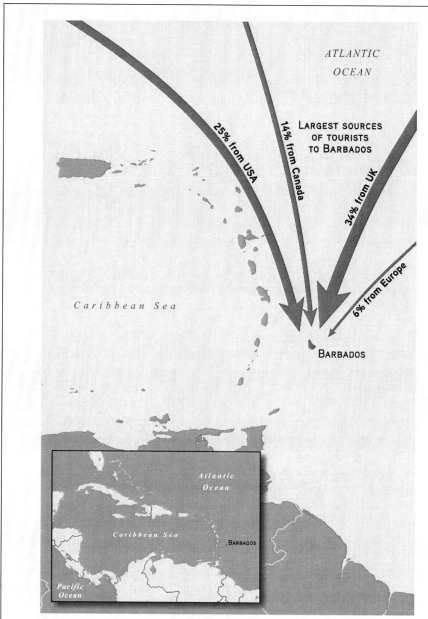

**Map 2.1.  Barbados, West Indies. The majority of tourists who visit this Caribbean island destination come from the significant generating regions in Europe and North America. (Source: XNR Productions)**

(*continued*)

---

### Box 2.3.  *(continued)*

## Note

1. Barbados Tourism Authority, "Perfect Weather," accessed February 4, 2011, http://www.visit barbados.org/perfect-weather.

## Source

Caribbean Tourism Organization. "2009 Country Statistics and Analysis [Barbados]." Accessed February 4, 2011. http://www.onecaribbean.org/content/files/Strep1.pdf.

---

either actual site contamination or fear of contamination. Similarly, this could include some type of a problem in the tourism infrastructure that would prevent tourists from reaching or being able to stay at their intended destination. Also in April 2010, the eruption of Iceland's Eyjafjallajökull volcano and subsequent ash cloud shut down airports across Europe and created a massive backlog of travelers. Many people who had plans to travel to a number of different destinations during this time were forced to cancel their trips.

It is important to understand what factors are going to allow demand to be fulfilled as well as what factors will prevent it. If tourism stakeholders understand those factors, then they can begin to see what strategies might help people with suppressed demand get past any barriers and have the experiences they are looking for. At least theoretically, suppressed demand can be converted into effective demand if the right opportunities are presented. This might involve offering discounts to students, such as Eurail discounted Youth Passes for people ages sixteen to twenty-four. Or it might involve targeted promotional campaigns, such as the US$87 million that BP paid to the Gulf Coast states for the purpose of tourism and promotion to get the word out about destinations that were not affected by the disaster.[4]

It may seem like it should be easy to assess demand because we often assume that if people are not already traveling, they probably want to. However, there is actually one additional category of demand: **no demand**. This refers to people who for various reasons really do not want to travel.

## FACTORS IN DEMAND

A person's demand for tourism may be shaped by the nature of the society in which he or she lives. For example, a country's government can help generate effective demand by creating opportunities for people to travel. Government-mandated holidays will give people more time to travel. The level of development in a society is an important factor shaping demand. Generally, higher levels of development will lay the foundation for more people to translate their desire for travel and tourism experiences into effective demand. Higher levels of economic development bring an increase in both discretionary income and leisure time. Higher levels of social development bring improvements in the health, well-being, and education of the population. These things give more people within that society greater means, interest, and opportunity to travel. The more developed countries of the world continue to account for the largest proportion of international tourists. However, some of the newly developing countries like Brazil and China have been experiencing conditions that allow more people to travel, and they are quickly becoming among the significant tourist-generating nations.

At the same time, individual factors—such as a person's view of the world and their childhood influences and experiences—as well as personality type play a distinct role in determining whether they have a strong desire to travel or prefer to spend their leisure time at home. Personal biases and even phobias—such as a fear of flying—will also shape an individual's demand. More generally, however, we can consider how a person's stage in the life cycle affects demand.

In the youth stage (i.e., children who have not yet reached the age of legal adulthood), interest in travel and tourism experiences vary. Younger children are most likely to have a demand for experiences that are specifically promoted to this demographic, like a trip to Disneyland or Disneyworld. Beyond this, demand is shaped by the travel patterns of family and friends. If travel is a part of their family life, they will come to expect and anticipate these experiences. Likewise, hearing about their friends' travel experiences can also stimulate demand. However, many children may have no demand for travel, not because they lack interest in other places but because they lack opportunity and therefore such experiences may not even be a part of their consciousness. Demand for travel typically increases during the teenage years with greater opportunities and a greater desire for independence. Still, decisions about whether the child's demand is effective or potential continue to be made by parents or guardians.

In the young adult stage (i.e., individuals who are legally of age but do not yet have the responsibilities associated with adulthood), there is typically a high demand for travel because of the pent-up desire for freedom and independence from the youth stage. These individuals may have fewer time constraints than adults with careers and families. Students, in particular, have long designated holidays between terms that provide the opportunity for travel. However, one of the greatest barriers to travel during this stage is financial; essentially, young adults may have less discretionary income available for travel. This may result in potential demand where they will travel in the future if their circumstances change, but many are nonetheless able to translate their desire into effective demand by using their limited disposable income to take short vacations and travel cheaply by using public transportation and staying in hostels.

The married/partnered (without children) stage can be associated with a complex set of variables that contribute to both effective demand and potential demand. With two incomes and accumulated vacation time, these couples may have both the time and money to travel. However, as they develop careers and set down roots in their home environment (e.g., buy a house, acquire pets, get involved in community activities, etc.), it may become increasingly difficult to get away for extended periods of time.

The family stage arguably has the greatest influence on whether demand is effective or potential. Couples and single parents with dependent children have increased household, childcare, educational, and other expenses and therefore less disposable income available for travel. At the same time, the cost of a trip increases as a family must purchase more transport tickets, book a larger hotel room or suite, pay for more activities, and others. Between the parents' work schedules and the children's school and activity schedules, it may be difficult to find an appropriate time when everyone will be free to travel. Moreover, family trips require more coordination and preparation to ensure that all members of the family are ready to go on the trip and various contingencies are accounted for (e.g., packing drinks and snacks, entertainment, favorite toys or blankets, various first aid supplies in case of illness or accidents, etc.). Because of these constraints, families may have the desire for travel and tourism experiences but decide to put it off or revise their expectations by traveling to destinations closer to home, taking trips of a shorter duration, or undertaking travel to visit family, such as grandparents.

Initially, effective demand increases in the empty nest stage. Once children become independent and no longer require financial support, these individuals may experience an increase in their disposable income and an increase in leisure time. This will continue to increase after they retire from their full-time jobs. As a result, empty nesters may translate their potential demand into effective demand, not only in terms of having the opportunity to travel but also to have the type of tourism experiences they desired. As this stage transitions into the elderly stage over time, effective demand decreases again. Retirees living on a fixed income may have to make choices about the experiences they can afford. Travel may become physically more difficult, and health concerns can present a distinct challenge. Some individuals may become more easily tired by journeys. This not only affects their experience of the destination but also requires a post-trip recovery period, which will affect the way they remember the trip. Others may not be physically able to undertake long journeys. For example, individuals experiencing back pain may be unable to sit in the confines of an uncomfortable seat for a lengthy period of time. The loss of one's spouse or partner during the course of this stage has the potential to affect demand. Ultimately, suppressed demand transitions into no demand as the individual feels that the experience of tourism is no longer worth the hassles of traveling.

While there are, of course, always exceptions to these general patterns, the life cycle variable provides some insight into why demand might be effective for some groups of people within a society and potential for others. This helps tourism stakeholders develop strategies to translate potential demand into effective demand. For example, many destinations have recognized that families are a significant potential tourist market with a demand for travel, if the right opportunities are presented. As a result, the tourism industry encourages family travel with the development of family-friendly resorts that offer activities for children and/or babysitting services to allow parents some alone time. These resorts may have specially priced family packages that allow children to stay or eat at on-site restaurants for free to make such a vacation seem more affordable—and therefore more accessible—to families.

# The Supply Side

Tourism may also be approached from the supply side with a focus on the industry. This, too, is a fundamental component of tourism: tourism necessarily involves the provision of services and experiences. Geography has generally had more to contribute to this side of tourism because of the discipline's focus on the places and place-based resources that play an important role in the supply of tourism. While issues of tourism resources will be the focus of the chapters in part II, the remainder of this chapter introduces some of the theories and concepts that have been put forth to help us understand tourism from the supply side.

## TOURISM

From the supply side perspective, one of the most important distinctions that we can make to help us understand many patterns in tourism is that of mass tourism and niche tourism. The concept of mass tourism is explained through Fordism, or the system of mass production and consumption, typically linked back to Henry Ford and the changes made in automobile manufacturing. Fordism refers to the manufacture of standardized goods in large volumes at a low cost. Thus, **mass tourism** is the production of standardized experiences made available to large numbers of tourists at a low cost.

At mass tourism destinations, the infrastructure is well developed to handle large quantities of tourists. There are typically good transportation links that allow people to easily reach the destination, whether it is interstate highway access, a major international airport, or a cruise terminal. There may be a spatial concentration of hotels and resorts to accommodate these tourists, as well as restaurants and entertainment facilities to meet their needs. These service providers are often dominated by large multinational corporations. Whether tourists visit the Bahamas, Italy, or Thailand, they can stay at a Best Western. When they are in Orlando, Beijing, or Casablanca, they can eat at a T.G.I. Friday's. To some extent, tourists can expect similar experiences at these places regardless of where they are actually located. Because the emphasis of mass tourism is on quantity, low-cost packages may be offered to make these destinations accessible to medium- and lower-income groups. In addition, the standardization of experiences means that destinations may be considered interchangeable. This leads to competition between destinations, which contributes to a further reduction in prices.

The most prominent mass tourism destinations have been in warm climates and coastal areas. The idea of mass tourism is also associated with key inversions discussed above, like relaxation and partying. As a result, mass tourism is often characterized as the worst of tourism and for stereotypical tourists. Yet, mass tourism has existed since the early eras of tourism and will continue to exist because it meets certain needs. The well-developed infrastructure facilitates tourism for large numbers of people, while the competition and economies of scale allow more people to participate in tourism than would otherwise be possible. Moreover, it provides the type of experiences that many tourists continue to demand.

Mass tourism is often contrasted with **niche tourism** (also sometimes called "alternative" or "special interest" tourism), which is based on the concept of post-Fordism. This concept reflects changes in the ways in which production and consumption are understood. Post-Fordism recognizes that there is not always a single mass market in which all demands may be met through mass production. As a result, there is a need for more differentiated or specialized products targeted at specific markets. Particularly as the tourism industry has developed and more people have had the opportunity to travel to different places, there has been a growing demand for new types of experiences outside of the mainstream. Niche tourism allows destinations to exploit a particular resource that they possess and create a sense of distinction so that tourists feel they must visit that destination to have that experience. It also allows tourists to choose a vacation experience that is more tailored to their specific interests rather than a one-size-fits-all package.

Many destinations become characterized by either mass tourism or niche tourism, although a destination has the potential to tailor its offerings to meet the demands of different types of tourists. Some tourism products that will be discussed in the next chapter lend themselves more toward one type of tourism over the other, and each type will affect tourists and tourism destinations in different ways.

## TOURISM ATTRACTIONS

**Tourism attractions** are aspects of places that are of interest to tourists and provide a pull factor for the destination. Attractions can include things to be seen, activities to be done, or experiences to be had. Some tourism attractions seem "given." For example, the most spectacular scenes of natural beauty, impressive architectural constructions, and places where significant historic events occurred are those that are natural for people to want to experience. However, these sites are attractions because they have been given meaning. This meaning may be given by the tourists themselves and the types of things they demand, but it may also be given by the tourism industry. Each potential destination has to find the attraction (or attractions) that makes it unique and will cause people to want to visit that place instead of another.

There are four broad categories of tourism attractions: natural, human (not originally intended for tourism), human (intended for tourism), and special events.[5] Natural attractions are obviously based on the physical geography of a place, such as the coast, mountains, forests, caves, inland water sources, flora, fauna, and so on. The first category of human attractions includes those places or characteristics of places that had some other purpose or function but have since become an attraction for tourism, such as historic structures, religious institutions, and aspects of local culture. The second category of human attractions include those places or aspects of places that were specifically designed to attract visitors, such as modern entertainment facilities like amusement parks, casinos, shopping centers, resorts, and museums. Finally, special events is a diverse category that can include religious and secular festivals, sporting events, conferences and conventions, and, in some cases, social events such as weddings and reunions.

Almost anything can be made into a tourist attraction, including a whole array of oddities and curiosities. For example, the Blarney Stone of Blarney Castle in Ireland has become a well-known tourism attraction visited by an estimated 400,000 people annually. Legend has it that those who kiss the Blarney Stone will gain the gift of eloquence, and visitors have reportedly gone through this ritual for more than two hundred years. Early visitors were held by their ankles and lowered head first over the battlements to perform this act, but safety measures have since been put into place so that visitors only have to lean backwards while holding on to an iron railing, often with the help of a guide. The origins of the stone—and this ritual—are much debated, and some reports suggest that the Blarney Stone was, in fact, once part of the castle's latrine system. Regardless of its origins, it has recently been called the most unhygienic tourism attraction in the world.[6]

Not all attractions are created equal; some have greater pull forces than others. There are a few prominent international sites that people all over the world would like to have the opportunity to see or experience at least once in their lifetime, whether it is the Eifel Tower or the Great Wall of China. These are the attractions that have the greatest pull force. Essentially, they are one of the most important reasons people choose to visit that destination. These sites are often featured on lists like the "new wonders of the world," compiled in 2007. This type of designation only increases the desirability of such sites as tourism attractions.

A secondary tier of tourism attractions also exerts some pull. These attractions may factor into tourists' decisions to visit a particular destination and will certainly be experienced when tourists visit that place, but they are not the primary reason. In the example given above, few people are likely to visit Ireland solely because of Blarney Castle, but clearly many tourists make a point to have this experience when they are there.

There are also other attractions that may exert little pull or have little influence on tourists' decision to visit that destination. These may be attractions that people only learn about once they arrive at the destination and may be experienced only by tourists who spend more time at the destination. These tourists have the opportunity to explore the destination in greater depth and visit sites beyond those that are well known. While the Matterhorn and Jungfrau are some of the well-known, frequently visited mountain sites in Switzerland, the lesser-known Mount Rigi could also be considered an attraction with equal opportunities for tourism activities (figure 2.5).

## TOURISM INDUSTRY

Attractions play an important role in creating the demand for travel, but they cannot exist alone. The services provided by the tourism industry facilitate travel to and experience of these attractions. For example, Stonehenge is a well-known United Nations

**Figure 2.5.  As this view from Mount Rigi, Switzerland, indicates, the destination is clearly a high-quality natural attraction. Yet, Rigi does not possess the re-nown, and therefore does not exert the same pull force on international tourists, as other Alpine destinations. (Source: Tom Nelson)**

Educational, Scientific, and Cultural Organization (UNESCO) World Heritage Site attraction that draws tourists from all over the world to the English county of Wilt-shire. Yet, English Heritage, the organization that owns and manages the site, is not in the business of organizing trips to Stonehenge. The site itself offers only minimal options for food and drink and does not offer visitors a place to stay. Thus, the needs of tourists visiting Stonehenge must be met by other service providers in the surround-ing area.

Correspondingly, attractions may account for only a small proportion of income at a destination. Some attractions operate on a pay-for-participation basis, but there are just as many attractions that are free or have only a minimal admission fee. As such, it is the tourism industry service providers that generate revenues. This can be so significant that tourism is frequently described as the world's largest industry. However, this claim is difficult to substantiate, given the lack of data regarding all aspects of the various travel, tourism, and hospitality-related economic activities ranging from transportation to accommodation, food and beverage, tours, enter-tainment, retail, and more. This is further complicated by the fact that there is considerable overlap between the services provided to tourists and those provided to nontourists. In addition, only part of tourism services takes place in the formal sector of the economy. The remainder is provided in the unregulated informal sector of the economy, as tourists utilize gypsy cabs, hire unlicensed tour guides, and/or

# Box 2.4.  Experience: A Hidden World in Thailand

I have been fortunate enough to visit Thailand several times, and in recent years, I began leading student study trips there. Bangkok is, of course, always part of our trips. It is an amazing and overwhelming place. There are so many contrasts and contradictions, with everything from elephants to Mercedes, ancient temples to modern skyscrapers, great wealth to terrible poverty. As with any trip, there are always certain "must-see's" for a place. In Bangkok, I always take students to visit the city's well-known tourist attractions, such as the Grand (King's) Palace, Wat Phrakaew (the Temple of the Emerald Buddha, which is considered one of the most sacred Buddhist temples in Thailand, although the statue of the Buddha is only about a foot tall and is actually made of jade), and Wat Pho (the Temple of the Reclining Buddha). These are incredible places to see, and I can't imagine that a visit to Thailand would be complete without them. But the experiences we have at these places are usually not the ones I remember most. Instead, it is often the unexpected—the chance encounters with people and the glimpses into places I never knew existed—that have the greatest impact on me.

On the last study trip I led, we traveled from Bangkok to Phang Nga (about five hundred miles). This is one of the southern provinces in the Malay Peninsula, which runs along the Andaman Sea. Much of the area around Phang Nga Bay, including some forty islands, is protected as a national marine park. This area has a distinctive and scenic environment with mangroves, caves, and massive rain forest–covered limestone cliffs. Over the years, it has become increasingly popular for tourism. The most well-known of its attractions is the Ko Khao Phing Kan islands and the iconic Ko Tapu tower islet just offshore, which is now popularly referred to as "James Bond Island" because it was featured in the 1974 film *The Man with the Golden Gun*. I had previously spent some time in this area and was happy to have the opportunity to go back. This time, to do some more in-depth exploring of the islands, I arranged a sea kayaking excursion for our group through a local tour company.

We took a boat into the bay and the kayaks from there. Our guide directed us to an island where there was a narrow opening at sea level. Given the water level at that time, we had to lie back, flat against the kayak, in order to pass through into the sea cave without running into the stalactites hanging down. From there, we crossed into a magical hidden world. The interior of the island was a collapsed cave system (*hong*), creating a sort of inner lagoon. It was an area the size of a small lake open to the sky but protected on all sides by limestone cliffs covered with tropical vegetation. It was quiet and beautiful and truly unique. I could have spent hours paddling around the calm waters, exploring the mangroves and listening for the sound of birds.

Although I think this experience is increasingly becoming part of the tourist offering in Phang Nga Bay, it's not why I chose to include that destination on our itinerary. As a geographer, I had always been fascinated by the sight of the towering karst islands I had seen in the bay, but I had no idea these incredible interior spaces existed. In a way, that made "discovering" them all the more special and more memorable than visiting something that I had seen pictures of and read about beforehand. It was an amazing experience and one that I won't soon forget.

*—Marcus*

buy goods from vendors they encounter on the street or at the beach. Thus, it may be more correct to identify tourism as the world's largest service sector industry, as American tourism geographer Alan Lew argues in his blog post "Tourism is NOT the World's Largest Industry—So Stop Saying It Is!"[7]

## Conclusion

Depending on our perspective and priorities, we may focus more on tourism demand than supply, or vice versa. However, the success of tourism depends on the demand-supply match, or the ability of the tourism industry at a particular destination to provide the services and experiences that tourists demand. The demand-supply match is not going to be the same for all places, and it will change over time as conditions change on both sides. This chapter discussed some of the key concepts that will help us understand both demand and supply and how they match up, which will provide the foundation for our examination of tourism throughout the rest of the chapters in this book.

## Key Terms

- deferred demand
- discretionary income
- domestic tourism
- drifter
- effective demand
- experience stage
- explorer
- inbound tourism
- individual mass tourist
- international tourism
- mass tourism
- movement stage
- niche tourism
- no demand
- organized mass tourist
- outbound tourism
- post-trip stage
- potential demand
- pre-trip stage
- pull factor
- push factor
- suppressed demand
- tourism attractions
- tourism stakeholders
- tourist inversions
- tourist typology

## Notes

1. Uncyclopedia, "Tourist—The Stereotype," accessed October 12, 2010, http://uncyclopedia.wikia.com/wiki/Tourist_-_the_stereotype.

2. Stephen Williams, *Tourism Geography* (London: Routledge, 1998), 12–14.

3. Nelson Graburn, "The Anthropology of Tourism," *Annals of Tourism Research* 10 (1983).

4. Kevin McGill, "Jindal: BP Funding Millions for Oil Spill Recovery," Associated Press, November 1, 2010, accessed November 4, 2010, http://www.businessweek.com/ap/financialnews/D9J7J43G1.htm.

5. John Swarbrooke, *The Development and Management of Visitor Attractions*, 2nd ed. (Burlington, MA: Butterworth-Heinemann, 2002).

6. Paul Thompson, "Blarney Stone 'Most Unhygienic Tourist Attraction in the World.'" *Daily Mail*, June 16, 2009, accessed November 13, 2010, http://www.dailymail.co.uk/news/article-1193477/Blarney-Stone-unhygienic-tourist-attraction-world.html.

7. Alan A. Lew, "Tourism Is NOT the World's Largest Industry—So Stop Saying It Is!" *Tourism Place Blog*, May 1, 2008, accessed February 4, 2011, http://tourismplace.blogspot.com/2008/04/tourism-is-not-worlds-largest-industry.html.

# Sources

Boniface, Brian, and Chris Cooper. *Worldwide Destinations: The Geography of Travel and Tourism*, 4th ed. Amsterdam: Elsevier Butterworth Heinemann, 2005.

Gregory, Derek. "Scripting Egypt: Orientalism and the Cultures of Travel." In *Writes of Passage: Reading Travel Writing*, edited by James Duncan and Derek Gregory, 114–50. London: Routledge, 1999.

Gunn, Clare A., with Turgut Var. *Tourism Planning: Basics, Concepts, Cases*. 4th ed. New York: Routledge, 2002.

Williams, Stephen. *Tourism Geography*. London: Routledge, 1998.

# CHAPTER 3

# Overview of Tourism Products

Eating, partying, praying, shopping, swimming, sightseeing, gambling, hiking, help-ing, and having sex—although it may seem like these things have nothing in common, they are all activities people participate in through tourism. Tourism is not a one-size-fits-all experience. People have different reasons for traveling, and they want different things from their experiences. Consequently, there is a distinct need for different types of **tourism products**. As a service industry, the primary "products" of tourism are not tangible goods but experiences. With more people traveling than ever before, the tour-ism industry has developed to provide an array of increasingly diversified and special-ized experiences to meet the demands of tourists across the spectrum, from organized mass tourists to drifters.

This chapter provides a brief introduction to some of the types of products that comprise the modern tourism industry. This discussion is by no means comprehen-sive; it is only a selection of tourism products that crosses different types of tourism and tourists. Many of these products overlap and share characteristics of other prod-ucts but have a unique emphasis or appeal to a specific market. Each product involves different resources and affects destinations in distinct ways. We will explore these issues further in the context of the thematic chapters throughout the rest of this text.

# Beach Tourism or Sun, Sea, and Sand (3S) Tourism

Perhaps the most widespread and recognizable tourism product around the world is beach tourism. This is often referred to as "3S tourism" in reference to the three key resources for the product: sun, sea, and sand. Sometimes additional S's are added to the mix—including sex and spirits—but for our purposes, we will consider sex tourism as a separate (albeit related) tourism product. Obviously the focal point of 3S tourism is the beach, which has served as an attraction since an early era in the modern tourism indus-try (see chapter 4). Yet, 3S tourism is more than just the beach. Beyond any other, this product has been used to characterize the tourism industry. Every major world region has 3S tourism destinations. Some of the largest, best-known, and most popular destinations are based on this product. Moreover, 3S tourism appeals to some of the most basic tourist motivations, including the pursuit of pleasure and self-indulgence.

Typical 3S tourism is mass tourism, which accounts for the temporary movements of large numbers of tourists from the more developed countries in the northern climates to well-established coastal destinations, often developing countries with warmer, tropical climates. This product is highly dependent on a well-developed tourism infrastructure to facilitate the mass movement of people and create the desired experience at the destination. Resorts are often a fundamental component of these destinations. They offer the comforts of home and the facilities to enjoy the three S's, including beachfront access, swimming pools, lounge chairs, water-sport equipment, and so on. Because a key goal of this product is relaxation and leisure, related facilities include restaurants, nightclubs, and other venues offering entertainment. Given these amenities, there may be little incentive to leave the resort to experience other aspects of the destination.

Characteristic of mass tourism, these destinations are relatively standardized, so there is a certain degree of interchangeability among similar destinations in different parts of the world. For example, Mexico's Cancún has come to epitomize mass 3S tourism with enormous resort developments, discounted products attracting large numbers of middle- and lower-income tourists, few place-based connections, and a reputation for a party atmosphere. In fact, the name Cancún has become synonymous with 3S tourism and has been exported to other parts of the world (figure 3.1).

**Figure 3.1. This advertisement for "Can Cun Beach" is not in Mexico or anywhere else in the Caribbean basin. In fact, it is halfway around the world in Port El Kantaoui, Tunisia, part of the world's other principal 3S destination region—the Mediterranean. (Source: Velvet Nelson)**

Not all tourism oriented around the beach is synonymous with organized mass tourism, however. Destinations with these resources may not have the capacity to develop this type of large-scale industry, and they may not want to. Correspondingly, individual mass tourists and explorers interested in vacationing at the beach may not want this type of experience. The demand-supply match allows some destinations to maintain the natural quality of their beaches with limited infrastructure to accommodate a smaller number of tourists who appreciate the quieter, more intimate experience. In contrast with major destinations in the Caribbean basin characterized by mass 3S tourism, some of the islands with less developed tourism industries, such as Grenada, offer this brand of beach tourism.

# Sex Tourism

Sex tourism is a product that takes place in destinations all over the world in a variety of forms. The most commonly recognized sex tourism product involves travel to a place to engage in commercial sex (i.e., prostitution). This brand of sex tourism is associated more with male tourists than female. For many destinations, sex is considered to be a by-product of travel rather than the primary motivation (e.g., business travelers using prostitutes at the destination during the course of their trip). However, other destinations have become known for the availability of commercial sex or a particular type of commercial sex (e.g., homosexual or child sex) and therefore attract tourists specifically for this purpose. While this may be a one-time encounter with the prostitute, he or she may also be hired for extended periods, perhaps as a travel companion for the duration of the tourist's vacation. Additionally, these destinations may cater to voyeurs looking for the opportunity to experience things that might not be available to them in their home environment. Well-known destinations for this brand of sex tourism are in Southeast Asia, predominantly Thailand and the Philippines.

The demand generated by sex tourists has become a driving force in the commercial sex trade and consequently trade in women and children. Recently, international agencies including the UNWTO and the United Nations Office on Drugs and Crime (UNODC) have recognized that there is a connection between the tourism industry and human trafficking.[1] In addition to sexual exploitation, trafficked persons often suffer from extreme violations of their human rights, such as the right to not to be held in slavery or involuntary servitude, the right to be free from violence and cruel or inhumane treatment, and the right to health. Various governmental and nongovernmental organizations as well as private companies have worked to develop codes of conduct for both tourism stakeholders and tourists. These codes are intended to promote responsible patterns of behavior to ensure that no one involved in the tourism industry is sexually exploited (for more on codes of conduct, see chapter 11). In particular, efforts have largely concentrated on preventing the trafficking of children and child sexual exploitation associated with tourism. Many countries like the United States have passed child sex tourism laws under which tourists who engage in sex with minors, even outside of the country, can face up to thirty years in a U.S. prison.

Sex tourism that doesn't involve commercial sex is harder to define and is therefore less commonly recognized. For example, this may be framed as seeking romance

# Box 3.1.  Case Study:
# Mass S Tourism in the Mediterranean

"You will either have the holiday of your life or a holiday from hell, all depending on your outlook on life."[1]

As this tour operator suggests, much of tourism experiences comes down to perspective. While some tourists avoid prototypical sun, sea, sand, sex, and spirits tourism, it clearly holds appeal for many tourists around the world, as evidenced by the tremendous popularity of resorts providing these experiences. In this case, the operator is describing Magaluf, one of the principal resorts on the Mediterranean island of Palma de Mallorca (map 3.1) and a destination often cited as having all of the excesses of S tourism in the region. Like many S destinations, Magaluf was once a small island fishing village. During the 1960s, the Mallorcan municipality of Calvià experienced significant investment in mass tourism infrastructure and high-rise resort development in both Magaluf and neighboring Palmanova. Today, the resort has little appearance of or connection to the rest of the island or the Spanish mainland. The municipality receives well over a million tourists annually, many of whom are foreign. In particular, Magaluf was developed specifically to cater to British tourists and has become a piece of Britain in the Mediterranean. Not only is English widely spoken around the resort, but hundreds of cafés and bars have British names, serve British foods and drinks, and even show British television programs.

Following a downturn in tourism during the 1990s, Mallorcan tourism officials developed a diversification strategy to get tourists involved in other activities throughout the destination. However, local tourism operators often discourage tourists from leaving the resorts as a result of possible inconveniences (e.g., crowded public transportation) or dangers (e.g., pickpockets). Most tourism promotions highlight Magaluf's beaches, with the promise of beautiful sand, clear water, and the relaxation of sunbathing during the day. While these S's may be the primary attraction for neighboring Palmanova, they are often only secondary considerations for Magaluf. Also known as "Shagaluf," this resort is better known for its other S's and the multitude of bars and nightclubs, cheap alcohol, the 24-hour party atmosphere, and casual sex. In fact, tourism researcher Hazel Andrews found that there was an "expectation that sexual activity was a reason, if not *the* reason, for being there."[2] The principal tourist market for Magaluf tends to be young adult (from age eighteen to the thirties) British working-class singles. Most arrive in groups on package tours, sometimes for stag and hen parties.

The atmosphere tends to be sexually charged, with references to and an abundance of naked bodies, including topless sunbathers, nudity in cabaret-type shows, exposure during bar crawl drinking games, and even in tourism-related imagery such as promotions and postcards. Tourists are warned about the noise levels of large quantities of inebriated tourists during the peak summer months. Females in particular are warned about unwanted attention, potential harassment, and possibly even rape. Yet, despite a negative reputation, Magaluf continues to appeal to a specific tourist market.

*Discussion topic*: Do you think that 5S tourism is a good strategy for Magaluf? What are the potential negative consequences of using this strategy?

*Tourism on the web*: Institut Balear del Turisme, "Mallorca, the Balearic Islands" at http://www.illesbalears.es/ing/majorca/home.jsp

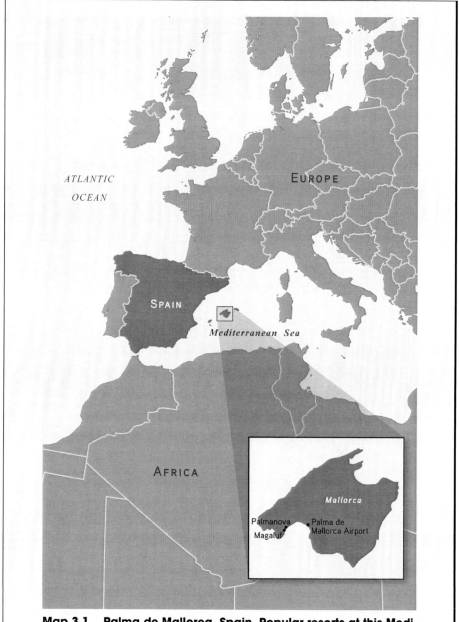

**Map 3.1.   Palma de Mallorca, Spain. Popular resorts at this Medi-terranean destination like Palmanova and Magaluf are based on tourism's S's. (Source: XNR Productions)**

(*continued*)

---

### Box 3.1.  *(continued)*

## Notes

1. Islas Travel Guides, "Welcome to Magaluf," accessed February 8, 2011, http://www.majorca-mallorca.co.uk/magaluf.htm.
2. Hazel Andrews, "Feeling at Home: Embodying Britishness in a Spanish Charter Tourists Resort," *Tourist Studies* 5, no. 3 (2005): 251.

## Source

Andrews, Hazel. "Feeling at Home: Embodying Britishness in a Spanish Charter Tourists Resort." *Tourist Studies* 5, no. 3 (2005): 247–66.

---

and/or a relationship rather than sex. This type of sex tourism is more often associated with women. In this case, money may not be exchanged for the act of sex. However, there may be an economic motivation nonetheless, as tourists offer their partners drinks, meals, entertainment, and/or gifts during the course of their time together. The relationship that forms may continue after the tourists leave the destination; they may return later or pay to bring the partner to their home. The Caribbean, namely popular 3S destinations like Jamaica and the Dominican Republic, has become associated with this phenomenon, where typically white female tourists become involved with black "beach boys." This has become so common that women traveling without a male companion at these destinations are assumed to be sex tourists.

In addition, tourists may travel to a destination with implicit or explicit intentions of having sex with other tourists. Again, the atmosphere of popular 3S destinations lends itself to this form of sex tourism, where the focus is on relaxation and pleasure. Clothing may be minimal—perhaps even optional—and alcohol and/or recreational drugs may be present. Inhibitions may be lowered, and tourists may feel freer to have sexual encounters with strangers than they would in their daily lives and home environments. While this pattern has been publicized in the context of students' spring break, it is certainly not limited to this demographic.

Perhaps not surprisingly, research has shown that, although many people have reported engaging in any one of the above behaviors, few would describe themselves as sex tourists.[2]

# Nature Tourism

Nature tourism is a product that represents a diverse set of activities set in or based on the appreciation of natural attractions. These attractions may include unique natural features, landscape scenery, or the wildlife of a particular place. Such features may be protected as parks and preserves; in particular, the national park designation plays a role in the creation of opportunities for nature tourism, as both domestic and international tourists make a point to visit these places. Nature tourism may be the primary tourism product for a trip or one type of activity participated in during the course of a trip. For example, birding is a specialized nature tourism product that has been growing in recent years. The practice of bird watching and listening is particularly popular among older, affluent tourists, traditionally from more developed countries such as the United States and the United Kingdom, who enjoy traveling to new places in search of opportunities to observe different species. Dedicated tour companies, such as Birding Africa, provide entire trips oriented around the practice.

Although nature tourism may be positioned as niche tourism in opposition to mass tourism such as 3S, this product can also provide a diversionary activity for mass tourists. In the case of the Caribbean, islands depend on sun, sea, and sand to attract tourists. However, these destinations also promote nature tourism as an activity tourists can participate in for a day, or part of a day, during their vacation. This is not the primary motivation for the trip, but it allows tourists to experience more of an island than simply resort areas on the coast. These products may be packaged as nature walks or hikes, in which guides highlight local flora and fauna (figure 3.2).

As the global tourism industry has been growing, more destinations around the world have utilized their natural attractions and developed a nature tourism product. There are, of course, good examples of nature-based tourism activities in which tourists have the opportunity to experience unique environments and/or wildlife with few negative impacts. At the same time, there are bad examples of nature being exploited for the purpose of tourism. This has generated considerable debate about how nature tourism should take place and resulted in the evolution of the ecotourism concept (see box 3.2).

# Adventure Tourism

Adventure tourism is a product that combines aspects of nature (above) and sport tourism (below). Like nature tourism, this product is typically predicated on natural attractions; however, the emphasis in adventure tourism is more on the activity that takes place in that environment as opposed to appreciation of that environment. Like sport tourism, adventure tourism is based on physical activity; however, the emphasis in adventure tourism is typically a physical activity that tourists wouldn't normally participate in at home and is more dependent on the natural resources of a place. These activities may require specialized equipment and training or skill, and there is some degree of excitement and/or perceived risk. Examples of adventure tourism might include zip-lining in rain forest canopies, kiteboarding, whitewater rafting or kayaking, mountain trekking, rock climbing, spelunking, and skydiving.

As with ecotourism, there are hard and soft variants, depending on the actual level of risk involved. Hard adventure tourism is more likely to be the focus of a trip that takes place in remote locations, while soft adventure tourism may be an activity for mass tourists closer to well-developed destination areas. Although these activities occur in destinations around the world, places that have become most associated with adventure tourism are some of the most remote. For example, Nepal offers adventure

**Figure 3.2.  Recognizing the most powerful pull factor for the Caribbean, one of the first attractions described for the island of Curaçao is its beaches. However, nature tourism provides a secondary attraction for many tourists, such as the ones shown in this photograph who are participating in a nature walk in Christoffel National Park. (Source: Tom Nelson)**

tourism activities such as mountain trekking and rock climbing in the Himalayas. Zimbabwe offers bungee jumping at Victoria Falls or whitewater rafting on the Zambezi River (figure 3.3).

## Sport Tourism

Sport and tourism have historically had a symbiotic relationship. Definitions of sport tourism include both travel to participate in sports and to watch sporting events, but for our purposes, we will consider the latter under event tourism (below). In the hard variant of this product, sport is the primary motivation for a trip; in the soft variant, sport may be a leisure activity that tourists participate in at some point during their

# Box 3.2.   In-Depth: The Ecotourism Concept

The term **ecotourism** is frequently used as a synonym for nature tourism. In theory, there is overlap between the two products; in practice, there may be little distinction between them. However, the concept of ecotourism is intended to go beyond activities in nature and/or appreciating nature. The International Ecotourism Society (TIES) defines ecotourism as "responsible travel to natural areas that conserves the environment and improves the well-being of local people."[1] The concept was intended to maximize the benefits of tourism and ensure both economic and environmental sustainability. An argument can be made for tourism if it is shown to be as profitable as other, more environmentally destructive activities, such as logging or mining—or in fact, more profitable in the long term. However, this depends on the preservation of environmental resources that provide the basis for tourism. At the same time, local people must be part of tourism. These people should be involved in activities to ensure that the tourism developed fits within their values and lifestyles. They should directly benefit from tourism, not only to improve their quality of life, but also to ensure that they have a stake in it and will provide the necessary support.

Destinations around the world have attempted to translate the ecotourism concept into a tourism product, with varying results. Places such as Costa Rica and Kenya have become associated with ecotourism, while others offer some type of experience called ecotourism. As such, researchers argue that it may be useful to make a distinction between hard and soft variations of ecotourism that exist in practice. In this model, "hard ecotourism" is a niche product involving small numbers of tourists who are explicitly interested in wilderness experiences as well as ensuring the sustainability of their actions. Typically categorized toward the drifter end of the spectrum, these tourists visit more remote destinations where there are few other tourists and tourist services. Ecotourism is the primary focus of the trip, which may be physically and/or mentally demanding. This may be done as part of a specialized tour package through a company such as Gap Adventures, but it may also be undertaken independently with the use of informal local resources.

"Soft ecotourism" has been criticized as just a different label for nature tourism, with little of the concept behind ecotourism. This variation provides mass tourists with an opportunity to have an "ecotourism" experience as part of their larger trip. These tourists have a more superficial interest in environmental issues. Their experiences are shorter and may be even just a day trip to a natural area that is relatively close to the principal destination region and has the appropriate infrastructure (e.g., paths, bathrooms, refreshments, etc.) to accommodate a large number of tourists. Consequently, interactions with nature are facilitated by a guide and tend to be more superficial. These hard and soft positions are, of course, two ends of a spectrum, and there are many examples of experiences that fall somewhere in between.

Thus, while ecotourism was intended to provide a sustainable framework for nature tourism, it has, to some extent, become just another buzzword to generate interest in tourism. This has led to the development of certification programs to help ensure that products being labeled ecotourism are, in fact, environmentally sustainable. For example, Ecotourism Australia is one of the most long-standing ecotourism accreditation systems. This organization developed a set of guidelines for various levels of environmentally sustainable tourism, from nature tourism that uses specific measures to minimize the impact of tourists' activities on the environment to a comprehensive form of ecotourism in which operators strive for the highest levels of sustainability. Businesses can then use this certification to support their claims of sustainability to knowledgeable tourists.

*(continued)*

---

## Box 3.2.   *(continued)*

*Discussion topic*: Search for an ecotourism product on the Internet. Do you think that the experience/activity described should be considered nature tourism or ecotourism? Why?

*Tourism on the web*: Ecotourism Australia, "Welcome to Ecotourism Australia," at http://www.ecotourism.org.au/

## Note

1. The International Ecotourism Society, "What Is Ecotourism?" accessed November 20, 2010, http://www.ecotourism.org/what-is-ecotourism.

## Source

Weaver, David B. "Comprehensive and Minimalist Dimensions of Ecotourism." *Annals of Tourism Research* 32, no. 2 (2005): 439–55.

---

**Figure 3.3.    Adventure tourism often involves physical activities in spectacular natural environments. Whitewater rafting on Class IV rapids provides enough adrenaline-inducing excitement, while the spectacular scenery of the river gorge further enhances the experience. (Source: Velvet Nelson)**

trip. This general product encompasses a range of activities that span not only different types of sports but also different seasons and environments. Sport tourism may be dependent on the resources of the local environment, as with adventure tourism, but this product may be more dependent on a specific type of infrastructure or facility. For example, the inherent physical geography of a place may play a role in golf, but the course design is often a more important factor.

The activity may be one that the tourist is involved in at home during his or her leisure time. Avid golfers often plan trips where they travel to play different courses. They may wish to try new courses or experience famous courses associated with major professional golf tournaments, such as Pebble Beach in California or Augusta National in Georgia. At the same time, the activity may be something that the tourist has only limited opportunity to participate in when they are in their home environment. In the flat states of the plains or the warm southern states, people may have a desire to participate in winter sports, but they don't have that opportunity at home. Therefore, they have to plan a trip to a mountain state, such as Colorado, to fulfill this demand.

Winter sport tourism is one of the most prevalent sport tourism products. Alpine skiing, cross-country skiing, and snowboarding are popular winter recreation activities that provide the basis for winter sport tourism. Some ski resorts in Europe date back to the late nineteenth century, while the oldest in North America date back to the early twentieth century. Many of the world's more developed regions have major winter sport industries. This is particularly true in Europe, where the Alps are one of the world's premier winter sports regions, and in North America, where many resorts are located in the Rocky Mountains. Other activities that tourists might participate in during a winter vacation might include snowshoeing, sledding, or ice skating; however, these activities are less likely to be the primary motivation for a trip.

Summer sport tourism, or warm weather sport, includes a much more diverse set of activities. Again, golf tourism is one of the largest summer sport tourism products that now have a presence in destinations around the world. Other activities may include bicycling (figure 3.4) or horseback riding tours. Water sport tourism is also immensely popular at coastal destinations and includes activities such as swimming, snorkeling, scuba diving, surfing, wind surfing, jet skiing, water skiing, sailing, fishing, and more. While these activities may take place at any number of coastal destinations, some have particularly been associated with water-sport tourism. For example, the island of Tortola in the British Virgin Islands is known as a sailing destination, while Grand Turk Island in the Turks and Caicos is known as a scuba destination.

# Rural and Agricultural Tourism

Rural tourism is an often hard-to-define product that may encompass many of the activities described above based on natural attractions; however, there is typically a human component as well. The U.S. Census Bureau defines rural areas as all of the land and people located outside of urbanized areas and urban clusters.[3] Therefore, this includes both small towns and wilderness areas, and very different types of tourism activities are likely to take place in each. Thus, rural tourism is more often associated

**Figure 3.4.   Variations of bicycle tours are now being organized in destinations around the world. In the case of this tourist, bicycling across Switzerland is the primary objective of her trip. At other destinations, tourists may have the opportunity to spend a day of their vacation sightseeing by bicycle. (Source: Sara Schnabel)**

with the general sensibility of "rural" that pertains to life in the countryside. Rural recreation activities such as scenic drives, country picnics, hunting, or fishing may be included in this product.

In particular, some of the best-known forms of rural tourism make use of local agricultural industries. This may also be described as farm or agricultural tourism (agritourism or agrotourism). Activities within this product vary widely. Tourists may participate in activities set in the farm environment, such as horseback riding or hiking farm trails. They may consume farm produce, such as eating at a farm restaurant, purchasing items at a farm market, or even doing the "pick-your-own" option. Tourists may also participate in farm activities. Some activities are simulated, such as tourist cattle drives and cowboy cookouts hosted by dude ranch resorts, but there are also working farms and ranches on which the tourist learns about and assists in daily chores or harvests. For these activities, tourists will stay on the farm in facilities converted to

## Box 3.3.  Experience: Europe by Bicycle

My husband and I have always been avid bikers. A few years ago, we learned about Bicycle Adventure Club—a nonprofit where members organize bicycle tours both in the United States and around the world for other members. We had just retired, so we had lots of free time, and the idea of biking in Europe appealed to us. We started with a tour in Italy and have since done others in Switzerland/France and Slovenia/Austria/Italy. We bike from town to town and spend one or two nights in a place before traveling to the next one. Each night at the hotel we read in our guidebook about the places we're going to visit the next day so that we know what we want to see and do along the way. A lot of the sightseeing that we do takes place from our bicycles during the ride, but we also have some additional time, especially after we arrive at a town for the evening, to visit other sites as well.

The tour organizers provide everyone a route sheet, a map, and GPS coordinates to get you from one town to the next, and then you're on your own. No one actually leads you as a group, so you have some flexibility to see what you want. You do occasionally get lost, though. On our trip through Switzerland, we arrived at the designated town in the late afternoon, but we couldn't find the hotel—it was around a corner behind another building, and the directions were pretty vague. It took us about a half hour of walking around, trying to ask people in English, showing them our map and the name of the hotel, before the tourist information office was finally able to get us there. But there were other people in the group who had even more trouble and didn't actually get in until about 8 p.m. We normally get to the hotel much earlier so that we can shower and relax a bit before a 7 p.m. dinner.

The tours are given a difficulty rating based on the number of miles covered and the amount of climbing involved per day. I think the first one we did in Italy was rated a 3B or 3C—that's up to 3,500 feet of climbing and 65 miles per day. Everyone is responsible for bringing their own equipment, so I had bought a folding bicycle that I could pack for the flight to Europe. It was a very small bicycle with twenty-inch wheels, which made this challenging ride extremely difficult. I now have a regular size breakaway bicycle where all of the parts actually fit into my suitcase, and I've never had to pay oversized/overweight luggage fees. There's a van that takes your luggage from one hotel to the next, and there may be a vehicle that picks people up who aren't going to be able to make it on that particular stage, but for the most part, you are expected to complete every ride as scheduled.

On one of our rides in the tri-border region between Slovenia, Austria, and Italy, I blew out a tire. It was stupid, but the road going down from the mountains in Slovenia to Austria was very steep and very bad with lots of potholes. It was a little scary, so I rode my brake too hard. The wheel overheated, the tire blew off, and the tube was ruined. I couldn't replace it, and I couldn't fix it. A nice couple—the woman was English—with a car stopped and ended up taking me back to the hotel. It turns out we had both taught in the same field.

Each of our trips has been amazing. Biking in Europe—especially places we've toured—can be extremely challenging. Vršič Pass in Slovenia, for example, is a route through the Julian Alps with steep grades and fifty switchbacks—twenty-four up and twenty-six down. Sometimes when I'm biking here in Colorado and I start to get tired, I think to myself, if I can bike Vršič, I can do anything! So it is also rewarding and a tremendous amount of fun. The scenery is beautiful, the towns are lovely, and it's such a different way of seeing a place than when you're traveling by car. One of our favorite experiences was on the Switzerland/France tour. It was so much fun for us to know that three different days of that trip we followed the same route as the Tour de France that year. Our trip was in June, and we watched the Tour on TV in July and saw all of the places we had just been. We definitely plan on doing more tours in the future.

*—Sara*

serve as a bed and breakfast or specially constructed facilities such as cottages. Farm tourism has a particularly strong tradition in Europe.

In addition, new products based on even more specific interests continue to evolve out of this product. For example, wine tourism has become so popular that it has grown into a distinct product. This involves traveling to wine regions to visit vineyards and wineries, participate in wine tastings, and purchase wine at the source. This supplements income generated from the production of wine and promotes the product to wider markets. Wine tourism now takes place all over the world, including traditional producers such as France and Italy, as well as the United States, Chile, Australia, and South Africa.

# Urban Tourism

As with rural tourism, urban tourism may encompass activities considered with other products, such as cultural and heritage tourism or event tourism (below). Towns and cities have an array of attractions upon which urban tourism may be based, and some of the largest tourism destinations in the world are major cities, such as Paris, New York City, Bangkok, and Dubai. These urban attractions fall under either category of human attraction (see chapter 2), including those that originally had some other purpose and those that were built for the purpose of tourism. In many cases, attractions will be spatially concentrated in particular parts of the city, such as historic neighborhoods, shopping and entertainment districts, or waterfront developments.

For example, cities all over the world attract tourists for their "old town" areas that feature historic buildings from ancient ruins to churches and cathedrals or castles and palaces. Serving different purposes over time, these areas may be preserved as attractions. Urban amenities such as upscale or boutique shopping, museums, art galleries, theaters, concert venues, sports arenas, restaurants, bars, nightclubs, and more serve the dual purpose of providing a desirable living environment for residents and an attractive environment for tourist visits. In some cases, an additional category of attraction has developed: those that originally served a specific purpose but have since been transformed into something else entirely. For example, the Meatpacking District in Manhattan developed based on the spatial concentration of slaughterhouses and packing plants. In recent years, this area has been redeveloped into New York's most fashionable neighborhood with diverse restaurants, trendy clubs, fashionable boutiques, and luxury hotels. This, combined with historic district designations, has given rise to walking and guided tours of the area.

# Cultural Tourism

Cultural tourism is arguably one of the oldest tourism products, as many of the earliest tourists traveled for the experience of other cultures and cultural attractions. As the tourism industry began to develop specialized products, cultural tourism was considered a niche tourism product oriented toward a small subset of affluent and educated tourists interested in authentic experiences of other cultures. Today, however, cultural tourism is recognized as one of the broadest tourism products, which encompasses a vast range of attractions and activities and has extensive overlap with other products. Some reports suggest that as many as 70 percent of international tourists today participate in cultural tourism.[4] Given its tremendous extent and importance, we will examine the cultural resources for tourism in greater depth in chapter 6.

Cultural tourism is based on human attractions, and in particular, elements of a society's culture. For the most part, cultural tourism pertains to the unique cultural patterns that have evolved in a specific place over time to serve a purpose for that group of people, not to attract tourists. This includes the patterns of lifestyles, cuisine, clothing, art, music, folklore, religious practices, and more that make a place distinct. In the modern world, with increased globalization and the perception of uniform contemporary lifestyles, there is often an interest in and a demand for experiences of different cultures. Although many of these patterns no longer have a role in the daily lives of these people, this demand means that they may in fact maintain elements of traditional culture for the purpose of offering a unique experience for tourists (figure 3.5). There is considerable overlap between this brand of cultural tourism and heritage

**Figure 3.5. Elements of traditional culture create a distinct attraction for foreign tourists. These people in an ethnic Miao village in rural Guizhou, China, are dressed in traditional costumes to greet a group of American tourists with music, dancing, and liquor. (Source: Velvet Nelson)**

tourism, as well as certain types of event tourism such as festivals. In addition, as elements of traditional culture are more likely to be an available attraction in rural areas, there may be overlap with rural tourism as well.

At the same time, the role of contemporary culture should not be underestimated in tourism. Elements of contemporary culture may be used specifically for the purpose of attracting tourists, but tourism may also be a side effect. This may be associated with some aspect of high culture, such as artistic works and performances. England is particularly known for its literary destinations—places specifically associated with a well-known writer or referenced in a widely read work. In these cases, tourism to a place is not a goal of the writer, yet tourism stakeholders in a place may use the work to their advantage. This may also be associated with popular culture. For example, some of the major film projects over the past decade, such as *Harry Potter*, *The Lord of the Rings*, and *Pirates of the Caribbean*, have all generated significant tourism to film sites. Again, tourism was not the primary object in producing the film but is clearly a by-product.

Although attractions developed specifically for the purpose of tourism do not fit traditional ideas of cultural tourism, they are nonetheless shaped by and represent aspects of contemporary culture. For example, Disneyland and Disneyworld are two of the most visited tourism destinations in the world and have been described as epitomizing American culture. Likewise, the theme park–like environment of Las Vegas is distinctly part of popular American culture. In contrast with tourism related to elements of traditional culture associated with rural areas, these activities are associated with urban areas and overlap with urban tourism.

# Heritage Tourism

As heritage tourism overlaps with cultural tourism, interest in cultural heritage has a very long history. However, heritage tourism only recently emerged as a distinct tourism product and is considered one of the fastest growing. Heritage tourism encompasses travel to varied sites of historic importance such as the Parthenon or the Taj Mahal, sites where important historic events occurred such as Gettysburg National Military Park or Auschwitz Concentration Camp, and sites that represent the stories and people of the past such as the South African Cultural History Museum or Mozart's Birthplace museum. These sites may be located in either rural or urban areas.

Given the considerable overlap between heritage and cultural tourism, the two may be combined into a single "cultural heritage tourism" product. However, that may unnecessarily limit heritage tourism. For example, heritage tourism activities may be oriented around United Nations Educational, Scientific, and Cultural Organization (UNESCO)–designated World Heritage Sites. These are sites deemed to be of outstanding universal value based on a specific set of selection criteria. These criteria are predominantly based on human/cultural factors, but there are also four criteria based on physical/natural factors that encompass those places of important natural history and biodiversity, as well as places of spectacular natural beauty.[5] While these places would likely serve as tourism attractions regardless, the World Heritage Site designation often raises the site's profile and increases visits.

# Visiting Friends and Relatives (VFR) Tourism

Visiting friends and relatives (VFR) is one of the most common tourism products in which most people participate. This product developed significantly in the second half of the twentieth century with increased mobilities. People in many parts of the world experienced greater abilities to move to new locations, within their own country or abroad, based on a variety of opportunities for school, work, or otherwise. This created dispersed networks of family and friends. At the same time, people experienced greater abilities to travel to visit these family and friends. VFR is often domestic tourism; however, this is also one of the largest tourist products for places with high rates of emigration. This form of international tourism links the place of origin, whether it is a small Caribbean island like Trinidad or a large country like India, with the places to which these people have migrated.

Still, VFR tourism is a product that generally receives little attention. Many people won't consider VFR trips to be tourism because it may be seen as an obligation rather than a vacation or simply "going home" rather than "going away." Moreover, VFR tourists are often seen as existing "outside" the normal tourism industry. Their patterns of behavior might be determined by different factors than those of other tourists. For example, their destination choice is based on where friends or relatives live as opposed to the attractions of a place. Their choice of activities is influenced by their friends' and relatives' regular activities, interests, and recommendations. In addition, they may be less reliant on the tourism infrastructure. They may stay in and eat at people's homes as opposed to staying in hotels and eating at restaurants. They may rely on their hosts' personal cars rather than renting one or using local transportation, and their hosts may serve as their guides rather than hiring one or taking a tour. Although these tourists may contribute less to the tourism industry at a destination, they are nonetheless contributing to the local economy.

There may be overlap between this product and others in terms of motivations. For example, people may travel to their birthplace for events such as weddings or reunions. In addition, there will be overlap with other products as people participate in tourism activities during the course of their visit with family and friends. Because of the tremendous variations within this product, some researchers have argued for it to be broken down into smaller segments, including domestic and international, short-haul and long-haul, or visiting friends and visiting relatives.

# Event Tourism

Event tourism is based on special events as a category of tourism attractions. Special events have long been an attraction for localized markets and have often generated day trips, for example, as people travel to neighboring towns to participate in local festivals. However, as more people are enabled to travel farther distances, this product has exploded. It now encompasses a diverse set of events that are global in nature or highly localized, always in the same location or at various locations, religious or secular, annual or one time only.

Kumbha Mela is a riverside festival held four times every twelve years at four different sites in India. It is considered to be one of the world's oldest religious festivals and the largest. The most recent Purna Kumbh Mela (the complete festival every twelfth year) in 2001 was attended by more than 60 million people over the course of the six-week celebration. This has been described as the largest human gathering in the recorded history of the world. Some traditional religious festivals also continue to be celebrated around the world but have evolved into new forms over time and in different places. For example, carnival has a long history, particularly in the Catholic religion, and pre-Lenten carnival festivals now attract visitors from all over the world. However, based on different traditions and influences, carnival in Venice is a much different experience than carnival in Rio de Janeiro. Moreover, popular events such as New Orleans' Mardi Gras have taken on a host of new activities and meanings.

Secular festivals take place all over the world based on a range of attractions, from popular culture—such as music or film festivals—to local heritage or even local produce. Oktoberfest, held in Munich over a seventeen-day period at the end of September and the beginning of October, is one of the most famous of these events. The two hundredth-anniversary celebration in 2010 saw approximately six and a half million visitors, who consumed an estimated seven million mugs of beer.[6] The Sauerkraut Festival started as a small local festival in Waynesville, Ohio, a town with less than three thousand residents, and has grown into a major event attracting approximately 350,000 visitors from all over the country. In addition to the more than 450 juried craft vendors, there are more than 30 food vendors offering everything from traditional pork and sauerkraut dishes to sauerkraut ice cream.[7]

Major sporting events are some of the most widely known forms of event tourism. In some cases, these are annual events that occur in the same place. As a result, these destinations are often closely associated with the event. For example, the Kentucky Derby is a world-famous thoroughbred horse race held in May at Churchill Downs in Louisville, Kentucky, that attracts approximately 155,00 visitors each year.[8] Wimbledon is one of the most prominent professional tennis tournaments, held in June at The All England Lawn Tennis Club in the London suburb of Wimbledon. The two-week-long tournament is attended by approximately 450,000 visitors.[9]

In other cases, these events take place at certain intervals and are hosted at different venues around the world. The Olympic Games are a global event held every two years, alternating between the summer and winter games. Major cities compete to host the games, not only to bring international attention to the city and country but also to bring investment and tourism. Vancouver, Canada, host to the 2010 Winter Olympic Games, was estimated to have received more than five thousand athletes and officials, ten thousand media representatives, and 2 million on-site spectators. The FIFA (Fédération Internationale de Football Association) World Cup is also a major world event that occurs every four years. The 2010 FIFA World Cup, hosted in South Africa, had an estimated 3 million people in attendance over the course of the month-long event.[10]

Professional conferences, conventions, congresses, and trade fairs have become so important that major cities all over the world have developed extensive convention facilities and actively compete to host organizations' events. These events range from just a few hundred participants to tens of thousands. For example, the 2010 Annual Meeting of the Association of American Geographers, held in Washington, D.C., saw more than eight thousand participants from eighty-one countries.[11] The majority of these participants must travel to and stay at the event site. While these are events that people may be required to attend for their jobs or for career advancement, the destination may encourage them to participate in other activities while they are there, such as evening entertainment activities, sightseeing, and shopping, or perhaps to stay longer than the required duration of their participation at the event.

The same increased mobilities that have created the dispersed networks of friends and families that play a role in VFR tourism have also generated a type of event tourism. While VFR tourism is considered tourism in which people travel to visit friends and family in their home environments, social events such as family reunions may also be planned so that each family member travels to a set location to meet the others. In some cases, this is a centralized location that is easily accessible to all, but increasingly reunions are being held at vacation destinations to take advantage of the tourism infrastructure as well as maximize the limited time and money many families have available for travel. Likewise, the rise of destination weddings has generated a type of event tourism where the couple, as well as friends and family, travel to a tourism destination for the ceremony as well as related activities.

# Service or Volunteer Tourism

Service or volunteer tourism involves traveling to another place to volunteer one's time providing aid, assisting with local development, contributing to conservation efforts, participating in research projects, and more. This is not always a clearly differentiated tourism product. We may not think of service work that takes place outside of the home environment as tourism because of our long-standing association of tourism with leisure activities and the pursuit of pleasure. Yet, these activities nonetheless fall under that broad definition of tourism consisting of travel to other places for various purposes. Moreover, many people will also participate in leisure activities during the course of their trip.

Service tourism generally involves the movement of tourists from the more developed countries of the world to the less developed ones. However, service tourism destinations may also be impoverished areas of developed countries or those devastated by a natural disaster, such as the hurricane-ravaged Gulf Coast region of the United States. Although the potential market for service tourism includes everyone, experiences may be oriented toward young people, particularly students or recent college graduates.

Service tourists do not easily fit into the tourist "types" (chapter 2). The tourists who are interested in this product will have characteristics in common with drifters and explorers: they wish to visit out-of-the-ordinary places, interact with local people, and have a deeper experience of place. Unlike drifters and explorers who create their own experiences, service tourists must rely on an organization to both create opportunities for service and facilitate their experience. Some activities will be set up by local groups, such as churches, but there are a variety of travel agencies and nonprofits that also organize experiences for various humanitarian, conservation, education, or research purposes. This may, in fact, open more doors for service tourists, allowing them to more effectively penetrate the back regions of a place than even drifters. These tourists have the opportunity to experience life as it is lived in that place by staying, eating, and socializing with local people.

Organizations that create service tourism opportunities may offer some type of sponsorship or financial support for participants, usually exceptional young people. Others may assist in fundraising that will both benefit the project and allow people to participate who wouldn't otherwise have the means, such as inner-city youth. However, most service tourists pay for their travel, accommodation, and other daily expenses in addition to donating their time and labor. In some cases, they may actually pay more for their experiences—while receiving fewer services—than they would for a traditional holiday. This may be because the tourism infrastructure at the places where service projects are conducted is less developed or because the area is more difficult to reach than a mass tourism destination. Their contribution to a project may also require that they stay at a place for a longer period of time than an average vacation. However, those interested in this experience believe that the intangible benefits are worth the monetary cost.

This product is sometimes considered "alternative tourism" in that it presents tourists with an alternative to other products that appeal to traditional touristic motivations. For example, the "alternative spring break" is targeted at students looking for something other than the typical spring break trip that covers all of the S's. Service tourists are motivated by their desire for a different type of experience and one that makes a positive contribution to the places they visit. This has more meaning to them than if they simply gave money to a cause, because they were a distinct part of the process and they can see and feel the effects directly. At the same time, service tourism holds distinct benefits for the tourists as well. This product allows for even greater interaction with and immersion in other places and cultures. The experience is not always an easy one, often requiring adjustments to the unfamiliar and the unexpected, but it can be exceptionally rewarding. Many service tourists argue that the personal development resulting from the experience has a more substantial and lasting impact on their lives after they return home than a typical vacation.

Although there are key differences in both motivations and experiences, there may be overlap between service tourism and other products discussed above, depending on the nature of the project. Earthwatch Institute's South African mammal conservation project could also be considered ecotourism. A Volunteer Latin America project, in which participants learn about and work on an organic farm in Ecuador, could be considered rural or agrotourism. A Go! Overseas Teach Abroad program at a school in one of Rio de Janeiro's *favelas* (figure 3.6) could be considered urban tourism, and a Cultural Restoration Tourism Project restoring an ancient Buddhist temple in Mongolia could be considered cultural tourism.

**Figure 3.6. In addition to contributions to the destination, service tourism can be a tremendously rewarding experience for tourists. This volunteer says goodbye to the children she taught at a primary school in Rio de Janeiro, Brazil. (Source: Heather Camacho)**

# Conclusion

Tourism is constantly evolving with ever more specialized products to meet the demands of tourists. This chapter introduces only a few of the products now offered by destinations around the world. Moreover, it should be evident from this discussion that each category could be further subdivided into tourism products that reflect a specific interest, activity, or experience (e.g., golf tourism as a part of summer sport tourism as a part of sport tourism), which would require a far more in-depth examination. Nonetheless, this overview contributes to our broad understanding of tourism. It also provides the necessary context for discussions of the geographic foundation for and the effects of tourism, since different types of tourism and tourism products rely on varied resources and have their own distinct effects.

# Key Terms

- ecotourism
- tourism products

# Notes

1. United Nations Office on Drugs and Crime, "United Nations Organizations Cooperate to Stamp Out Human Trafficking and Sex Tourism," April 2012, accessed December 7, 2012, http://www.unodc.org/unodc/en/frontpage/2012/April/united-nations-organizations-cooperate-to-stamp-out-human-trafficking-and-sex-tourism.html.

2. Martin Oppermann, "Sex Tourism," *Annals of Tourism Research* 26, no. 2 (1999).

3. United States Census Bureau, "2010 Census Urban and Rural Classification and Urban Area Criteria," accessed April 28, 2011, http://www.census.gov/geo/www/ua/2010urbanruralclass.html.

4. Bob McKercher and Hilary du Cros, *Cultural Tourism: The Partnership between Tourism and Cultural Heritage Management* (New York: Haworth Hospitality Press, 2002), 1.

5. United Nations Educational, Scientific, and Cultural Organization, "The Criteria for Selection," accessed September 10, 2011, http://whc.unesco.org/en/criteria/.

6. Oktoberfest, "The Oktoberfest Is Over!" accessed November 23, 2010, http://www.oktoberfest.de/en/article/About+the+Oktoberfest/About+the+Oktoberfest/The+Oktoberfest+is+over!/2205/.

7. Ohio Sauerkraut Festival, "Festival History," accessed November 23, 2010, http://www.sauerkrautfestival.com/.

8. Kentucky Derby, "2011 Kentucky Derby," accessed November 23, 2010, http://www.kentuckyderby.info/.

9. Wimbledon 2010 Official Website, "About Wimbledon," accessed November 23, 2010, http://aeltc2010.wimbledon.org/en_GB/about/guide/club.html.

10. Fédération Internationale de Football Association, "Lessons from 2006," July 9, 2010, accessed November 23, 2010, http://www.fifa.com/worldcup/archive/southafrica2010/news/newsid=1270860/index.html.

11. Association of American Geographers, "Washington, D.C: Building Partnerships for Geography," May 2010, accessed December 1, 2012, http://www.aag.org/galleries/meridian-files/201005Meridian.pdf

# Sources

Fennell, David A. *Ecotourism*. 3rd ed. London: Routledge, 2008.

McKercher, Bob, and Hilary du Cros. *Cultural Tourism: The Partnership between Tourism and Cultural Heritage Management*. New York: Haworth Hospitality Press, 2002.

Moscardo, Gianna, Philip Pearce, Alastair Morrison, David Green, and Joseph T. O'Leary. "Developing a Typology for Understanding Visiting Friends and Relatives Markets." *Journal of Travel Research* 38, no. 3 (2000): 251–59.

Oppermann, Martin. "Sex Tourism." *Annals of Tourism Research* 26, no. 2 (1999): 251–66.

Smith, Melanie K. *Issues in Cultural Tourism Studies*. 2nd ed. London: Routledge, 2009.

Wearing, Stephen. *Volunteer Tourism: Experiences That Make a Difference*. Wallingford, UK: CABI, 2001.

Williams, Stephen. *Tourism Geography*. London: Routledge, 1998.

# Part II

# THE GEOGRAPHIC FOUNDATION OF TOURISM

Tourism is not simply a product of the modern world. People have been traveling for various reasons since ancient times. However, patterns of tourism have historically been spatially concentrated. Certain places became destinations for tourists, because those places were accessible based on the transportation systems available at the time and because they possessed the physical and/or cultural resources that were valued by people in the principal tourist-generating societies during that period. Today, we see the dynamic reshaping of tourism patterns. Places all over the world are more accessible than ever, and new tourist markets are demanding different types of experiences. Trying to understand these ever-changing patterns in places with widely varied circumstances can seem overwhelming. Yet the framework of geography—with its diverse set of topical branches across both physical and human geography—provides us with the means of exploring all of these issues.

This section begins our examination of tourism through the topical branches of geography. In particular, these chapters consider the geographic foundation of tourism. Chapter 4 discusses the historical geography of tourism. While we cannot make a comprehensive study of the historical geography of tourism in this introductory text, this chapter provides an overview of tourism in key past periods and examines some of the geographic factors that contributed to the development of the modern tourism industry. Chapter 5 discusses the transport geography of tourism. It examines the components of the transport system and some of the fundamental issues in tourism transport. Chapter 6 discusses the physical geography of tourism. This chapter illustrates how we can use the tools and concepts of branches in physical geography to understand the physical resources that provide the basis for tourism at destinations around the world and the physical factors that present a barrier to tourism. Finally, chapter 7 discusses the cultural geography of tourism. It draws on the tools and concepts in one of human geography's most prominent branches to understand the cultural resources used in tourism, as well as cultural barriers.

# CHAPTER 4

# The Historical Geography of Tourism

Some of us may daydream about hopping in our car and driving across the West, cruising the Caribbean for four days and three nights, or getting on a plane and flying to Australia. Of course, we may never take these trips, for any number of reasons. But it's easy for us to imagine because we *can* do these things, which is something we often take for granted. If we look back, say, two hundred years, it is an entirely different story. At this time, the first expeditions across the American West had only just been completed by explorers like Lewis and Clark. The round trip journey took over two years of difficult travel on foot, on horseback, and in small boats. A sail to and around the Caribbean would take many months, dependent on wind and weather conditions. It could be a dangerous journey, with threats of hurricanes, tropical diseases, slave revolts, pirate attacks, or naval battles. Traveling to Australia would have been virtually unthinkable for an American.

Yet, as hard as it may be for us to comprehend, tourism was already a well-established phenomenon in the world. Clearly there are significant differences between this early tourism and today, but there are surprising parallels as well. Thinking about the past is not just a matter of idle curiosity; it is essential if we are to truly understand modern tourism in all of its complexity.

**Historical geography** is a topical branch of geography. Like the other branches, historical geography uses the framework of geography to examine topics in and contribute to the study of a particular field—in this case, history (see figure 1.1). Therefore, we can consider historical geography to be the study of the geography and geographic conditions of past periods. Yet, historical geography has another vital role to play. Geography is a means of understanding the world. However, as we examine current patterns and circumstances of places, we cannot truly understand them if we do not understand how they came to be. Thus, historical geography can also be used to examine the processes of change that have taken place over time so that we might better understand the geography of the present. Perhaps taken a step further, if we understand this evolution over time, we might be able to project the geography of the future. As such, historical geography has a part to play in all geography, including the geography of tourism.

Research in tourism studies has often focused on contemporary issues, and tourism has typically been a neglected topic in historical research. Likewise, there has been little relationship between tourism geography and historical geography, despite the fact that the latter framework clearly has potential to contribute to both the study of tourism in past periods and the evolution of tourism over time. Consequently, historical tourism research has been somewhat uneven, focusing on tourism during specific time periods or in particular places. Yet, the evolution of tourism as a mass phenomenon is considered one of the most significant social developments in recent history. The importance of studying the past to understand the factors that allowed the development of tourism, and the origins of many of the patterns we see today, should be clear.

This chapter continues to lay the foundation for our discussion of the geography of tourism. It provides an overview of tourism in key past periods and the development of the modern tourism industry (figure 4.1). The framework of geography can help us understand the factors that allowed this development to take place. We will consider some of these factors here so that we may begin to develop an appreciation for broad patterns and trends in tourism; however, we will continue to examine these issues as they pertain to the topical branches discussed in the following chapters.

**Figure 4.1. We can examine patterns and trends of tourism in past periods to help us understand the circumstances of modern tourism. (Source: Nancy Shumaker)**

# Studying Historical Tourism

The origin of tourism is a subject of debate among scholars. This is partially attributed to the lack of a clear definition and what motivations and/or activities should (or should not) be considered tourism. Travel has taken place throughout human history, leading some scholars to argue that we can trace this history back to the Sumerians some six thousand years ago.[1] Most scholars don't go back so far, as little is known about this period. However, some scholars point to evidence found in the ancient Mediterranean world among the Greek and Roman civilizations as some of the earliest examples of tourism. Others consider health-related travel and religious pilgrimages as important predecessors of tourism.

The beginning of modern tourism development is commonly placed in eighteenth-century Western Europe. The verb *tour* had come into usage in the English language in the seventeenth century, and by the eighteenth century, the noun *tourist* had developed to describe those who traveled, typically for pleasure or culture. At this time, tourism became a popular activity among the elite upper classes that had sufficient disposable income and leisure time. In particular, Britain is cited as not only one of the first nations to develop tourism but also one of the largest sources of tourists during this early era. With new innovations in transportation, tourism was increasingly expanded to the middle classes as well. As a result, the greatest quantity of research has focused on the emergence and expansion of tourism that started in the eighteenth century and accelerated throughout the nineteenth and twentieth centuries.

There is also a distinctly practical reason for this regional and temporal bias in historical tourism research. Eighteenth-century European Grand Tour travel is the first era of tourism in which there is significant source material for analysis. In that era and since, a tremendous amount of source material—including tourists' personal diaries, letters, and published narratives, as well as travel company literature and promotions—was produced and provides us with insights into why people traveled, where they went, how they got there, and what their experiences were.

We have considerably less information about tourism in earlier time periods. Likewise, we have little information about tourism in different geographic regions. For example, we know comparatively little about tourism in Asian cultures, such as China, Japan, and India, despite indications that activities such as religious pilgrimages have been taking place there over an even greater scope of time than in Europe. Even the sources that are widely available for historic tourism research are limited in perspective. Most of the sources from the Grand Tour era were produced by tourists themselves. Considerably less data is available from a supply side perspective, including from individuals providing services to these tourists. Thus, the following discussion is necessarily selective.

# Roman Tourism

Although examples of travel for health, culture, or pleasure may be found in other ancient civilizations, such as Greece, the Romans may be considered the first true tourists based on a number of parallels with later—even modern—eras of tourism. We do not have the benefit of historical sources, such as letters and diaries, to provide in-depth perspectives on tourists and their activities during this era; however, information can be obtained from archaeological evidence and the writings of scholars and social commentators that have survived the passage of time.

There were several key factors that laid the foundation for tourism in the Roman Empire. One of the most important was the two-hundred-year long period of peace and stability that the empire enjoyed (called the Pax Romana—from the end of the first century BCE to the end of the second century AD), which is typically a precondition for tourism. This helped create a prosperous society that was able to develop an interest in traveling to other places for health or pleasure without fear of having to cross hostile territory.

At the same time, the Roman Empire had a well-developed transportation infrastructure. This extensive network of paved roads was originally built for military purposes and to connect the empire's vast land area, as well as providing the basis for commercial trade. Increased patterns of movement within the empire also generated new developments in public transportation, with organized relays of horses at five- or six-mile intervals, by which a person could travel up to one hundred miles per day. Likewise, inns were established along the roads to accommodate traveling government officials and merchants. This infrastructure also facilitated travel for pleasure.

The Romans had various motivations for travel, many of which had a distinctly practical basis. For example, one motivation was military tourism. Soldiers had explicit reasons for traveling, but these expeditions could also be combined with pleasure. Women and children might be allowed to travel with their husbands and fathers, and families could visit attractions along the way. The Romans had developed an appreciation for leisure and entertainment activities. This meant that at least part of the population had free time outside of work and necessary daily chores and that they enjoyed celebrations that were distinct from religious rituals or ceremonies.

Health tourism was also widely practiced among the Romans. Some invalids traveled to places with distinct physical properties, such as mineral waters or hot springs, that would be beneficial to those with certain health conditions. Perhaps more significantly, people traveled to escape places with conditions that would be detrimental to their health. All but the poorest citizens left Rome during the summer due to extreme heat and the rampant spread of disease among the crowded urban population. These middle- and upper-class citizens would retreat to the surrounding countryside in lower altitudes of mountainous regions, where temperatures would be lower and the air fresher. Similarly, seaside resorts in the coastal region between Rome and Naples became popular destinations for those seeking to get away from the city. These fashionable resorts replicated the best parts of social life from Rome and offered entertainments including baths, dining, concerts and theater performances, and even gladiator games.

Only a few privileged groups had the time and resources to be able to travel farther afield in the Mediterranean region. This included the most affluent families, high-ranking government officials, and young men from the upper class in the process of completing their education. Cultural attractions such as temples and ancient monuments formed the basis of many destinations. Most cities had temples that not only represented a god or goddess but also served the function of museum with collections of statues, paintings, and artifacts. The list of the Seven Wonders of the World created some of the most sought-after destinations and formed the basis for an early version of the Grand Tour. This was a tourist itinerary, typically through Greece, Asia Minor, and Egypt, comprised of the most important sights. Egypt, in particular, boasted of wonders such as the Pyramids of Giza and the Lighthouse of Alexandria, as well as landscapes and a culture that would have seemed different and exotic to Roman tourists. In contrast, the mountainous landscapes of the Alps were generally avoided, as they were considered barriers to travel rather than attractions.

Roman tourism has been described as being "typically modern" and having "nearly all of the trappings of its late-twentieth century counterpart, even to the final ironies."[2] Roman tourists visited many of the same sites popular among tourists today. They had the benefit of guidebooks to instruct them on what they were to see; however, they had to read about the sites before their travels because the books were expensive, large, heavy, leather-bound volumes of papyrus sheets. During the course of their travels, Roman tourists would hire guides. To remember their experiences, they would sketch the scenes they saw or purchase souvenirs, such as paintings, artifacts, or miniature replicas of statues or monuments.

# Religious Pilgrimages

Despite the apparent familiarity of the type of tourism seen during the Pax Romana, it was not to last. The collapse of the Roman Empire brought an end to these patterns. The transportation infrastructure fell into disrepair, and traveling became a dangerous proposition with the poor condition of roads; closed inns; and various threats of wild animals, thieves, and hostile territories. As such, there was little thought of traveling for pleasure. Only the most adventurous, the most determined, or those who absolutely had to would risk travel.

In particular, one of the most common forms of tourism during the Middle Ages (from the fifth to the fifteenth centuries) was undertaken by devout individuals with strongly held spiritual beliefs. Some of the best-known and frequently visited shrines included Santiago de Compostela in Spain (as early as the ninth century) and Canterbury in England (from the twelfth century). Pilgrimages were also undertaken to the Holy Land, although this was a much more difficult, time-consuming, expensive, and dangerous journey for those traveling from Europe. At this time, travel for health reasons became intertwined with religious pilgrimages. The Roman Church had an extremely powerful influence over life during the Middle Ages, and people increasingly turned to faith healing. They traveled to shrines with the express purpose of appealing to the patron saint for miraculous cures. Given the generally poor living conditions during this period, with high rates of malnutrition and disease, this became a relatively common practice.

By the late medieval period, pilgrimages were being undertaken on such a large scale that they became more organized. The demand for information about the places pilgrims would visit and the routes they would have to take gave rise to a new type of travel guide, including directions, descriptions of places, and even possible accommodations. One of the problems that pilgrims faced was a lack of inns and certainly a lack of quality inns. The local gentry would typically house travelers from the upper classes. Charitable hospices were formed to accommodate travelers from the lower classes, but eventually the sheer number of travelers overwhelmed these institutions. As a result, there was a renewed demand for paid accommodations by the middle classes, and inns began to be established once more. Eventually, regular tours were organized where guides would take pilgrims to the most popular sites and shrines on designated routes and stay at preapproved inns.

At the dawn of the Renaissance, pilgrimages were still extremely popular, but the nature of the journeys was beginning to change. Many people had the desire to make a pilgrimage, and pilgrims came from all social classes except the poorest. The pilgrimage became very attractive as one of the few justifiable reasons for leaving home, and the expanding infrastructure helped make travel a bit easier. These factors combined gave rise to other motivations for travel, including pleasure. Moreover, the Protestant Reformation in the sixteenth century diminished the belief in the miraculous shrines that pilgrims had visited en masse. Interest in travel was maintained, but tourists now looked for new experiences.

# Spa Tourism

Starting in the seventeenth century, many concurrent developments began to take place in tourism that contributed to the evolution of the modern tourism industry. The first of these developments was spa tourism. Health had long been a primary motivator for travel. Physicians put forth many theories about which environments possessed the best curative properties for various conditions, most notably tuberculosis. Spas—places usually possessing mineral springs—had been used intermittently over time as destinations for invalids seeking cures for different ailments. The important role of faith healing during the medieval era led to a decline in early spas, but by the seventeenth century, they experienced a resurgence with visits from members of royal and noble families. There was a growing interest in balneotherapy, or water therapy, and physicians widely promoted cures from either drinking or bathing in mineral waters. Thus, spas had the dual benefit of possessing health-giving properties and providing an escape from the poor environmental conditions of the increasingly polluted industrial cities. As a result, by the eighteenth century, English spas such as Bath and Tunbridge Wells had become immensely popular.

Although spas were initially developed for those seeking cures, and in some cases prevention, soon they increasingly became known as fashionable and exclusive resorts. As the socialization function became more and more important, resorts increasingly built promenades and assembly rooms and offered theater performances, concerts, dances, receptions, card parties, and gambling. Eventually, "seasons" developed in which the upper classes would converge on spa towns for the entertainment and to both see and be seen. These spas reproduced many aspects of London society.

The earliest resorts were located around mineral springs in areas that were inland and relatively accessible to London. At this time, the coast and the sea were seen as dangerous places to be avoided if possible. It was a wild landscape full of hazards, from unpredictable weather to pirates and smugglers. However, by the late eighteenth century, several factors contributed to a change in attitudes and allowed new spa resorts to emerge. First, a new appreciation began to develop for rugged natural scenery and the forces of nature that had formerly generated fear. Second, physicians began to advocate the health advantages of the seaside, including taking brisk walks along the beach, drinking seawater, and even sea bathing. Sea bathing was a carefully regulated activity, typically undertaken with the aid of bathing machines. These wooden structures allowed the bather to be gradually immersed in the water safely and privately, the latter being especially important for ladies.

As seaside spas began to develop, they provided a complement to inland resorts. Visits to the seaside would take place at different times of the year than the social season at the fashionable inland destinations. However, the seaside spas were increasingly developed into resorts with the same comforts and entertainments and thus started to compete with the traditional inland resorts for status and clientele. Sill, overall numbers visiting the seaside remained relatively small. As with the inland resorts, the most successful spas, such as Brighton, were those that were relatively accessible from London. Transportation by stagecoach often made farther resorts impractical because this mode was expensive, and poor roads made travel both slow and uncomfortable.

Over the course of the nineteenth century, seaside spas experienced a number of changes. The development of resort towns changed the nature of the coastline, which had once been characterized by scattered fishing villages. These resort towns began to be connected by new modes of transportation, including steamship travel and passenger trains. These innovations shortened travel time and reduced the expense of travel, allowing more people from the middle classes to make the trip. This brought further changes in the nature of the resorts. The earlier, upper-class tourists rented houses for the season and established a temporary residence complete with their own serving staff. The increase in middle-class tourists, who spent a shorter amount of time at the destination, created a demand for the development of accommodation facilities such as hotels and boarding houses.

By the second half of the nineteenth century, even the working classes were able to travel to the resorts. In some cases, the trip could be made for just a day with faster and more reliable rail service. This meant that more people could travel, even if they weren't able to get away for extended periods of time or didn't have the money to stay in a hotel. These tourists brought ever more changes to the resorts. Less emphasis was placed on curing illnesses and more on promoting well-being. Sea bathing with the use of expensive bathing machines fell out of favor, and tourists were encouraged to get out and enjoy the fresh sea air. Perhaps the most important component of a seaside holiday was the pursuit of pleasure, as these tourists sought to emulate the life of leisure displayed by the upper classes—at least for a short time.

Once these resorts were seen as less exclusive, the upper class, followed by the middle class, began looking for new destinations, often abroad. The same transportation innovations that made traditional resorts more accessible also helped open up new resorts across Europe. These tourists particularly looked to the new winter resorts developing in the Mediterranean region, such as the Côte d'Azur in France. As with the coastal resorts in Britain, these areas were previously underutilized for tourism. However, with the development of spa tourism, the region's mild climate was highly desirable among northern tourists and was popularized by the British royal family. Likewise, members of the Austrian royal family made other resorts fashionable, particularly within their own empire, such as Opatija on the Istrian Peninsula.

Although these resorts provided relief from the cold, damp northern winters, they were generally to be avoided during the summer. In the Victorian era, tanned skin was highly unfashionable and considered a sign of the working classes. In addition, clothing styles were tight and made from heavy materials that would have been unsuitable for the Mediterranean summer heat.

By the early twentieth century, new developments contributed not only to additional changes at these existing resorts but also the creation of new destinations around the world. As the latest craze in health remedies, some physicians began recommending heliotherapy, based on exposure to sunlight. However, it was perhaps fashion that played the greatest role. Clothing styles evolved to become less restrictive and hot, which allowed people to spend more time in the sun. As more people swam freely in the ocean, swimwear was also needed. Suntans became fashionable, as the upper classes had time to spend at resort destinations in the sun, while the working classes were stuck inside in factories.

Thus, a new tourism product, based on the combination of sun and sea, became enormously popular. The Mediterranean was at the heart of this new trend. Developments in air transport and relatively inexpensive foreign package vacations made the Mediterranean more accessible. At the same time, new and exotic resorts were developed around the world, including the Caribbean basin and Southeast Asia. Interestingly, the original coastal resorts in England experienced a decline. Upper- and middle-class tourists had the opportunity to visit new resorts, which left the old resorts to day-trippers and lower-income tourists who could not afford to travel abroad. Moreover, with little new investment, the infrastructure became outdated. For example, at some of the early resorts where tourists had arrived by train, there were few parking facilities to accommodate those now arriving by car.

# International Tourism

At the same time spas were developing in Britain, international tourism was also developing in the form of the Grand Tour. A variation of the Grand Tour took place as early as the Elizabethan era in the sixteenth century and evolved into the traditional Grand Tour era from the mid-seventeenth century through the eighteenth century. This was originally intended to provide young British men from the aristocratic class with a classical education. Often traveling with tutors, they would visit the cultural centers of Renaissance Europe and sites of classic antiquity. Italy, above all, was the focal point of such a tour, with destinations such as Venice, Florence, Rome, and Naples.

The average length of the Grand Tour was forty months, and the journey often followed a designated route through France, Italy, Germany, Switzerland, and/or the Low Countries (modern Belgium, the Netherlands, and Luxembourg). Few tourists strayed from this route into other areas. Particularly early in this era, traveling conditions were difficult, so the route was distinctly shaped by geographic conditions and available transportation technologies. As with Roman tourism, the Alps were considered a barrier to be crossed en route to the highlighted destinations rather than an attraction in themselves. A widespread, efficient network of transportation that met the needs of these tourists was slow to develop. Likewise, there were few accommodations. Although some of the main cities on the tour developed hotels, these Grand Tourists generally had to use the same inns, hostels, and post houses as other travelers.

Toward the end of the eighteenth century, the Grand Tour began to experience a number of changes. The demographics of the Grand Tourists steadily expanded to include aristocrats from other Northern European countries as well as the sons of the growing class of affluent but not titled British families. Some of the earliest groups of tourists began to expand the territory of the tour in search of newer and more exclusive destinations, such as Greece, Portugal, and even modern-day Turkey. At the same time, the focus of the Grand Tour began to shift. Education continued to play a role, but sightseeing also gained in importance. Tourists visited archaeological sites, museums, and art galleries, and they attended concerts and theater performances. Socialization and the development of social contact with others in the same class at assemblies and balls also came to be a part of the Grand Tour. Given the increasing importance of these latter activities, some critics argued that the Grand Tour had become nothing more than the pursuit of pleasure.

The onset of the French Revolution in 1789, followed by the conflict surrounding the Napoleonic Wars, effectively halted Continental travel for a time. While this interval brought a boost in British domestic travel, it also created a pent-up demand for experiences abroad. Napoleon's defeat at Waterloo and the Second Treaty of Paris in 1815 created a host of new opportunities for international travel. Many of the changes to the Grand Tour that had begun before the Napoleonic Wars continued after travel resumed. This effectively ended the Grand Tour era and ushered in a new era of international tourism in the nineteenth century in which more people participated than ever before.

The demographics of tourists continued to change. In the post-Napoleonic period, more adults began to travel, as well as families traveling together. This also meant that more females were traveling than ever before, a trend that would continue as travel became easier with an increasingly organized tourism infrastructure.

Likewise, more members of the middle class were able to travel. This generated even more changes in the nature of international tourism. Middle-class tourists didn't have the advantage of invitations from local nobility, so they had to rely on the developing tourism infrastructure, such as accommodations. Correspondingly, they were less likely to travel with servants and household staff, which created a demand for local serving staff at the places of destination. These tourists had less time and money available to travel, so before the middle of the nineteenth century, the average length of a

## Box 4.1.   In-Depth: The Rise of Organized Mass Tourism

Thomas Cook is often described as the father of modern mass tourism because of the role he and his company played in organizing tourism services that made tourism easier and more accessible to more people. Cook was a bookseller and a Baptist preacher who got his start by organizing a train trip for 570 people to attend a temperance meeting in 1841 England. With the success of this trip, he began to organize excursions for other groups, which quickly evolved into organizing low-cost pleasure trips primarily utilizing rail transport and the growing accommodation industry. Within a few years, Cook's Tours had opened up new opportunities for tourism among the working classes, as well as for females traveling without male companions. Travel by rail was quick, cheap, and generally considered safe. All aspects of the trip were preplanned by the company. The tourists did not have to know anyone at the destination, and they did not have to worry about whether the accommodations would be suitable.

Based on the existing popularity of seaside resorts, they were one of the key destinations for Cook's Tours. However, preferences were changing, and demands for new experiences were arising. Cook's Tours were responsive to these demands and consistently offered trips to destinations that were becoming popular, such as England's Lake District. In addition, his tours helped create new destinations not only in England but also in Wales, Scotland, and Ireland. These destinations were quickly followed by Continental tours. By the middle of the 1850s, Cook was organizing tours in France and Germany, followed by Switzerland and Italy. Thus, a new generation and a new class of tourists could experience many of the same places as the Grand Tour, albeit on a far more compressed time frame and with ever more of the comforts of home.

Thomas Cook was the innovator, but his company was soon joined by others providing similar types of experiences. However, a century later, Thomas Cook & Sons Ltd. remained at the forefront of organized mass tourism when the company launched a new type of packaged trip: instead of traveling by chartered rail transport, this trip was based on chartered air transport. The company began with trips from Britain to Corsica and continued to expand into new destinations.

*Discussion topic*: What do you think was the most significant development of Cook's Tours in the evolution of modern tourism, and why?

European tour had been reduced to four months. As tourists had less time to spend at the destination, seeing the sights took precedence over learning about them. Nonetheless, the route generally remained the same, and many of the same cities continued to be popular destinations because of the varied, well-known attractions ranging from classical antiquity to the Renaissance.

During this same period in the nineteenth century, Europeans also began to extend their reach into new regions. British travelers had already visited parts of Asia and Africa, but these experiences were typically framed as travel or exploration rather than tourism. However, European tourists increasingly visited the newly independent countries of North America and the colonies of the West Indies for pleasure. Transatlantic travel had become safer following the end of the Napoleonic Wars, as well as easier and faster with the development of steamships. These destination areas had replicated many of the institutions and patterns of life at home, and, for the most part, hostile native populations had already been eliminated. Moreover, landscapes that were far different than anything these tourists would have encountered in Europe provided a distinct attraction. Some of the remaining concerns about transatlantic travel were the hazards of tropical storms and the fear of diseases such as yellow fever and malaria.

Some critics have considered the large numbers of British tourists arriving in other parts of the world a new form of colonialism. Soon after the arrival of the first tourists at a destination, their numbers steadily increased. On one hand, this had the positive effect of creating a demand for new businesses to cater to the needs of these tourists. On the other hand, local residents and even other tourist groups complained about negative effects ranging from increased use of the English language to higher costs of living.

International tourism continued to grow steadily until the outbreak of World War I in 1914. During the interwar period, there was still considerable geopolitical uncertainty that created some unfavorable conditions for travel. In Europe, boundaries were redrawn and disputed, the transportation network was fragmented, food and fuel were in short supply, and rumors abounded of places that were unsafe. All of these factors had the potential to create problems for tourists. Then, the outbreak of World War II effectively put an end to pleasure travel once more. By the time the war was over, the pent-up demand for international travel was released and tourism grew to ever greater proportions. Air travel had been improved by the war and could now be used for mass passenger transport. Particularly as the price of air travel came down, destinations around the world were suddenly far more accessible (figure 4.2). As of 1948, there were an estimated 14 million international tourists. By 1965, that number had grown to 144 million.[3]

This tourist boom lasted until the 1970s. At that time, the Middle Eastern oil crisis that brought fuel shortages and increased prices, followed by a global recession, caused a sharp decline in tourism. However, once global economic conditions stabilized, tourist numbers not only recovered but continued to grow. The terrorist attacks in New York City and Washington, D.C., on September 11, 2001, caused another decline. Although tourism began to increase once more, the industry was further affected by the global recession that started in 2007.

## Scenic Tourism

There is one final development during the same time period that contributed to changes in patterns of travel and tourism. From the late eighteenth and early nineteenth centuries, artistic and literary movements helped change attitudes toward the natural environment. In particular, concepts such as the sublime, picturesque, and romantic allowed people to see and appreciate landscapes in new ways. These changing attitudes helped create a demand for new types of tourism experiences in new destinations. People began to seek out natural landscape scenery, which became an increasingly important component of tourism experiences. This resulted in a shift away from the cultural centers of the Grand Tour to less explored destinations with natural beauty.

The concept of the sublime created a demand for new types of destinations, at first in Britain but also throughout Europe, North America, and various colonial territories. These were places that previously might have been seen as hazardous and experienced

**Figure 4.2. By the 1970s, international air transport was becoming increasingly accessible, allowing more people to travel than ever before. This group of international tourists is preparing to board a plane in Columbus, Ohio, for a European tour in 1971. (Source: Carolyn Nelson)**

with feelings of fear, but now they could be interpreted with awe or delight—so long as such scenes were observed from a safe distance. For example, the Alps, which had long been considered a dangerous barrier to travel between Northern and Southern Europe, could be seen in a new light under the sublime. However, it would still take time for ideas to evolve and the infrastructure to develop before tourism experiences in the Alps could be appreciated.

The concept of the picturesque is most closely associated with tourism. Upper- and middle-class tourists were encouraged to travel in search of appropriate natural scenery and appreciate it in accordance with the specific framework laid out by Gilpin. This **picturesque tourism** dictated what types of places made for suitable destinations and taught tourists how to experience these places. For example, the Wye Tour in the border region between England and Wales became popular with picturesque tourists based on Gilpin's *Observations on the River Wye and Several Parts of South Wales, etc. Relative Chiefly to Picturesque Beauty: Made in the Summer of the Year 1770* (1782). These tourists would then "capture" the landscape by describing it in writing and sketching or painting the scene.

Some of the greatest changes in travel patterns came with the Romantic Movement. Romanticism has been considered as important as any economic, political, or demographic changes in shaping the development of tourism, first in England but throughout the world as well.[4] In reaction against rapid industrialization and urbanization, travel and tourism experiences came to be seen as a key means of escaping

---

## Box 4.2.  Terminology: Aesthetic Landscape Concepts

With the rise in popularity of landscape painting, people began to look at landscapes in new ways. Writers attempted to classify landscapes and instruct others in how to appreciate them. Edmund Burke's *A Philosophical Inquiry into the Origins of Our Ideas of the Sublime and the Beautiful* (1757) was one of the most influential works. According to Burke, **beautiful** landscapes were soft, smooth, and harmonious; often associated with scenes of domesticity; and the experience of these landscapes was typically reassuring and pleasurable. In contrast, **sublime** landscapes were rugged, vast, and dark places. Although such scenes were likely to induce anxiety or fear, they could also be thrilling—when experienced from a safe distance. Following Burke's example, Reverend William Gilpin wrote a series of essays, including *Essay on Prints* (1768). According to Gilpin, **picturesque** landscapes had a rough, varied, or irregular quality, giving them an interesting character that could be observed and effectively illustrated in painting.

By the turn of the nineteenth century, the Romantic Movement began to emerge among intellectuals, writers, and artists as a reaction to the changes that had come with industrialization. For them, **romantic** landscapes were wild and untouched by humans. They were places in which people could reclaim something that had been lost in the modern world—but it was no longer enough to simply observe landscapes from a distance. People were encouraged to immerse themselves in nature for a personal connection that would refresh mind, body, and soul.

*Discussion topic*: Identify tourism attractions that could be classified as beautiful, as sublime, as picturesque, and as romantic. Explain your choices.

society and modern life. In particular, travel to natural places was seen as wholesome, authentic, and inspiring. These ideas were popularized by the writings of English poets like William Wordsworth, Percy Bysshe Shelley, and John Keats, as well as American authors like Washington Irving, James Fenimore Cooper, and Henry David Thoreau. The places these authors described were also depicted by English painters such as John Constable and those of the American Hudson River School, especially Thomas Cole. All of these created an idea and an image of new places (e.g., the English Lake District and the Hudson River Valley) that people wanted to experience for themselves, creating a demand for new types of tourism experiences.

Whereas picturesque tourism was goal oriented in finding appropriate vistas to record, **romantic tourism** taught people to enjoy the experience. In the eighteenth century, walking was something that the upper classes didn't do, because they had other modes of transport available to them. However, in the nineteenth-century Romantic era, walking came to be seen as a way of immersing oneself in nature. More and more people took to walking, hiking, and roving the countryside. Yet, there were still some barriers to these activities, not the least of which was getting lost. This was especially a hazard for tourists who were unfamiliar with the territory. Consequently, a new infrastructure had to be developed to meet the demand for these experiences. For example, in the 1830s, Claude François Denecourt marked the trees in Fontainebleau Forest, near Paris, with painted arrows that directed visitors along paths that highlighted the most interesting sights. Thus, a place that would have been impractical, and perhaps dangerous, for urban and foreign visitors could now be experienced with pleasure and without fear.[5]

Throughout the nineteenth century, the ideas of Romanticism were transported around the world, which reshaped tourism. The Alps, for example, became a destination in their own right, not just to see but to experience. The classical continental route of the Grand Tour was adjusted to accommodate this new demand, and new resorts were developed in Switzerland, Austria, and parts of Italy and France. This demand for romantic mountain scenery was extended to other mountainous regions as well.

## American Tourism

In many respects, the American experience parallels the British one. The American upper classes sought to emulate their European counterparts, and intellectual and artistic ideas were often transferred across the Atlantic. However, American tourism soon took on a life of its own, and by the twentieth century, new patterns emerged in the United States that would influence tourism development in other parts of the world.

Travel and tourism were relatively slow to develop in North America. Through the first decade of the nineteenth century, tourism had little place in the United States. The newly independent country lacked an aristocratic class that did not work and had sufficient leisure time to be able to undertake long journeys for pleasure. Unlike Europe, which had a history of organized transportation routes, the United States had to develop a national transportation infrastructure. Until this infrastructure could be established, travel was difficult and undertaken only as necessary. In addition, it would take time for Americans to think of their own places in terms of tourism. America was a young nation that many believed lacked history and culture, which were the types of attractions that had long been fashionable in Europe. Following British tradition, physicians recommended European spas for health tourism, and the wealthiest citizens were able to join in the classical Grand Tour.

By the 1820s, however, tourism had reached America, and those who could afford to travel did so. This was based on an increase in available leisure time and a desire for leisure activities, as well as an ever expanding transportation infrastructure. At the same time, Americans were beginning to experience the same changes in attitudes toward the natural environment that had already influenced tourism development in Britain. Throughout the history of Euro-American colonization of the continent, the wilderness had been viewed as a dangerous place to be subdued by eliminating predators, cutting down the forest, cultivating fields, and building towns. The idea that nature could be anything else was hard for Americans to accept. The concept of the sublime came to the region in the early nineteenth century, but it was the compromise position of the picturesque, and the associated artistic movements such as the Hudson River School, that really helped Americans see their environment in new ways.

In this early stage, tourism was, for the most part, spatially concentrated in the Northeast. Prior to the Civil War, there were only a few Southern resorts; they were hard to reach, relatively small in scale, and primarily catered to the regional gentry. In contrast, the transportation infrastructure was more developed in the North, allowing greater accessibility, especially among the large potential tourist market in the more densely populated cities. This accessibility also helped reduce travel costs, and some resorts offered lower-cost options, both of which allowed greater opportunities for the middle classes to participate.

Some of the earliest destinations in this region were spas based on mineral waters. Beliefs about the curative properties of mineral waters carried over to American society. One of the first spas was Ballston Spa in Saratoga County, New York, which boasted the first hotel in the country built outside of one of the major cities. As travel opened up in the nineteenth century, these spas began to develop in much the same fashion as earlier British spas. New accommodations and entertainments drew ever more tourists, who came for leisure and socialization rather than health. As these spas became overrun with visitors, the original and wealthy tourists sought newer, more exclusive resorts, and they were replaced at existing resorts by the middle classes.

Travel was disrupted by the Civil War, but subsequent opportunities for travel in the United States continued to increase through the end of the century. There was a steadily growing middle class that had more leisure time and disposable income to travel. The national transportation infrastructure was constantly being expanded, not the least by the completion of the Transcontinental Railroad. This was a key factor in making nature, particularly in the West, more accessible. In fact, the railroad was a crucial mediator of scenic tourism experiences in the American West. Until the tourism infrastructure could be more fully developed, early tourists may have only had the opportunity to view the landscape from railroad passenger cars; landscapes lying outside of the rail corridor often remained inaccessible.

## Box 4.3.   Case Study: Tourism at Niagara Falls and Taming the Sublime

Reports of Niagara Falls began to circulate by the beginning of the seventeenth century, describing the scene as simultaneously beautiful and frightening. For more than two centuries, few Europeans and Euro-Americans would have the opportunity to see the falls for themselves. It was a difficult journey through often uncharted territory controlled by the Iroquois Nation until the Revolutionary War. Accessibility increased slowly with the development of paths and roads that would allow for horse and later carriage traffic. This brought the development of inns to accommodate those making the trip, which could last over ten days. While both roads and inns remained of questionable quality, only the most determined and intrepid travelers would undertake the journey. However, those who did felt that they were rewarded by the experience of the awesome and spectacular nature of the site.

As tourism continued to grow in the United States, more people from the upper and middle classes looked to the nearby mountains as an escape from the city during the summer months. With the increasing accessibility brought by steamboats and railways, and changing attitudes toward the natural environment, new destinations emerged in the Catskill, White, and Adirondack Mountains. Niagara Falls emerged as one of the most popular of these destinations in the 1830s. Americans had a growing desire for sublime experiences, and Niagara was considered one of the finest examples in the still-growing nation. As a result of this demand, the tourism infrastructure was quickly developed. The completion of the Erie Canal, followed by new rail connections, helped increase the site's accessibility. Likewise, construction began on hotels to accommodate visitors.

As more people visited the falls, its reputation continued to grow. The sublime thrill of the experience soon became equated with feelings of passion and romance, and Niagara emerged as a popular destination for honeymooners. This marked a significant change in the site's tourist demographic, which brought further changes to the destination. New sightseeing platforms were built to make the experience of the falls easier, especially for women constrained by the norms of fashion. Moreover, as it was now considered a fashionable social spot, new entertainment facilities were also built. By the end of the nineteenth century, Niagara Falls was the country's most popular destination among not only domestic tourists but foreign ones as well.

Yet, as Niagara became increasingly popular as a distinctly American tourism destination, there was also a growing dissatisfaction with the experience. The experience of a sublime landscape was intended to be thrilling because of the sense of adventure it involved, as well as the potential danger. Yet, the developments of tourism at the falls irrevocably changed the nature of the experience. Tourists of all ages, genders, and physical abilities could arrive at the site with relative ease on a steamship or in a passenger rail car, stay in the comfort of a nearby hotel, and "experience" the falls from designated paths and strategic platforms. The peace and solitude of the experience was lost in competition with not only countless other tourists but also the many vulgar developments brought to the site by opportunistic entrepreneurs.

Niagara Falls is considered to be one of the first examples of over-commercialization of a tourism destination in the United States. Both the sheer volume of tourists and the nature of tourism developments contributed to the dissatisfaction and, for perhaps the first time, began to generate concerns about the negative impacts of tourism. On the one hand, people had the desire to experience sites with spectacular natural features. On the other hand, in order for people to be able to experience these sites, some developments were necessary but would also necessarily alter the experience. This tension would subsequently become an issue for many of the country's other leading tourism destinations as well.

*Discussion topic:* What lessons can modern tourism destinations learn from the historic case of Niagara Falls?

## Sources

Gassan, Richard H. *The Birth of American Tourism: New York, the Hudson Valley, and American Culture, 1790–1830.* Amherst: University of Massachusetts Press, 2008.

Löfgren, Orvar. *On Holiday: A History of Vacationing.* Berkeley: University of California Press, 1999.

After the war, ideas of the Romantic Movement had firmly taken hold. This was particularly true among the upper-class urbanites of the large Northeastern cities that already saw the problems of congestion and pollution and craved the experience of the strange, remote, and wild parts of the country. Intellectuals and writers began to argue that the country's unparalleled natural features were—or at least should be—the basis of America's unique identity and compensated for its lack of history. This argument was successful, and the first national park, Yellowstone, was created in 1872.

From that time on, domestic tourism was advocated as a sort of ritual of American citizenship in which Americans could see, know, and appreciate the nation in which they lived. This ritual became increasingly important with the outbreak of World War I in Europe in 1914. With traditional European destinations temporarily unavailable to American tourists, they looked to their own emerging destinations (figure 4.3). With the explosion of automobile ownership and highway construction that took place during the

**Figure 4.3. The development of automobile transport created new opportunities for tourism, especially in early-twentieth-century America. Personal cars allowed this family to get together for a reunion in 1916. (Source: Carolyn Nelson)**

interwar years, this tourism experience was increasingly accessible. With the popularity of autotouring, a park-to-park tour was promoted as a new type of Grand Tour.

From the 1920s to the 1960s, resort tourism experienced a resurgence. These resorts served the primary purpose of getting out of the city during the hot summer months. Women and children would relocate to cabins in resort communities, while men would spend weekends there but continue to work in the cities during the week. As with earlier health spas, the Catskill Mountains provided one of the primary locations for these resorts. They were a reasonable distance from New York City but provided a vastly different environment. There was often a distinct ethnic component to these destinations: Germans, Czechs, and Jews each established their own resorts. In fact, the area was sometimes referred to as the Borscht Belt or the Jewish Alps, due to the presence of several large Jewish resorts. Similarly, Idlewild was a significant destination in Michigan because it was one of the few resorts available to blacks until discrimination was prohibited.

As more Americans took to the road for travel after World War II, a host of new tourism destinations emerged across the country. Unlike many of the earlier destinations that were built on natural attractions, such as spas and national parks, these destinations were often built around human features. For example, there was a growing interest in American history, such as Revolutionary War sites. However, many new destinations were designed expressly for the purpose of tourism. Disneyland—opened in 1955 in California—became a prominent tourism destination that set the precedent for other destinations solely oriented around entertainment and pleasure.

## Conclusion

Much research on tourism in past periods has focused on several key eras considered instrumental in the evolution of modern tourism. In particular, the Grand Tour is often cited as the origin of modern international tourism. In fact, some scholars argue that the Grand Tour lives on:

> The true descendants of . . . the Grand Tour tradition, however, consist of the young interrailers who roam the city in search of other interrailers and the groups of American and Japanese college students doing the modern version of the Grand Tour. Just as in the seventeenth century, they are here with the blessing of their parents. A season of interrailing or a European tour is still supposed to be a good investment in a middle class education.[6]

The historical geography of tourism is a fundamental component in the geography of tourism. Historical geography provides the framework for examining the geographic patterns of tourism in past periods and the changes that have taken place over time, which is the foundation for the patterns that we see today. Although it is often hard for us to imagine tourism in earlier periods, clearly many parallels may be seen. Moreover, starting from the early nineteenth century, we can trace the evolution of infrastructure, organization, experiences, and even many of the problems of tourism directly to the patterns that we see today and will be exploring in greater depth in the remaining chapters.

## Box 4.4.   Experience: A 1950s Family Road Trip

Some of my oldest memories are of the annual family road trip. It was the early 1950s, and I was only about five or six years old. We were living in Central Ohio at the time, and every summer, our family vacation would involve a trip down to South Carolina to visit my grandmother. Today, that trip is no big deal. Although it is a good day's drive, our cars are efficient, reliable, and comfortable. We have air conditioning for when it's hot, and we can plug in an iPod for a steady supply of music or even pop in a DVD to keep the kids entertained. It's all highways with at least four lanes of 65 mph traffic or better. We're never far away from a gas station, fast food restaurant, or roadside rest stop to take care of any of our needs. But back then, the experience was quite different.

The family car was a 1950 Chevrolet. It had a good-sized trunk for our luggage and plenty of room for me and my brother in the backseat. We might play games along the way, but I remember standing on the floor in the backseat for much of the trip. Cars didn't have seat belts then, and I liked to look over the front seat to watch where we were going. There were roadside rest stops where we could pull off of the road for a while and possibly have lunch if we'd packed a picnic for the first day, but there were no facilities. If we needed to use the toilet, we had to stop at a gas station and get the bathroom key from the attendant. There were no fast food restaurants, only local diners and truck stops. We usually ate at the truck stops because my dad always swore that wherever the truckers went would have the best food.

To start the trip, we had to leave home first thing in the morning and begin the drive south. We crossed the Silver Bridge over the Ohio River at the border between Ohio and West Virginia (that bridge collapsed in 1967). We would then spend the rest of the day in West Virginia crossing the Appalachian Mountains. This was the longest and most difficult part of the trip. At that time, the only road was a treacherous, winding, hilly, two-lane road that essentially followed the path of least resistance through the mountains. On the best parts of the road, I don't think we averaged better than 30 mph. For this part of the trip, my parents gave us Dramamine to keep us from getting motion sickness, but that just made us sleepy. I know my dad was happy when the West Virginia Turnpike was built. Even though we had to pay tolls to use the road and it was still only two lanes, the trip became a little bit easier and safer.

We had to make it to Bluefield, West Virginia, that first night. There were no motels along the way, so our only option was to stop in the city of Bluefield where there was a hotel. It was a typical, although now old-fashioned, hotel with a proper lobby, elevator, and inside access to rooms. In the morning, we would eat breakfast in the hotel's dining room, and then set out for another long day. We were able to cover more distance that day, as the roads leveled out in Virginia and North Carolina, and we would arrive in Whitmire, South Carolina, by dinnertime. We would stay there with my grandmother for about a week. The main things to do were to go swimming at the municipal pool or to hang out at the local drugstore, where I would sit on the floor and read their comic books.

Sometimes, we would continue on to Myrtle Beach. Crossing South Carolina to reach the coast took another whole day of driving. We would spend another four or five days there. Back then, it wasn't much more than a fishing village that was just starting to attract tourists. None of the resorts had been developed yet, and there weren't even any hotels—only "guest cottages" for visitors. These were essentially individual, self-contained cottages near the beach. My mom cooked for us in the cottage's kitchen, and occasionally we would go out to one of the town's chicken or seafood restaurants. We spent our days at the beach or fishing off the pier, and at night we went to the Pavilion Amusement Park, which had been built only a few years before and has now been torn down.

*(continued)*

---

## Box 4.4.  (continued)

I hated the long drive home. At least at the beginning of the trip we had the beach to look forward to. I suppose the lack of traveler's conveniences that we have today makes the trip back then sound like an ordeal, but we didn't know any better, and it was the only vacation away from home that we took. Chevrolet had a slogan, "See the USA in your Chevrolet." Well, that was the part of the USA that I saw in our Chevrolet.

*—John*

---

# Key Terms

- beautiful
- historical geography
- picturesque
- picturesque tourism

- romantic
- romantic tourism
- sublime

# Notes

1. Charles R. Goeldner and J. R. Brent Ritchie, *Tourism: Principles, Practices, Philosophies.* 9th ed. (Hoboken, NJ: Wiley, 2006), 41.

2. Loykie Lomine, "Tourism in Augustan Society (44 BC–AD 69)," in *Histories of Tourism: Representation, Identity, and Conflict*, ed. John Walton (Clevedon, UK: Channel View Publications, 2005), 69; Maxine Feifer, *Tourism in History: From Imperial Rome to the Present* (New York: Stein and Day, 1986), 8.

3. Gareth Shaw and Allan M. Williams, *Critical Issues in Tourism: A Geographical Perspective*, 2nd ed. (Malden, MA: Blackwell, 2002), 30.

4. James Buzzard, *The Beaten Track: European Tourism, Literature, and the Ways to Culture, 1800–1918* (Oxford: Clarendon Press, 1993).

5. Orvar Löfgren, *On Holiday: A History of Vacationing* (Berkeley: University of California Press, 1999), 49–51.

6. Löfgren, *On Holiday*, 160.

# Sources

Aitchison, Cara, Nicola E. MacLeod, and Stephen J. Shaw. *Leisure and Tourism Landscapes: Social and Cultural Geographies.* London: Routledge, 2000.

Andrews, Malcolm. *The Search for the Picturesque: Landscape Aesthetics and Tourism in Britain, 1760–1880.* Stanford, CA: Stanford University Press, 1989.

Baum, Tom. "Images of Tourism Past and Present." *International Journal of Contemporary Hospitality Management* 8, no. 4 (1996): 25–30.

Beckerson, John, and John K. Walton. "Selling Air: Marketing the Intangible at British Resorts." In *Histories of Tourism: Representation, Identity, and Conflict*, edited by John Walton, 55–68. Clevedon, UK: Channel View Publications, 2005.

Berghoff, Hartmut, and Barbara Korte. "Britain and the Making of Modern Tourism: An Interdisciplinary Approach." In *The Making of Modern Tourism: The Cultural History of the British Experience, 1600–2000*, edited by Hartmut Berghoff, Barbara Korte, Ralf Schneider, and Christopher Harvie, 1–20. Houndmills, UK: Palgrave Macmillan, 2000.

Bermingham, Ann. *Landscape and Ideology: The English Rustic Tradition, 1740–1860.* Berkeley: University of California Press, 1986.

Buzzard, James. *The Beaten Track: European Tourism, Literature, and the Ways to Culture, 1800–1918.* Oxford: Clarendon Press, 1993.

Chu, Petra ten-Doesschate. *Nineteenth-Century European Art.* New York: Abrams, 2003.

Cohen-Hattab, Kobi, and Yossi Katz. "The Attraction of Palestine: Tourism in the Years 1850–1948." *Journal of Historical Geography* 27, no. 2 (2001): 166–77.

Feifer, Maxine. *Tourism in History: From Imperial Rome to the Present.* New York: Stein and Day, 1986.

Gassan, Richard H. *The Birth of American Tourism: New York, the Hudson Valley, and American Culture, 1790–1830.* Amherst: University of Massachusetts Press, 2008.

Goeldner, Charles R., and J. R. Brent Ritchie. *Tourism: Principles, Practices, Philosophies.* 9th ed. Hoboken, NJ: Wiley, 2006.

Higgins-Desbiolles, Freya. "More Than an 'Industry': The Forgotten Power of Tourism as a Social Force." *Tourism Management* 27 (2006): 1192–1208.

Kevan, Simon. "Quests for Cures: A History of Tourism for Climate and Health." *International Journal of Biometeorology* 37 (1993): 113–24.

Korte, Barbara. *English Travel Writing from Pilgrimages to Postcolonial Explorations*, translated by Catherine Matthias. Houndmills, UK: Macmillan, 2000.

Koshar, Rudy. "'What Ought to Be Seen': Tourists' Guidebooks and National Identities in Modern Germany and Europe." *Journal of Contemporary History* 33 (1998): 323–40.

Löfgren, Orvar. *On Holiday: A History of Vacationing.* Berkeley: University of California Press, 1999.

Lomine, Loykie. "Tourism in Augustan Society (44 BC–AD 69)." In *Histories of Tourism: Representation, Identity, and Conflict*, edited by John Walton, 69–87. Clevedon, UK: Channel View Publications, 2005.

Prideaux, Bruce. "The Role of the Transport System in Destination Development." *Tourism Management* 21 (2000): 53–63.

Roskill, Mark. *The Languages of Landscape.* University Park: The Pennsylvania State University Press, 1997.

Shaffer, Marguerite. *See America First: Tourism and National Identity, 1880–1940.* Washington, DC: Smithsonian Institution Press, 2001.

Shaw, Gareth, and Allan M. Williams. *Critical Issues in Tourism: A Geographical Perspective.* 2nd ed. Malden, MA: Blackwell, 2002.

Simmons, Jack. "Railways, Hotels, and Tourism in Great Britain, 1839–1914." *Journal of Contemporary History* 19 (1984): 201–22.

Towner, John. "The Grand Tour: A Key Phase in the History of Tourism." *Annals of Tourism Research* 12 (1985): 297–333.

Walton, John K. "Prospects in Tourism History: Evolution, State of Play, and Future Development." *Tourism Management* 30 (2009): 783–93.

Whyte, Ian D. *Landscape and History since 1500.* London: Reaktion Books, 2002.

Williams, Stephen. *Tourism Geography.* London: Routledge, 1998.

# CHAPTER 5

# The Transport Geography of Tourism

Although it is easy to daydream about the places we'd like to visit, our travel decisions are often based on far more practical logistical issues. Few of us have the luxury of traveling without constraints. We may be limited by our travel budget, the amount of vacation time available, even our personal preferences or biases. Consequently, we have to consider how accessible the places are that we want to go by asking questions like: How would I get there? How long would it take? How much would it cost? Then we have to negotiate between where we *want* to go and where we *can* (reasonably) go. Much of this is contingent upon transportation.

While the transportation infrastructure may shape *where* we travel today, in the early eras of travel discussed in the last chapter, it determined whether people could travel at all. The development and improvement of transportation was one of the most important factors in allowing modern tourism to develop on a large scale and become a regular part of the lives of millions of people around the world. Technological advances provided the basis for the exponential expansion of local, regional, and global transportation networks and made travel faster, easier, and cheaper. This not only created new tourist-generating and -receiving regions but also prompted a host of other changes in the tourism infrastructure, such as accommodations. As a result, the availability of transportation infrastructure and services has been considered a fundamental precondition for tourism.[1]

**Transport geography** is a topical branch of geography that evolved out of economic geography. Like tourism, transportation is, of course, inherently geographic because it connects places and facilitates the movement of goods and people from one place to another. Transport geography fundamentally depends on some of the basic geographic concepts introduced in chapter 1, such as location or scale. For example, location shapes patterns of movement, including whether movement is possible from and/or to a given location and how that movement might occur. Transportation networks exist at local and regional scales and, in the modern world, are increasingly being connected into a global system. In addition, there are many geographic factors of places—both physical and human—that either allow or constrain transportation.

There is a distinct and reciprocal relationship between tourism and transport. Tourists constitute an important demand for transportation services and therefore play a role in the study of transport geography. At the same time, transportation is a fundamental component of tourism and thus is important for our purposes in the geography of tourism. We need to understand the means of connection between the people who demand tourism experiences and the places that are able to supply those experiences. As tourism is based on the temporary movements of people across space, the transportation that facilitates these movements is key in converting suppressed demand to effective demand. Beyond getting tourists to a destination, transportation also facilitates their experience of that destination. Given the extent of interconnection between tourism and transport, a recent "progress report" on the state of transport geography argued that there should be a closer relationship between this topical branch of geography and the geography of tourism.[2]

This chapter further develops the geographic foundation of tourism by examining transportation as a fundamental component of tourism through the concepts of transport geography. This topical branch provides us with the framework to examine the transport system, particularly the role of different transportation modes in tourism, the geographic factors that facilitate movement, and the spatial patterns of movement in tourism. In addition, we will look at some of the new ways researchers are examining the intersection between tourism and transport.

## Studying Tourism Transport

It is widely recognized that transport is a vital element in tourism, but its role is not always well developed in the literature. In fact, there are some inherent difficulties in trying to understand tourism transport. It can be difficult to even identify what would be considered "tourism transport." Tourists use a multitude of different types of transportation in varied contexts for a wide array of purposes. In some cases, these tourists may be able to use a personal form of transport. In others, they must pay for the services of government-subsidized public transport or those provided by a private company. Although there are several examples of dedicated tourism transport at a destination or specific attraction, tourists are typically only one group of users of transportation facilities and services. Employees of the tourism industry, local residents, and other transit passengers may also use the same transportation. Generally, no distinction is made between these different passengers, which provides us with little data on how tourists are using transportation. Moreover, tourism and transport are typically managed by different governmental agencies with little in the way of collaboration.

The approach to studying issues in tourism transport is not always clear either. Tourism studies and transport studies are interdisciplinary fields that have drawn upon concepts and theories from different perspectives.[3] Geography has been one of the common areas. Spatial concepts in geography have been applied to understanding the role of transport in facilitating tourists' movements, both from tourist-generating regions to receiving regions and within receiving regions.

Yet, the application of geographic models to tourism has not always been successful. For example, urban transportation models for commuting patterns are based on the assumption that the majority of people will take the most efficient route possible from home to work. This is predicated on commuters' knowledge of the situation, including the type of transportation available to them, potential routes, traffic, and congestion patterns.[4] However, these assumptions cannot be made in the context of tourism. The decision-making process of tourists about where to go and how to get there is not always rational. They frequently have little or no knowledge about the place they are visiting. They rely on guidebooks, maps, tourist information services, hotel personnel, and random strangers to provide them with information about how to get to a particular destination. Those tourists who try to take the most efficient route may get lost several times along the way, and many others will voluntarily choose a route that is less than direct because they consider exploration to be part of the experience. Even when tourist routes can be modeled for a specific destination, there is typically little transferability to other contexts.

Nonetheless, geographers argue that an understanding of the distribution of accommodations and attractions at a destination, as well as the transportation network that connects these places, can be extremely valuable. This type of data should allow the destination to efficiently plan and manage the transportation system to meet the needs of tourists and better provide them with the information they need. In particular, geographers cite the potential for geospatial technologies to more effectively understand the patterns of and opportunities for tourism transport in the context of specific destinations.

# The Evolution of Transportation and Tourism

From the historical geography of tourism, we can begin to appreciate how vital transportation has been to the development of tourism. For example, the ancient Romans were among the earliest societies to travel, and an extensive road network—combined with an organized system of horse-and-cart transport—was one of the key factors in this development. Likewise, the deterioration of these roads after the collapse of the Roman Empire was one of the issues that brought all nonessential travel to a halt.

Over time, new transportation systems developed throughout Europe that allowed greater opportunities for travel. From the mid to late Middle Ages, while roads remained poor, water transport provided some means for travel. Major river systems such as the Rhine, Danube, and Loire, as well as canal networks, formed the basis for transportation within the region and provided regular passenger services. New options for travel over land also gradually developed and expanded across the region. In the fifteenth century, the post system was developed in France, where travelers could change horses at relay stations established at regular intervals. This evolved into a widespread network of coach services by the middle of the eighteenth century.

The innovations with the greatest impact on tourism came at the beginning of the nineteenth century with the development of commercially successful steam locomotion. Regular steamboat service offered faster, more reliable, and increasingly comfortable transportation. Steamboats operated along river systems and supplanted earlier, slower, riskier oceanic sailing vessels. Steam packets traveling regular transatlantic routes were the most efficient means of travel throughout much of the nineteenth century. Originally intended for transporting the mail, they also began carrying cargo and passengers. Then, as rail service developed and expanded, it trumped all previous means of transportation. Although railways were originally intended for carrying heavy freight, like coal, they also proved extremely successful for passenger travel. Not only were railroads faster and more efficient than other available modes, they could also routinely carry ten times the number of passengers as a horse-drawn coach.[5] In addition, the typical charge of one penny per mile for rail travel was substantially lower than coach fares.[6]

Both forms of steam locomotion reshaped patterns of tourism in a myriad of ways. Due to decreased travel time and cost, more people from the middle and lower classes were enabled to participate. This increase in tourism raised concerns among the earlier generations of tourists. In some cases, these earlier tourists sought new destinations in previously distant or inaccessible places. In other cases, they fought to limit the changes that were taking place at existing destinations. For example, prominent English poet William Wordsworth strongly objected to the proposed rail development in the Lake District on the grounds that it would destroy the natural beauty of the area that he and other visitors came there for. Although this line was not built, rail stations on the periphery of the area nonetheless brought substantial numbers of tourists, who traveled into the area on foot or by coach.

The invention of the sleeping car provided greater opportunities for long, uninterrupted train trips. This idea evolved into the Pullman car—luxury sleeping cars that effectively served as a hotel on wheels and allowed the upper classes to travel longer distances in comfort. However, rail travel created new challenges as well. For example, where it formerly took weeks for a tourist to travel from locations in northern Europe to destinations in southern Europe, trains reduced the trip from London to Nice to just one and a half days. Prominent physicians claimed that this was not enough time for passengers, particularly those traveling for health reasons, to adjust to changing environmental conditions. To avoid potentially serious health complications, these physicians argued that travelers should break the journey down into intermittent stages.[7]

Steam-based transportation also changed the ways people experienced places. Tourists had the opportunity to see different landscapes in locations farther afield and to see them in a new way. Instead of stopping at strategic vantage points, tourists viewed the landscape through glass windows on scenic cruises and railroads, and they had to learn to focus on a moving landscape. These tourists were also somewhat restricted in what they saw along transportation corridors, whether it was a river, canal, or rail line. Additional modes of transport were necessary for further exploration. Tourists would have to take horse-drawn carriages or buses to nature sites and scenic vistas. Secondary transport was even needed to reach downtown centers, as rail stations were typically located outside of town. Consequently, enterprising innkeepers invested in shuttle services and opened inns near the station to capture the in-transit market.

At the beginning of the twentieth century, the automobile further reshaped and expanded tourism. Widespread personal car ownership is considered to be key in the development of modern mass tourism. In the United States, this—combined with the expansion of the interstate highway system—allowed tourists increasing freedom to visit multiple destinations during the course of a single trip and to explore new areas of the country. New attractions and destination regions emerged, leading to the development of new types of accommodation, such as the motor hotel (motel), to meet tourists' needs.

Finally, air transportation created ever more opportunities for tourism—especially mass international tourism—in the second half of the twentieth century. Air travel had been made available to a select group of affluent tourists following the end of World War I, but it was greatly expanded in the years following World War II. Innovations in air transportation, such as the jet engine and wide-bodied passenger jets, allowed planes to increase both the distance traveled and the numbers of passengers carried. As such, all parts of the world have been opened up to tourism, including many destinations that are almost entirely dependent on air transportation for international tourist arrivals.

While these innovations in transportation were not driven by tourism, the tourism industry directly benefited from improvements in safety and efficiency as well as reductions in cost. The framework of historical geography helps us examine these changes that have taken place over time to better understand the interconnections between transport and tourism. This gives us valuable insight because the transport industry continues to evolve with new technological developments. In turn, this will present ongoing opportunities and challenges for the tourism industry. For example, the development of commercially viable supersonic transport would reduce long-haul travel times, thereby creating new destinations and opening up new markets. Conversely, stricter regulations and/or prohibitive emissions taxes could result in significant changes to travel patterns, from where tourists go to what types of transportation they use.

# The Transport System

Transport geography recognizes transport as a system that involves networks, nodes, and modes and is based on demand. For tourism, the primary function of this transport system is to facilitate the movements of passengers to and from destinations. Secondary functions include getting tourists to the transport terminal and supporting the movements of tourists within the destination. Since tourism is typically considered to be nonessential travel, transport services must be safe, relatively convenient and comfortable, and competitively priced to support tourism. However, the networks, nodes, and modes of this system will not be solely used for the purposes of tourism. Instead, the tourism industry generally takes advantage of existing transport systems, with the exception of new destinations that were specifically planned for the purpose of tourism. Yet, even in this case, when the transport infrastructure must be developed to facilitate tourism, the network will serve other transportation needs as well.

A **transportation network** is the spatial structure and organization of the infrastructure that supports, and to some extent determines, patterns of movement. The transportation infrastructure has been expanding at both the local and global scales, becoming an ever more complex web of interconnections. At the same time, the relative cost of transportation has declined. These factors have allowed more movement to take place than ever before.[8] The nature of the network can encourage people to travel along one route or discourage them from traveling along another. These networks may be highly dependent on geography. For example, the physical geography of a place will affect patterns of transportation, whether it is physical features like mountains, river systems, and ground stability; atmospheric conditions such as wind directions; or oceanic conditions such as currents. The human geography of a place, such as the circumstances of political geography, can also have an effect on transport. National boundaries may affect the ability to create a transportation network and efficiently connect places, either on the ground or in the air through no-fly zones.

**Transportation nodes** are the access points to the network. These nodes may be **terminals**, where transport flows begin or end, or **interchanges** within a network. Population geography often plays the most significant role in determining the location of nodes. In general, nodes are likely to be situated in areas with high population densities, and terminals in particular will be located in or near major cities. **Transportation modes** are the means of movement or the type of transportation. Broadly, there are three categories of modes based on where this movement takes place—over land (surface), water, or air—with different types within each category[9] (see table 5.1).

In comparison with the other primary categories of mode, surface transport is more dependent on geography because the development of a network is restricted by land area, infrastructure, and possibly even national boundaries. Yet, surface transport continues to be the most widely used mode of tourism transport to reach the destination and to move around the destination. Self-powered surface transport, such as walking or bicycling, is used to get around a destination or as a form of transportation-as-experience (e.g., bicycle tours). Additionally, surface transport can be broken down into rail and road transport.

Today, the use of rail transport in tourism is highly uneven. Countries like the United States that have placed an emphasis on expansion of road networks have seen some of the greatest declines in passenger rail transport. Few developing countries have invested in creating rail networks. However, throughout Europe and parts of East Asia, extensively developed rail networks continue to be used on a wide scale. Some countries have even made new investments in this infrastructure (e.g., high-speed trains, figure 5.1), to improve rail transport and provide a competitive means of getting to or from a destination.

Personal vehicles (figure 5.2) are now the dominant mode of tourism transport, accounting for approximately 77 percent of all trips.[10] Still, road transport has not been as significant in developing regions of the world where fewer people have access to private cars. Recreational vehicles (RVs) are a subcategory of personal vehicles that offer a unique form of tourism contingent upon transport. Scheduled bus services account for a small amount of tourism transport to and from destinations, while local bus services and taxis may be used to reach a major transport node or for travel within a destination. Charter bus services are used in package tours and excursions from a resort area, and specialized tourism transport, such as sightseeing and hop-on hop-off buses that stop at major attractions, provide an additional option at major destinations.

**Table 5.1. Summary of the Advantages and Disadvantages Associated with the Modes and Types of Tourism Transport.**

| Mode | Tourist Considerations | Destination Considerations |
|---|---|---|
| **Surface** | | |
| Walk | • Free<br>• Flexibility<br>• Required in traffic-free zones | • Requires investment in some infrastructure (e.g., paths, sidewalks, signs) |
| Rail | • Well suited for short-to medium-haul travel<br>• Ease of navigation versus driving<br>• May facilitate tourism experiences (e.g., historic or scenic trains) | • May require investment in infrastructure, new technology, and/or maintenance<br>• Reduces traffic congestion and pollution<br>• Increases access to businesses<br>• Schedules and routes can be modified based on demand<br>• May serve as an attraction |
| Personal car | • Flexibility<br>• Privacy<br>• Well suited for short- to medium-haul travel<br>• Associated with varied costs (e.g., fuel, tolls, parking)<br>• May be difficult to navigate unfamiliar roads | • May require investment in roads and parking facilities<br>• Brings fewer visitors per vehicle<br>• May generate congestion and pollution<br>• Increases accessibility of destinations not served by mass transit |
| Scheduled bus | • Low cost<br>• Ease of navigation versus driving<br>• May be used for short- or medium-haul travel<br>• Constrained by schedules and routes<br>• Lack of privacy, personal space, and security | • May be subject to significant perceptual constraints (e.g., location of stations, prevalence of crime)<br>• Requires little additional investment<br>• Schedules and routes can be modified based on demand |
| **Water** | | |
| Ferry | • Provides access to small destinations<br>• Offers the ability to take personal cars<br>• Slow<br>• Not used for long-haul travel | • Requires docking and terminal facilities<br>• Increases access to small destinations |
| Cruise | • Allows travel to multiple destinations<br>• Provides a vacation experience<br>• Requires travel to port<br>• Slow<br>• Not well suited for long-haul travel | • Requires a deepwater harbor or ferry service, docking and terminal facilities<br>• Increases access to island/coastal destinations<br>• Has the potential to bring large quantities of tourists |
| **Air** | | |
| Scheduled | • Provides access to more destinations<br>• Well suited for long-haul travel<br>• May have high costs<br>• May contribute to increased stress levels<br>• May have health risks (e.g., jet lag, deep-vein thrombosis) | • Requires space for/ investment in runway and terminal facilities<br>• Must be regulated<br>• Generates pollution (e.g., air, noise)<br>• Increases access to remote or hard-to-reach destinations<br>• Has the potential to bring large quantities of tourists |
| Sightseeing | • Offers a unique experience<br>• May have high costs | • May be disruptive<br>• Facilitates access to large-scale attractions |

**Figure 5.1.** France's Train à Grande Vitesse (TGV) high-speed service network is centered in Paris and helps tourists easily reach the leading destination regions across the country. (Source: Kim Sinkhorn)

**Figure 5.2.** Personal cars provide tourists with the greatest flexibility to travel and experience the destination the way they choose. (Source: Velvet Nelson)

Developments in other modes, particularly air, have changed the role of water transport in tourism. Ferries may be used as a means of reaching a destination, particularly those areas that are not large enough to support an airport. For example, ferries and hydrofoils are used to transport tourists to some of the islands off the coast of southern Europe, such as the Greek island of Hydra. Yet, in other cases, ferries have been replaced with "island hopper" flights, which is a common occurrence in places such as the Hawaiian Islands.

Nonetheless, water transport continues to play an important role in tourism with the cruise ship industry, where transportation constitutes the tourism experience rather than serving as a means to an end. The Caribbean continues to be the most popular cruising region, followed by the Mediterranean; however, new routes are being developed all over the world. Cruises were once marketed to older age groups, but many lines have expanded their target markets by offering various price options, attractions for younger markets, and theme cruises for special interest groups (figure 5.3). In addition, water transport can provide the means of participating in activities at the destination, such as sunset cruises, whale watching, and snorkeling or scuba-diving expeditions.

Air transport is the most recently developed mode and has primarily been used in tourism as a means of reaching the destination (figure 5.4). In fact, this mode has

**Figure 5.3.  Although water transport has become less significant as a means of getting to and from a tourism destination, the cruise industry has become one of the tourism industry's biggest sectors. Today, cruise lines offer a diverse set of experiences for different target markets. For example, the Disney Cruise Line appeals to families. (Source: Amber Fisher)**

**Figure 5.4. Air transport provides the means of reaching destinations that are isolated by poor surface transportation networks—in this case, Dangriga, Belize. (Source: Tom Nelson)**

been vital in increasing the accessibility of remote and poorly connected destinations. Due to high costs, air travel has been unavailable for much of the world's population. However, recent developments such as the introduction of low-cost carriers have started to make changes in the way airlines do business. In fact, cheap regional flights have begun to compete with both rail and road transport. Air transport can also be an integral part of a tourism experience, such as a panoramic helicopter flight over large scenic attractions like the Grand Canyon or Iguazu Falls on the border between Argentina and Brazil.

These modes serve different roles in tourism, and trips frequently require the use of multiple modes. For example, personal cars, taxis and shuttle services, or inner-city train systems may be used to get to and from the terminal node (i.e., a train station, airport, or seaport). Likewise, tourists may rent a car, take taxis and tour buses, or use public transportation systems to reach and get around their destination. As such, it is important that a destination develop a comprehensive transportation system in which the networks of the different modes used in tourism are integrated. This will allow tourists to change from one mode to another as seamlessly as possible.

As tourists, we typically evaluate our options instinctively, with little reflection; therefore, these issues often seem self-evident. However, there are many factors that determine the appropriate mode(s) of transportation for a trip. There are both practical considerations involved (i.e., what modes are available for a trip) and a variety of perceptual considerations (i.e., personal preferences and constraints).[11]

## Box 5.1.  Case Study: The Swiss Travel System

Switzerland is widely recognized for having not only one of the most extensive public transport systems in the world but also one of the most efficient. While this system serves local and domestic needs, it also provides an incredible foundation for tourism. Few countries have the same potential to offer tourists such easy access to their destinations through both comprehensive connections between places and regular timetables. Although air transport provides access to the country for regional and global tourists, the public transport system within the country spans both water and surface transport. Water transport consists of boat routes on rivers and lakes, while surface transport includes a road network used by cars, intercity buses, and metro buses, as well as the internationally renowned rail network that provides the foundation for the entire system.

In an effort to both increase use of this network and promote international tourism, the Swiss Federal Railways (SBB) created the Swiss Travel System. This system provides a range of ticket options for foreign travelers and increases the ease of travel within the country by providing access to each of the train, bus, and boat routes within a network that spans some 12,500 miles. For example, the Swiss Pass (the most comprehensive option) allows unlimited travel on any of the modes for a specified number of days and discounted fares on specialized transport (e.g., cog trains or aerial cable cars) in destination areas. In addition, the pass offers free entry to approximately four hundred museums in the country and discounts at some hotels. Discounted fares are also provided to youth (defined as under the age of twenty-six) and free fares for children (defined as under the age of sixteen) when accompanied by a parent.

While most routes in Switzerland could arguably be described as scenic, there are specifically designated scenic rail and water routes. Additionally, restored "nostalgia" trains have been developed for the use of tourists. Some railways, such as the Jungfraujoch, which takes visitors to the "Top of Europe," Europe's highest railway station, were constructed especially for the purpose of tourism. The Swiss Travel System network provides an excellent example of the interrelationship between tourism and transport. In addition to simply facilitating travel from one place to another, this network can also be considered a distinct part of the tourism experience.

*Discussion topic*: What role do you think intra-destination transport (such as the Swiss Travel System) plays in tourism decisions?

*Tourism on the web*: Swiss National Tourism Office, "Switzerland Tourism," at http://www.myswitzerland.com

(*continued*)

## Box 5.1.  *(continued)*

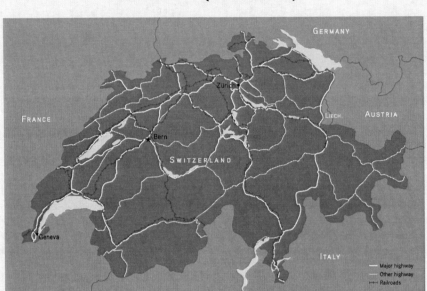

**Map 5.1.  Switzerland. This popular European tourism destination is well connected by a comprehensive and efficient transportation network. The major surface transport links (road and railroad) shown here are further connected by numerous minor ones. (Source: XNR Productions)**

## Source

Swiss Travel System. "Switzerland by Train, Bus and Boat." Accessed October 13, 2011. http://www. swisstravelsystem.com/en/.

Distance is one of the most important practical considerations that may automatically eliminate one or more modes. Greater distances require longer travel times and/ or higher transportation costs. Monetary cost is one of the most important perceptual considerations. Transportation accounts for some of the largest expenditures in tourism. For many trips, the experience stage begins when the tourists reach the destination; thus, they are interested in reaching their destination as quickly and efficiently as possible. However, for tourists with a limited budget for a trip, it may come down to a choice: spend more money on transportation or on the experience at the destination. For example, a direct flight may be the option that requires the shortest amount of travel time, and, by extension, often the least amount of hassles and potential problems in the form of lines, security screenings, delays, lost luggage, and so on. This allows the maximum amount of time spent at the destination. Yet, a flight with multiple connections or even other modes of transport, such as a personal car, may be lower-cost options that are longer or less convenient but could allow the tourists to spend an additional day at the destination, participate in a particular tourism activity, or make other expenditures. Likewise, if transportation cost is a significant factor, tourists may need to consider a second- or third-choice destination as an alternative.

Personal goals and preferences also play a role in transportation decisions. As we saw above, we cannot assume that tourists will take the most efficient route from the point of origin to the destination based on shortest distance or travel time. Rather than being primarily concerned with getting from point A to point B in the fastest manner possible, tourists might be interested in seeing things along the way, where the movement stage is as important as the experience stage in the tourism process. Consequently, they might choose to drive a personal car to get a better view of the landscape through which they are passing, as well as to have the freedom to make stops or take intentional detours along the way. Additionally, tourists who are afraid to fly will take an alternative mode of transportation to get to their destination, regardless of whether air transport is the quickest, easiest, or cheapest mode.

This choice of mode affects the level of interaction tourists will have with both people and places. The development of new modes of transportation changed the ways in which people experienced places. The faster the mode, the less of the passing landscape is seen. For air transportation in particular, observing the landscape is generally not considered a part of travel; therefore, tourists only have the opportunity to experience the place of the destination as opposed to the places of travel as well. The choice of mode also has the potential to create opportunities for interaction with other people or limit it. Personal cars tend to isolate tourists, both from locals and from other tourists. Specialized tourism transport, such as charter and sightseeing buses, fosters interaction with other tourists, while walking and taking public transportation often allows tourists the greatest opportunities to interact with local people.

# Patterns of Movement in Tourism

Transport geography also considers spatial patterns of movement. Movement is a fundamental part of the tourism process. Depending on the type of **tourism itinerary**, or the planned route or journey for a trip (figure 5.5), movement may comprise two distinct stages in the tourism process: travel to and travel from the destination. While perhaps just a means to an end, travel to the destination may hold a certain measure of excitement and anticipation. This is less likely the case for travel home. After the experience at the destination, tourists may be tired and ready to just get home. The length of the trip, and any potential hassles that arise during the course of travel, can shape the post-trip stage, in which people remember their trip (see box 5.2). Yet, movement may also be an integral part of the trip and encompass the entire experience stage.

Tourism scholars have identified many different types of tourism itineraries. The most basic type is **point-to-point**. In this itinerary, people travel from their home to a destination where they stay for the duration of their vacation and then return home. The selected mode for such a trip will depend on the transportation infrastructure and relative locations of the tourist's origin and destination. Typically, movement will be a means to an end with this type of itinerary. For example, tourists traveling

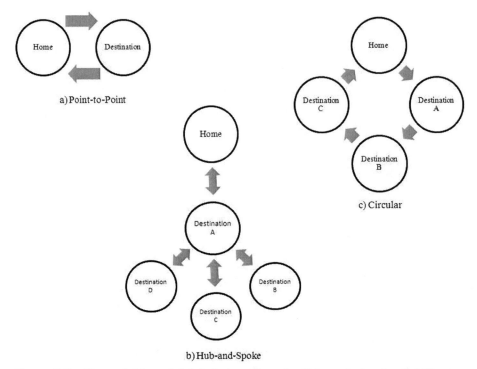

**Figure 5.5.    The point-to-point (a), hub-and-spoke (b), and circular (c) itineraries provide three examples of tourism itineraries. There are many variations on these patterns that are, to some extent, dependent on the available transport system for the destination.**

from New York City to an all-inclusive resort in the Dominican Republic will follow a point-to-point itinerary using air transport to reach the destination, at which point the experience stage will begin. However, the movement stage can nonetheless be incorporated into the experience stage. For tourists using road transport to drive from New York City to the Finger Lakes region in Upstate New York, the scenery witnessed en route may be considered part of the experience, in addition to the time spent at the destination.

A variation on the point-to-point is the **hub-and-spoke itinerary.** This involves travel from home to a destination. That destination then becomes a base for visiting other destinations, each time returning to the first destination before returning home. For example, the Shannon International Airport in Ireland provides international tourists access to the country's west coast. According to the Tourism Ireland website, although it is not a primary attraction in itself, "Shannon Town is a vibrant place and a good base from which to explore the delights of Clare and Limerick."[12] In particular, the Shannon Region includes Ireland's leading tourism attraction: the Cliffs of Moher. In this case, movement is interspersed with experience.

The **circular itinerary** is the pattern most dependent on transportation, as travel is distinctly part of the tourism experience. In this itinerary, tourists travel from home to one destination and then another (and perhaps another) for varying lengths of time before returning home. At one end of the tourist spectrum, drifters and explorers such as backpackers may follow a circular itinerary as they utilize public transportation

## Box 5.2. Experience: What Do You Mean, *Wednesday?*

I think everyone has a travel disaster (or at least near-disaster) story. Mine happened over ten years ago now, but I will always remember it. My husband and I had just moved to Columbia, Missouri. I immediately started a new job, but my husband, who was working on his PhD, took off for the Black Hills for a summer of fieldwork. By the beginning of July, we hadn't seen each other in about six weeks. I was able to take a few vacation days around the Fourth of July holiday so that I could spend a week in the field with him. I was really looking forward to it. I didn't know it at the time, but my husband had splurged to surprise me with a night at a nice bed and breakfast after I arrived in Rapid City, South Dakota.

Columbia only has a small airport with very limited service, so most people would either drive to St. Louis or Kansas City to catch flights. I was scheduled to leave out of Kansas City around midday on Friday, fly to Denver and catch a connection to Rapid City. I didn't want to leave my car at the airport for a week, and I found out about a shuttle service that would pick me up at my house and deliver me to the Kansas City airport. It was only about a two-hour drive, but the shuttle ended up picking me up around seven o'clock in the morning in order to pick up other passengers and meet everyone's departure times. I don't normally eat breakfast, so I just got up, checked with the airline to make sure everything was running on schedule, and left. After the shuttle dropped me off, I went to check in and the ticket agent told me that I wasn't going to make my connection. The flight to Denver was now delayed. It wasn't weather-related. It wasn't mechanical. In fact, I don't think I ever knew why. So I asked when was the next flight to Rapid City. She calmly told me that they could not get me there until Wednesday.

What do you mean, *Wednesday?* It was Friday. I was going to have to leave Rapid City the following Friday! I asked if they could make arrangements for me to get there on another airline. No, my ticket was with them; I would have to buy a new ticket. What was I supposed to do for five days? Was the airline going to put me up in a hotel, give me food vouchers? Of course not. I was basically stranded in Kansas City. I was getting ready to get a cab and pay whatever astronomical fee it was going to cost to go back home when I finally got ahold of my husband in the field. He told me to get to Denver, and we'd figure things out from there. Because the agent was unable to tell me when, exactly, my flight was actually going to leave, I went straight to the gate to wait. On the other side of security, it was literally just the gates. No bathrooms, no restaurants, no vending machines, not even a water fountain. And my flight left six hours late. There was no food on the plane, and by the time I arrived in Denver, all of the vendors were closed for the night.

After I called from Kansas City, my husband left his field site in South Dakota and drove all day to get to Denver. I don't know what he had to do to get there, but he arrived within a half hour of me. I literally hadn't eaten anything all day, so we stopped at the first twenty-four-hour diner we could find and then crashed at the motel next door. I finally got to South Dakota Saturday evening and spent the next few days of my "vacation" on the phone, on hold, long distance, trying to reach the airline's customer service. I suspected that my return flight had been canceled since I didn't take their Wednesday Rapid City flight. I was right, and they tried to convince me I needed to purchase a new return ticket—for $2,000! I finally managed to get them to put me back on the flight, but I was still worried that I wasn't going to be able to get home. Needless to say, it was an extremely stressful trip.

Afterwards, I wrote several letters of complaint. In return, I was awarded a $75 airline inconvenience voucher that I never used. It didn't come close to the $175 bed and breakfast reservation that we lost or the money we spent in gas driving to and from Denver. And it certainly didn't compensate me for my "inconvenience." The next year, I decided to make the twelve-hour drive, by myself, just to avoid the hassles of flying.

*—Kristin*

systems like trains or buses to travel from destination to destination. At the other end of the spectrum, a common pattern for organized mass tourists is to follow a circular itinerary on a charter bus tour of multiple destinations, possibly even in multiple countries. Cruises are the ultimate transportation-as-tourism experience (see box 5.3). However, it must be noted that for tourists who do not live near a deepwater port, their tourism process still involves movement to and from the terminal port.

---

## Box 5.3.    In-Depth: The Cruise to Nowhere

The "cruise to nowhere" is an interesting case in the geography of tourism. Cruises are perhaps the most conspicuous example of how the mode of transportation and the act of travel can be more important than the destination (i.e., any ports of call) itself. Moreover, in the case of the cruise to nowhere, there is no destination. The entire itinerary involves sailing to and from the port of origin. In some cases, these are localized experiences that may be river-based day trips or overnight excursions. These experiences may have a specific purpose or theme, such as gaming and gambling or a musical concert.

However, most of the major international cruise lines now offer a cruise to nowhere as well, which are typically oceangoing experiences that last around three days. For example, Carnival is one of the many cruise lines that offer this type of experience. The company's website suggests:

> Where's the best place for you to spend a few fun-filled days? Nowhere! A Carnival "Cruise-to-Nowhere" is the perfect way to get away for a couple of days. It's also a fantastic opportunity to sample everything that makes our cruises so great, including: delicious dining options, luxurious spas, exciting entertainment, friendly casinos, duty-free shopping and—of course—superb service. No one does Nowhere better than Carnival![1]

As indicated here, this type of cruise to nowhere has often been promoted as an opportunity for first-time cruise tourists to try the cruise experience without a significant commitment of time and money. It is also increasingly reflecting the fact that there is so much to do onboard today's cruise ships and that many people don't want to deal with the hassles, expenses, or potential safety concerns often associated with shore excursions. In the modern cruise industry, it may be argued that the destination is the ship itself. Indeed, many of the new megaships are considered floating resorts with an enormous range of amenities, including waterparks, surf simulators, rock climbing walls, full-sized basketball courts, miniature golf courses, or ice-skating rinks, in addition to the standard dining and entertainment options. This is particularly the case with the cruise to nowhere itineraries.

Yet, while most tourism experiences are distinctly and uniquely place-based, place is entirely removed from this experience. Cruises are rarely questioned as tourism experiences—they involve the temporary movement of people from one place to another primarily based on the pursuit of pleasure. Thus, cruises are, in fact, often considered to be the epitome of mass tourism.

*Discussion topic:* Do you think place is a necessary component of tourism? Why or why not?

## Note

1. "Cruise to Nowhere," Carnival Corporation, accessed November 6, 2010, http://www.carnival.com/cruise-to/cruise-to-nowhere.aspx.

These models are, of course, simplifications. In reality, the possibilities are endless. Itineraries are typically shaped by factors such as the distance traveled and the mode of transport used. However, the specific itinerary often comes from individual choices about visiting a single destination or spending time at several, taking a direct route or making detours and side trips, or following the same route to and from the destination or returning by a different path.

# Transportation and Destination Development

Practically, transport geography can be used to provide valuable information about specific patterns for destinations. New destinations seeking to establish tourism, as well as existing destinations looking to expand their industry, need to consider issues such as where their potential tourist markets are located and how accessible the destination is to those markets. This is entirely contingent upon the transport system.

Potential destinations must analyze the existing system to determine if the appropriate framework already exists and can be utilized for the purposes of tourism. If not, they will have to invest in the development of new networks, nodes, and/or modes. In most cases, at least part of the existing system can be used for tourism purposes. For example, a nation may have an international airport located in the capital city that can accommodate international tourists, but a regional airport or surface transport may need to be developed to connect these tourists with the country's destination regions. In the case of Switzerland, discussed in box 5.1, Zürich is the largest city and a prominent international business center, and the Zürich airport is considered to be the country's international gateway. Yet, many of the country's international tourists continue on to other destinations, such as Lucerne, Interlaken, or Grindewald, via its well-developed transportation network.

Similarly, destinations targeting new markets must consider their distance from that market and the available transportation modes between the two places, with the associated travel time and cost factors. The geographic concept of **distance decay** indicates that demand for a product or service decreases as the distance traveled to obtain that product or service increases. In other words, if a consumer perceives that two products or services are comparable, he will choose the one that is easier to obtain. In theory, then, the increased time and cost of greater distances will decrease the desirability of a destination. However, tourism represents a special case that requires some modification of the model. Tourism demand does not "decay" immediately. In fact, demand is highest at a certain distance from the tourists' home.[13] After that point is reached, increasing distance will result in decreasing demand, unless there is a high degree of **complementarity**. Complementarity refers to the relationship between people in one place who have the desire for certain travel experiences and a place that has the ability to satisfy that desire.

It is also important that destinations analyze tourists' patterns of movement and itineraries, preferences in modes, cost thresholds, and any factors that might influence their decision-making process. For example, drifters and other categories of tourists interested in niche tourism products like nature and adventure tourism, may specifi-

**Figure 5.6. Wildlife tourists interested in viewing animals in their natural habitat are more willing to accept poor transportation infrastructure. (Source: Velvet Nelson)**

cally seek out undeveloped destinations and therefore have lower expectations from the transportation infrastructure (e.g., unpaved roads; see figure 5.6). However, mass tourists from the major generating regions, specifically Europe and North America, are used to a modern and efficient transportation infrastructure where they can get from one place to another quickly, comfortably, and safely. If these tourists perceive that transportation at a destination is unreliable, slow, difficult, and possibly even dangerous, they are likely to choose an alternative destination. As such, destination stakeholders may need to coordinate their efforts to increase investment in the infrastructure and regulate the provision of transportation services to create a better environment for tourism.

Data on these patterns can identify transport flows and places where traffic is concentrated at a destination. This information can aid destination planners to formulate effective strategies to eliminate potential bottlenecks or alleviate problems with congestion and overcrowding during peak seasons. These solutions may include designating alternative routes, directing tourists to alternate attractions, or creating new policies such as the establishment of restricted or traffic-free zones. This will help reduce the negative impacts on the destination created by traffic and pollution and improve the visitor experience.[14] Management strategies such as these will be discussed in greater detail in chapter 11.

In addition, destination stakeholders need to consider usage patterns, profitability, and competition for limited mass transportation resources due to seasonality.

For most destinations, tourism is a seasonal industry with highs and lows. During the high season, mass transportation may run at capacity or in fact, over capacity. If the supply of transport services is not expanded to meet the increased demand, systems can become congested. Thus, all users experience decreased access to and quality of transportation services. For example, tourists arriving at major urban destinations are often reliant on public transportation systems due to prohibitive costs (e.g., car rental, insurance, parking, congestion charges for driving in the city center, and the like) or unfamiliarity with roads and traffic patterns. Tourists' usage can complement commuters' usage when they visit on weekends and holidays. However, during peak tourism seasons, typically during the summer months, tourists compete with residents. For residents, this can generate animosity toward tourists. For tourists, this can have a negative impact on their ability to visit the desired attractions and their overall satisfaction with the destination.

Conversely, mass transportation is a perishable product because on regularly scheduled routes, unsold seats "expire"—in other words, those seats are not available to be sold at another time or on a later date. Transportation systems may experience losses during the low or off tourism season. As a result, operators may need to reduce the number of scheduled routes to the destination. They may also advertise discounted fares or work with other stakeholders to offer package deals (e.g., combining transport with accommodation or activities) in an effort to increase off-season visitors.

# New Directions in Research

Over the past few years, researchers have begun to explore the intersection between tourism and transport in new ways. While it is important that we continue to try to understand the patterns of where tourists are going and how they are getting there, this new research is also taking into consideration the implications of current trends in tourism on transportation and the role of tourist transport in issues of global human and environmental significance.

For example, growth in some of the tourism products discussed in chapter 3 has created new opportunities and challenges with regard to transport. In particular, both heritage and event tourism have been cited as bringing the relationship between tourism and transport even closer. There is a significant niche market of "transport enthusiasts." Interest in appreciating historic transport has generated a demand for themed museums, exhibitions, and car shows. Interest in experiencing these modes has generated a demand for tourist trips on horse-drawn carriages, historic trains, vintage cars, gondolas, paddle steamers, and others.[15] At the same time, interest in advances in transport technology has generated a demand for opportunities to experience the newest planes or very fast trains.

Conversely, the rise of products like nature, rural, and sport tourism has at times strained the relationship between tourism and transport. These products typically involve the transfer of tourists from an urban market or a centrally located terminal node (e.g., an airport) to remote locations that are not well served by public transportation. In addition, tourists participating in various sports activities may be carrying heavy or bulky equipment, such as golf clubs, skis, surfboards, and bicycles. These items are difficult to take on public transportation, if in fact they are permitted at all. As such, these tourism products are heavily reliant on private cars. Tourists must either be able to reach the destination in their own vehicles or rent one upon their arrival at the terminal, and destination stakeholders must plan accordingly to manage vehicles in an area that is perhaps unaccustomed to high volumes of traffic.

Another new direction considers tourism, transport, and health. Although early health concerns about the faster speeds of rail travel proved to be unfounded, the increase in long-distance air transport associated with tourism has generated new risks. This can range from the comparatively mild effects of jet lag to traveler's thrombosis, which, in the most serious cases, can result in a potentially fatal pulmonary embolism. In addition, new attention is being given to the increased levels of stress that can result from anxiety about flying, the threat of terrorism, missed flights, lost baggage, and more. While this can lead to occasional (and well-publicized) incidents of aggression or violence, it also can exacerbate existing conditions, resulting in in-flight medical emergencies. Finally, geographers have begun to study the rapid diffusion of infectious diseases, like severe acute respiratory syndrome (SARS), by air travel.[16]

Other researchers are considering issues of access to tourism transport and inequality. Tourism is dependent on transport to facilitate experiences. As such, tourism becomes unavailable to populations without ready access to or the ability to pay for transportation—lower-income groups in inner-city areas, remote rural areas, or developing countries. Tourism transport can become a symbol of inequality and a means of segregating tourists from residents. For example, the modes used for tourists are typically modern, safe, and comfortable, whereas the public transportation used by residents may be old, deficient, and overcrowded. Tourist transport does not generally serve the needs of residents and may, in fact, be off-limits to them.

Finally, a significant new direction in research focuses on the environmental impacts of tourism transport, management policies, the adaptations to and potential effects of regulations, and attempts to change patterns of tourist behavior. Some of these issues will be discussed further in chapter 10, "The Environmental Geography of Tourism."

# Conclusion

Transport is a fundamental component in tourism, as it facilitates the movement of tourists from their place of origin to their destination. Transportation systems were a precondition for tourism, and new innovations helped usher in several key eras in tourism. In particular, transport was one of the factors in the development of modern mass tourism, which allows more people—in more parts of the world—to travel than ever before. At the same time, transportation can distinctly shape the tourism experience. As transport geography provides the means of exploring the spatial patterns of movement and the geographic factors that allow or constrain this movement, we can apply the concepts of this topical branch to contribute to our understanding of the role transport plays in tourism.

# Key Terms

- circular itinerary
- complementarity
- distance decay
- hub-and-spoke itinerary
- interchange
- point-to-point itinerary

- terminal
- tourism itinerary
- transport geography
- transportation mode
- transportation network
- transportation node

# Notes

1. Bruce Prideaux, "The Role of the Transport System in Destination Development," *Tourism Management* 21 (2000): 54.

2. David J. Keeling, "Transportation Geography: New Directions on Well-Worn Trails," *Progress in Human Geography* 31 (2007): 221.

3. Stephen Page, *Transport and Tourism: Global Perspectives*, 2nd ed. (Harlow, UK: Pearson Prentice Hall, 2005), 34.

4. Alan Lew and Bob McKercher, "Modeling Tourist Movements: A Local Destination Analysis," *Annals of Tourism Research* 33 (2006): 405.

5. Jack Simmons, "Railways, Hotels, and Tourism in Great Britain, 1839–1914," *Journal of Contemporary History* 19 (1984): 207.

6. Charles R. Goeldner and J. R. Brent Ritchie, *Tourism: Principles, Practices, Philosophies*, 9th ed. (Hoboken, NJ: Wiley, 2006), 56.

7. Simon M. Kevan, "Quests for Cures: A History of Tourism for Climate and Health," *International Journal of Biometeorology* 37 (1993): 118.

8. Jean-Paul Rodrigue, Claude Comtois, and Brian Slack, *The Geography of Transport Systems*, 2nd ed. (New York: Routledge, 2009), 5, accessed February 10, 2011, http://people.hofstra.edu/geotrans.

9. Rodrigue, Comtois, and Slack, *The Geography of Transport Systems*.

10. Rodrigue, Comtois, and Slack, *The Geography of Transport Systems*.

11. Lew and McKercher, "Modeling Tourist Movements," 407.

12. Tourism Ireland, "Shannon—Clare County," accessed March 2, 2011, http://www.discoverireland.com/us/ireland-places-to-go/placefinder/s/shannon-clare/.

13. Bob McKercher and Alan A. Lew, "Tourist Flows and the Spatial Distribution of Tourists," in *A Companion to Tourism*, ed. Alan A. Lew, C. Michael Hall, and Allan M. Williams (Malden, MA: Blackwell, 2004), 40–42.

14. Lew and McKercher, "Modeling Tourist Movements," 420.

15. Derek R. Hall, "Conceptualising Tourism Transport: Inequality and Externality Issues," *Journal of Transport Geography* 7 (1999): 182.

16. Les Lumsdon and Stephen J. Page, "Progress in Transport and Tourism Research: Reformulating the Transport-Tourism Interface and Future Research Agendas," in *Tourism and Transport: Issues and Agenda for the New Millennium*, ed. Les Lumsdon and Stephen J. Page (Amsterdam: Elsevier, 2004), 11–12.

# Sources

Albalate, Daniel, and Germà Bel. "Tourism and Urban Public Transport: Holding Demand Pressure under Supply Constraints." *Tourism Management* 31 (2010): 425–33.

Dickinson, Janet E., and Derek Robbins. "Representations of Tourism Transport Problems in a Rural Destination." *Tourism Management* 29 (2008): 1110–1121.

Duval, David Timothy. *Tourism and Transport: Modes, Networks, and Flows.* Clevedon, UK: Channel View Publications, 2007.

Hall, Derek R. "Conceptualising Tourism Transport: Inequality and Externality Issues." *Journal of Transport Geography* 7 (1999): 181–88.

Henderson, Joan. "Transport and Tourism Destination Development: An Indonesian Perspective." *Tourism and Hospitality Research* 9, no. 3 (2009): 199–208.

Khadaroo, Jameel, and Boopen Seetanah. "The Role of Transport Infrastructure in International Tourism Development: A Gravity Model Approach." *Tourism Management* 29 (2008): 831–40.

Lew, Alan, and Bob McKercher. "Modeling Tourist Movements: A Local Destination Analysis." *Annals of Tourism Research* 33 (2006): 403–23.

Löfgren, Orvar. *On Holiday: A History of Vacationing.* Berkeley: University of California Press, 1999.

McKercher, Bob, and Alan A. Lew. "Tourist Flows and the Spatial Distribution of Tourists." In *A Companion to Tourism*, edited by Alan A. Lew, C. Michael Hall, and Allan M. Williams, 36–48. Malden, MA: Blackwell, 2004.

Page, Stephen. "Transport and Tourism." In *A Companion to Tourism*, edited by Alan A. Lew, C. Michael Hall, and Allan M. Williams, 146–58. Malden, MA: Blackwell, 2004.

———. *Transport and Tourism: Global Perspectives*, 2nd ed. Harlow, UK: Pearson Prentice Hall, 2005.

Prideaux, Bruce. "Links between Transport and Tourism—Past, Present, and Future." In *Tourism in the Twenty-First Century: Reflections on Experience*, edited by Bill Faulkner, Gianna Moscardo, and Eric Laws, 91–109. London: Continuum, 2001.

———. "The Role of the Transport System in Destination Development." *Tourism Management* 21 (2000): 53–63.

Reilly, Jennifer, Peter Williams, and Wolfgang Haider. "Moving towards More Eco-Efficient Tourist Transportation to a Resort Destination: The Case of Whistler, British Columbia." *Research in Transportation Economics* 26 (2010): 66–73.

Rodrigue, Jean-Paul, Claude Comtois, and Brian Slack. *The Geography of Transport Systems.* 2nd ed. New York: Routledge, 2009. Accessed February 10, 2011. http://people.hofstra.edu/geotrans.

Shaffer, Marguerite. *See America First: Tourism and National Identity, 1880–1940.* Washington, DC: Smithsonian Institution Press, 2001.

Shaw, Gareth, and Allan M. Williams. *Critical Issues in Tourism: A Geographical Perspective.* 2nd ed. Malden, MA: Blackwell, 2002.

Simmons, Jack. "Railways, Hotels, and Tourism in Great Britain, 1839–1914." *Journal of Contemporary History* 19 (1984): 201–22.

Towner, John. "The Grand Tour: A Key Phase in the History of Tourism." *Annals of Tourism Research* 12 (1985): 297–333.

Williams, Stephen. *Tourism Geography.* London: Routledge, 1998.

# CHAPTER 6

# The Physical Geography of Tourism: Resources and Barriers

As tourists, we routinely evaluate the physical geography of potential destinations. From this perspective, it isn't important that we understand the science behind how or why a place is shaped by the earth's physical processes. Rather, we simply need to know enough to determine if a place has the physical setting we're looking for, if its physical conditions will provide us with the opportunity to participate in the activities we want, or if its conditions might keep us from doing those things. Armed with a little knowledge about the patterns of a place, we can try to make informed decisions about where to go as well as when. This same knowledge is also needed by stakeholders at both emerging and existing destinations to assess (and reassess) the physical resources for tourism in that place. However, for these stakeholders, it may be more important that they have some understanding of physical geography, especially when it comes to negotiating the physical barriers to tourism in that place.

Because tourism is a human phenomenon, greater emphasis is placed on examining tourism through the topical branches of human geography. Nonetheless, it is still important to consider the physical side of geography. Physical geography is the subdivision of geography that studies the earth's physical systems. As in human geography, physical geography is further organized into topical branches, including meteorology and climatology, hydrology and oceanography, geomorphology, and biogeography. This chapter introduces each of these topical branches and examines how the elements in the earth's physical system affect tourism, either as a resource that provides the basis for tourism or as a barrier that prevents tourism. In addition, it considers how global environmental change is also affecting patterns of tourism. First, however, we will discuss the concept of resources as applied in the context of tourism.

## Resources, Barriers, and the Tourism Resource Audit

In general terms, resources refer to some type of product that is perceived to have value and may be used to satisfy human needs and/or wants. Geographic research on resources recognizes that these products are relative and subjective. This means that what is considered a resource depends on the cultural, political, economic, and/ or technological circumstances of a society at a given point in time. Consequently, something that might be considered a resource for one group of people might not be for another due to different cultural values, political priorities, economic conditions, or levels of technology. Likewise, what is considered a resource in one time period might not be in another due to changes in all of these factors. While resources may be human or cultural, we typically think of physical or natural resources that are elements in the earth system. The availability of these resources is dependent on physical processes but also human efforts.

Applied to the context of tourism geography, **tourism resources** are those components of a destination's environment (physical or human) that have the potential to facilitate tourism or provide the basis for tourism attractions. Physical tourism resources are considered to be "an invaluable tourism asset and . . . fundamental to the development of tourism for virtually all destinations. They tend to be the foundation from which other resources are developed, and thus often play both a principal and key supporting role in tourism."[1] Moreover, tourism activities are contingent on not one but a combination of resources. These resources may be readily available tangible features in the geography of a place, but for many resources, destinations must still develop them to be used in tourism. This is based on the goals and values of the target tourist market to meet their demands and create that complementarity between places discussed in chapter 5.

Whereas the presence of resources can allow a destination to develop, the presence of barriers can prevent it. A barrier refers to something material in the environment that constitutes a physical impediment or something immaterial that creates a logistical or perceptual impediment. As with resources, what is considered a barrier—and the extent to which it functions as a one—varies with different cultural norms, political policies, economic circumstances, or technological advancement. Elements in the earth-ocean-atmosphere system can present distinct physical barriers, but they also have the potential to become perceptual barriers as well.

In tourism, both physical and perceptual barriers may prevent tourists from visiting certain destinations. Additionally, these barriers have the potential to shape the ways in which destinations develop. Thus, a destination needs to evaluate its physical geography not only for potential resources but also for any barriers and to find ways of overcoming them—whether it is grading the landscape, installing artificial snowmakers, or convincing potential tourists that the weather's really not as bad as they think it's going to be.

Tourism stakeholders, especially those at emerging destinations, frequently fail to fully understand the conditions of their own resource base. With economic benefit as the goal, stakeholders may take shortcuts in the development process. They may choose to model their industry on that of a successful destination, even though circumstances are different for each place. They may conduct only a superficial analysis of the area's resources, or they may simply assume that they already have all of the information they need. Yet, it's never that simple. Some resources are attractions in themselves; these are the ones that are often easy to spot (e.g., Mount Everest). Others, however, simply provide the framework that allows for tourism. It can be much more difficult to understand how the quality, quantity, distribution, accessibility, seasonality, and so forth of these resources are going to affect tourism in that place.

The **tourism resource audit** (TRA) is a tool that can be used by destination stakeholders to systematically identify, classify, and assess all of the features of a place that will impact the supply of tourism. Because resources are subjective, however, this can be tricky. Typically, a range of stakeholders, coming from different perspectives, should be involved to create the most comprehensive and appropriate dataset. This will include experts to provide scientific data and analysis, community members to contribute local knowledge, industry analysts to assess market potential, and even tourists to offer the demand-side perspective. A variety of strategies can be used to create an exhaustive list of resources that are critically evaluated to understand how they might affect tourism. In recent years, geographic information systems (GIS) have been used to manage the often large datasets created by a TRA. Analysis of this data allows stakeholders to determine the strengths and weaknesses of tourism at the destination, improvements that need to be made, and strategies that should be put in place for both immediate and long-term development.

Although this process is, perhaps, less exciting than other aspects of tourism development and promotion, it is fundamental. According to the authors of *The Tourism Development Handbook*, "The effort put in at this stage should be well rewarded later on with the development of a more successful and sustainable tourism destination."[2] Still, a TRA only captures the condition of resources at a given time. Resources, and what are considered resources, are not static. Consequently, the TRA database should be updated regularly, and tourism strategies reevaluated accordingly.

# The Physical System, Physical Geography, and Tourism

A *system* is defined as an interrelated set of things that are linked by flows of energy and matter and are distinct from that which is outside the system. This is an important organizing concept in physical geography, as the earth is made up of interrelated physical systems, including the abiotic systems (i.e., the overlapping, nonliving systems consisting of the atmosphere, hydrosphere, and lithosphere) that provide the basis for the biotic system (i.e., the living system made up of the biosphere). Specifically, the atmosphere is the thin, gaseous layer surrounding the earth's surface. The hydrosphere encompasses the waters that exist in the atmosphere, on the earth's surface, and in the crust near the surface. The lithosphere includes the solid part of the earth. Finally, these three spheres form the basis for the biosphere, which is the area where living organisms can exist.

Each of these spheres can be studied through different but ultimately interrelated topical branches in geography, including meteorology and climatology (atmosphere), hydrology and oceanography (hydrosphere), geomorphology (lithosphere), and biogeography (biosphere). Table 6.1 provides a summary of the resources and barriers associated with each of these branches of physical geography, and the issues are discussed below. In the past, there have been fewer links between tourism and these topical branches of geography, in comparison with those on the human side of geography. Nonetheless, physical geography plays a crucial role in our understanding of the earth and our place in it, and geographers recognize that these physical systems have distinct impacts on all aspects of human life. Thus, there is clear potential for greater research connecting physical geography and tourism geography.

## METEOROLOGY, CLIMATOLOGY, AND TOURISM

While it may seem like the atmosphere is beyond the scope of geography, it is still an integral part in the earth system. Not only do atmospheric processes affect what happens in other spheres, these phenomena also affect human life every day. Geographers are interested in both weather and climate to understand how patterns vary from place to place, how they shape those places, and how they affect human activities on the earth's surface. Meteorology and climatology are interrelated atmospheric sciences. **Meteorology** is the study of weather, which refers to the atmospheric conditions (e.g., air temperature and pressure, humidity, precipitation, wind speed and direction, cloud cover and type, etc.) for a given place and time. Because these conditions are dynamic, in an almost constant state of change, there is a distinct focus on short-term patterns. **Climatology** is the study of climate, which refers to the aggregate of weather conditions for a given place over time. Climatology expands upon meteorology by considering longer-term trends, making generalizations about average weather conditions, and identifying variations or extremes.

In one introduction to physical geography, the distinction between weather and climate is bluntly put in this way: the idea of a place's climate is what attracts people to that place, but it is the reality of day-to-day weather conditions that makes them leave.[3] While overly simplistic, this does raise an important consideration for the demand perspective in the geography of tourism. Tourists depend on information about the climate of a destination to try to make an informed decision about whether or not that place generally has the right conditions for the desired tourism activities at the time of year in which they intend to visit. Yet, climate data does not predict specific weather conditions. Forecasts become increasingly unreliable beyond just a few days, and most trips will be planned well in advance of that. Consequently, tourists may find that the actual weather conditions at the destination during their vacation aren't what they expected. This can be simply an inconvenience or prompt small changes in their plans, but it can also fundamentally alter or even cancel a trip.

One tourism scholar notes: "It is generally accepted that climate is an important part of the region's tourism resource base, but the role of climate in determining the suitability of a region for tourism or outdoor recreation is often assumed to be self-evident and therefore to require no elaboration."[4] Another argues that tourism planning rarely considers anything more than "simple, general descriptions of the climate, which are often unconnected to the needs of tourism."[5] When we consider all of the ways in which weather and climate impact tourism, we should begin to realize that this

**Table 6.1. Summary of How Features in Each of the Topical Branches of Physical Geography Can Become Resources for or Barriers to Tourism.**

| Branch | Resources | Barriers |
|---|---|---|
| Meteorology and climatology | **Attraction** <br>• In general, good weather conditions <br>• Perceptual depending on individual and cultural preferences and desired activities <br><br>**Basis for activities** <br>• Moderate temperatures <br>• Sun (e.g., sunbathing) <br>• Precipitation (e.g., skiing)/ lack of precipitation (e.g., most outdoor activities) <br>• Wind (e.g., windsurfing)/ lack of wind (e.g., swimming) | **Detraction** <br>• Perceptual depending on individual and cultural preferences and desired activities <br><br>**Disrupt activities** <br>• Extreme temperatures <br>• Precipitation/lack of precipitation <br>• Wind/lack of wind <br>• Natural hazards (e.g., thunderstorms, hurricanes, blizzards) |
| Hydrology and oceanography | **Attraction** <br>• Unique water features (e.g., waterfalls, geysers) <br>• Specific characteristics (e.g., meandering rivers for floating, rapids for whitewater rafting and kayaking) <br>• Distinct properties (e.g., thermal or mineral springs for medical treatments) <br>• Foundation for attractive tourism landscapes (e.g., green golf courses, landscaped resorts, decorative fountains) <br><br>**Basis for activities** <br>• Swimming and bathing <br>• Boating and rafting <br>• Watersports <br>• Fishing <br><br>**Necessary quantity and quality** <br>• Drinking and bathing <br>• Cooking and cleaning | **Detraction** <br>• Perceptual (e.g., lack of available water to create attractive tourism landscapes) <br>• Physical (e.g., poor water quality) <br><br>**Disrupt activities** <br>• Lack of available water to participate in tourism activities <br>• Health risks from poor water quality <br>• Natural hazards (e.g., flooding, tidal surges, tsunamis) |

(continued)

**Table 6.1.** *(continued)*

| Branch | Resources | Barriers |
|---|---|---|
| Geomorphology | Attraction | Detraction |
| | • Unique landforms (e.g., islands, mountains, canyons, caves)<br>• Cultural values (e.g., sacred landscapes)<br>• Landform processes (e.g., erupting volcanoes) | • Perceptual (e.g., cultural and personal perceptions of uninteresting or ugly landscapes) |
| | Location for resorts | Prevent accessibility |
| | • High-altitude summer retreats and health resorts | • Physical (e.g., landforms that cut a destination off from major markets and/or make transportation difficult) |
| | Basis for activities | Disrupt activities |
| | • Mountain hiking/climbing<br>• Winter sports | • Natural hazards (e.g., earthquakes, volcanic eruptions) |
| Biogeography | Attraction | Detraction |
| | • Distinct biomes (e.g., tropical rainforest, temperate rain forest, desert)<br>• Attractive vegetation (e.g., flowering plants, fall colors)<br>• Unique, rare, or endangered plant and animal species | • Lack of expected vegetation (e.g., barren instead of lush)<br>• Deforested landscapes<br>• Diminished wildlife populations due to habitat loss, overhunting, and poaching |
| | Basis for activities | Disrupt activities |
| | • Nature hikes, canopy tours<br>• Fruit picking, truffle hunting<br>• Bird watching, wildlife safaris | • Natural hazards (e.g., wildfires)<br>• Outbreaks of animal diseases (e.g., foot-and-mouth disease) |

cannot be taken for granted. While the intersection between the geography of tourism and climatology has been explored in greater depth than the other branches of physical geography, the literature still clearly argues for more work to be done.

It is said that weather and climate have a greater influence over what can and cannot be done in a given place than any other physical feature, and this applies to the development of tourism. These elements determine the time and length of the tourism season, the products that can be developed, the location of activities and infrastructure, and more. Generally speaking, climate is the feature that a destination is least able to manipulate to provide the desired conditions for tourism. An exception might be a snowmaker that ensures tourists can have the experience they came

## Box 6.1.   Experience: Irish Blue, Tuscan Rain, and Memories of European Weather

A few years ago, my husband and I decided that we had the time and money to start travel-ing more. I had traveled in Europe years ago, before I got married and had children, but my husband had never been. The first destination that we chose was Switzerland. It was wonder-ful. Every day we had beautiful sunny skies and perfect pleasant temperatures for the kinds of activities we wanted to do: exploring the historic cities and hiking in the mountains. We had such an amazing experience that we decided to make a trip to Europe an annual event.

The next year we chose Ireland. Obviously we knew that this was going to be a differ-ent kind of experience. Everyone told us to expect that the weather wouldn't be very good. But it was even worse than we anticipated. Apparently, for the duration of the week that we were there, a front coming off the North Atlantic got stalled over the island. Temperatures were colder, and the rain heavier, than normal. It literally rained every day, and almost all day at that. On the day that we visited the Rock of Cashel, which we were looking forward to as the highlight of our trip, we had horrible, wind-driven downpours. Throughout the course of the trip, we got excited anytime we saw small patches of blue sky, which we dubbed "Irish blue." We had one afternoon with some skies like this and temperatures that might have made it up to 60°F. Of course, after everything else, we were grateful for some not-entirely-unpleasant conditions. However, we were still somewhat amused by the fact that the locals kept commenting on how great the weather was and headed in droves to the ice cream shops. This isn't to say that we don't have good memories of Ireland—we do—and we generally liked it, in spite of the weather.

We chose Slovenia after that, and honestly, we didn't know quite what to expect from the weather. We had some days of nice weather, especially in the Julian Alps, that reminded us of Switzerland. We also had some days of rain. There was one day in particular that we will always remember. We had taken the train to the city of Maribor. We had heard that some of the area's famous ski slopes were open for hiking during the summer, so we found a place to ride the cable car up the side of a mountain with the intention of hiking down. It was a sort of gray, overcast kind of day, but we assumed (mistakenly) that it was going to stay that way. Shortly after we reached the top and got off, it started to drizzle. At this point, our only option was to start walking. As it turns out, there wasn't exactly a path, so we just followed the other people down the side of the mountain. As we passed through cow pastures, the rain started getting harder. And harder. Fortunately, we did have rain ponchos with us that kept us from getting completely soaked—on the top half at least. I think I could have poured the water out of my running shoes. It seemed like an awfully long trip down the side of that mountain, and after we reached the bottom, we were on the wrong side of the slope, so we had to walk farther still to the place where we could catch a bus to take us back to the train station. Finally, we stopped at a restaurant and ordered some drinks just to get out of the rain for a little while. We felt rather conspicuous, wearing our silly ponchos and dripping water, as we sat down among the nicely dressed Slovenes there for dinner. I wouldn't say that this ruined our experience of Slovenia. But it is defi-nitely something that we vividly remember about that trip.

Finally, we headed to Italy. We chose Tuscany expressly for its reputation as a warm, sunny destination. On the day that we arrived, it was just that. But after that, we didn't see the sun again, and we saw even less "Irish blue" than we had in Ireland. It was just plain cold, with driving rain, and we were unable to do any of the things that we had planned to do. We

*(continued)*

## Box 6.1.   *(continued)*

**Figure 6.1.   Trying to make the best of the situation while hiking in the rain in Maribor, Slovenia. (Source: Carolyn Nelson)**

were most looking forward to taking several days to hike in the Cinque Terre, but the paths between the towns were closed because all of the rain had made them treacherous. So we were forced to stick to the cities. Of course, it's hard to appreciate the spectacular medieval and Renaissance architecture of places like Florence when all you can see is the underside of your umbrella. And because we had expected to spend our time outside, we hadn't made reservations at any of the museums, and it was too late to do it at that point. Needless to say, it was not a fun trip and the biggest disappointment of all.

It's been a few years, but we haven't been back to Europe since then. It wasn't exactly the weather that put us off Europe for a while—although that was definitely part of it. We'll go back sometime in the next few years, and you can be sure that we will choose both where we go and when carefully to give us the best possible chance of having good weather. We can say from experience that it absolutely does make a difference.

*—Carolyn*

for, although natural conditions, such as a day of sun with five to ten inches of fresh powder, are still considered to be the best.

Whether it is nature-based or in an urban area, much of tourism takes place outside. As such, elements of weather and climate can be a resource that does not generate tourism but provides the conditions that allow for tourism activities to take place. Tourism is voluntary; tourists will only participate in an activity if the conditions allow it to be done safely and relatively comfortably. Consequently, there is an important correlation between weather and tourism revenues, either directly (e.g., financial losses due to poor or unexpected weather conditions) or indirectly (e.g., financial gains in secondary tourism activities that are less sensitive to the weather).

These elements of weather and climate can also be the resource on which tourism depends. Obviously, sun is a vital resource for sun, sea, and sand tourism. For these elements of the physical system, though, what is considered a resource for or a barrier to tourism is variable, depending on the activity and perceptions. This means that the same feature can, in fact, be both. For example, in the case of Tarifa, Spain, located between the popular 3S resorts of Costa del Sol and Costa de la Luz, the presence of high winds was a barrier to the development of sun, sea, and sand tourism. However, stakeholders turned this feature into a tourism resource by promoting the destination as the "capital of wind" and developing niche tourism activities like windsurfing.[6]

Destinations seek to reassure potential tourists in target markets of their conditions, such as in the case of Barbados and their "perfect weather" (box 2.3). However, even destinations with notoriously poor weather conditions for tourism activities try to make the most of it. For example, Scotland's National Tourism Organization website, Visit Scotland, cheerfully encourages tourists to "explore Scotland's landscape of lochs and mountains, its interesting geography and its gloriously unpredictable climate."[7] Moreover, rather than shying away from their bad weather, they make light of it while highlighting other attractions. In breaking down the seasons, the site declares that hospitality is "something that improves as the weather worsens."[8]

Finally, extreme weather events such as hurricanes or blizzards present a barrier to tourism. As a perceptual barrier, tourists may avoid destinations when and where there is the potential for a hazard to occur (e.g., the low tourism season for destinations in the Caribbean and the Pacific corresponds to the hurricane season). As a physical barrier, these events have the potential to prevent tourists from reaching a destination or participating in the desired activities at a particular time. In addition, the damage and destruction caused by an extreme weather event has a long-term effect on the destination. It will face not only the cost of repairs but also the lost revenues while it is partially or completely closed to tourists. Additionally, the destination may have to work to recover those tourists who went elsewhere for the duration by advertising that they are open again or by offering discount specials.

## HYDROLOGY, OCEANOGRAPHY, AND TOURISM

The hydrosphere includes the surface water in oceans, lakes, and rivers; subsurface water; frozen water; and even water vapor in the atmosphere. As a result, there is significant overlap between this sphere and the others. Broadly, **hydrology** is the science of water and considers the properties, distribution, and circulation of water in the hydrosphere. However, modern hydrology is specifically concerned with fresh water. Fresh water is incredibly important in shaping human activities; consequently, the study of hydrology provides us with the means of understanding the availability of fresh water so that this fundamental resource can be appropriately managed to provide people with both the quality and quantity of water that they need. At its most basic, oceanography is the study of processes in oceans and seas and is therefore concerned with saline water. The global ocean is the most extensive feature of the hydrosphere. Covering 71 percent of the earth's surface, oceans make up approximately 97 percent of the earth's surface water.[9]

Water is a tremendously significant resource for tourism. Combined with the environments surrounding it, this feature provides the basis for countless tourism attractions and activities around the world. Features such as waterfalls and geysers are often scenic attractions, while thermal and mineral springs have long provided the basis for health resorts. Rivers and lakes (both natural and artificial) allow for recreational activities, such as boating, fishing, rafting, kayaking, wildlife viewing, and more. Today, some of the most significant destinations are located in coastal areas. The beach, in particular, is considered to have a powerful appeal to the physical senses. For many societies, it is considered to be an aesthetically pleasing place that provides the potential for recreation from sunbathing to water sports.

Knowledge about these environments is important for stakeholders in the development and maintenance of a destination. The characteristics of a coast can shape the attractiveness of the area for tourism as well as its potential for tourist activities. Depositional coastlines characterized by beaches are common mass 3S destinations, while the more rugged erosional coastlines can be a resource for scenic tourism. White sand is often perceived to be the most desirable for beach tourism (figure 6.2), although volcanic black sand can be found on beaches in the Caribbean and Hawaiian islands, and

**Figure 6.2. White sand beaches, such as this one at Verdado, Cuba, are distinct tourism resources and often the basis for modern 3S tourism destinations. (Source: Velvet Nelson)**

some popular beaches in the Mediterranean are composed of rocks and pebbles. The calm waters of sheltered coves may be an important resource for mass tourism but not for niche tourism based on adventure and sport. Stakeholders also need to be aware of the physical processes at work along coastlines that can affect these resources and other infrastructure. Tourism destinations may need to periodically undertake beach nourishment to artificially replace lost sand or improve sand quality. For example, nearly US$70 billion have been spent in efforts to maintain, rebuild, and replenish beaches in Miami-Dade County, Florida.[10]

Finally, stakeholders need information about these resources to provide a safe and suitable environment for tourism activities. Data about tides, currents, and waves should be used to identify the optimal times to participate in water sports (e.g., swimming, snorkeling, scuba diving, surfing, etc.) and provide tourists with warnings about potentially hazardous conditions.

A lack of water—in terms of appropriate quality or quantity—can present a tangible barrier to tourism development; however, this can be overcome. Water is a necessary precondition for tourism because it is a fundamental human resource. A destination needs to ensure adequate levels of water quality for both tourism resources (e.g., quality of surface water for aesthetic purposes and tourism activities) and human resources (e.g., quality of water for drinking and bathing). At the same time, stakeholders must understand the constraints of water supply at the destination and consumption patterns to balance the needs of local economic activities, the resident population, and tourists. Las Vegas, a desert destination that receives over 37 million tourists per year, is unable to provide enough water to support this demand from locally available surface and groundwater reservoirs and must import water with expensive diversion systems. Small island destinations (e.g., Curaçao, Cyprus, and Mauritius), as well as dry coastal destinations (e.g., Australia, Dubai, southern California), are increasingly looking to desalination of seawater (see box 6.2) to meet their needs.

Water also presents a barrier to tourism in the form of hazards, although this is tied to meteorological or geomorphic hazards. For example, coastal destinations are affected by tidal surges caused by hurricanes or tsunamis as a result of earthquakes. One of the most devastating disasters in recent times was the 2004 Indian Ocean tsunami that killed approximately 230,000 people across fourteen countries, including an estimated 9,000 tourists enjoying a beach vacation. In the case of Sri Lanka, this disaster was estimated to have cost the tourism industry US$250 million and 27,000 tourism-related jobs. Across the region, countless small and medium-size tourism businesses did not have insurance that would allow them to rebuild.[11] In addition, many tourists stayed away from these popular beach destinations out of fear due to the traumatic and highly publicized nature of the event.

## GEOMORPHOLOGY AND TOURISM

**Geomorphology** is the study of landforms, which refers to the shapes of the earth's surface. This includes identifiable forms such as mountains and hills, valleys and plains. In particular, the study of geomorphology considers the characteristics and

# Box 6.2.   In-Depth: Desalination to Meet Increased Water Demand in Egypt's Red Sea Resorts

Over the past few decades, Egypt has experienced tremendous population and economic growth. This has put significant pressure on its water resources, and the country is now facing increasing problems with water scarcity. This is especially an issue for the Red Sea coast and the Sinai Peninsula, where there are extremely limited fresh water resources, and the distance from the Nile River makes the cost of transporting potable water via pipeline prohibitive. The peninsula's traditional population has been nomadic Bedouin tribes, who migrate based on the availability of water and pastures. The remainder of the historically small population has, in the past, been concentrated in the northern part of the peninsula where there is greater access to fresh water. However, the development of tourism over the past few decades has brought many changes to the peninsula.

Following the return of the Sinai Peninsula to Egypt in 1982, the southern and coastal regions were targeted for economic growth and development, fueled by foreign investment. These areas were considered to have a good tourism resource base, including a consistently warm and dry climate year-round, beaches, and renowned coral reefs for scuba diving and snorkeling. While the lack of fresh water presented the greatest barrier to tourism development, this was something that the destination was able to overcome. In particular, desalination was identified as the most appropriate means of meeting the need for water to accommodate tourism.

Resorts such as Sharm El Sheikh developed at the southern tip of the Peninsula and experienced dramatic growth. It emerged as one of Egypt's most popular destinations and expanded beyond niche tourism based on diving into one of the world's significant mass tourism destinations. Hotel construction continued until the destination was nearly at capacity, which prompted the development of new resorts in the region. Sharm El Sheikh now receives over three million tourists annually, with little seasonal fluctuation. The city's resident population has also grown as more people have been attracted to the area by the influx of jobs in tourism and related industries. The growth of this industry has led to ever greater demands for desalinated water. These demands quickly outstripped the state-owned facilities' ability to supply enough water. Private companies also began to build desalination facilities in the region and sell water to the resorts at a relatively high cost.

Despite the vital need for desalination to meet the water needs of this region, there are some concerns about the process and its outcomes. Some studies have shown that the desalination process is highly efficient at removing the salts from the water; however, the process does not necessarily produce bacteriologically safe water for drinking, which can create a health risk for international tourists. Other studies have focused on the environmental effects of the process. Desalination yields approximately 30 percent drinking water and 70 percent brine, which contains all of the salt. This brine can't be discharged back into the sea because of the effect it would have on the highly diverse coral reef ecosystem that is one of the most significant tourism resources for the destination. Instead, the brine is discharged back into the aquifer by injection wells, which increase the groundwater salinity over time. This causes a decrease in the efficiency of desalination plants and an increase in costs. In addition, these plants require significant inputs of energy and therefore contribute to the destination's greenhouse gas emissions.

*Discussion topic:* Give another example of a physical feature that can be both a resource for and a barrier to tourism in a specific place. How does one weigh against the other?

*Tourism on the web:* Egypt Tourism Authority, "Sharm El Sheikh: The Classic Red Sea Destination," at http://en.egypt.travel/city/index/sharm-el-sheikh.

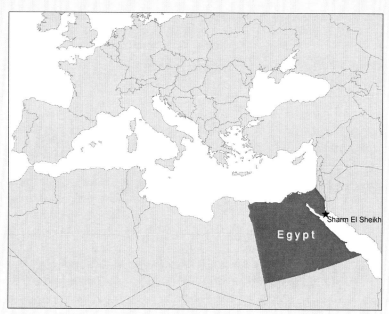

**Map 6.1. Sharm El Sheikh, Egypt. For this destination located on the Red Sea, water is both a resource for and a barrier to tourism. (Source: Gang Gong)**

## Sources

Awwad, Ramadan A., T. N. Olsthoorn, Y. Zhou, Stefan Uhlenbrook, and Ebel Smidt. "Optimum Pumping-Injection System for Saline Groundwater Desalination in Sharm El Sheikh." *WaterMill Working Paper Series* 11 (2008). Accessed October 26, 2011. http://www.unesco-ihe.org/WaterMill -Working-Paper-Series/Working-Paper-Series.

Diab, Atef M. "Bacteriological Studies on the Potability, Efficacy, and EIA of Desalination Operations at Sharm El-Sheikh Region, Egypt." *Egyptian Journal of Biology* 3 (2001): 59–65.

Rayan, Magdy Abou, Berge Djebedjian, and Ibrahim Khaled. "Water Supply and Demand and a Desali-nation Option for Sinai, Egypt." *Desalination* 136 (2001): 73–81.

spatial distribution patterns of landforms, as well as the internal and external geo-graphic processes that create and shape them. Landforms are changing constantly as a result of a variety of forces in the atmosphere, hydrosphere, and biosphere that are continuously at work on the surface of the lithosphere. The internal forces are generally constructive in nature, meaning that they increase the relief (the changes in elevation and slope) of the earth's surface, while the external forces are more likely to be destructive in that they wear features down and decrease the relief of the surface. Over time, the action of these forces has created the landforms that form the basis of destinations we know today—for example, the Hawaiian Islands (formed by a hotspot or magma plume), the Alps (formed by compressional folding and faulting), or Arches National Park (formed by erosion).

As a resource, landforms and landform processes can be a natural tourism attraction. One of the most well-known examples of a landform-based natural attraction is the Grand Canyon (box 6.3), but others include Uluru (also known as Ayers Rock) in Australia, the Rock of Gibraltar on the Iberian Peninsula, or the fairy chimney rocks at Göreme, Turkey. Cultural values are often attributed to these landforms, and they are visited for that reason. For example, Mount Emei is one of the Four Sacred Buddhist Mountains in China (figure 6.3). Places where we can safely see the physical (internal) forces of landscape formation at work can also become tourism attractions. Arenal Volcano became one of Costa Rica's most popular sites, where tourists witnessed the almost constant effusive eruptions—with ash plumes and lava flow—that occurred up until 2010.[12] Likewise, landforms can also be a tourism resource by providing opportunities for tourism. Mountain resorts around the world are extraordinarily popular destinations for both the scenery and activities such as hiking, climbing, and winter sports.

Landforms can also present a barrier to tourism, primarily by preventing people from reaching the place of destination. In particular, mountain destinations around the world have long had to manage accessibility issues. It can be a difficult and costly process to extend ground transportation lines to a resort or to construct the necessary infrastructure for air transport. In one example, Yeager Airport in the Appalachian Mountains of West Virginia was built on a hilltop in the 1940s. The project cost $8.3

**Figure 6.3.   Mount Emei in Sichuan Province is one of the Four Sacred Buddhist Mountains in China. The first temple was built on the mountain in the year 401. Today, the site is a popular tourism attraction for the combination of scenery, cultural value, and heritage. (Source: Velvet Nelson)**

# Box 6.3.  Case Study: External Processes in Landscape Formation as a Tourism Attraction? The Grand Canyon

While neither the steepest nor the longest canyon in the world, the Grand Canyon is widely recognized to be one of the most significant geomorphic features in the United States and, arguably, the world. It is also considered to be one of the most impressive natural tourism attractions based on the combination of the size, scale, and visual appearance of the landscape, which is attributed to the external processes of landscape formation.

The canyon itself is considered to be geologically young, in that it is has been carved within the last six million years. The region's Colorado Plateau Province is characterized by nearly horizontal sedimentary rocks that have been lifted between five thousand and thirteen thousand feet above sea level and then carved by erosion. In particular, the erosive processes of the powerful Colorado River that carved the depth of the canyon along a 277-mile stretch of the Kaibab Plateau are considered the primary forces in the formation of the landscape. As a result, elevations along the rim of the Grand Canyon extend from six thousand to eight thousand feet above sea level. The different types of rocks erode in different ways, creating the shape of the canyon walls. In particular, the hard metamorphic rocks at the base of the canyon are more resistant to erosion than the softer sedimentary rocks above, which creates a step-like appearance. However, other external processes, such as weathering and mass wasting, have also played important roles in shaping the landscape that we see. Moreover, regional patterns of climate and vegetation contribute to the stark, dramatic character of the landscape.

Perception of what is and is not a resource at different times has played a role in the development of the Grand Canyon. One of the first American expeditions to survey the area took place in the mid-nineteenth century, led by Lieutenant Joseph Ives of the U.S. Army Corps of Topographical Engineers. Although his *Report upon the Colorado River of the West; Explored in 1857 and 1858* made note of the wild and spectacular character of the region, he was widely quoted for stating, "The region . . . is, of course, altogether valueless. It can be approached only from the south, and after entering it, there is nothing to do but leave. Ours has been the first and the last party of whites to visit this profitless locality."[1] At this time, Americans were primarily interested in use value rather than scenic value. Subsequent studies of the geography and geology of the region increasingly recognized its unique physical properties, and the Grand Canyon was finally designated a national park in 1919.

Today, the Grand Canyon is recognized as one of the most impressive landforms in the world and has been designated one of the Seven Natural Wonders of the World. Grand Canyon National Park is visited by between four and five million tourists a year. While the majority of visitors are Americans, this internationally recognized site is an attraction for foreign tourists as well.

*Discussion topic:* Among all of the interesting and unique landforms in the United States and around the world, why do you think the Grand Canyon is considered such a highly desirable natural attraction for tourism today?

*Tourism on the web:* U.S. National Park Service, "Grand Canyon National Park," at http://www.nps.gov/grca/index.htm; Arizona Office of Tourism, "Grand Canyon Vacations & Info," at http://www.arizonaguide.com/things-to-do/grand-canyon

(continued)

## Box 6.3.   (continued)

**Figure 6.4.  Formed by a combination of external processes, the Grand Canyon makes a unique and dramatic natural attraction for tourism. (Source: Marcus Gillespie)**

# Note

1. Joseph C. Ives, *Report upon the Colorado River of the West; Explored in 1857 and 1858* (Washington, DC: Government Printing Office, 1861), 30.

# Sources

McKnight, Tom, and Darrel Hess. *Physical Geography: A Landscape Appreciation*. Upper Saddle River, NJ: Prentice Hall, 2000.

National Park Service. "Grand Canyon Trip Planner." Accessed October 26, 2011. http://www.nps.gov/grca/parknews/upload/trip-planner-grca.pdf.

Seven Natural Wonders. "Grand Canyon." Accessed October 27, 2011. http://sevennaturalwonders.org/the-original/grand-canyon.

million and required two million pounds of explosives to move nine million cubic yards of earth to create a large enough area of level land for a runway.[13] At the same time, natural hazards caused by the dynamic processes of landscape formation have the potential to damage the tourism infrastructure and disrupt tourism activities. At a local scale, tourists were evacuated from El Hierro, one of the Canary Islands, due to the threat of a volcanic eruption in mid-2011. Globally, the massive ash cloud from the eruption of Iceland's Eyjafjallajökull volcano in 2010 had a ripple effect, disrupting travel and tourism around the world.

Tourism stakeholders will benefit from the expert knowledge of geomorphologists during the TRA not merely to identify the potential features of interest but to provide guidance on how these features can be developed for tourism. At the same time, scientific information about landform processes should be used to help the destination create an effective disaster response plan.

## BIOGEOGRAPHY AND TOURISM

**Biogeography**, combining principles from both biology and geography, is the study of living things. Alexander von Humboldt, a leading figure in the development of modern geography, is widely considered to be the founder of biogeography. This topical branch considers the spatial patterns and physical processes of these living things in the collection of ecosystems contained within the earth's biosphere. Biogeographers are interested in the extent of diversity among the earth's species, broadly described by the term biological diversity (biodiversity). Moreover, biogeographers are concerned with explaining the changes in these patterns and processes that have taken place over time and understanding the impact of human activities on the diverse species and their habitats.

The biogeography of a place is primarily considered a resource for tourism. For example, the presence of unique animal species and/or plant species becomes a key resource for products such as nature and wildlife tourism. Tourists to southern Africa are interested in viewing the "Big Five" game animals in their natural habitat: the African elephant (figure 6.5), Cape buffalo, leopard, lion, and rhinoceros. Tourists from the temperate zones have long been interested in the tropical rain forest biome.

However, these characteristics of physical geography can, in some cases, present a barrier to tourism. This is largely based on perception. Consider destinations that lack the "right" kind of vegetation—or the vegetation that tourists expect. Tropical island destinations around the world have been subject to Western perceptions of an island paradise (i.e., lush, green environments typically epitomized by palm trees). Of course, not all of these islands exhibit these patterns. The comparatively flat "ABC" islands of Aruba, Bonaire, and Curaçao are characterized by desert scrub and cactus vegetation. To some extent, this barrier can be overcome as destinations, and particularly resorts, artificially plant nonnative trees and flowers in an effort to create the perceived desired appearance.

Tourism stakeholders will benefit from the knowledge generated by biogeographers about the factors that contribute to the success or failure of a particular species

**Figure 6.5. Wildlife is a vital resource for tourism at many African destinations. Tourists look for the "Big Five" game animals, such as these elephants on Lake Kariba, located on the border between Zimbabwe and Zambia. (Source: Gareth Rawlins)**

so that they may adequately protect these resources. In particular, research in biogeography has examined the potential for tourism to be used as a tool in environmental preservation with the goal of preventing habitat and/or species loss. Much of this work has focused on the ecotourism concept introduced in chapter 3. In addition, biogeographers have been instrumental in studying the effects of tourism on ecosystems. This will be discussed further in chapter 10.

# The Impact of Global Environmental Change on Tourism

One of the recent directions in tourism research focuses on the relationship between global environmental change and tourism. Part of this research considers the role of the tourism industry in environmental change. This will be discussed in chapter 10, "The Environmental Geography of Tourism." Yet, another part of this research focuses on the ways in which global environmental change is affecting patterns of tourism and will continue to do so in the future. The tourism industry is considered to be highly sensitive to changing environmental conditions, and some of the world's most popular tourism destinations are considered among the most vulnerable places (e.g., islands, other coastal areas, and mountains). Even UNESCO World Heritage Sites—ranging from the Great Barrier Reef to Glacier-Waterton International Peace Park—are considered threatened by the effects of climate change.

These changes have the potential to dramatically reshape patterns of tourism, in some cases creating new opportunities for some destinations and new challenges for others. For example, warmer temperatures can present an opportunity for destinations at higher latitudes or in higher elevations to develop or expand their summer tourism offerings. However, this may be at the expense of existing summer resorts that experience even hotter temperatures and heat waves that are uncomfortable at best and deadly at worst. Moreover, any increases in summer tourism may be offset by declines in winter tourism. Many popular ski resorts, such as those in the Alps, are facing increasingly unreliable snowfalls and may, in fact, become unfeasible in the future.

In other cases, projected changes will most likely have negative impacts for tourism destinations. Rising sea levels are likely to have an adverse effect on coastal resources through coral bleaching, beach erosion, or loss of beachfront properties. Shifting climate regions may accelerate the loss of biodiversity. Some areas are projected to experience drier conditions or longer droughts. This has the potential to create new, or exacerbate existing, problems of water shortages as well as increase the risk of wildfires. Conversely, other areas are projected to experience wetter conditions. This may bring an increase in pests, such as mosquitoes, as well as epidemics of malaria. These areas are also projected to see more frequent and intense storms.

These changes in the physical resource base will affect tourism in many ways. For destinations, revenues from tourism may become more unreliable, while operating costs are likely to increase. Depending on the type of changes experienced, a destination may have to rely more heavily on cooling systems for a longer period of the year, use snowmaking equipment more often, use irrigation and watering systems, and/or pay higher hazard insurance premiums. If these costs are passed on to tourists, travelers will have to reevaluate their decisions, not only about where they go but whether they go. Those tourists who are able to continue to travel may be forced to choose different destinations for their desired activities or to participate at different times of the year. Essentially, all tourism stakeholders will be affected, and all need to adapt.

In particular, **climate change adaptation** refers to the technological, economic, and sociocultural changes intended to minimize the risks and capitalize on the opportunities created by climate change. Tourists generally have the greatest ability to adapt because, at least in theory, they have the ability to choose when and where they travel. Destination stakeholders, however, must work within the constraints of their resource base. Research indicates that both tourism officials and operators currently have a low level of concern for the implications of climate change and overestimate their ability to adapt in the future. Nonetheless, some destinations may require physical solutions to reduce their vulnerability to the effects of changing environmental conditions, while most should begin to consider policies and educational strategies to manage effects. For example, in light of recent disasters at tourism destinations, it is clear that destinations around the world should work to increase awareness and preparedness for hazards and establish disaster contingency plans. As such, there is a distinct need for greater research and communication between the scientific community and tourism stakeholders.

Many places around the world are already being affected by environmental changes. This has been widely documented and publicized in the media. As a result, concerns that these places might be fundamentally changed or destroyed altogether have, in a sense, created a new opportunity in tourism. Playing upon these concerns, tourism stakeholders have begun to encourage tourists—at least those who have the means—to see such places before they are gone. This is sometimes referred to as disappearing tourism, doom tourism, or **last chance tourism**.[14] Last chance tourism provides individuals with the opportunity to see a particular place, geographic feature, or species in its natural habitat while they still can. It also allows them to witness the changes that are taking place and, ultimately the end, firsthand. For some tourists, last chance tourism is a manifestation of their genuine interest in the specific resource and concern for its impending demise. Destinations may choose to promote their vulnerability as a means of generating attention and aid in efforts to protect their vanishing resources. In fact, there are positive examples in which tourism has contributed to the recovery of environments or species. Yet, for other tourists, this is considered to be an expression of egocentrism. Destinations may capitalize on these tourists' desire for exclusivity, and their willingness to pay for the privilege of rarity.

Nearly all of the types of resources discussed in the sections above have become the focus of last chance tourism in various parts of the world. Although tourists have long visited the UNESCO World Heritage Sites identified earlier, there is a new imperative to scuba dive on the Great Barrier Reef while it is still one of the world's most biodiverse ecosystems and to hike in Glacier-Waterton International Peace Park while there are still glaciers. Tourists are interested in skiing historic resorts under natural conditions and seeing endangered wildlife in their natural habitat, whether it is polar bears in Canada or mountain gorillas in Rwanda. They are increasingly visiting the Arctic and Antarctic regions for the experience of sea ice before it melts and possibly even to witness the drama of a calving glacier. They want to have the opportunity to sit on the beaches of small island destinations like Tuvalu or the Maldives before they are submerged. That such tourists might ultimately be contributing to the demise of these destinations will be discussed in chapter 10.

# Conclusion

As a place-based phenomenon, tourism is shaped by and to some extent dependent on the earth's physical features and processes. These things can be either a resource that allows for tourism to take place or a barrier that prevents it. The factors that determine whether something is a resource or a barrier vary between places, societies, and even periods of time depending on the particular circumstances, perceptions, and perhaps level of technology. The topical branches of physical geography provide the means of examining the earth's physical systems across the atmosphere, hydrosphere, lithosphere, and biosphere. The knowledge generated by meteorology, climatology, hydrology, oceanography, geomorphology, and biogeography can be used to better understand how elements in the physical system affect patterns of tourism. This knowledge will become even more important in the future in light of global environmental change.

## Key Terms

- biogeography
- climate change adaptation
- climatology
- geomorphology
- hydrology

- last chance tourism
- meteorology
- tourism resource
- tourism resource audit

## Notes

1. Kerry Godfrey and Jackie Clarke, *The Tourism Development Handbook: A Practical Approach to Planning and Marketing* (London: Cassell, 2000), 66.

2. Godfrey and Clarke, *The Tourism Development Handbook*, 72.

3. Tom McKnight and Darrel Hess, *Physical Geography: A Landscape Appreciation* (Upper Saddle River, NJ: Prentice Hall, 2000), 67.

4. C. R. De Freitas, "Tourism Climatology: Evaluating Environmental Information for Decision Making and Business Planning in the Recreation and Tourism Sector," *International Journal of Biometeorology* 48 (2003): 45.

5. María Belén Gómez Martín, "Weather, Climate, and Tourism: A Geographical Perspective," *Annals of Tourism Research* 32, no. 3 (2005): 587.

6. Gómez Martín, "Weather, Climate, and Tourism," 576.

7. Visit Scotland, "All about Scotland," accessed October 20, 2011, http://www.visitscotland.com/guide/scotland-factfile/.

8. Visit Scotland, "Scottish Climate," accessed October 20, 2011, http://www.visitscotland.com/guide/scotland-factfile/geography/climate/.

9. Steve Kershaw, *Oceanography: An Earth Science Perspective* (Cheltenham, UK: Stanley Thornes, 2000), 5, 17.

10. Robert W. Christopherson, *Geosystems: An Introduction to Physical Geography*, 7th ed. (Upper Saddle River, NJ: Pearson Prentice Hall, 2009), 516.

11. Andrew Holden, *Environment and Tourism*, 2nd ed. (London: Routledge, 2008), 222.

12. "Arenal Volcano Costa Rica," accessed October 29, 2011, http://www.arenal.net/.

13. Central West Virginia Regional Airport Authority, "Yeager Airport History," accessed October 29, 2011, http://yeagerairport.com/about.html.

14. Raynald Harvey Lemelin, Emma Stewart, and Jackie Dawson, "An Introduction to Last Chance Tourism," in *Last Chance Tourism: Adapting Tourism Opportunities in a Changing World*, ed. Raynald Harvey Lemelin, Jackie Dawson, and Emma J. Stewart (London, Routledge, 2012).

## Sources

Christopherson, Robert W. *Geosystems: An Introduction to Physical Geography*. 7th ed. Upper Saddle River, NJ: Pearson Prentice Hall, 2009.

Davie, Tim. *Fundamentals of Hydrology*. 2nd ed. London: Routledge, 2002.

De Freitas, C. R. "Tourism Climatology: Evaluating Environmental Information for Decision Making and Business Planning in the Recreation and Tourism Sector." *International Journal of Biometeorology* 48 (2003): 45–54.

Godfrey, Kerry, and Jackie Clarke. *The Tourism Development Handbook: A Practical Approach to Planning and Marketing*. London: Cassell, 2000.

Goh, Carey. "Exploring Impact of Climate on Tourism Demand." *Annals of Tourism Research* 39, no. 4 (2012): 1859–1883.

Gómez Martín, María Belén. "Weather, Climate, and Tourism: A Geographical Perspective." *Annals of Tourism Research* 32, no. 3 (2005): 571–91.

Gregory, Derek, Ron Johnston, and Geraldine Pratt. *Dictionary of Human Geography*. 5th ed. Hoboken, NJ: Wiley-Blackwell, 2009.

Hall, Michael C., and Alan Lew. *Understanding and Managing Tourism Impacts: An Integrated Approach*. New York: Routledge, 2009.

Lemelin, Raynald Harvey, Emma Stewart, and Jackie Dawson. "An Introduction to Last Chance Tourism." In *Last Chance Tourism: Adapting Tourism Opportunities in a Changing World*, edited by Raynald Harvey Lemelin, Jackie Dawson, and Emma J. Stewart, 3–9. London: Routledge, 2012.

Priskin, Julianna. "Assessment of Natural Resources for Nature-Based Tourism: The Case of the Central Coast Region of Western Australia." *Tourism Management* 22, no. 6 (2001): 637–48.

Scott, Daniel, Bas Amelung, Suzanne Becken, Jean-Paul Ceron, Ghislan Dubois, Stefan Gössling, Paul Peeters, and Murray C. Simpson. *Climate Change and Tourism: Responding to Global Challenges, Summary*. Madrid: World Tourism Organization and United Nations Environment Programme, 2007. Accessed February 22, 2011. http://www.unwto.org/climate/support/en/pdf/summary_davos_e.pdf.

# The Human Geography of Tourism: Resources and Barriers

When we consider potential vacation destinations, our assessment of the human geography of those places is probably more instinctual and less analytical than that of the physical geography. If we dislike the cultural characteristics of a particular group of people, we will simply avoid those destinations where we're most likely to encounter them. If we find big, crowded cities overwhelming and stressful to navigate or if we find the rural countryside boring and uneventful, we won't consider such places in our destination search. If a country is going through a bloody civil war, it would never even enter our thought processes to consider it a vacation spot. From the demand perspective, clearly the human characteristics of a place play an important role in shaping what we want or expect from the destinations we visit. From the supply perspective, these characteristics are also important in determining, first, if tourism will occur in a place, and second, how it will occur.

As we established in the previous chapter, tourism resources are those components of *both* the physical and human environment of a destination that have the potential to facilitate tourism or provide the basis for tourism attractions. While that chapter focused on the physical components of the environment, we turn our attention to the human components in this chapter. In particular, we introduce several new topical branches in geography—including cultural, urban, rural, and political geographies—for the purpose of identifying and examining the human resources that provide the basis for tourism as well as the human factors that present a barrier to tourism. These topical branches are clearly interrelated. Many of the resources and barriers discussed through each of the branches below could easily be approached from a different perspective through the framework of another.

## Cultural Geography and Tourism

The subject of cultural geography and issue of cultural tourism are both widely discussed and the focus of entire books. Most, quite naturally, begin with a discussion of culture. The concept of culture is considered problematic, hard to define, and open to multiple interpretations. Culture is global and local, historic and contemporary, material and symbolic. It can be considered high (oriented toward a select audience educated to appreciate it), or it may be defined as mass, popular, or low and consumed by a wide audience. It is dynamic and ever changing. Thus, we can think of culture as encompassing the way of life for a group of people, with its roots in the past but evolving with present circumstances. Everything, from their artistic expressions to their daily activities, contributes to this way of life and helps create and re-create the meanings and associations they have, as well as their values and identity.

In geography, culture has long been an important topic as we try to understand the world. Cultural geography is a dynamic topical branch that has often been influential in shaping trends in wider geographic research. Today, it is one of the most widely recognized topical branches; in fact, it is sometimes considered synonymous with human geography as a whole. To some extent, this is a reflection of the wide-ranging approaches to and issues in cultural geography. For example, **cultural geography** may be considered the study of how cultures make sense of space, how they give meanings to places, how they create landscapes, how they spread over space, how their identities form, how they are different from others, or how institutions shape culture.

Culture has also long been an important tourism resource, whether in ancient times or today. Because the concept of culture is so ambiguous, there has been much debate about the definition of cultural tourism and/or cultural tourists. Some favor a narrow, idealized view: "To be a cultural tourist is to attempt, I would suggest, to go beyond idle leisure and to return enriched with knowledge of other places and people. . . . In this way cultural tourism is clearly demarcated as a distinct form of tourism."[1] Others argue that, under a broad definition of culture, almost all of tourism today could be considered cultural tourism. We can, perhaps, consider a point somewhere in between. Certainly the cultural resources for tourism are extraordinarily important for much of tourism, and there may be significant overlap between cultural tourism and other products. However, it may be simply a matter of emphasis.

Given the vast scope of cultural geography, there has been considerable interconnection between it and the geography of tourism. Within the context of this discussion, we can use the framework of cultural geography to help us identify cultural resources for tourism and analyze potential barriers that exist between cultures. Cultural geography also has a part to play in helping us understand the effects of tourism on societies (part III) and factors that shape interactions between tourists and places (part IV).

The cultural resources for tourism are virtually limitless. Remnants and symbols of a place's cultural heritage have been some of the most significant resources for tourism throughout history. For example, ancient Roman tourists and modern international tourists alike have been fascinated by the Pyramids of Giza, both for the spectacle of the archaeological site and for its mythology. Cultural heritage resources can be specific sites within a place (e.g., Stari Most or Old Bridge in Mostar, Bosnia and Herzegovina, a UNESCO World Heritage Site based on its symbolic importance in connecting and reconnecting the ethnically divided city) or encompass entire cities (e.g., Valparaíso, Chile, a UNESCO World Heritage Site based on its history as a cultural melting pot and its unique, colorful character). Religious sites, which are often tied to cultural heritage, can also be resources for tourism. Cathedrals, mosques, and temples all over the world are recognized within their respective belief systems for their religious importance. However, they are also more widely appreciated for their history and their aesthetic design. Thus, well-known sites like the Barcelona Cathedral, Hagia Sophia, or Potala Palace and Jokhang Temple Monastery (figure 7.1) have become significant tourism attractions visited by adherents and other international tourists.

Not all elements of cultural heritage need to have a long history or be significant in the greater scope of world affairs to be considered a potential resource. For example, Abbey Road's place in England's cultural heritage dates back to 1969 with the release of the Beatles' final studio LP recorded at Abbey Road Studios and given the same title. The album cover, showing the band members crossing the street, has become iconic, even among younger generations. Even Harry Potter has become an integral part of England's cultural heritage today, and any place that has a part to play in his story—or which served as the inspiration for a place in the story—becomes a resource. These places, such as Gloucester Cathedral, the Glenfinnan Viaduct, or Leadenhall Market, would have otherwise remained unknown to potential tourists around the world.

Various aspects of the arts, whether based on traditional or modern culture, can serve as a resource as well. While these resources may not be the primary attraction that

**Figure 7.1. The iconic Potala Palace, former winter palace of the Dalai Lama, and the Jokhang Temple Monastery, is a significant Buddhist religious complex in Lhasa, Tibet. Recognized as a UNESCO World Heritage Site, this complex is highly desired by international tourists of all belief systems. (Source: Velvet Nelson)**

draws tourists to a place, they constitute a part of the experience and something that tourists may see or do during their visit. Visual arts are often used as a basis for a destination's attraction: famous museums (e.g., the Louvre in Paris or the Metropolitan Museum of Art in New York City), city-level art districts (e.g., the Short North in Columbus, Ohio), and open-air sculpture parks (e.g., Vigeland Park in Oslo, Norway). Likewise, the production of arts and crafts—and these items themselves—can be a resource for tourism. For example, tourists may visit a traditional "factory" in Tunisia to watch the skilled crafts workers make carpets and potentially purchase one to take home with them. The same applies to the performing arts. Tourists may try to see a play or musical (for some, any play or musical will do) in a famous theater district, such as New York City's Broadway or London's West End. In other cases, tourists may wish to see the performances that are specific to the place visited. For example, tourists to Chengdu, China, may attend a Sichuan opera, the highlight of which is typically *bian lian*, or face-changing. In this unique and highly protected art form, performers rapidly change a succession of brightly colored masks.

The varied characteristics of traditional cultures—such as distinctive appearances, clothing styles, livelihood patterns, housing types, cuisines, and more—can individually or collectively be considered tourism resources (figure 7.2). These may be indigenous peoples, minority groups, or other populations that live outside of the wider society such as the Amish in parts of Pennsylvania, New York, and Ohio. At the same time, the characteristics of a modern society can be a resource, as international tourists

**Figure 7.2. The Kuna are an indigenous tribe in Panama and Colombia. One element of their culture—their molas—can be considered a tourism resource. The people have become known for these brightly colored and intricately designed textiles that are used to make the women's distinctive traditional clothes. (Source: Fred McGinnis)**

seek to do things like experience a "typical" Irish pub or ride one of London's double-decker buses. Likewise, aspects of a society's popular fashion, musical culture, culinary styles (see box 7.1), and more can constitute tourism resources.

Additionally, less tangible elements of a place's culture can either contribute as a resource for tourism or constitute a barrier. For example, language is a basic element of culture. A common language, whether the native language or one that is widely spoken, between the sending and receiving countries or regions may be considered a resource for that particular destination. In contrast, the lack of a commonly spoken language can become a barrier. This, of course, is perceptual. For many tourists, the idea of not being able to communicate with people at the destination is a source of anxiety and stress; thus, they will be more likely to choose destinations where they feel confident they know the majority of people will be able to speak the same language.

The same can apply to religious beliefs or cultural value systems. Many societies, particularly those seeking to develop tourism, are open to and tolerant of cultural differences in physical appearance, patterns of dress, or codes of behavior. However, this is not always the case. Tourists are often requested to observe the norms of the society they visit, which may involve changes in the ways they dress (e.g., wearing more conservative clothing or covering one's head) or the ways they act (e.g., refraining from holding hands with one's partner or other public displays of affection). Many tourists are willing to respect these practices so that they may have the experience of that place and culture. However, others may be reluctant to visit a place where they feel they are restricted or concerned about reports of harsh punishments for those who, perhaps unintentionally, violate one of these social rules.

# Urban Geography, Rural Geography, and Tourism

Urban geography and rural geography are distinct topical branches of geography that study specific geographic areas. Yet, these areas—and the studies of them—are not unrelated. Ideas about and definitions of urban and rural areas are often contingent upon each other. They may be negatively defined (i.e., the definition of one is predicated on *not* being the other) or simply defined in opposition with one another (i.e., the characteristic of one is the opposite for the other). For example, using the 2010 United States Census Bureau urban and rural classifications as an example, the basic criteria for an urban area is at least 2,500 people. Correspondingly, a rural area "encompasses all population, housing, and territory not included within an urban area."[2]

Urban geography and rural geography are topical branches in human geography that have clear ties to population and economic geographies. In addition, these branches deal with themes that are shared by social, cultural, political, and even environmental geographies. **Urban geography** may be defined as the study of the relationships between or patterns within cities and metropolitan areas. Urban geography is considered to be a relatively recent development in the field. Over time, trends in the study of geography have reflected the reality of human settlement and livelihood patterns. Consequently, as long as the majority of the world's population lived in rural areas and was dependent on environmental resources for their survival, greater atten-

# Box 7.1.   In-Depth: Food as a Cultural Resource in Italian Tourism

Italy ranks as the world's fifth-largest tourism destination both in terms of international tourist arrivals, numbering at 43.6 million in 2010, and tourism receipts, accounting for US$38.8 billion.[1] Along with history, art, and architecture, food is one of the first things that we think about for Italy. In fact, there is no other destination more closely associated with its cuisine than Italy. Other destinations may have a reputation for good food or a wide variety of dining experiences to choose from, but none bring to mind a specific type or style of food so clearly as the pizzas and pastas of Italy. Thus, while food may not be the primary reason these tourists visit Italy, it is undoubtedly part of their expectations for the experience.

As the country spans a long geographic territory with different landforms and climate regions, differences in cooking styles have naturally evolved based on readily available ingredients. For example, northern Italian cooking uses more beef and butter, while southern Italian styles incorporate more seafood and olive oil. In between the two, and blending traditions from both, Tuscan cuisine is often viewed as quintessentially Italian, with pastas, light sauces, and fresh vegetables. Regardless of these regional variations, however, food and wine make up a distinct part of Italian culture. It is part of the cultural heritage that is passed down from generation to generation, as parents teach their children to make the recipes they learned from their parents and grandparents. It is the central point around which life revolves and the basis for family gatherings as people come together to eat, drink, linger, and socialize.

At the same time, food and wine—with everything from production regions to places of consumption—makes up an important part of the cultural landscape. Vast vineyards and olive groves characterize the countryside, such as Tuscany's Chianti area. Located between Florence and Siena, Chianti is the largest and most popular area in this premier wine-producing region. Small family gardens can easily be seen throughout the small towns and villages. Fresh produce and seafood markets are an integral part of the cities, from the large, well-known ones like Florence's San Lorenzo Mercato Centrale to the small markets that serve the local neighborhoods. And, of course, countless restaurants and cafés can be found in every town and on every city street. They are a distinct part of the character in these places, and they represent a piece of Italian life.

The majority of these restaurants are family owned and operated, and they serve as a place for family members and people from the neighborhood to get together. At the same time, they are generally small in size but open, possibly even spilling out onto the sidewalk, with an inviting atmosphere for tourists. While they often have much the same to offer in terms of food, they give tourists the opportunity to sample classic cuisine for the region. With their ready access to fresh produce from gardens and markets, even simple dishes can seem extraordinary, especially to those tourists for whom freshness is a distinctly foreign concept. The social space of the restaurant and the slow pace of the meal create a sense of an intimate and unique cultural experience. As such, tourists to Italy often find that some of their most memorable experiences revolve around food.

*Discussion topic:* Identify and discuss another example of how food can serve as a cultural resource for tourism.

*Tourism on the web:* Ministro per gli Affari Regonali, il Turismo en lo Sport, "Official Website for Tourism in Italy," at http://www.italia.it/en/home.html; Regione Toscana, "Tourism and Holidays in Tuscany: Official Tourism Site of Tuscany," at http://www.turismo.intoscana.it/intoscana2/export/TurismoRTen/

**Figure 7.3.    From the production regions in the countryside to the innumerable restaurants around every corner in cities such as this one, food is a vital cultural resource for tourism in Italy. (Source: Barret Bailey)**

# Note

1. United Nations World Tourism Organization, *UNWTO Tourism Highlights 2011 Edition* (Madrid: World Tourism Organization, 2011), accessed February 7, 2012, http://mkt.unwto.org/sites/all/files/docpdf/unwtohighlights11enlr_1.pdf, 6.

tion was given to these issues. Although the earliest cities emerged some six thousand years ago, it has been only recently that the majority of the world's population has lived in cities. Reflecting these changing spatial patterns, urban geography began to emerge as a topic of inquiry in the mid-twentieth century and become a recognized topical branch in the subsequent decades.

Correspondingly, issues of tourism in urban areas received increasing attention in geographic research, as well as in other fields, starting in the late 1980s. While this too reflected the increasing importance of cities in the modern world, it also was an indication of the rising significance of urban tourism. Although it could be argued that urban tourism dates back to the Grand Tour in classical cities such as Paris, Vienna, Venice, and Rome, the growth in heritage tourism over the past several decades generated a new demand for these types of urban attractions. At the same time, cities began to see the value in revitalizing rundown urban areas to create an attractive environment for tourism.

**Rural geography** may be defined as the study of contemporary rural landscapes, societies, and economies. The rural had long been a focus of much human geography research, as the majority of people lived in these areas and depended on rural liveli-hoods. In particular, rural areas were an important site for research in the regional tradition of geography. Because of this association with primarily descriptive studies, rural geography fell out of favor in the field. As with regional geography, however, a subset of geographers argued for the development of a more critical approach to regional geography that would go beyond describing rural patterns to try to explain the changing nature of rural areas. These studies have taken various approaches, from cultural (e.g., to understand the concept of rural that has been romanticized as idyllic) to economic (e.g., to understand changing patterns of rural production and consump-tion) and social (e.g., to understand serious issues such as rural poverty).

Although rural geography continues to be under-recognized as a distinct topical branch in the field, these studies have clear implications for the geography of tour-ism. Rural tourism also has a long history. The pastoral ideal was popularized in art and literature based on beautiful rural settings and romanticized country life. In fact, through the eighteenth century, cultivated landscape scenery was viewed as more at-tractive than scenes of wild nature. Interest in experiences of the rural gained even more momentum with the Romantic Movement (see chapter 4), which was primarily a response to the tremendous rise in both industrialization and urbanization. Today, tourism is a vital component in the economic changes that have been taking place in rural areas around the world.

Urban/rural and city/country can be powerful concepts, and despite a general lack of clear definitions, we often have distinct ideas about them. Whether these ideas are positive or negative, vivid or vague, depends on our individual backgrounds and preferences. However, these ideas will nonetheless play an extraordinarily important role in our choice of destinations. In some cases, tourists will assess the generalized resources for tourism in urban or rural areas and rule out entire categories of destina-tions based on that alone. For example, the person who considers only the stereotypes of major cities (e.g., crowds, noise, smog, crime, unfriendly people, etc.) will avoid many popular destinations around the world. In other cases, tourists may decide to visit a destination solely on the basis of that place's most well-known resources. The person who has always wanted to see the Colosseum may not consider any destinations other than Rome once he or she has the opportunity to travel to Europe. Of course, it is important that tourists consider the resources and barriers associated with specific destinations in either of these areas to make the most informed decision.

## URBAN GEOGRAPHY AND TOURISM

Urban geography's focus on the spatial patterns of cities has much to contribute to the geography of tourism. For example, we can consider the extent and nature of a city's connections. While these connections are generally not created for the purpose of tourism, they facilitate it nonetheless. Given the corresponding high level of acces-sibility, cities often serve as an entry point—if not the main attraction—for tourism across the regional, national, and international scales. Likewise, we can consider the spatial organization of a city. Borrowing from the central business district (CBD) concept, the central tourism district (CTD) refers to the spatial concentration of tourism facilities—from attractions to accommodations—within an urban area. This not only helps us understand the nature of tourism at such destinations but also provides the framework for understanding the potential effects of tourism (see part III).

The urban tourism product is based on a wide range of resources. In fact, one of the strengths of this product is the tremendous extent of urban resources that can be made into various categories of attractions (human—not originally intended for tourism; human—intended for tourism; and special events). Thus, urban tourism overlaps with many other products (e.g., cultural, heritage, VFR, event, etc.), and it draws from a number of different tourist markets (e.g., leisure tourists, business tourists, etc.).

Many attractions are derived from the history of cities around the world, from the ancient (e.g., the Acropolis in Athens, Greece, used as a fortress from the second millennium BCE, with the present temples dating back to the fifth century BCE, now a UNESCO World Heritage Site and major tourism attraction) to the more modern (e.g., Robben Island, offshore from Cape Town, South Africa, used as a prison until the mid-1990s with prisoners such as Nelson Mandela, now a UNESCO World Heritage Site and museum). Indeed, these attractions have become so vital that in many cases a city's "old town" or historic district is also the CTD. The spatial concentration of attractions prompts the development of other tourist facilities and services to meet the needs of this ready-made market. Likewise, markets or bazaars were key places for residents to obtain needed products but now serve as an attraction for tourists (e.g., Seattle's Pike Place fish market) and a place to buy souvenirs (e.g., the straw market in Nassau, the Bahamas). Ethnic neighborhoods once served a distinct purpose for immigrants; today, they are highlighted in tourism as part of the city's unique and colorful character (e.g., Miami's Little Havana).

At the same time, cities all over the world have also recognized the potential to create new attractions for tourism from existing resources. In some cases, this involves a physical redevelopment of the urban infrastructure. Tourism has frequently been seen as an important vehicle for urban revitalization, such as the redevelopment of a harbor or former industrial site into a fashionable shopping and/or entertainment district (e.g., Baltimore's Inner Harbor). In other cases, this involves creating new ways of looking at the urban infrastructure. For example, Rio de Janeiro has been at the forefront of slum tourism, an offshoot of the urban tourism product that involves tours of the city's infamous favelas.

Cities also hold countless special events, from neighborhood festivals to hallmark events like the Olympics or the FIFA World Cup, all of which constitute a tourism attraction. In particular, the hallmark events are extraordinarily important, as can be seen by the intense competition between major world cities to be named host sites. These events are significant in generating a vast number of tourist visits when they occur, but they are also significant in raising international awareness of and interest in the destination.

Urban tourism destinations depend heavily on their reputations, both nationally and internationally. A widespread reputation is a distinctly positive factor, as it creates a demand for the experience of that specific destination. However, based on this reputation alone, cities may suffer from the perception that they have a finite number of resources to offer. Every major city has certain attractions that are well known; tourists to these destinations will be sure to see or experience them. In fact, it may be considered a "crime" to visit a city without seeing them—whether it is the Alamo in San Antonio, Texas, or the Little Mermaid statue in Copenhagen, Denmark. However, these types of destinations are prone to one-time visits, where tourists feel that they've "been there, done that" and are ready to experience the main attractions in other cities. Thus, a destination may have to continually work to create new attractions, revitalize existing ones, or promote lesser-known and alternative attractions. For example, the Amsterdam Tourist Board argues, "Took the picture, got the T-shirt? For all those visitors who've seen Amsterdam's beautiful canals, visited the red light district, pioneered the Jordaan and gotten the hang of the city's non-stop nightlife . . . here's news for you: Amsterdam is bigger than you think! There's still plenty to see, do and experience."[3]

The principal barriers to urban tourism are typically perceptual, based on stereotypes of major cities, although there may be a real basis behind this. For example, tourists may feel that pollution, such as smog and litter, render urban destinations unattractive. They may be put off by having to experience high-profile destinations with hundreds, if not thousands, of other tourists (figure 7.4). Tourists may also be concerned by reports

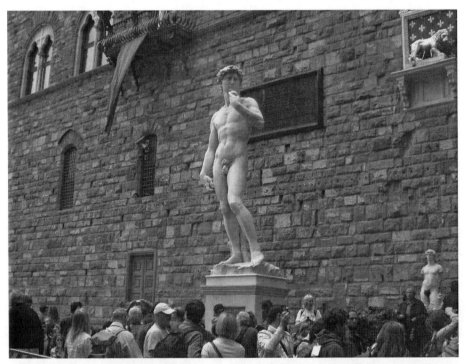

**Figure 7.4.   Michelangelo's *David* is considered the most famous statue in the world. Today, the original is housed in the Galleria dell'Accademia in Florence, Italy. But, for the thousands of tourists who don't want to wait to get inside, they can view a copy of the statue in its original location in the Piazza della Signoria. (Source: Velvet Nelson)**

of a local population that is hostile to foreign tourists or by high crime rates. While tourists are more likely to be affected by petty crime in tourist areas—such as pickpocketing or scams—than violent crimes, it can be a deterrent nonetheless.

All destinations must try to offset the real or perceived barriers with the resources it has to offer. Claiming that a destination is a cosmopolitan center with a distinctly local (not big-city) character is a widely used strategy in urban tourism. Cities of various sizes across the globe have made this case, whether it's Santa Fe, New Mexico (which "has all the markings of a cosmopolitan city in its offering of art, culture, and cuisine, but still has a small-town feel"[4]), or Toronto, Canada ("From cosmopolitan chic to country charm, Toronto's neighbourhoods offer an eclectic mix of architecture, food and shopping"[5]).

## RURAL GEOGRAPHY AND TOURISM

Many of the issues raised in rural geography apply to the geography of tourism in rural areas as well. Understanding the rural ideal—what it is and why it is appealing—is vital in tourism. Much of this is geographically contingent. In large countries with vast areas of undeveloped land, such as the United States or Canada, interest in rural tourism has more often focused on the wild lands protected as national parks. As such, there may be considerable overlap between natural tourism resources and rural ones. Conversely, in smaller countries with extensive cultivated landscapes, such as those in Europe, there is a greater appreciation for experiences in settings that combine natural and human resources. For example, natural resources, ranging from clean air to open spaces, are extraordinarily important in creating the foundation for these tourism products. Yet, these products are often oriented around rural economic activities. Farm tourism, in particular, has been immensely popular.

Rural tourism serves as an umbrella for a diverse set of more specialized tourism products. Although the extent of resources is, perhaps, less varied than in urban areas, each resource is used in a specific way to meet the demands of a particular group of tourists. For example, both farm tourism and wine tourism are based on agricultural production, but tourists interested in farm stays are different from tourists interested in vineyard tours and wine tastings (figure 7.5). Each experience is considered unique; these tourists often participate in the same activities at different farms or estates. Similarly, the tremendous geographic scale of rural areas means that activities are often time consuming, and tourists only have the opportunity to experience a part of the landscape. If they are satisfied with this experience, they may be interested in returning to experience more. In fact, rural tourists often develop an attachment to place based on their experiences that lead them to return to the same places over and over again. This may become a factor in tourists' decisions to purchase or build a second home in their preferred rural settings (e.g., a country house or a lake house).

While the diversity of activities has the potential to appeal to different tourist markets, rural tourism draws almost exclusively from leisure tourists; opportunities to receive business tourists are far more restricted than in urban areas. Rural tourism businesses are more likely to be locally owned, but they are also more likely to operate

## Box 7.2.   Case Study: A Bit of
## Both Worlds in Vancouver, Canada

Some destinations are a natural fit with either urban or rural tourism products. Tourists who visit New York City are clearly interested in experiencing all that the city has to offer, from the lights and busy streets of Times Square to the high-end shopping of Fifth Avenue to the nightlife of East Village. In contrast, tourists who visit Maine will be primarily interested in experiencing the state's rural character, from small towns and villages to pick-your-own orchards to scenic drives. Yet, not all destinations are this clear-cut. In fact, many places around the world thrive on their ability to offer visitors experiences of both urban and rural attractions and opportunities to participate in activities in both urban and rural areas.

Vancouver, Canada's third-largest city, is an urban destination that claims attractions rivaling other such destinations. As one of the country's cultural centers, the city has many cultural resources for tourism, from the performing arts to festivals. Vancouver's high level of ethnic diversity gives the city a unique character and provides many of its attractions. Various museums and art galleries highlight elements of First Nations culture. Vibrant ethnic neighborhoods, such as Chinatown and the Punjabi Market, bring in visitors with distinctive shops and restaurants as well as temples (Buddhist and Sikh, respectively) and special events like the Chinese New Year celebration or Vaisakhi, an ancient harvest festival that originated in northern India. Other urban tourism resources can be found at Robson Street, the city's premier shopping district with popular, high-end, and boutique stores, and Granville Street, the main entertainment district with its concentration of bars and nightclubs. Many of these popular urban districts can be explored on foot; however, many visitors choose to utilize the "Big Bus"—the city's fleet of vintage double-decker and open-top sightseeing buses. The hop-on, hop-off tour allows visitors to maximize their time and visit up to twenty-two of the city's best-known attractions.

Yet, despite all of these resources and potential, tourists rarely visit Vancouver solely for the purpose of urban tourism. In fact, some of Vancouver's most frequently visited attractions are not within the urban center but just outside of the city. Some of these attractions, based on a range of physical and human resources, can be reached within an hour or two; some can be reached in as little as fifteen minutes from downtown. Promoted rural tourism activities consist of visits to farms, farmers markets, and wineries, as well as scenic drives along the Sea-to-Sky Highway and in the Okanagan Valley during the fall colors season. Hiking trails surround the city, from the popular site of the Capilano Suspension Bridge to Grouse Mountain, and many farther afield. Fort Langley National Historic Site, twenty-four miles from the city, pays homage to the province's heritage at the site of a Hudson's Bay Company trading post, originally constructed in 1827, through reconstructed facilities and demonstrations. And, certainly, the area around Vancouver is a well-known destination for winter sports, highlighted by the city's selection as the host site for the 2010 Olympic Games.

The destination's promotional literature makes the most of this dual character. In just one example, the provincial tourism authority Tourism BC claims: "Renowned for its scenic beauty and endless opportunities for outdoor activities, Vancouver is also a cosmopolitan city with all the urban amenities—fine dining, shopping, museums, galleries, music and theatre."[1] This shows potential tourists the city's range of resources, which appeals to a wide tourist market and creates an attractive idea of a distinct place. Thus, unlike tourists visiting other major urban areas, those visiting Vancouver come with the expectation of experiencing more than just an urban destination.

*(continued)*

## Box 7.2.  (continued)

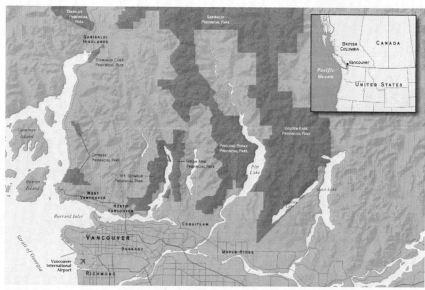

**Map 7.1.  Vancouver, British Columbia. This Canadian destination has the resources that allow tourists to participate in both urban tourism in the downtown district and rural tourism in the surrounding area. (Source: XNR Productions)**

*Discussion topic:* Take and argue a position: do you think urban and rural tourism are compatible or incompatible tourism products?

*Tourism on the web:* Tourism Vancouver, "Vancouver: Spectacular by Nature" at http://www.tourismvancouver.com/

# Note

1. Tourism BC, "Vancouver Things to Do," accessed February 1, 2012, http://www.hellobc.com/vancouver/things-to-do.aspx.

on a small scale. Rural tourism also tends to be highly seasonal in nature. The majority of these activities take place out-of-doors, and they may be dependent on the stages of agricultural production (e.g., planting or harvest).

Some of the greatest issues in rural tourism relate to accessibility. With the exception of vast publicly owned spaces, found in areas such as the western United States, much of the rural landscape is privately owned. Even when some owners are willing to give tourists access to their land, activities may be disrupted or even rendered impossible by owners who don't permit access. Second, rural areas are generally less connected than urban ones. It may be more difficult and more time consuming to

**Figure 7.5. The rural landscape—such as this scene from wine country in Napa Valley, California—provides an attractive setting for recreation. (Source: Velvet Nelson)**

reach these places, and it is dependent on transportation. Areas that aren't served by public transportation, such as a rail network, must be reached by personal vehicles. This becomes a form of social exclusion, where certain social groups such as the poor segments of the population aren't able to participate.

# Political Geography and Tourism

Traditionally, political geography has focused on the study of the spatial structure of states and their struggle for territory and resources. Political geography has existed as an academic study for more than a hundred years, but the changes it has experienced over the years reflect changes in both the field of geography and the world. Today, globalization has become one of the greatest processes of change in the world and requires new ways of looking at the policies of and connections between places. Thus, we might consider **political geography** to be the study of the ways states relate to each other in a globalized world. Clearly this topical branch overlaps with others in human geography, namely economic and social geography but also urban geography.

Studies in tourism have considered the political factors in tourism; however, few studies have focused on the geography of political factors in tourism. Examinations of tourism from the perspective of political geography have primarily considered the relationship between national identity and tourism.[6] Yet, there are various ways we can examine the policies that shape tourism through the framework of geography.

So far, we have primarily considered tourism resources as those components of a destination's environment that have the potential to provide the basis for tourism attractions, but we can also consider those factors that have the potential to facilitate tourism. For the most part, this applies to political tourism resources. A government's policies at the national, regional, or local scale have the potential to shape tourism development. The public sector may determine which areas will be targeted for development. For example, in the 1970s, the Mexican government selected the state of Quintana Roo to be the site of the country's first master-planned resort: Cancún.[7] The public sector can support tourism development by investing in the construction or upgrade of basic infrastructure (e.g., transportation facilities, electricity, water and sewage supply, etc.) and protection of the appropriate resources (e.g., natural, cultural, heritage, etc.). It may also offer tax breaks or subsidies to encourage private sector investment in the tourism industry. At the same time, a government can create barriers to tourism development through bureaucratic red tape.

A stable political environment can also be considered a tourism resource or an important precondition for tourism. Conversely, an unstable political environment will present a barrier to tourism. Although some of the most intrepid drifters may be undeterred from traveling in a potentially volatile country, most tourists will avoid any destination that is unstable or that they perceive to be unstable—at least until the situation changes. At best, they may find their vacation disrupted; at worst, they may find themselves caught up in the middle of a conflict. Early in 2011, some four thousand European tourists were forced to cut short their vacations in Tunisia, a popular Mediterranean destination. This was due to unexpected protests and riots that marked the beginning of the Arab Awakening. Shortly thereafter, many governments around the world issued warnings for their citizens to avoid all nonessential travel to the country.[8]

Good international relations between countries and open entry policies, such as eliminating visa requirements for some or all inbound international tourists, can improve accessibility and facilitate the movement that is a fundamental component of tourism. In particular, open borders can be advantageous for tourism. The Schengen Area is a "borderless" region encompassing twenty-six European countries, primarily European Union members. Tourists entering the Schengen Area must pass through border control, but any international travel within the area can be done without undergoing these procedures. This greatly facilitates ease of travel, both for international tourists who are citizens of any of the member countries and for other tourists traveling in the area.

In some cases, poor relations between two countries will simply restrict travel from one to the other but not necessarily have an adverse impact on the industry as a whole. For example, American policies have restricted travel to Cuba (to varying degrees depending on the administration) since the Cuban Revolution; thus, the island has been deprived of this potentially large tourist market with a good relative location. Yet, Cuba's tourism industry attracts approximately two million visitors a year from Canada and Mexico, as well as from countries in South America and Europe. Of course, the "forbidden" nature of tourism may generate tourist visits, even with the threat of fines and/or imprisonment. However, the tourism industry will be seriously affected in a country that has been widely sanctioned by the international community for its policies and actions. At the same time, tourists from that country may also experience problems traveling abroad (see box 7.3).

Entry regulations and border controls can also effectively serve as a barrier to tourism. A country may discourage travel to their destinations by imposing strict regulations on travel, such as requiring all tourists to check in with the police upon entry or traveling with a guide at all times. The same is true if the country has difficult and confusing procedures, long wait times, and/or high fees for applying for entry visas. A country's reputation for long lines at border checkpoints and rigorous customs and security inspections may also serve as a deterrent.

# Conclusion

Just as the physical features and processes of place shape tourism, so will the varied human features and processes of that place. There are countless factors that will act as resources for or barriers to tourism; these chapters have barely skimmed the surface. Nonetheless, we can begin to see how we can use a geographic framework to help us identify and explore these issues. In part III, we will build on this foundation by examining the geographic effects of tourism. The nature of these effects for any destination will undoubtedly be influenced by the characteristics of both the physical geography and the human geography of that place. Thus, we will continue to draw upon these topical branches that we have already discussed, even as we turn our focus to a few new ones.

# Key Terms

- cultural geography
- political geography
- rural geography
- urban geography

# Box 7.3.  Experience:
# Traveling on an African Passport

I was born in Zimbabwe. I am fortunate to have had the opportunity to travel quite a bit, but I wasn't prepared for what I had to go through on this particular trip. At the time, I was living in Harare, the capital, and after a very stressful period at work, I was ready to leave with my girlfriend on a well-deserved Christmas holiday to the United Kingdom to meet my girlfriend's family.

I had chosen to fly on Ethiopian Airways, as I had heard good things about the service, and they offered 40 kg baggage allowance! I decided to fly through Addis Ababa, the capital of Ethiopia and hub of the airline, and spend the night there. We could have gone on directly to England, but I wanted to get another stamp in my passport and experience that part of Africa. We waited over an hour and a half for the bus to take us to our hotel. Coming from Zimbabwe, where we have a lot of poverty and suffering, I was amazed and slightly horrified that, in a twenty-minute bus journey, most of what I saw was shanties and squalor. Things didn't improve, as it turns out that all three-star hotels are not created equal—the showers didn't work, the roof was falling down in places, and the bed was horrendously uncomfortable. Coupled with a 4 a.m. wake-up call for our flight and some rather odd ideas of what constitutes decent food in Ethiopia, it was not an auspicious start to our holiday.

Our next flight, full of East and Central Africans heading off for their Christmas holidays, took us through Rome. We touched down at Rome International for a quick layover to collect more passengers, and that's where the fun really started. A forty-five-minute layover suddenly became a lot longer. We were told there was a problem with the engine—but it would be fixed shortly. Two hours later, with no more explanation, some of the passengers started to get a little rowdy. The flight attendants served dinner and drinks, and more time passed. Having watched the technicians shine flashlights into the engine for several hours, we were beginning to think that the engine was not as fixable as the attendants said. At this stage, there was a volatile mix of Christmas spirit, alcoholic spirit, and a healthy dose of African spirit. We declared that we wanted the captain to come out and explain exactly what the problem was and how long it was going to take to fix. It was suddenly announced that we would be allowed to enter the airport terminal, and everyone deplaned with great alacrity.

Inside the terminal we were met by a very courteous Ethiopian Airways agent who told us that the plane had an engine fault which would be fixed in a few hours when the part arrived from Switzerland. While they didn't think it would take too long, the airline would put us all up in a hotel for the night. In the meantime, we were to separate: European Union, American, and Australian passport holders on one side and all other passports on the other. The reason was that the first group was legally allowed to enter Italian soil without visas, so they would go to the hotel first. The rest of us, mainly African passport holders, would follow once the airline cleared it with Italian immigration.

My girlfriend travels on a British passport, so she was in the first group to leave for the hotel. She didn't want to leave without me and offered to stay. But I am a gentleman, so I told her to go ahead, get a nice room, and I would join her as soon as I could. She gave me her pillow and left with all the other First World citizens for a four-star hotel in Rome. There were about eighty Africans from various countries left waiting hopefully for our bus to take us to the hotel. We were very tired now; from the 4 a.m. wake-up call, it was now 9 p.m., and there was no airline representative to be seen. Upon asking the immigration personnel, we

*(continued)*

## Box 7.3.   (continued)

were informed that the Ethiopian Airways desk was on the other side of the terminal—but we couldn't go there because we didn't have visas. Several passengers demanded to be let through or bring a representative to us. This was actually a difficult process; the passengers' English was fragmented, at best, and the Italian immigration officials barely spoke any English.

By this time, we were all very irritated and handwrote a petition signed by all present that our human rights had been infringed upon. When the airline representative finally returned, she was given our complaint. She explained that we would not be able to leave the airport, as we did not have visas. We would, however, be given food and drinks and allowed to call someone should we wish, but we would have to stay in the terminal for the night. This announcement nearly resulted in a riot. The food was a measly sandwich and cold beverage. Having left tropical Africa in the morning, we were wearing light clothes, but the terminal in Italy on a frosty December night was close to freezing. And, of course, our luggage was still on the plane. The chairs in the terminal all had solid armrests, so we couldn't lie down. I eventually pulled four solid wooden chairs together in the dining area and slept fitfully till about 5 a.m. At that time, the cleaning staff started to arrive, turned on the lights, and woke those of us who were trying to sleep.

We were tired, miserable, hungry, and very cold—but mostly highly irritated. No Ethiopian Airways representatives had been seen for several hours. We had had enough. This massive troupe of Africans stormed the wrong way down the stairs, surrounded the Italian immigration officials, and demanded to be let out so we could give the airline a piece of our minds. The officials got very excited (again, they spoke very little English), and we were all nearly arrested. Eventually someone got word to Ethiopian Airways, and someone new arrived. He apologized and announced that we would receive breakfast, the other passengers would join us shortly from the hotel, and our flight would depart. We were skeptical but decided that a meal would certainly help ease our suffering. We were given a small sandwich and a warm beverage, then left to our own devices again!

An hour after breakfast, a passenger delegation was sent downstairs to wrangle with the immigration officials again. When the agent showed up, he apologized profusely for the delay and allowed us to wait in the Alitalia First Class lounge. Finally something was going right! There were comfortable leather couches to sleep on, free food and drinks, and even a hot shower. We spent the rest of the day waiting there. Still, I had not been able to speak to anyone at home, in the UK, or even my girlfriend in Rome.

Nearly twenty-four hours after touching down in Rome the day before, the next flight from Addis Ababa arrived, and we were put on it to England instead. The flight to London's Heathrow airport was uneventful, but after we disembarked we learned that our luggage was still on the original plane. We waited two more hours for the bags, and then it took another two hours to get to the family's home. Well over sixty hours after leaving Harare, we finally got to bed on Christmas morning. I have always been very proudly Zimbabwean and African by birth, but to be treated like an afterthought due to my passport was a very frustrating and distasteful experience.

*—Gareth*

# Notes

1. Kevin Meethan, *Tourism in Global Society: Place, Culture, Consumption* (Houndmills, UK: Palgrave, 2001), 128.

2. United States Census Bureau, "2010 Census Urban and Rural Classification and Urban Area Criteria," accessed April 28, 2011, http://www.census.gov/geo/www/ua/2010urbanruralclass .html.

3. Amsterdam Tourist Board, "Amsterdam Metropolitan Area," accessed February 1, 2012, http://www.iamsterdam.com/en/visiting/amsterdam-metropolitan-area.

4. New Mexico Tourism Department, "North-Central Region," accessed February 1, 2012, http://newmexico.org/explore/regions/northcentral.php.

5. Tourism Toronto, "Places to Explore," accessed February 1, 2012, http://www.seetoronto now.com/Visitor/Explore/City-Neighbourhoods.aspx.

6. See, for example, Duncan Light, "'Facing the Future': Tourism and Identity-Building in Post-Socialist Romania," *Political Geography* 20 (2001).

7. Rebecca Maria Torres and Janet D. Momsen, "Gringolandia: The Construction of a New Tourist Space in Mexico," *Annals of the Association of American Geographers* 95, no. 2 (2005): 315.

8. Elaine Ganley and Bouazza Ben Bouazza, "Tunisia Riots: Tourists Evacuated As Protests Continue." *Huffington Post*, January 14, 2011, accessed February 4, 2012, http://www .huffingtonpost.com/2011/01/14/tunisia-riots-tourists-ev_n_809118.html.

# Sources

Blacksell, Mark. *Political Geography*. London: Routledge, 2006.

Chang, T. C., and Shirlena Huang. "Urban Tourism: Between the Global and the Local." In *A Companion to Tourism*, edited by Alan A. Lew, C. Michael Hall, and Allan M. Williams, 223–34. Malden, MA: Blackwell, 2004.

Crang, Mike. *Cultural Geography*. London: Routledge, 1998.

Duncan, James, Nuala C. Jackson, and Richard H. Schein. "Introduction." In *A Companion to Cultural Geography*, edited by James Duncan, Nuala C. Jackson, and Richard H. Schein, 1–9. Malden, MA: Blackwell, 2004.

Kaplan, Dave, James Wheeler, and Steven Holloway. *Urban Geography*. 2nd ed. Hoboken, NJ: Wiley, 2009.

McKercher, Bob, and Hilary du Cros. *Cultural Tourism: The Partnership between Tourism and Cultural Heritage Management*. New York: Haworth Hospitality Press, 2002.

Meethan, Kevin. *Tourism in Global Society: Place, Culture, Consumption*. Houndmills, UK: Palgrave, 2001.

Sharpley, Richard. "Tourism and the Countryside." In *A Companion to Tourism*, edited by Alan A. Lew, C. Michael Hall, and Allan M. Williams, 374–81. Malden, MA: Blackwell, 2004.

Shaw, Gareth, and Allan M. Williams. *Critical Issues in Tourism: A Geographical Perspective*. 2nd ed. Malden, MA: Blackwell, 2002.

Sheller, Mimi. *Consuming the Caribbean: From Arawaks to Zombies*. London: Routledge, 2003.

Smith, Melanie K. *Issues in Cultural Tourism Studies*. 2nd ed. London: Routledge, 2009.

Taylor, Peter J. "New Political Geographies: 'Twixt Places and Flows." In *The Student's Companion to Geography*, 2nd ed., edited by Alisdair Rogers and Heather A. Viles, 113–17. Malden, MA: Blackwell, 2003.

Williams, Stephen. *Tourism Geography*. London: Routledge, 1998.

Woods, Michael. *Rural Geography*. London: Sage, 2005.

# Part III

# THE GEOGRAPHY OF TOURISM EFFECTS

While tourism began as an activity, it quickly became an industry. Peoples and places all over the world—now more than ever—looked to tourism as a means of development. The promise of economic benefits from tourism, namely job creation and income generation, has been extremely alluring. Likewise, with the evolution of the environmental movement, the potential for environmental preservation has also been a strong motivator. Today, these arguments for tourism can be heard in places all over the world, whether on a small island with chronic high unemployment rates or in a remote wilderness area under pressure from the extractive industries. Tourism is held up as the panacea for all sorts of problems. Indeed, properly planned and developed, tourism can have a positive impact on both the peoples and the places involved. However, this is not always the case. The benefits of tourism are not always evenly distributed, and it can have unforeseen consequences. Both the potential costs and benefits for a particular place must be carefully considered and weighed to understand the net result of tourism. Ultimately, this knowledge should be used to determine the most appropriate strategies to maximize the benefits of tourism at the destination and to minimize the costs.

This section examines the geography of tourism effects. In particular, chapter 8 discusses the economic geography of tourism. Chapter 9 considers the social geography of tourism, and chapter 10 explores the environmental geography of tourism. Each of these chapters uses the tools and concepts of the respective topical branches to help us understand both the benefits and the costs of tourism on the human and physical resources of the destination. In addition, they will address some of the factors that play a role in determining what the outcome of tourism will be for a particular place.

# CHAPTER 8

# The Economic Geography of Tourism

Tourism is big business. The UNWTO estimates that the international tourism industry—without considering the value of domestic tourism in countries around the world—generated US$1,030 billion in 2011.[1] With figures like this, it's not surprising that the economic impact of tourism is considered so important. However, neither the economic benefits nor the economic costs of tourism are evenly distributed between countries, communities, or even segments of the population. Consequently, who benefits from tourism and who is hurt by it are issues that need to be carefully considered.

The economic geography of tourism gives us the means to examine the economic effects of tourism at the individual, local, and national scales. **Economic geography** is a topical branch in human geography that is related to the field of economics and intersects with other branches such as social, political, and urban geographies. Broadly, economic geography is the study of the spatial patterns, human-environment interactions, and place-based effects of economic activities. Economic geography has a long-standing focus on issues of production. Traditionally, production has been used to describe production in the primary (e.g., agriculture) or secondary (e.g., manufacturing) economic sectors. Yet, with the tremendous rise of the tertiary sector (i.e., services) in the modern world, the study of economic geography has adapted to reflect this change.

Given this emphasis on understanding the patterns that have developed with the service sector, it would stand to reason that there should be a close relationship between economic geography and the geography of tourism. In today's world, tourism is undoubtedly one of the most significant economic activities and arguably the most significant service sector industry. As such, tourism geographers have naturally drawn from the theories and concepts of economic geography. Yet, the exchange has not always been mutual. Despite calls for greater connections between economic geography and the other topical branches of geography[2] and specifically tourism geography,[3] economic geographers have given little attention to either tourism geography research or tourism as a topic of inquiry.[4] Tourism geographer Dimitri Ioannides suggests several potential barriers to greater interaction between the two branches, including the inability in many cases to distinguish between tourism and other related services, the conglomeration of industries and services that make up the production of the tourist experience, and the greater emphasis that has been placed on demand-side perspectives in tourism studies.[5]

Economic geography has a vital part to play in our understanding of the geography of tourism. The potential economic benefits of tourism are extraordinarily important in the development of tourism destinations around the world. Yet, the promise of such benefits should not be adhered to blindly; they must be weighed against the potential costs to determine if net benefits will, in fact, be received. This chapter utilizes the tools and concepts of economic geography to consider the potential for tourism to contribute to economic development at a destination, as well as the failure of tourism to live up to this potential or have other negative consequences for the destination. Additionally, it also discusses the factors that influence the outcome of these effects.

# Economic Benefits of Tourism

Particularly since the post–World War II era, tourism has been seen as an attractive option for **economic development**. Economic development is typically described as a process. It encompasses the various changes that create conditions for improvements in productivity and income and therefore the well-being of the population. Essentially, economic development has the potential to bring many changes to the economic geography of a place. For many less developed countries based on predominantly low-income primary sector activities, tourism has provided new opportunities for economic diversification. For example, countries that weren't considered to have a cost-effective location for industrial development might now be identified as having attractive locations and/or resources for tourism. This allows the development of tertiary activities, which may be accompanied by an increase in income. As such, the benefits of tourism have primarily focused on job creation and the interrelated factors of income, investment, and associated economic development.

## TOURISM EMPLOYMENT

One of the principal benefits of tourism is job creation. This is particularly emphasized by countries that have traditionally experienced problems with high unemployment rates, as well as rural and peripheral regions of countries where jobs are limited. For example, the Caribbean has a history of chronic unemployment and high rates of labor-based emigration. Thus, the creation of new jobs for tourism has been a distinct advantage for many islands.

There is considerable potential for direct employment in the tourism industry, which is considered to have a relatively high demand for labor. For example, the Venetian Resort Hotel Casino in Las Vegas, Nevada (figure 8.1), combined with the Palazzo Resort Hotel Casino, is the largest five-diamond hotel/resort complex in the world and employs a virtual army of nearly ten thousand people.[6] This one complex alone maintains a larger workforce than many traditional manufacturing facilities, which have been experiencing declines in labor demand as a result of increased

**Figure 8.1.  Massive resort complexes such as the Venetian Las Vegas maintain thousands of employees in a vast range of capacities, from hotel management to casino dealers, bartenders, maintenance crews, security forces, and even these gondoliers. (Source: Velvet Nelson)**

mechanization. By way of comparison, Hyundai Motor Manufacturing Alabama employs three thousand people.[7]

Direct employment in the tourism industry varies widely. Some people may be employed, often in the private sector, to facilitate destination planning, development, or promotion. Others provide services to tourists by working at local information offices or serving as guides. As in the case of the Venetian, hotels and resorts employ countless people; depending on the scale of the hotel and the services provided, these employees may function as valet parking attendants, bellhops, check-in clerks, concierges, housekeepers, groundskeepers, maintenance crews, security forces, bartenders, servers, kitchen staff, salespeople in in-house retailers, spa therapists, casino dealers, or entertainers. Tourist attractions also employ a range of staff to maintain facilities and to facilitate the tourism experience.

In addition, there is considerable potential for indirect employment generated by the tourism industry. In some cases, these jobs support tourism development but are not directly involved in serving tourism. This includes jobs in the construction industry that are required to build both the general infrastructure that will allow tourism (e.g., airports or highways) and the specific tourism infrastructure (e.g., hotels). Likewise, this can include manufacturing jobs that produce the goods that are sold to tourists. In other cases, these jobs are created in related service industries that both support and benefit from tourism but do not solely cater to the tourist market. This includes jobs in transport services, general retail businesses, local restaurants, or others.

The tremendous diversity of services provided in the context of tourism constitutes an added benefit; it allows jobs to be created in a variety of capacities and at different skill or education levels. This opens up tourism employment to a wider range of people, rather than a subset of the population. For example, a higher proportion of tourism-related jobs go to women compared to jobs in other modern industries. Particularly in less developed countries, less skilled work is accessible to women, who may not have had the opportunity to obtain a formal education. In addition, the domestic nature of many of the services provided in tourism may be seen as an acceptable form of employment in parts of the world where women have not traditionally had a place outside of the home and in the formal economic sectors (figure 8.2).

**Figure 8.2. Tourism is often promoted as creating new employment opportunities. This woman is working at a tourist restaurant and entertainment venue at Victoria Falls, Zimbabwe. (Source: Velvet Nelson)**

## INCOME, INVESTMENT, AND ECONOMIC DEVELOPMENT

For most places, the potential financial benefits of tourism are an important factor driving tourism development. However, these benefits come in different forms with different effects. Tourism has the potential to bring investment to a place or region. A place may possess the resources for tourism, but varying degrees of development will be required before tourism can take place. This is typically infrastructural development to allow people to reach the destination, to stay there (if appropriate), and to appreciate attractions. The public sector is likely to invest in the basic infrastructure, such as transport systems and utilities, and some attractions, such as local/national parks, monuments, or museums. The private sector is likely to invest in specific tourist infrastructure, such as accommodations, as well as attractions. For many destinations, particularly those in poorer regions seeking to use tourism as a strategy to improve the economy and income levels, the local private sector may not have the capital to invest in tourism development. As such, external—often foreign—investment may be a crucial catalyst for growth and starting the development process in that place, when it would not have been possible otherwise.

Tourism also has the potential to bring currency to a destination. Thus, tourism geographers are concerned not only with the movement of people from one place to another but also with money. In the case of domestic tourism, this signifies a spatial redistribution of currency within the country. This is particularly significant when destinations are developed in poorer, peripheral regions of a country. Tourism is considered an important means of allowing some of the wealth that is typically concentrated in the country's primary urban area to be channeled into these destinations, thereby decreasing regional inequalities. In the case of international tourism, this indicates an influx of currency that contributes to the country's gross domestic product (GDP) and has the potential to improve its trade balance (i.e., increase its surplus or decrease its deficit). Similarly, this signifies a means of redistributing some of the wealth from the more developed countries of the world to the less developed ones.

The **travel account** is defined as the difference between the income that the destination country receives from tourism and the expenditures of that country's citizens when they travel abroad. The recent trend toward tourism in less developed countries such as Honduras, Mozambique, or Cambodia has allowed these destinations to develop a positive travel account. In other words, such destinations receive international tourists and therefore derive income from these tourists, but because international tourism is beyond the financial means of much of their population, they send relatively few tourists to other countries. In contrast, more developed countries such as Germany and Japan have traditionally had a negative travel account. These countries are significant tourist-generating areas and send substantial numbers of tourists abroad every year who spend money in other countries, yet they are not among the world's leading destinations. As smaller numbers of tourists visit these destinations, the income derived from them is less than the amount being spent abroad.

The **direct economic effect** of tourism is often used to refer to the initial introduction of currency into the local economy by tourists themselves. This is in the form of **tourist dollars**, or the money that tourists bring with them and spend at the destination on lodging, food, excursions, souvenirs, and more. The **indirect economic effect** of tourism refers to the second round of spending that is a direct result of the tourist dollars. The recipients of tourist dollars use this money to pay expenses, employees, taxes, and so on, as well as reinvestment in the tourism business. This involves buying the goods and services demanded by tourists or the new equipment that will allow them to better serve the tourist market. This round of spending is primarily intended to improve or expand the tourism industry in a way that will encourage future visitation and spending (i.e., greater direct effects) at the destination. As long as the additional spending takes place within the local economy (e.g., hiring local workers, buying locally produced goods), it can create additional economic benefits for the destination. Finally, the **induced economic effect** constitutes an additional round of spending. For example, recipients of tourist dollars pay taxes, licenses, or fees on their business; then the government may use this money to subsidize local development projects. Likewise, recipients may use tourist dollars to pay their employees, who then purchase the goods and services that they need for their own consumption.

This process of spending and respending may be quantified by the **multiplier effect**. This is typically expressed as a ratio. For example, the ratio of 1 to 1.25 means that for every tourist dollar that is spent directly on tourism, an additional 25 cents is created indirectly in the local economy. The multiplier effect may be used to estimate the economic benefits of tourism because it provides an indication of how the income from tourism is distributed throughout the economy. The greater the ratio, the more likely it is that money is staying within that economy. Consequently, the ratio will generally be higher at the national scale rather than at the local scale, where some money will necessarily be spent outside of the community. Businesses will be required to pay federal taxes, which may not be reinvested in that particular place. Not all goods can be obtained locally, and not all employees live at the destination and spend their earnings locally. The multiplier effect is often criticized because it can be extremely difficult to calculate depending on a wide range of factors. As such, it should be considered with caution, as a general guide to describe the potential for additional economic benefits to the destination as opposed to a precise measure.

The development of tourism has the potential to contribute to further economic development and diversification. The tourism industry can take advantage of existing local industries or encourage the development of new ones to support tourism and provide the goods or services demanded by tourists. These are called **linkages** and are typically part of the indirect economic effects. For instance, tourism has the potential for strong linkages to local agricultural industries where foods typical to a particular region are produced and prepared locally for tourist consumption at markets, restaurants, or resorts (figures 8.3 and 8.4). These linkages may be used to create a sense of place-based distinctiveness for the destination, where tourists will have the opportunity to experience things that they would not be exposed to at home. In the case of agricultural linkages, this may be a type of cuisine that is based on local ingredients not readily accessible or commonly used at the tourists' place of origin. Thus, tourists feel like they tried something new and authentic. At the same time, linkages may be used to appeal to a particular brand of "responsible" tourists, typically those socially conscious consumers interested in things like organic and fair trade products.

Figure 8.3. Kiosks and market stalls selling locally grown/made products can be an important part of the attraction at tourism destinations, which also helps support other local industries. This vendor in Ljubljana, Slovenia, has pršut (prosciutto) and wine, which are well-known products from the country's Mediterranean region. (Source: Leo Zonn)

Figure 8.4. Touring Viña Montes La Finca de Apalta in the Colchagua Valley, Chile. (Source: Barret Bailey)

# Box 8.1.  Experience: Wine and Tourism in Chile

I can't say that I ever planned on going to Chile, but when my girlfriend had to go to Santiago for her job, I decided that I would meet her there. After she finished her work, we would spend a few days in the city, but we both wanted to get out and explore some more of the country. I didn't know much about Chile before this trip, but I knew about Chilean wine. I manage a restaurant, and we have a selection of South American wines, including a Chilean Malbec. It was my idea to visit the wine regions in the Central Valley. I did some research and found that the company that produces this wine had several vineyards in the region. I chose one of them to visit; it was the largest of their vineyards and located in the area where we wanted to go, south of Santiago in the less-visited Colchagua Valley.

The smog had been getting worse every day we spent in Santiago, and when we drove out of the city, visibility was low. We couldn't even see the mountains that surround the city. As the morning went on and we got farther from the city, the haze began to burn off. By the time we reached the site, it had turned out to be a beautiful day with clean air and clear skies. We first toured the vineyard; they took us up the vine-covered hillside for a spectacular view of the valley's scenery. Then we toured the winery and had a tasting. They produce mainly red wines at this winery, and we had the opportunity to try the Cabernet Sauvignon, Syrah, and Carmenère, which is a variety I'd never heard of before. We also tried a Sauvignon Blanc from another one of the company's vineyards. Although our guide for the tour had limited English, she was plainly knowledgeable about viticulture. She did her best to answer some good questions from our group about the valley's soils, climate, and varieties of grapes, as well as the processes of hand-picking the grapes and producing the wines.

We were somewhat surprised to learn that taxes make the wines very expensive to purchase locally, so the majority is exported. Because the white wines have a much more limited distribution in the United States, we purchased a few of these bottles at the winery and brought them home with us. In particular, we wanted to try their award-winning Chardonnay, and we didn't think we'd be able to get it here. The reds are pretty widely distributed, though, like the Malbec we have at the restaurant, and some of the varieties can also be found at the grocery stores in town.

Wine is clearly an important part of the economy, but at the same time, I think it really adds to what Chile has to offer in terms of tourism. The two industries are, in fact, a perfect complement to each other. For me, our tour of the vineyard and winery was one of the highlights of our trip. We wanted to see some of the countryside beyond the city, and the landscape scenery of the vineyard set in the valley was exceptionally beautiful. As food and wine are my passion, I am always interested in learning more about and trying things that are unique to the places I visit. It gave us a distinctly local experience as well as something local to bring home with us. In addition, I can tell my customers more about the Chilean wine we sell at the restaurant because I've actually been to the winery, and my girlfriend has been buying these wines at the store since we've been back. While this is partially because she is familiar with them, it also has more meaning for us because it reminds us of our trip.

*—Barret*

# Box 8.2.    In-Depth: Pro-Poor Tourism

Critics have said that those who are already economically better off in a community are more likely to receive the benefits of tourism, while the poorest segments of the population are more likely to experience the costs of tourism. As the tourism industry, particularly those segments driven by the private sector, is a profit-oriented venture, tourism development has done little to consider the relationship between tourism and poverty or to view poverty elimination as a goal. Moreover, the poor are not a homogenous group; there is a tremendous range of factors that may prevent people from participating in tourism. The poor may not have access to the education and/or training—including language skills—that would allow them to obtain tourism jobs or to understand and work within the legal framework to start a tourism business. They may not have access to the capital or credit they need to start or expand a tourism or related business. Similarly, they may not have access to or control over the land and other resources that could be used for the purposes of tourism. They may be only small-scale producers of goods or services, and tourism businesses may seek to deal with a single, large supplier of the products they need. Additionally, they may be excluded from the tourism planning and development process.

Yet, there is an undeniable relationship between tourism and poverty. In particular, the regions of the world that have experienced some of the highest tourism growth rates are also the regions that have the highest concentrations of poor people. Particularly since the beginning of the twenty-first century, new studies have been undertaken to better understand this relationship. The Pro-Poor Tourism Partnership was formed as a collaborative research initiative to develop the concept of **pro-poor tourism** (PPT). PPT is defined as tourism that results in increased net benefits for poor people and ensures that tourism growth contributes to poverty reduction. PPT is not a tourism "product" like those discussed in chapter 3; rather, it is an approach to tourism. It seeks to expand the economic benefits of tourism to the poor by addressing those barriers that prevent them from participating in tourism. Yet, PPT is also intended to help limit the various economic, social, and environmental costs of tourism that are most likely to affect the poor.

Proponents of PPT argue that the tourism industry is better suited to contribute to poverty reduction than many other economic activities because it is a diverse, labor-intensive industry that often utilizes freely available resources (e.g., natural environments or elements of culture). Tourism brings the consumer to the producer, which opens up opportunities for poor people who may not have the ability to take their goods or services to a place of consumption. In addition, tourism has the potential to complement and supplement existing economic activities (e.g., agriculture or fishing), thereby increasing income-earning potential.

Although there may appear to be little incentive for a tourism venture to take PPT measures, especially profit-oriented private sector ventures, tourism is nonetheless dependent on a supportive and stable local community, and the issues associated with high rates of poverty have the potential to erode this foundation. Furthermore, it may be argued that there is a subset of tourists who are socially conscious and would be interested in supporting such a project. Small-scale, socially responsible niche tourism products (e.g., community-based eco-tourism) have been most likely to incorporate PPT strategies. However, it is argued that the full potential of the PPT approach will not be realized until its strategies are also expanded to mass tourism.

*(continued)*

## Box 8.2.    *(continued)*

# Sources

Ashley, Caroline, Charlotte Boyd, and Harold Goodwin. "Pro-Poor Tourism: Putting Poverty at the Heart of the Tourism Agenda." *Natural Resource Perspectives* 51 (2000): 1–6.

Ashley, Caroline, Dilys Roe, and Harold Goodwin. "Pro-Poor Strategies: Making Tourism Work for the Poor." *Pro-Poor Tourism Report* 1 (2001).

Torres, Rebecca, and Janet Henshall Momsen. "Challenges and Potential for Linking Tourism and Agriculture to Achieve Pro-Poor Tourism Objectives." *Progress in Development Studies* 4, no. 4 (2004): 294–318.

Although some existing economic activities might have the potential for linkages as the tourism industry becomes well established, at least initially the local economy may not be sufficiently or appropriately developed to support the tourism industry. Existing activities may require adaptations to meet the specific demands of tourism. The local agricultural industry may make a transition from a single crop (e.g., corn) to more diversified agriculture to supply the range of products in demand by the tourism industry (e.g., lettuce, tomatoes, jalapeño peppers). Likewise, the local fishing industry may need to expand in order to supply the quantity of products demanded by the tourism industry. Additionally, activities may need to be wholly developed; until then, products must be imported. However, to maximize the economic benefits of tourism, local linkages should be created as soon as it is feasible to minimize the dependence on external suppliers.

# Economic Costs of Tourism

Places all across the globe would like to get a share of the trillion-dollar international and domestic tourism industry. Consequently, much emphasis is placed on the economic benefits of tourism. Yet, the *potential* for these benefits must be carefully considered to understand what the *actual* effect will be on a destination (i.e., who will receive the benefits and what will be the consequences). As such, we need to take a closer look at the nature of the jobs created in the tourism industry at a destination, the extent of economic effects, and the changes that occur in the local economy.

## TOURISM EMPLOYMENT

The jobs created in the construction industry, the tourism industry, and the various supporting industries can attract immigrants from other regions of a country or other countries. This is particularly the case when tourism is developed in peripheral areas where there may not be a large enough local population to fill the new demand for labor.

However, this labor-induced migration may quickly outstrip available jobs and result in a labor surplus. In fact, areas with a high dependence on tourism may have higher levels of unemployment than surrounding regions. This is due to the number of people who move to the destination based on the promise of employment, or the hope of higher-paid employment than would be available to them in their home community.

In addition, tourism is both seasonal and cyclical, which has the potential to affect employment patterns. Even popular tropical destinations, such as the islands of the Caribbean, have a distinct tourist season. Higher rates of precipitation during the wet season, as well as the increased risk of hurricanes, are considered barriers to tourism (chapter 6). At the same time, the majority of tourists come from the Northern Hemisphere during the winter months for the inversion of cold to warm weather (chapter 2). Consequently, at these destinations, there is a high demand for labor during peak months, and tourism businesses may need to hire additional workers. Yet, during the low season, some of these workers may have to find temporary employment in other sectors or face unemployment.

Tourism employment is entirely based on the success of the industry. When a destination is experiencing growth, new jobs will be created in both tourism and related industries. For example, when a destination is developing or expanding, a tremendous amount of local and/or tourism infrastructure may be built, creating a boom in the construction industry. However, when the industry as a whole, or a specific destination, is experiencing a decline, jobs will quickly disappear. Moreover, tourism businesses may only provide services to tourists on an on-demand basis and will therefore require fewer full-time employees and fewer supplies.

One of the most common criticisms of the tourism industry is based on the type of jobs created. Many jobs are unskilled and low-wage, which can have few benefits for the local population. Tourism businesses may seek to minimize costs by providing services to tourists on an on-demand basis. Therefore, instead of a staff of full-time employees, businesses may rely on independent contractors who are paid an hourly wage or per job and who receive no benefits like health care or pension plans. For example, rather than maintaining a salaried staff of tour guides who are available to give regularly scheduled tours whether or not any tourists have signed up, a company is likely to hire guides for specific tours once they have filled. In addition, some of these contract jobs may be in the informal sector of the economy.

Many countries do not have minimum wage laws, do not enforce these laws, or generally have a low wage standard. Like other industries, multinational tourism companies take advantage of this. Tourism is an extremely competitive industry; there are many destinations around the world competing for investment from the same companies and visits by the same tourists. If the cost of wages at a destination reduces companies' profit margins, they will choose to locate elsewhere. If it raises the cost of vacationing at that destination too much, tourists will choose to visit someplace less expensive. As such, to ensure that the destination continues to receive the income—particularly foreign income—from tourism, local or national governments may be reluctant to pressure companies for higher wages.

Highly paid managerial positions represent a smaller proportion of overall tourism jobs, and these positions may not go to local people. Particularly when tourism is developed in rural or peripheral regions of a country and/or less developed countries, the population may not have the necessary education, training, or experience to be able to hold these types of jobs. Additionally, multinational companies may prefer to import workers who are already familiar with company policies or who may be more likely to understand the needs of the targeted tourist market. Unless a concerted effort is made to develop the local resource base to be able to successfully hold higher-level tourism positions, a destination can become dependent on foreign expertise.

Finally, the growth of jobs in the tourism industry may have negative consequences in other areas of the economy. Jobs in the tourism industry may have higher wages than other local employment opportunities. They may be perceived to be less physically demanding than manual labor jobs or more stable than activities like agriculture that are highly dependent on unpredictable environmental conditions. As people choose tourism employment over others, this can contribute to labor shortages and declines in other parts of the local economy. Thus, tourism will not necessarily result in an increase in employment opportunities or produce a net gain in the local or national economy.

## INCOME, INVESTMENT, AND ECONOMIC DEVELOPMENT

While tourism has the potential to support other economic activities, the reality is that tourism often grows at the expense of other activities around the destination. For example, land traditionally used for agriculture may be sold, voluntarily or under coercion, for commercial tourism development. Depending on the terms of the sale, this may present an opportunity cost for the farmer, as he or she exchanges the value of the land for the income that he or she would have derived from the annual produce of that land in the years to come. Furthermore, the potential for creating economic linkages between agriculture and tourism at the destination is diminished or lost altogether.

This can also lead to an overdependence on tourism as the principal source of income in a local or national economy. Rather than promoting economic diversification, this trend toward tourism growth at the expense of other economic activities can result in greater concentration in a single economic sector. As a result, the economy is more vulnerable to fluctuations in the industry, and tourism is a sensitive industry that may be adversely affected by any number of unforeseen factors that the destination has little or no control over.

Although foreign investment may initially provide an important source of income that allows for destination development, an overdependence on multinational companies can have a long-term impact on the nature of economic effects at the destination. The income these companies generate is more likely to be transferred out of the region or country instead of contributing to the multiplier effect. This is referred to as **leakages**. These are the part of tourism income that does not get reinvested in the local economy. Some leakage occurs with each round of spending after tourist dollars are introduced into the economy, until no further respending can take place. The direct effect will be mitigated if the tourism businesses are externally owned, because profits will be transferred out of the region or country. The indirect effects will be reduced if tourism businesses seek external suppliers for their products. Likewise, the induced effects will be eliminated if local people spend their earnings outside of the region or country or on imported goods.

The classic example of leakage is seen in the all-inclusive package mass tourism resorts. These large-scale chain resorts are owned by multinational companies based in the more developed countries of the world. When tourists travel from these same countries and spend their tourist dollars at the resort, those dollars may, in fact, be returning to the country of origin. Take, for example, the context of food. In some cases, despite the higher transportation costs of importing food, the company may be able to obtain food items at a lower cost from a subsidized mass producer at home as opposed to the higher per unit cost of a local producer. In other cases, local producers simply may not be able to sell their products to the resorts because they do not have the appropriate contacts, contracts, or the ability to provide buyers with receipts.[8] Whether it is true or not, the perception exists that mass tourists don't care where their food came from or that they will have concerns about the quality and integrity of local foods. They may suspect that this food was produced and/or processed under unhygienic conditions or that it will not be up to the same standards they are accustomed to at home. These types of resorts may also assume that mass tourists prefer the types of foods eaten at home and won't try new types of foods for fear of getting sick.[9]

The result is that, although countries like Honduras, Mozambique, or Cambodia may have a positive travel account, they may not receive the full economic benefits of tourism. These less developed countries have little capacity to develop tourism on their own; therefore, they are likely to rely on multinational companies to do it for them. Even though they receive international tourists, there are typically high levels of leakages that reduce the multiplier effect. As a result, little money is retained or reinvested at the destination, and the goal of redistributing wealth between parts of the world remains unrealized.

Moreover, rather than redistributing a country's wealth and economic opportunities, tourism may contribute to a further spatial concentration. This may be in an area that already has a stronger development base, such as a major metropolitan area, or it may be the development of a tourist zone. This can create or contribute to regional inequalities, as that area develops, modernizes, and experiences the economic benefits of tourism while other areas remain marginalized.

Likewise, tourism will not necessarily result in a redistribution of wealth among the population. Much of the money that is not leaked out of a region or country tends to stay in the hands of the upper- and middle-income groups. Despite concepts like pro-poor tourism (PPT) and the potential for tourism to improve the economic well-being of traditionally marginalized populations such as indigenous peoples, few of the economic benefits of tourism actually accrue to the poorest segments of a population. For the most part, tourism development does not incorporate poverty elimination objectives. This is because tourism is largely driven by the private sector and companies whose primary objective is profit.

In fact, tourism has the potential to further harm the local population, especially the poorest segments of that population. As a destination develops, it may experience increasing land costs and costs of living. Land is often assessed for tax purposes on its market value rather than its use. As land at an emerging destination is sold to tourism developers at a relatively high cost, the value of all of the land in the area may be reassessed, resulting in an increase in property taxes. This may make it increasingly difficult for landowners to be able to afford to live on and/or use their land as they had in the past. For example, a farmer may have a piece of land that has been in his family for generations. He would like to maintain this land for both the heritage it represents to him and its use as a working farm. However, his income from the farm may no longer be enough to support his family and pay the increased taxes to keep the land.

The value of goods and services may be adjusted based on the amount of money tourists will pay for such things as opposed to the local population. For example, property owners at a destination may have the opportunity to rent houses or apartments/flats to tourists at a high per week price. As such, local residents might not be able to afford to rent living space within the destination area, and they will be forced to move elsewhere. Similarly, stores may cater to tourists who are able and/or willing to pay more for certain products. Again, residents might not be able to afford to buy these products, at least from these stores. Consequently, they may have to travel outside of the destination to obtain the products they need, and if this is not an option for them based on transportation constraints, they will have to find alternatives or go without.

Finally, a destination may experience a range of hidden economic costs associated with tourism. For example, there may be a financial cost associated with managing the social or environmental effects of tourism that will be discussed in the following chapters.

# Factors in Economic Effects

In some cases, we will be able to clearly see the effects of tourism on the economy. This is most likely in communities or countries with relatively undeveloped or undiversified economies. For example, small island developing states (SIDS), whether they are located in the Caribbean, the Mediterranean, the Indian Ocean, or the Pacific, face similar constraints to economic development (e.g., limited resource bases, lack of economies of scale, reduced competitiveness of products due to high transportation costs, few opportunities for private sector investment, etc.).[10] The development of tourism in the SIDS can result in clearly identifiable economic impacts, such as an influx of foreign investment, a decrease in the unemployment rate, and an increase in the per capita gross domestic product. In other cases, the impact of tourism on a country's overall economy can be more difficult to determine. The development of tourism may reflect a redistribution of resources, such as an investment or employment in tourism instead of other economic activities.

The specific economic effects of tourism at a destination, and the extent of these effects, will likely vary widely. The often interrelated factors that may determine these effects can include the nature of the local economy and the level of development at the destination, as seen in the example above. Similarly, the type of tourism, ownership in the tourism industry, and tourist spending patterns at the destination can have an impact on these effects.

For example, mass tourism destinations are more likely to be characterized by large-scale multinational companies that may use foreign staff and rely on imported supplies. As such, leakages are going to be high. In contrast, niche tourism destinations are more likely to be characterized by small-scale, locally owned tourism businesses with significant local linkages and therefore a higher multiplier effect. However, many destinations have a combination of both, typically a higher proportion of small local businesses (e.g., hotels or restaurants), but the large companies will have the greatest capacity (e.g., the most beds or tables).

Organized mass tourists typically contribute the fewest tourist dollars to the local economy. One of the most prominent examples can be seen in the cruise industry. The large quantities of cruise tourists notoriously contribute very little to the local economy at the visited ports. Tourists may not venture farther than the markets at cruise terminals, which are often characterized by cheap, mass-produced, imported souvenirs like T-shirts. They may be reluctant to spend additional money on destination excursions when the majority of activities that take place onboard are included in the purchase price. Some never even leave the ship when it's in port. In contrast, drifters and explorers, who spend longer at a single destination and rely less on the explicit tourism infrastructure, have greater opportunities to support local businesses.

# Knowledge and Education

For the majority of tourists (actual and potential) around the world, money is one of the most important concerns. We may have a demand for tourism, but it is a nonessential expense. We have to determine how much of our disposable income we can devote to travel and what experiences we can afford. While this may be the only consideration for many tourists, there is a subset of socially conscious individuals who would be interested in supporting the local economy at the places they visit. However consumers may be faced with a choice: if they can't afford a niche destination (one with a higher cost due to the lack of economies of scale but strong local linkages), do they accept a cheaper vacation at a mass destination (one with a lower cost due to economies of scale but higher levels of leakages) or stay home?

Even if tourists are interested in and willing to pay more for destinations that are economically beneficial to local people, they may not be knowledgeable enough to make an informed decision. In contrast to fair trade commodities, there is little in the way of widely known or recognized certification of tourism products. There are a few examples, such as Fair Trade in Tourism South Africa, which is considered to be the first program to certify that tourism enterprises have fair wages and working conditions and an equitable distribution of benefits.[11] However, it often falls to individual tourism businesses to advertise their own policies on their website or other promotional literature, such as local ownership, fair wages, support of local farmers and craftspeople, and so on.

Tourism businesses must also weigh the higher cost of policies that support the local economy against the cost of not doing so. These are profit-oriented businesses, and paying higher wages or higher costs for locally produced supplies can reduce their

## Box 8.3.  Case Study: A Differentiated Price Structure at Tourism Attractions in Zimbabwe

Zimbabwe is an interesting case in tourism. The southern African country has a strong tourism resource base. Historically, wildlife has been the primary natural tourism resource, including the "Big Five" game animals that provide an attraction for safaris and hunting expeditions. This is complemented by other unique natural and cultural attractions, including four UNESCO World Heritage Sites (Great Zimbabwe, Khami Ruins, Mana Pools National Park, and Victoria Falls). From this base, tourism emerged as one of the country's most significant economic activities, and Zimbabwe became one of the largest international tourism destinations in Africa. Today, however, the tourism industry faces numerous challenges.

Both domestic and international tourism have experienced significant declines. Zimbabwe has been in severe economic crisis since 2000. The country has experienced falling income levels and rampant inflation; both unemployment and poverty rates are as high as 80 percent. As a result, emigration, particularly among the educated middle and upper classes, and "capital flight"—where Zimbabweans with money have invested it outside of the country—have been a problem. Given these conditions, few Zimbabweans have the means to participate in tourism. Additionally, the country's political turmoil led many countries to issue travel warnings recommending that their citizens avoid any nonessential travel to Zimbabwe. Other highly publicized issues, such as reports of human rights violations, high crime rates, high rates of HIV/AIDS infections, a cholera epidemic, and more, have all contributed to a generally poor international reputation that discourages international tourism.

The remaining vestiges of the country's tourism industry are characterized by a differentiated price structure. In other words, different categories of tourists are charged different rates for the same activities or services. Theoretically, this type of policy is argued to open up opportunities for local people to participate in tourism when they might not be able to otherwise. In particular, it is argued to have social benefits, where local people can appreciate their own natural or cultural heritage instead of reserving it for the exclusive use of foreigners. It is also argued that foreign tourists who are able to visit the country should be able to afford the higher rates and be willing to pay for the privilege of the experience. This income can be used to maintain the attraction and support the local economy. Moreover, higher fees for international tourists can be used to offset lower numbers of tourists received.

While this practice is not unique to Zimbabwe, the country provides an interesting case for examining its use. For example, admission at Zimbabwe's most popular tourism attraction—Victoria Falls—is US$30 for foreign visitors and only US$7 for Zimbabwean residents. At Hwange National Park, the country's largest game reserve, the difference is US$25 (US$30 for nonresidents versus US$5 for residents). However, even nominal admission fees can be beyond the means of much of the population and prevent them from visiting important national sites. At the same time, foreign tourists may come to resent being charged substantially higher fees on top of all of the other money spent on expected expenses like transportation, accommodation, food, activities, souvenirs, and more. This resentment can compound, considering that they have already found themselves subject to visa fees, airport taxes, and other costs not directly associated with tourism services. Faced with these costs, they may choose alternative destinations, such as game parks in neighboring Botswana. This is particularly applicable in the example of Victoria Falls. Shared with Zambia, the admission fee on that side of the border is only US$20 for foreign tourists.

The situation gets more complicated when foreign and domestic tourists travel together. For example, many upper- and middle-class Zimbabweans (and therefore the ones who are most likely to be able to participate in tourism) are educated abroad. They make friends and contacts with foreign nationals whom they may encourage to visit them when they return to their homeland. The differentiated price structure can make the hosts uncomfortable, as they have to ask their guests to pay more money. Beyond that, when tourism facilities or services are shared between residents and their guests, the locals may find themselves charged the foreign rate simply because they are traveling with a foreigner. Personal vehicle entry at a national park, for instance, is double for nonresidents of Zimbabwe (US$10 versus US$5 for residents). Accommodations can run as much as US$50 more per night for foreign tourists (e.g., the per night rate at a bed-and-breakfast located around Victoria Falls is US$120 for foreigners versus US$70 for residents). These concerns lead to the practice of borrowing Zimbabwean identification cards for their guests to ensure that everyone receives the local rate.

In theory, the concept of a differentiated price structure would appear to maximize the economic benefits of tourism—and to some extent, the social benefits. Domestic tourism is made available to an increasing number of residents who are able to appreciate and enjoy their national resources. While the per-tourist rate is lower, the higher numbers of tourists accounts for significant economic benefits. At the same time, international tourists are enabled to experience another country's attractions. While their numbers are lower, the higher rates also account for significant economic benefits. As seen in this case, though, a differentiated price structure can have unintended effects that are revealed on closer examination.

*Discussion topic*: Do you think domestic and foreign tourists should be charged different rates? Why or why not?

*Tourism on the web*: Zimbabwe Tourism Authority, "Welcome to a World of Wonders," at http://www.zimbabwetourism.net/

**Figure 8.5.   This sign shows the difference in tourist rates between Zimbabwean residents and foreign visitors at Chinhoyi Caves, a Category III National Park site. (Source: Velvet Nelson)**

*(continued)*

## Box 8.3.   (continued)

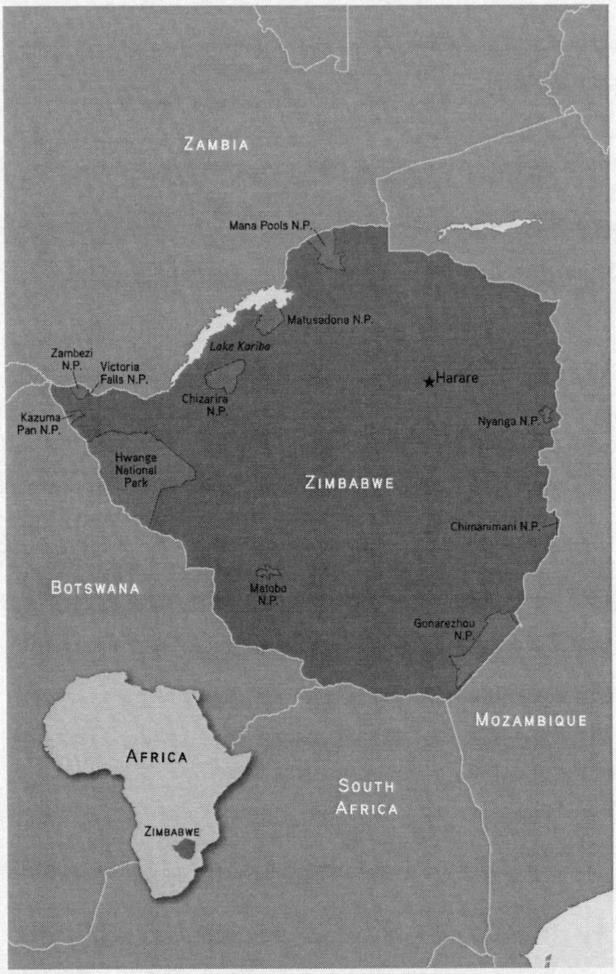

**Map 8.1.   Zimbabwe. This southern African destination uses a differentiated price structure at attractions such as the national parks. (Source: XNR Productions)**

# Source

Manwa, Haretsebe A. "Is Zimbabwe Ready to Venture into the Cultural Tourism Market?" *Development Southern Africa* 24, no. 3 (2007): 465–74.

profit margin. Alternatively, if these expenses are built into the price of the tourism product, the venture may become less competitive and lose business to other companies or destinations offering similar products. Yet, there can be value in promoting ethical business practices. Moreover, as seen in the discussion of PPT, the local population has the potential to undermine tourism if they feel they aren't receiving enough benefits from the industry. Consequently, it is important to understand the nature and distribution of the economic effects at a destination.

# Conclusion

Tourism has emerged as one of the world's most significant economic activities; consequently, a foundation in economic geography is a vital component in the geography of tourism. It can be easy to focus only on the positive economic effects of tourism. In fact, it is often the case that those who are better off to begin with are the ones who are most likely to benefit from tourism. As they have the greatest voice and power in decision making, the positive outcomes may be the only ones considered. Yet, it may be that a substantial proportion of the population will never see the benefits of tourism and may not want to see it take place. Ultimately, both the public and the private sector should undertake efforts to see that more segments of the population are able to benefit from and therefore support the industry.

# Key Terms

- direct economic effect
- economic development
- economic geography
- indirect economic effect
- induced economic effect
- leakages

- linkages
- multiplier effect
- pro-poor tourism
- tourist dollars
- travel account

# Notes

1. United Nations World Tourism Organization, *UNWTO Tourism Highlights: 2012 Edition* (Madrid: World Tourism Organization, 2012), accessed December 10, 2012, http://dtxtq4w60xqpw.cloudfront.net/sites/all/files/docpdf/unwtohighlights12enlr_1.pdf.

2. Sharmistha Bagchi-Sen and Helen Lawton Smith, "Introduction: The Past, Present, and Future of Economic Geography," in *Economic Geography: Past, Present, and Future*, ed. Sharmistha Bagchi-Sen and Helen Lawton Smith (London: Routledge, 2006), 1.

3. Dimitri Ioannides, "Strengthening the Ties between Tourism and Economic Geography: A Theoretical Agenda," *Professional Geographer* 47 (1995).

4. Dimitri Ioannides and Keith G. Debbage, "Introduction: Exploring the Economic Geography and Tourism Nexus," in *The Economic Geography of the Tourist Industry*, ed. Dimitri Ioannides and Keith G. Debbage (London: Routledge, 1998), 5.

5. Dimitri Ioannides, "The Economic Geography of the Tourist Industry: Ten Years of Progress in Research and an Agenda for the Future," *Tourism Geographies* 8 (2006).

6. The Venetian Las Vegas, "Human Resources," accessed March 31, 2011, http://www.venetian.com/Company-Information/Human-Resources.

7. Hyundai Motor Manufacturing Alabama, "HMMA Employment," accessed March 31, 2011, http://www.hmmausa.com/jobshmma/hmma-employment/.

8. Rebecca Torres, "Linkages between Tourism and Agriculture in Mexico," *Annals of Tourism Research* 30, no. 3 (2003): 555.

9. Rebecca Torres, "Toward a Better Understanding of Tourism and Agriculture Linkages in the Yucatan: Tourist Food Consumption and Preferences," *Tourism Geographies* 4, no. 3 (2002): 293.

10. United Nations Office of the High Representative for the Least Developed Countries, Landlocked Developing Countries and the Small Island Developing States, "Small Island Developing States," accessed January 15, 2012, http://www.unohrlls.org/en/sids/43.

11. Fair Trade in Tourism South Africa, "Welcome to Fair Trade in Tourism South Africa," accessed January 15, 2012, http://www.fairtourismsa.org.za/index.html.

# Sources

Hanson, Susan. "Thinking Back, Thinking Ahead: Some Questions for Economic Geographers." In *Economic Geography: Past, Present, and Future*, edited by Sharmistha Bagchi-Sen and Helen Lawton Smith, 25–33. London: Routledge, 2006.

Williams, Stephen. *Tourism Geography*. London: Routledge, 1998.

# CHAPTER 9

# The Social Geography of Tourism

For those of us who don't live in (or at least in the vicinity of) a tourism destination, we probably give very little thought to what tourism means to the people whose lives it directly affects on a daily basis. In the last chapter, we began to examine some of the effects of tourism as an industry: we saw how tourism can impact peoples' lives directly, through personal income from work in the tourism industry or related fields, or indirectly, through economic development at the destination resulting from tourism. However, tourism affects peoples and societies in far more ways than this.

The social geography of tourism gives us the means to explore more of the effects tourism has on people and their lives. **Social geography** is a topical branch in human geography that encompasses a range of perspectives on the relationships between society and space. Although society is a commonly used term, it is used in so many different ways that it can be difficult to conceptualize. Broadly, society refers to the ties or connections people have with others. More specifically, we can consider the ties between people either occupying a geographic space or connected by networks across space (e.g., common values, ways of life, political systems, or perceived identities). Thus, social geography might consider space as a setting for social interactions or the ways in which spaces are shaped by these interactions. In particular, the focus in studies of social geography is on issues of inequality.

Social geography is the topical branch most closely related to the discipline of sociology and clearly overlaps with other branches of human geography, including economic geography, political geography, and especially cultural geography. To some extent, social geography has had a weaker relationship with the geography of tourism than some of these other branches. As we saw in the previous chapter, the positive economic effects have been the biggest factors driving tourism; therefore, a strong case may be made for the relationship between economic geography and tourism geography. Likewise, the negative environmental effects have been the most visible effects of tourism; thus, human-environment interactions have long been important in the geography of tourism, as we'll see in the next chapter. In contrast, the social effects of tourism have received less attention in tourism geography studies. Historically, tourism took place within societies or between relatively similar societies (e.g., North American tourists in Western Europe), which generated few readily apparent social effects. In the modern world, it can be difficult to distinguish what effects might occur in a society as a direct result of tourism from changes that might occur as a result of the wider processes of globalization.

Nonetheless, social geography has an important part to play in our understanding of the geography of tourism. Tourism presents an opportunity for social interaction; tourism brings together groups of people who have little historic contact and/ or little in common. Tourism can also be a catalyst for social change; the development of tourism activities may reshape long-standing cultural patterns and ways of life. As such, this chapter continues our discussion of the geographic effects of tourism by utilizing the tools and concepts of social geography to consider the potential benefits of tourism for tourists and local peoples. It also considers the potential costs of tourism, particularly with regard to people in the community in which tourism is taking place. Finally, it discusses the factors that might determine the type and extent of these effects, as well as possible measures to maximize the positive effects while minimizing the negative.

# Social Benefits of Tourism

Much attention is given to the negative implications of the social interactions that take place in the context of tourism and the social changes that result from tourism. Yet, tourism can have positive outcomes as well. At its most idealistic, tourism has been promoted as a means of promoting global understanding and international peace. On a large scale, this goal is considered naive and improbable. However, it should not be considered unrealistic that the experience of other places and their peoples can have a beneficial impact on tourists at a personal level. This, of course, is contingent upon both tourists and locals approaching the experience with civility and a willingness to learn about the other.

Tourism may also be argued to have the potential for social development at a destination. Although development is typically discussed in economic terms, the concept can be extended to nonmaterial indicators as well. As such, tourism can generate positive social changes at a destination, such as new opportunities for segments of the local community or new developments that could improve the quality of life for local people. At the same time, tourism development may serve as a catalyst for movements to protect against wider (negative) social changes by supporting traditional ways of life and reinforcing social identities.

## PERSONAL DEVELOPMENT

Tourism can provide the opportunity for interaction between groups of people that might not otherwise occur. If this is undertaken with an openness and a sensitivity to other peoples and ways of life, tourism can be a beneficial experience for both tourists and local people at the destination visited. Tourists have the opportunity to not only meet other people but to experience life in their society firsthand. This allows them to gain a better understanding of, and perhaps even empathy for, that society. Consequently, tourism can—even if only subconsciously—promote a greater geographic literacy of the world. Conversely, these experiences will also give tourists a new perspective on life in their own society and possibly even generate changes in their daily lives. These may be small changes, such as a desire to eat different kinds of foods, but it can also lead to major changes, such as moving to a place that he or she has visited, or marrying someone from that place. In fact, some tourists—particularly explorers and drifters—participate in tourism because of the potential for such transformative experiences. Although such potential effects on tourists are generally recognized, there has been little research on these effects.[1]

At the same time, residents at a destination also have the opportunity to interact with other groups of people (figure 9.1). This is particularly applicable in the case of countries or communities that have a positive travel account (i.e., they have high rates of inbound tourism and low rates of outbound tourism). Thus, although they may not have the opportunity to travel to and experience other societies, these people still have the opportunity to meet and learn about the tourists who visit their destination.

**Figure 9.1. This lunch presented a unique opportunity for the American tourists and the ethnic Miao villagers to interact with and learn about each other. (Source: Velvet Nelson)**

## SOCIAL DEVELOPMENT

Arguments for tourism have often cited the potential for new opportunities within a community. The economic benefits of tourism, such as jobs and income, can lead to social benefits as well. New types of jobs associated with tourism and the income from these jobs can provide local people with greater freedom to choose not only where they live but how they live. This, of course, depends on one's perspective. For example, rural communities around the world have been experiencing declining opportunities for employment and livelihood. This creates a push factor, in other words, pushing people out of the region to other areas—typically urban ones—that might have greater potential for access to more and/or better jobs. In some cases, people, especially those who are young, are attracted to the promise of a new and different life in these areas. For these people, the development of tourism might provide the ability to leave a traditional or stagnated community, with its real or perceived restrictions, for a more modern or vibrant community with access to jobs as well as other opportunities. Yet, in other cases, people prefer to maintain their life with family and friends in their home community. The extension of tourism into rural areas might provide them with this opportunity.

Access to jobs and income can create new opportunities for traditionally marginalized populations. For example, in many parts of the world, women have had little opportunity for employment outside of the home (i.e., in the private sphere) and in the formal sector of the economy. To some extent, the jobs created by tourism have not been incompatible with traditional roles for women, while giving them the opportunity for employment in the public sphere, increased social interaction, increased income to support themselves and/or their families, and possibly even financial independence from their family or spouse (figure 9.2). As women gain a greater value in society and greater freedom, this can lay the foundation for additional social changes and ultimately reduce gender inequalities.

We have already seen that income from tourism can be reinvested in the destination. While this investment may be directed at improvements in the destination that will create and maintain an attractive environment for tourism, the local community can also benefit from these improvements. Improved public transportation systems that will facilitate the movement of tourists at the destination can also be used to increase the motilities of local people. Increased police protection and measures to reduce incidents of both petty and violent crimes may be done as a means of trying to promote a safe and stable environment for tourism investment and tourist visitation, but local people can benefit as well. The creation or beautification of open-access public spaces to ensure an attractive environment for tourism can contribute to increased community pride, satisfaction, and general quality of life among local people.

In addition, there is potential for a destination to use the income from tourism to invest in local and/or domestic social development. Again, these improvements may not be entirely unrelated to the tourism industry, but local people can be the beneficiaries nonetheless. For example, a destination might choose to invest in the human resource base by building or expanding schools, education, and training programs. This

**Figure 9.2. Tourism can create new opportunities for women, especially in societies where women have not traditionally had a place in the public sphere. This woman is working at a tourist resort in Salvador, Brazil. (Source: Jason Fisher)**

increasingly well-educated population will have more opportunities to improve their lives and contribute to the local/national economy, including in the tourism industry.

## PRESERVATION

Perhaps the most frequently cited argument for tourism is preservation—in this case, the preservation of local ways of life, traditions, and identities. Tourism is a distinctly place-based activity. The trend away from the standardization of mass tourism has emphasized the need for destinations to be able to offer the unique combination of physical and human attributes that constitute a place. Accordingly, a place seeking to develop this type of tourism will have an impetus to maintain these attributes. In such a case, the place may resist the processes of globalization that contribute to a sameness between different parts of the world—a sense of placelessness. This place might choose to limit the development of chain restaurants or big box stores and use tourism to support local businesses, like independent restaurants or mom-and-pop shops. Likewise, this need for a sense of distinctiveness at destinations can help reinforce or rejuvenate social identities that might otherwise be lost.

Tourism can support traditional ways of life or simply be more compatible with them than other forms of economic development. This might be in the form of the backward linkages discussed in the previous chapter with local farmers or fishermen

# Box 9.1.   Case Study: Tourism and the Sámi Reindeer Herd Migration

The Sámi are considered to be Europe's only indigenous people. Research indicates that these people have lived in the northern Scandinavian Peninsula for nearly ten thousand years. Yet, they do not have a state of their own. Instead, Sápmi—the Sámi homeland—spans Sweden, Norway, Finland, and part of Russia (map 9.1). The traditional lifestyle of the Sámi was well adapted to the arctic environment in which they live, based on fishing, hunting, and reindeer herding. Throughout much of their history, they were able to live outside of mainstream Scandinavian society.

**Map 9.1.   Sápmi. The homeland of the Sámi people spans the northern regions of Norway, Sweden, Finland, and Russia. (Source: XNR Productions)**

However, as with indigenous populations across the globe, their way of life was threatened throughout the nineteenth and twentieth centuries. The creation of modern nation states and controlled boundaries divided the Sámi homeland. Governments denied the nomadic peoples legal land ownership and encouraged nonnative settlement of traditional land areas. Development programs, such as logging, eroded the natural resource base on which their lifestyle depended. Missionaries sought to convert traditional belief systems to Christianity. Government-sponsored assimilation programs restricted elements of Sámi culture; for example, the use of Sámi languages in schools was prohibited. While some Sámi were displaced and forced farther northward, many became settled and largely assimilated into mainstream society. As a result, population figures vary, with most estimates ranging from seventy thousand to eighty thousand.

In recent years, the governments of countries with a Sámi population have recognized these peoples as an indigenous minority and increased their rights to land, livelihood, and culture. While some elements of Sámi culture have been lost (e.g., extinct dialects) or severely eroded, the population has made concerted efforts to renew and promote culture heritage. In particular, the traditional livelihood of reindeer herding is considered one of the key components of Sámi culture and fundamental in maintaining the group's traditional heritage. In Norway, this practice is legally reserved for the Sámi, while in the other countries, the Sámi are the primary practitioners. Only a minority of Sámi continue to practice reindeer herding, generally estimated at 10 percent of the population. Yet, in the modern world, even this extent might not be feasible without the supplemental income provided by tourism.

With this rejuvenation, Sámi culture serves as an attraction for a growing number of international tourists. While some tourists visit the region for cultural festivals, many experiences are organized around the group's reindeer traditions. From a few hours to a full trek, these tours and excursions give tourists the opportunity to learn more about Sámi culture from reindeer herdsmen/guides and experience it firsthand. Tourists can learn to drive a reindeer sled, travel along migratory routes, see unique landscapes, eat typical foods, stay in a traditional lavvu (teepee) or wilderness camp, listen to folk stories or yoik (chanting/music), and purchase slojd (handicrafts).

Of course, the social benefit in which tourism allows the tradition of reindeer herding to continue is contingent upon the way in which it is developed. While there are positive examples of reindeer tours that promote Sámi culture and support traditional patterns of livelihood, there are other examples in which non-Sámi have taken advantage of tourists' interest in indigenous culture to sell inauthentic experiences and/or souvenirs. In these cases, not only do Sámi communities fail to receive the economic benefits of tourism but they are also subject to the exploitation of their culture and heritage.

*Discussion topic*: What advantages does tourism have for traditional and/or indigenous communities? What are the disadvantages?

*Tourism on the web*: Visit Finland, "About Finland," at http://www.visitfinland.com/web/guest/finland-guide/about-finland/overview/detail/-/article-detail/10123/36492919; Visit Norway, "Explore Norway," at http://www.visitnorway.com/us/; Visit Sweden, "Welcome to Sweden," at http://www.visitsweden.com/sweden-us/

who are able to continue their livelihood, with the tourism industry serving as a ready market for their produce. In the case of traditional societies, livelihood and culture may be linked. Therefore, if these societies can continue to practice long-standing patterns of livelihood, then they have greater ability to maintain their cultural heritage.

Tourism is cited as having the potential to maintain or even revitalize aspects of traditional culture, such as artistic performances or crafts. One of the criticisms of globalization is the loss of such traditions. However, certain categories of tourists seek unique experiences of places and souvenirs of these experiences. As such, tourism can provide the motivation for local people to continue to practice rituals, songs, dances, or theatrical performances (figure 9.3), when these things might otherwise be aban-

**Figure 9.3.   Although the Tunpu people of Guizhou Province are considered an ancient clan of Han Chinese, and therefore are not an officially recognized minority group, they have been relatively isolated from outside influences for some six hundred years. As a result, they have maintained traditional aspects of culture and lifestyle. These Tunpu are performing Dixi, an ancient opera, for both a group of American tourists and villagers. (Source: Velvet Nelson)**

doned in favor of the patterns of modern global culture. Similarly, the production of local arts and crafts for tourists' consumption has the potential to keep traditions and skills alive when local craftspeople might otherwise find higher-wage industrial employment and local consumers have increased access to cheap, mass-produced merchandise. Even in light of the production of cheaper copies of traditional crafts, there is still likely to be a demand for high-quality, "authentic" items produced by local people using local materials.

# Social Costs of Tourism

Depending on how tourism takes place at a given destination, each of these potential social benefits of tourism could also be potential social costs. Social interactions through tourism can result in culture clash and misperceptions about the other group. Tourism development can contribute to a decrease in the quality of life for a local community by marginalizing certain sectors of the population, introducing social problems in communities that had few previously, and limiting local peoples' access to certain sites. Finally, tourism can also contribute to irreversible changes in traditional societies and cultural patterns, or ultimately their destruction.

## CULTURE CLASH

Although tourism can have a positive effect on both tourists and locals if both approach the experience with an openness and a respect for others, it can also have a negative effect if one or both groups are closed-minded and/or hostile to the other. Tourists and local people alike have been guilty of this. Tourists may travel to a place in which they are not familiar with the language or customs. Whether this is merely a source of annoyance to the local community or a serious offense, tourism may come to be viewed as a detriment to the community rather than an asset. Local people may not treat outsiders with civility. The way tourists are received by local people can have a significant impact on how they view the destination and represent the destination to other potential visitors. As such, a place can develop a poor reputation, which can affect future tourism.

When different social groups come together—especially groups with significant differences in languages, ethnicities, religions, or lifestyles—the potential exists for misunderstandings and culture clash. For tourists, the interaction with these different groups can contribute to culture shock. This may be as minor as a feeling of uneasiness in the unfamiliar setting of the destination or as significant as a sense of complete disorientation. Culture shock is most likely to occur among tourists who have had little previous opportunity to interact with other social groups or those who are ill prepared for the differences they encounter. The greater the culture shock, the more likely it is that the tourist will be dissatisfied with the experience.

To some extent, local people may also experience culture shock; however, culture shock generally occurs with the initial encounter of another social group. Locals are likely to have more sustained contact with the tourist culture. Thus, local people are more likely to experience significant effects from tourism. For example, the **demonstration effect** is a term used to suggest that local people will experience changes in attitudes, values, or patterns of behavior as a result of observing tourists. Although it may be argued that the demonstration effect can be positive, it is far more likely to be negative. In particular, the image that is presented by tourists on vacation is often substantially different from their patterns of behavior and consumption at home. This can be seen in the tourist inversions discussed in chapter 2, where tourists may dress more casually, behave more freely, and spend more money on food, alcohol, or luxury items than they would at home. As such, local people may develop considerable misconceptions about life in other parts of the world and, given the demonstration effect, may strive to emulate the worst parts of tourist culture.

The young people in a community are generally most susceptible to the demonstration effect, as they are quick to adopt outside values, dress codes, or lifestyles. This has the potential to cause significant problems within the local community. These new patterns may conflict with traditional views held by older generations, which can contribute to the creation of new social divisions between young people and elders. Yet, even as people aspire to emulate a particular lifestyle with attendant material possessions, these things may remain inaccessible to them—they may be deemed incompatible with traditional lifestyles, unavailable through local distribution channels, or too expensive for local income levels. Consequently, seeing this lifestyle on a regular basis without being able to obtain it can lead to frustration and resentment.

## LOCAL DECLINE

While tourism can create new job opportunities when it is developed in a community, tourism developed outside a community can create a push factor for migration. This contributes to problems of brain drain, where these people are no longer contributing their human capital to their home community. Certain subsets of the population may be more likely to migrate. Depending on the location, this may be a gendered migration, where one gender may be more likely to migrate for work than the other. This can contribute to a breakdown of family systems. Young people may be attracted to destination regions for the opportunities of new or higher-paying jobs, greater wealth, access to material possessions, or the ability to change their lifestyles. As a result, the remaining aging community may experience problems with stagnation and decline, further perpetuating the problem of emigration.

Tourism may introduce new preferences and patterns of behavior or consumption that can contribute to a decline in quality of life. For example, a tourism destination may experience an increase in fast food restaurants and restaurants catering to Western tastes (figure 9.4). As local preferences change accordingly, people may eat more of these high-calorie, processed foods as opposed to fresh, healthy local options. This can create new problems like obesity, type 2 diabetes and heart disease. Likewise, tourism can create the conditions that allow social problems that may or may not already exist—such as alcoholism, the sale of illegal drugs, prostitution,

**Figure 9.4.   Major fast food chains such as McDonald's can now be seen in tourism destinations all over the world. (Source: Velvet Nelson)**

and/or gambling—to flourish. The arrival of affluent tourists may provide the inducement for local people to get involved in the provision of one of these activities. Conversely, wage labor from tourism may give local people increased disposable income to participate in such activities.

While some destinations may take measures to decrease crime, tourism can also contribute to an increase in crime. Differences in wealth between tourists and the local community may lead to a rise in robbery and muggings, and tourists are often seen as easy targets for these types of crimes in destinations around the world. The introduction of or increase in the drug trade, prostitution, or gambling may be associated with the rise of organized crime at a destination. Moreover, tourists indulging in the excesses of a destination have the potential to be either the victims or the perpetrators of physical and/or sexual assault.

Although tourism development can lead to improvements at a destination, local people may not always benefit from these improvements. The construction of tourist facilities or the designation of parks or reserves can lead to the displacement or segregation of local people. For example, in less developed countries, groups of people, often ethnic minorities, may have lived in a certain area for generations without having modern, legal land ownership. As this land becomes targeted for tourism development, this lack of legal ownership allows the government to sanction their removal. Similarly, tourism developments may limit local peoples' access to certain sites or facilities, such as beaches or parks. In some cases, this may be a result of the transition from public to private lands where the new owners prohibit local people. In other cases, this may be a function of a newly introduced fee structure that local people are unable to afford. The destination might see an increase in new goods available at local stores, but these goods may replace the ones traditionally used and may be beyond the means of local people.

## CULTURAL EROSION

If efforts are not consciously made to preserve culture and ways of life, they can be eroded or even destroyed by tourism. The development of standardized mass tourism, particularly by multinational companies with globally recognized brands, can overwhelm and fundamentally alter the unique character of a place. A rural area or village may become more urbanized, and local businesses may be replaced. Traditional patterns of livelihood may be diminished or supplanted as people turn to tourism as easier (i.e., less physically demanding) or more lucrative employment.

Elements of local culture may be lost as people adopt elements of the tourist culture. For example, it is typically unrealistic to expect that tourists will learn a significant amount of the language spoken at their intended destination. It is, of course, also unrealistic to expect local people to learn all of the native languages spoken by the tourists they receive. As a result, there is a distinct need for a **lingua franca**, or a language that is used for the purpose of communication between people speaking different languages. As local people learn and speak this lingua franca to communicate with tourists in various service capacities, less emphasis may be placed on using local languages.

The very elements of culture that are intended to be preserved through tourism may also be destroyed by it, as they are changed to meet tourists' demands. Local cuisine may be made more palatable to tourists' tastes. Local objects that once had use and meaning within a society may be turned into something to be produced and sold as souvenirs (box 9.2). The mass production of these objects—possibly outsourced to factories with cheap labor—may result in a decline in the need for local skilled craftspeople. Rituals, songs, dances, or theater shows may be held for profit rather than for their original spiritual or social functions. Such events may be reformulated to make them easy to be performed for and understood by tourists. In some cases, they may be created specifically to fit tourists' preconceived ideas. Eventually, those within the society, including the craftspeople and performers, may lose their understanding of the original significance and/or meaning.

Finally, even those practices that continue to be undertaken by local people may be disrupted by the presence of tourists and tourism activities. For example, churches, temples, mosques, and other sacred sites may be presented to or perceived by tourists as attractions to be seen rather than places for practitioners to worship. These tourists may fail to respect religious ceremonies taking place or disturb those who came to pray (figure 9.5). Although these sites may not be logistically off-limits to local people, as in the case of site privatization, they become effectively unavailable to people who wish to use them for their original purpose.

# Box 9.2.   In-Depth: Authenticity and Commodification of Culture in Tourism

Authenticity and commodification are frequently used and much discussed terms in examinations of the sociocultural impacts of tourism. Authenticity can refer to the genuineness of something (e.g., an authentic artifact) or the accuracy of the reproduction of that thing (e.g., an authentic replica). Authenticity is a socially constructed concept, meaning that it is not inherent. People will have different ideas about what is authentic and what is not, and these ideas may change over time as peoples' values change. Some social scientists have argued that life in the modern world is often perceived as superficial and inadequate. Consequently, people may feel the need to search for authenticity, and tourism may be seen as providing the means of doing so.[1] Yet, as we have seen, tourism will affect that place and therefore will affect what is seen as authentic for that place.

The term **commodification** (sometimes also referred to as commoditization) is used to describe the way in which something of intrinsic or cultural value is transformed into a product with commercial value that can be packaged and sold for consumption (i.e., a commodity). Although almost all aspects of a place—physical and human—may be commodified for the purposes of tourism, attention has particularly been focused on the commodification of culture. Commodification of culture can take place for many different reasons, but, as one scholar notes, "The most important characteristic is its *purposeful production* for tourism consumption."[2] In other words, a tourism company or a local community may deliberately make changes or adaptations of aspects of culture based on the potential economic benefits that can be derived from tourism.

Some researchers have argued that tourism inevitably results in cultural commodification. This is seen as particularly applicable in cases of mass tourism, in which the emphasis is on mass production and consumption of both tangible goods and experiences.[3] As the objects, performances, and so on are commodified for tourists' consumption, they are irrevocably changed. Many scholars have viewed these changes as a loss of authenticity. Yet, others argue that this need not be the case. A society can use—and perhaps adapt—an element of their culture in tourism, to receive the economic benefits of the industry. At the same time, they will be able to keep the most important, closely guarded elements of culture for themselves, with their original meanings or for their intended purposes. Indeed, there are some cases in which communities have entirely created cultural works (e.g., items to be sold as souvenirs) or practices (e.g., festivals) for the purpose of tourism that have no traditional basis in the culture. These works or practices are empty of meaning, but they may be presented to tourists as authentic.

Issues of authenticity and commodification raise many questions about culture and its role in tourism (What is authentic culture? Should authentic culture be turned into a saleable commodity? Is it ethical to present something as authentic to tourists when it isn't?) as well as the nature of cultural change (Do efforts to "preserve" culture render it static instead of allowing it to evolve? Is tourism responsible for cultural change, or is it simply one part of the wider process of globalization?).

*Discussion topic*: Can you think of an example of commodified culture in tourism?

(*continued*)

---

## Box 9.2.   *(continued)*

# Notes

1. Dean MacCannell, "Staged Authenticity: Arrangements of Social Space in Tourist Settings," *American Journal of Sociology* 79, no. 3 (1973).
2. Milena Ivanovic, *Cultural Tourism* (Cape Town: Juta, 2008), 121 (emphasis added).
3. Robert Shepherd, "Commodification, Culture, and Tourism," *Tourist Studies* 2, no. 2 (2002): 185.

# Sources

Cohen, Erik. "Authenticity and Commoditization in Tourism." *Annals of Tourism Research* 15 (1988): 371–86.
MacLeod, Nicola. "Cultural Tourism: Aspects of Authenticity and Commodification." In *Cultural Tourism in a Changing World: Politics, Participation, and (Re)presentation*, edited by Melanie K. Smith and Mike Robinson, 177–90. Clevedon, UK: Channel View Publications, 2006.

---

# Factors in Social Effects

Similar to the economic effects, there are some cases in which it is easy to see the direct effects of tourism on a community. This is particularly the case when tourism activities are developed in relatively isolated and undeveloped communities. For example, the development of tourism in remote Amazonian indigenous communities will bring a host of changes to their society. This might include the construction of new infrastructure to support tourism (e.g., roads or modern bathroom facilities) and the importation of new products for tourists' consumption (e.g., bottled water), which might create further problems like package waste. It might require minor changes, such as in traditional patterns of dress (e.g., women covering their breasts), but it might also bring devastating consequences, such as diseases. Yet, in many cases, it may be difficult to separate what effects are a direct result of tourism and what would have occurred as a result of large societal changes. This is particularly the case when tourism activities occur in areas that are already well connected to modern, global culture. These destinations may be experiencing an erosion of local culture and unique social identities, but tourism's contribution may be indistinguishable from the effects of multinational corporations and the global media.

The specific social effects of tourism at a destination, and the extent of these effects, will vary widely. The often interrelated factors that may determine these effects can include the type of tourists a destination receives, the quantity of tourists, the capability of the destination to handle these tourists, the spatial distance between tourists and local communities at the destination, and the type of interaction that takes place between tourists and local people. In addition, other factors might include the extent

**Figure 9.5. Tourist information and guidebooks often highlight churches, temples, or mosques as tourism attractions and encourage visitation for historic and/or cultural reasons. As such, these sites may be perceived as open for tourists' pleasure, as opposed to being a place with a specific function for local people. (Source: Tom Nelson)**

of similarities between tourists and locals, the origins of tourists, and the duration of exposure to other cultures.

The general typology of tourists discussed in chapter 2 (drifters, explorers, individual mass tourists, and organized mass tourists), may give us an indication of the quantity of each type of tourists a destination receives, the character of the destination, and/or the type of interaction that will take place between tourists and locals. Drifters and explorers typically arrive at a destination in relatively small numbers, whereas the categories of mass tourists account for large numbers of visitors at a destination. Thus, it might be anticipated that the larger quantities of mass tourists will have more effects on the local community at the destination than the smaller quantities of independent tourists. In some cases, this assumption might be accurate. For example, local residents in a small, emerging destination may be willing to welcome the drifters and explorers who seek to immerse themselves in the community and thereby have minimal negative impacts. In contrast, once that destination is "discovered" and increasingly visited by mass tourists who are less conscious of their impact on the destination, the community may begin to experience more negative social effects.

However, the number of tourists alone does not provide a complete picture. The character of the destination will affect its ability to handle the tourists it receives. In the example above, the emerging destination may have little infrastructure in place to accommodate even the slightest temporary increases in population associated with its tourism growth (e.g., overcrowding on local roads and public transport or at local restaurants and establishments). Tourists will be much more conspicuous, and local people may have little experience in dealing with outsiders. Consequently, the potential for incidences of culture clash is increased. In contrast, a well-developed tourism destination or a destination in a large urban area may be able to receive large quantities of mass tourists with little effect. The infrastructure is already in place to accommodate the demands of tourists without adversely affecting the needs of local people. Tourists may blend in to the existing population densities of the area, or they may simply be considered to have a normal presence in the community. Likewise, local people may be accustomed to dealing with tourists on a regular basis.

In addition, some mass tourism destinations were developed specifically to spatially isolate tourists from the local community. In this case, large quantities of tourists may visit the destination, but they will be concentrated within designated areas. This is particularly applicable in the case of enclave resorts and self-contained hotel complexes, such as those characterizing many popular S destinations like the Dominican Republic, which were constructed separate from existing communities. The only local people who have interactions with tourists are those who are employed in the resort community. As such, the effects of tourism are largely spatially contained, and local people may be able to live their lives as they choose and experience relatively few negative consequences from tourism. However, the potential for positive social exchange between tourists and locals will also likely be lost.

The type of tourist will also affect the type of interaction between tourists and locals. These interactions typically fall into one of three broad categories. The first category is the most formal and clearly demarcates the difference between tourists as consumers and local people as service providers. In this case, interaction takes place as tourists purchase goods and/or services from local people from street stands, at shops, in restaurants, or within the hotel/resort complex. In the second category, the distinction between insider and outsider becomes more blurred as both tourists and local people visit and use the same facilities, including beaches, parks, restaurants, or other entertainment venues. This spatial proximity increases the opportunity for contact between tourists and locals but does not necessarily indicate that meaningful interaction will occur. Finally, in the third category, tourists—and in some instances locals—seek interaction for the purpose of talking to, getting to know, and exchanging ideas with the other. This might take place in a structured experience, for example, when tourists take a guided tour not only to experience a place but to gain from the perspective of a local guide. This can also be something far more intimate and personal, such as when a local person invites a tourist to his or her home for a meal.

As we have already seen, organized mass tourists are primarily motivated by relaxation and self-indulgence and less interested in experiencing the place visited. They are more likely to stay at large multinational resorts. Local people typically have very little presence at these resorts, with the exception of those who are employed by the resort, due to financial barriers as well as physical ones. With a range of amenities available to them, these tourists have little need or desire to leave the resort. As such, their opportunities for contact with local people are extremely limited and most likely fall under the first category. Individual mass tourists and explorers may have greater interaction in the second category as they seek new places to experience outside of the resort/tourist areas. In addition, the nature of the destinations visited by explorers and drifters lends itself much more to this type of interaction. Because these destinations are less developed with tourism infrastructure, tourists will necessarily share spaces and facilities with local people. This automatically creates opportunities for interaction. Moreover, these tourists tend to be more interested in the experience of place, including experiences with people in the local community. Thus, they are most likely to seek out the type of interaction described in the third category.

The similarity or difference that exists between both the cultures and the levels of development for tourists and local people may also play a role in the type and extent of social effects from tourism. When tourists visit places where there are few major differences in cultural characteristics and levels of socioeconomic development, the potential for tourism to have distinct social effects is lessened. Tourists who have a similar appearance and patterns of dress and speak the same language as people at the destination are less likely to stand out as outsiders. Historically, this was often the case, as international tourism developed among the societies of Western Europe and North America. As people traveled within these regions, there was little evidence of social effects that would not have otherwise occurred within these societies. Yet, once these tourists began visiting new destinations in the less developed parts of the world, the social effects of tourism became far more apparent. In particular, the greatest social effects are likely to be seen in destinations where the local community is relatively small, isolated, and less developed both socially and economically.[2]

To some extent, the social effects discussed above are based on the assumption that the tourists who visit a particular destination are coming from similar regions of origin and therefore have a common culture. This is the case for some destinations. Based on the particular cultural influence, the destination begins to adapt and reflect that particular culture, as in the example of British tourists to Magaluf on Palma de Mallorca, Spain, discussed in chapter 3. However, destinations frequently receive tourists from different regions who all bring their own distinct cultural characteristics. This diversity of cultural patterns may weaken the influence of any one group of people on the destination, or it may simply reshape the destination in different ways.

Finally, one of the key differences between the impacts on tourists and locals is the duration of exposure to other peoples, cultures, and ways of life. The concept of

# Box 9.3.  Experience: Life around Tourism

I've lived in different parts of the country over the years, but most recently, life brought me to a small town in Alabama. It's a one-stoplight town with a dollar store, and that's about it. It was a good location for us, since my husband's commute to Mobile in one direction was about the same amount of time as my commute to Gulf Shores in the other. The town itself is definitely not on any tourist map, but the county it's in is very much shaped by tourism, with destinations such as Gulf Shores and Fairhope.

Gulf Shores is the primary destination with its location on the Gulf of Mexico. I work for a local real estate company that manages approximately sixteen hundred properties in the area, mostly houses and condos that are used for vacation rentals. It's a pretty laid-back, warm-weather destination, where the beach is the main attraction. It is far less commercialized than other popular southern coastal resorts, like Myrtle Beach, South Carolina. There isn't much in the way of big hotels. In fact, there are only a handful of hotels on the beach at all. Most of the restaurants are independent and locally owned as well. Tourists who want to eat at one of the well-known chain restaurants have to drive ten or twelve miles north of Gulf Shores to Foley.

Fairhope is a very different type of destination in the county, located just off Mobile Bay. It's an attractive small town that has become a center for the arts. A local committee is dedicated to making works of art available to the public by placing them around town along a walking trail. The downtown business district is made up of art galleries, high-end boutique shops, and nice restaurants. Some tourists will visit for the day just for these things, but the town also attracts visitors for the monthly art walks and the many different art shows, fairs, and festivals that they host over the course of the year.

You quickly learn the in's and out's of living and working around here. Summer is the big season, when we get a steady supply of families coming for a week. During this time, I know it's a good idea to leave for work early in the morning and to take back roads. I definitely avoid State Route 59 on Saturdays from late morning on; most tourists come Saturday to Saturday so traffic is always heavy. If I want to go out to eat for lunch, I need to make a reservation. Otherwise, it's going to take longer than my lunch hour with the increased wait times to get a table and to be served. In the winter, Gulf Shores sees a smaller number of snowbirds who come down from the north and stay for maybe a month, maybe three or four. Because of these tourists, the place doesn't "shut down" like some other summer destinations. Business is obviously slower, and some stores and restaurants change their hours of operation. A few places close their doors for a while: Jake's Steakhouse and Grill puts out a sign that reads "Gone fishing, eat at Bubba's (Seafood House)," which is next door and has the same owner.

Some of these things associated with the tourism industry can be an inconvenience when it comes to living in and around this area. But, in the end, I like life here. I appreciate the type of destinations we have; they are places I would like to visit if I were a tourist. I'm able to enjoy the same amenities as the tourists who visit for a week or a winter, whether it is the beach, the nature trails, the art galleries, the shopping (even if it's just window shopping when I can't afford the upscale boutiques), the fresh seafood, and more. I would actually prefer to live in Gulf Shores. Since much of my time is spent there with work and other daily activities, I would love to be closer and cut down on my commute time. There's not much difference in the cost of living across the county. In fact, the primary disadvantage to living in Gulf Shores is not related to tourism at all: the cost of home ownership is considerably higher due to its coastal location and risk of hurricanes.

> I had a friend who grew up in Gulf Shores once point out to me that they—the locals—had done something amazing with the tourism industry. They somehow managed to convince tourists to come in large numbers during the most uncomfortable (hot and humid) time of the year. This means that the locals are able to make a living off of the tourists during the season when they didn't really want to do anything outside anyway. Then, once the summer ends, the masses go home, and the locals are free to enjoy the beach, the town, and all of the other tourism resources during the best parts of the year!
>
> —*Nancy*

**acculturation** is used to describe the process of exchange that takes place when two groups of people come into contact over time. Yet, this is rarely an equal exchange. One group is likely to have more of an impact on the other, and the second group will experience the greatest changes. Tourist-local interactions present an interesting case in acculturation. Although the potential exists for tourists to be influenced by what they experience at the destination, they are less likely to be affected and experience any real changes to their daily lives because each individual tourist experiences only short-term exposure to the destination culture. In contrast, local people experience sustained (at least for a portion of the year) exposure to tourists and their patterns. As a result, the local community is more likely to adopt these patterns and to experience more significant cultural changes.

# Knowledge and Education

In comparison to the economic and environmental effects of tourism, there is relatively little knowledge about the social effects. Because the private sector is typically most concerned with economic effects, it has traditionally done little in the way of assessing the potential social effects of tourism development. If a private sector developer does undertake any form of assessment, it is most likely mandated by the public sector at the local, regional, or national scale.[3] The public sector may have a greater stake in ensuring the social well-being of its population; however, it too has often neglected to consider the social effects.

Although these social effects may seem to be distinct from the economic ones, they are interrelated. In particular, a successful tourism destination, which is often judged on economic criteria, depends on the support of the local community. These are the people who will have to deal with the consequences of tourism. If the local community is concerned about the negative social effects of tourism, they will not support its development. Moreover, if the local community experiences these negative effects, they may actively undermine or sabotage the tourism industry. While it is extremely difficult to predict what will happen as tourism develops at a particular destination, there is nonetheless a clear need for both the public sector and the private sector to investigate and understand what consequences might emerge from tourism in that place.

As there are traditionally few efforts to assess potential social effects, these effects are generally poorly incorporated into the planning process. Yet, a better knowledge of the social geography of the community under consideration can be used by both the public and the private sector to maximize the social benefits of tourism and to minimize the costs. This can contribute to general public policy decisions that protect local people and their rights, such as landownership and access to public lands, resources, or sites. It might involve destination policy decisions that seek to manage both the numbers of tourists and the circumstances in which interaction between visitors and locals takes place. Likewise, the destination might seek to establish policies that will control tourists' behavior (e.g., dress codes, codes of conduct, etc.) to fit within the cultural norms of the resident population.

Education can go a long way in preventing the negative outcomes of tourist-local interactions at a destination. One of the most common complaints levied against tourists is ignorance of the place, its people, and their customs, which contributes to the process of culture clash. At the same time, this ignorance can be one of the key contributors to culture shock. Tourists are almost always encouraged to learn about a place before they visit. This helps ensure that the tourists are able to make an informed decision that their chosen destination will meet their expectations. Moreover, it helps the tourists understand what is expected of them so that they do not generate undue hostility toward themselves or cause offense to people in the local community. In addition, they should be willing to learn about the place through their experience of it. Although the situation is a bit more complicated for local people, education about tourists can help reduce misperceptions that also have the potential to contribute to culture clash.

## Conclusion

Although the tourism literature has increasingly recognized the sociocultural impacts of tourism, there has been relatively little interface between social geography and the geography of tourism. While there may be some exceptions of tourism in extremely remote wilderness areas with little to no population, tourism will impact the local community in a multitude of minor and major ways. As is often the case, the worst examples of tourism—ignorant tourists, hostile locals, poorly planned developments—and their negative consequences typically get the most attention. Yet, these consequences are not necessarily unavoidable. Concerted efforts can be made by both tourists and tourism stakeholders to ensure that the negative social effects of tourism are minimized.

## Key Terms

- acculturation
- commodification
- demonstration effect
- lingua franca
- social geography

# Notes

1. Susan Horner and John Swarbrooke, *International Cases in Tourism Management* (Burlington, MA: Elsevier Butterworth-Heinemann, 2004), 22.

2. Stephen Williams, *Tourism Geography* (London: Routledge, 1998), 156.

3. Michael C. Hall and Alan Lew, *Understanding and Managing Tourism Impacts: An Integrated Approach* (New York: Routledge, 2009), 58.

# Sources

Del Casino, Vincent J. *Social Geography: A Critical Introduction*. Malden, MA: Blackwell, 2009.

Hall, Michael C., and Alan Lew. *Understanding and Managing Tourism Impacts: An Integrated Approach*. New York: Routledge, 2009.

Pain, Rachel, Michael Barke, Duncan Fuller, Jamie Gough, Robert MacFarlane, and Graham Mowl. *Introducing Social Geographies*. London: Arnold, 2001.

# CHAPTER 10

# The Environmental Geography of Tourism

Tourism frequently gets linked to much-discussed environmental issues in the mass media. It is cited as an economic alternative to logging in the Amazon rain forest. It is used to argue against drilling for oil in the Arctic National Wildlife Refuge. It is considered to be the best chance for protecting rare and endangered wildlife species in sub-Saharan Africa. This connection between tourism and environmental issues brings together some of the topics that we've already discussed. In particular, it recognizes that the physical resources of a place can constitute very powerful attractions for tourism. It also recognizes that tourism is a viable economic activity that can be as profitable as or, in fact, more profitable in the long term than other, less environmentally sustainable economic activities.

The environmental geography of tourism allows us to explore this connection. Like tourism geography, **environmental geography** is a topical branch of geography that can be difficult to place within the field. Some scholars consider environmental geography to provide the geographic perspective on environmental science and therefore approach the topic as a "hard" science. Yet, this approach neglects a crucial component of environmental geography: people. Environmental geography is distinguished from other branches of physical geography in the recognition of and focus on the earth as the human environment. In other words, it considers the ways in which the environment affects people and people affect the environment. As such, environmental geography lies at the intersection of human and physical geography. Human-environment interactions is one of the long-standing traditions in geography and one of the key themes identified in chapter 1. Environmental geography provides the means of exploring this theme. While some geographers may approach the topic from a physical geography background (e.g., the science of human-induced climate change), others will do so from a human geography background (e.g., the human response to climate change).

Environmental geography has an important part to play in the geography of tourism. Natural attractions based on physical resources have long provided the basis for different tourism products in destinations around the globe. In the modern world, where millions of people live in highly developed urban areas, tourism provides a distinct opportunity for people to interact with the environment. To some extent, the

201

relationship between tourism and the environment may be described as symbiotic: because tourism benefits from being located in high-quality environments, those same environments ought to benefit from measures of protection aimed at maintaining their value as tourism attractions. However, the incredible growth of the tourism industry has made it difficult to sustain this symbiosis. While tourism does indeed have the potential for enhancement and protection of the environment, it has also, in many cases, become a major source of environmental problems that have threatened to destroy those resources on which tourism depends.

This chapter continues our discussion of the geographic effects of tourism. Specifically, this chapter utilizes the tools and concepts from environmental geography to consider the possibility for tourism to positively contribute to the maintenance of high-quality environments, as well as the potential negative environmental consequences of tourism. It also discusses the factors that shape the nature of these effects and the need for education to maximize the positive effects while minimizing the negative effects.

# Environmental Benefits of Tourism

The actions of tourists in a place are unlikely to result in any direct benefits for the environment. Essentially, when we undertake any type of activity—including tourism—in an environment, we cannot help but impact it in some way. Instead, it is tourism planning and development that is often seen as holding the potential to improve the environmental quality of the destination, maintain environmental standards, and/ or preserve the environmental resources of that destination.

## IMPROVEMENT

Tourism can provide a distinct impetus for cleaning up the environment of a place. Obviously the environment must be safe enough to allow tourist visits. Thus, the destination must ensure an appropriate level of environmental quality. When an existing destination has experienced damage or contamination as a result of, say, a natural disaster or an industrial accident, the affected sites must be cleaned up and/or restored before tourists can return. For example, in the aftermath of the 2004 Indian Ocean tsunami, the affected destinations had to manage the disposal of debris and other solid wastes and to purify water sources that were contaminated by damaged septic tanks and sewage treatment infrastructure. Yet, sometimes even recovery efforts aren't enough. In 1984, a toxic chemical leak at a Union Carbide pesticide plant in Bhopal, India, poisoned an estimated half a million people in what has been regarded as one of the worst industrial disasters in the world. Bhopal once had a reputation as a tourism destination based on its history, culture, and natural landscape. Although toxins are no longer in the environment, the perception of the city as "poisoned" persists.

A potential destination must restore the environmental quality of a brownfield site (land previously used for industrial purposes that may have been contaminated by low levels of toxins or pollutants) before tourism can be developed. Mines, factories, warehouses, and other industrial facilities may be abandoned after their operations have been shut down. While these places are often considered a form of visual or aesthetic pollution, there may also be a correlation between such derelict facilities and physical pollution or contamination. The land itself may have been damaged by industrial uses; hazardous chemicals may have leached into the soil or water sources; or the decaying infrastructure, such as buried or rusted pipes, may continue to contribute to environmental degradation. As long as the quality of the environment has not been irreparably damaged, these abandoned facilities may be reclaimed and redeveloped for tourism and recreation in a number of forms.

In some cases, the infrastructure may be preserved, essentially in its original state with some modifications to accommodate visitation, as a tourism attraction to highlight the heritage of the industry in that place. For example, the Idrija Mercury Mine in Slovenia operated for five hundred years before it was shut down in response to a growing awareness of the toxicity of mercury as well as new regulations about its use. Now it is a "tourist mine" and proposed UNESCO World Heritage Site, and guided tours offer visitors the chance to experience the mine and learn about its history (figure 10.1).

In other cases, some of the infrastructure may be maintained but adapted for new purposes. Baltimore's Inner Harbor revitalization project is cited as a prime example of transforming derelict waterfront warehouses into an attractive shopping and entertainment district that, to some extent, maintains the industrial character of the area. Visit Baltimore, the official destination development and marketing organization for Greater Baltimore, considers the Inner Harbor to be "the crown jewel of the city's active tourism industry, it is an attraction all by itself."[1]

**Figure 10.1.  This guide is providing a tour of the Anthony Mine Shaft in Idrija, Slovenia. Once the second-largest mercury mine in the world, it has now been converted to a tourist mine to highlight the historic importance of the mine. (Source: Velvet Nelson)**

Finally, landscapes may also be cleared, leveled, contoured, and replanted to reestablish native flora, recreate habitat for native fauna, and develop an appropriate landscape for recreation, such as multiuse paths. Although landscape reclamation can be a costly process, it is increasingly required by law in many parts of the world for environmental protection. In addition, grants and other resources may be made available for local communities to convert these areas for tourism as an alternative means of development once resources have been exploited by other economic activities. The Wilds provides an example of a tourist attraction on nearly ten thousand acres of reclaimed mine land in Ohio. A nonprofit organization initially received the land as a donation from the Central Ohio Coal Company in 1986 and has since redeveloped it as a conservation center and open-range habitat for rare and endangered species from all over the world. Visitors to The Wilds can take a "safari," an interactive wildlife tour, stay at the lodge, or participate in outdoor recreation activities like mountain biking or fly fishing.[2]

The environment must also be attractive enough to encourage and sustain tourist visits. This may be as simple as cleaning up litter on a beach or along a nature trail. However, it may also be as involved as improving wastewater treatment systems to prevent untreated discharge from reaching the ocean. This is fundamental in improving the quality of water at beaches that might be used for recreation. Otherwise, these areas would, at best, be perceived by tourists as dirty; at worst, visitors would be at risk for contracting waterborne diseases like gastroenteritis, hepatitis, dysentery, and typhoid. In either case, tourists would be dissatisfied with their experience of the destination. As they express this dissatisfaction during the post-trip stage—either personally to family and friends or publicly on blogs and travel-rating sites—the destination will obtain a negative reputation that can be extremely difficult to overcome.

## MAINTENANCE

Tourism can provide the means of maintaining the environmental quality of a place. Tourism is often accompanied by infrastructure development. For example, the development of hotels and resorts, as well as the corresponding influx of tourists that temporarily increases the size of the population at a destination, can overwhelm environmental quality systems, such as wastewater treatment facilities. As a result, the developer may be required by the applicable government agency to either construct or contribute to the construction of these facilities. This may be a new facility that did not previously exist at the destination or an expanded facility better equipped to handle increased usage. This may also be an improved facility to ensure that the quality provided meets the standards of foreign tourists. Although tourism is the explicit reason for these changes, local residents may benefit from them as well.

Tourism revenues may also be reinvested in an environment. As tourism activities will likely have an impact on the environment in which they take place, a portion of the income from these activities may be allocated for measures to minimize impacts or repair damage from tourism. For example, nature trails need to be adequately planned and subsequently maintained to limit the extent of erosion, especially in areas expected to receive large quantities of visitors. Such practices include stabilizing slopes, using natural vegetation to form buffers, and maintaining erosion control measures. These measures need not be expensive or high-tech: in the case of Grenada, the Caribbean island uses nutmeg shells—one of their primary agricultural products—as an organic means of mulching paths that are prone to get muddy and slippery with high traffic.

## PRESERVATION

Tourism can also provide a clear rationale for preserving the environmental resources of a place. Environmental preservation has been one of the most significant arguments for tourism development. Many places around the world would be lost to industrial, commercial, or residential development if they were not set aside for the purpose of tourism. Tourism constitutes a viable economic alternative to these other, often more damaging forms of development. As a result, the land can be made economically productive while it is kept, more or less, in its original state. Trees are a resource that can be exploited by removing them from the land and selling them to paper and pulp mills, furniture manufacturers, the construction industry, and so on. However, the forest as a whole may be seen as a resource to be enjoyed by hikers, birdwatchers, and other nature enthusiasts. If tourism and recreation in a place is thought to be as valuable—or perhaps even more valuable in the long term—then the argument for preservation has greater weight, and the landscape can be maintained as a whole.

In some cases, private tourism stakeholders will recognize the potential for protecting the natural features of a place, and they will invest in nature tourism with the intention of ultimately generating a profit. The private sector has an important part to play in tourism. Particularly in less developed countries where local and/or national governments may have few resources to devote to preservation efforts, private individuals and companies may be better able to achieve these goals. For example, the Makasutu Culture Forest in the West African country of The Gambia is a project that began in 1992, when two individuals initially purchased four acres of land to build a small backpackers' lodge. When the surrounding forest became the target of deforestation, they realized the need for preservation of a much wider area. Today, the forest is a thousand-acre private reserve and the site of nature-based tourism activities.[3]

In other cases, the public sector takes a leading role in the landscape preservation and resource protection that is needed to create the foundation for tourism. Local and/or national governments may invest in or subsidize preservation, and at the same time, income generated from operator licenses or visitor fees can help finance site maintenance, resource protection from developers or poachers, and additional preservation. There are many categories of **protected areas**. The Convention on Biological Diversity's definition of a protected area, accepted by 187 countries, is "a geographically defined area which is designated or regulated and managed to achieve specific conservation objectives."[4] The six overarching categories represent different levels of protection and allow for different types of activities. Category I

# Box 10.1.   Case Study: A Proposed Oil Refinery on the "Nature Island" of Dominica

Dominica is a volcanic island in the eastern Caribbean, characterized by rugged mountains and lush tropical rain forest vegetation. Despite these restrictions in physical geography, the island was developed for export-oriented agriculture as early as the late eighteenth century and remained dependent on these industries for nearly two hundred years. However, agriculture fell into decline in the second half of the twentieth century with political independence and the end of preferential access to the United Kingdom market for bananas. As with the other islands in the region at that time, Dominica looked to tourism as a potential economic alternative. Unlike many of these islands, though, Dominica lacked the white sand beaches upon which mass 3S tourism is based. Thus, the national tourism organization sought to utilize the island's stunning natural landscape to develop small-scale nature-based tourism products. As such, they created a new identity for themselves as the "nature island," which was used to promote these tourism products.

Yet, Dominica's development policies have not always been consistent with this identity and vision. For example, in an effort to increase visitation rates, the government made significant investment in its cruise terminal facilities to allow more—and bigger—ships. However, mass cruise tourism is a less sustainable form of tourism, which brings large quantities of tourists to a destination for a short time. These tourists overwhelm the environment and may provide little economic benefit for the destination.

Then, in 2007, the government of Venezuela proposed the construction of an oil refinery on Dominica. The government of Dominica forged a temporary agreement with Venezuela, contingent upon additional information, including an environmental impact assessment. While some local stakeholders argued for the economic benefits the refinery would bring to the island, others argued that any economic benefits would be negated by the loss of tourism. Organizations such as the island's Waitukubuli Ecological Foundation and the Dominica Hotel and Tourism Association perceived the proposed project as a dual threat: the threat of actual environmental degradation that would destroy the quality and aesthetic appearance of the nature island and the threat that the *idea* of an oil refinery would have on the concept of Dominica as the "nature island."

Among project opponents, it was taken for granted that an oil refinery would pollute the island's environment—particularly the air but also potentially land and water as well. More than that, however, opponents felt that an oil refinery was inconsistent, incongruous, and quite simply incompatible with Dominica's nature island identity and the nature-based tourism products that had been built on that identity. It was argued that even the possibility of constructing a refinery would irreparably damage Dominica's international reputation and that the tourists who had been drawn to the island's unique environment would no longer visit. This argument was supported by blogs and online chats where international contributors claimed that they would, indeed, go somewhere else if the refinery was built. It proved to be a powerful argument. The following year, the government postponed the project indefinitely.

*Discussion topic*: Identify an island tourism destination that has an oil refinery. Do you think that these two things are incompatible? What factors would allow or prevent tourism and industry from coexisting?

*Tourism on the web*: Discover Dominica Authority, "Discover Dominica, the Nature Island," at http://www.dominica.dm

**Figure 10.2.   Dominica is characterized by rugged terrain, steep cliffs, and black volcanic sand beaches. Although the island lacks the resources for mass 3S tourism development that characterize other Caribbean islands, it clearly possesses a different set of tourism resources that are particularly well suited to nature-based tourism products. (Source: Velvet Nelson)**

# Sources

Nelson, Velvet. "'R.I.P. Nature Island': The Threat of a Proposed Oil Refinery on Dominica's Identity." *Social & Cultural Geography* 11, no. 8 (2010): 903–19.

# Box 10.2.  Experience: Twenty Years in the National Parks

There are 397 areas in the National Park System, including everything from national parks to historical parks, battlefields, monuments, recreation areas, seashores, and more. I have been to 290 of them. The "Passport to Your National Parks" program was started in 1986, where you can purchase a "passport" book that includes information about all of the areas in the park system and a space for your book to get stamped at each park you visit. It's a fun way of recording where you've been. I began visiting parks shortly after the program was started, and now I'm on my fifth book.

I think it's neat that we, as a country, have understood that our heritage is important and worth preserving. I'm glad that we have protected our many unique and diverse environments and that I have had the opportunity to experience them. There are so many simply wonderful parks, including places that few people know exist. I enjoy visiting all categories of parks, but I really love the big, wide-open backcountry parks in the West. These are the ones I will visit year after year.

Yellowstone National Park is one of my favorites. I've been there twelve times in the past twenty years. I usually go for about a week and either camp in the park or stay in a lodge. I get up early to see the sunrise, and then I spend my days hiking on some of the backcountry trails. The landscape is so unique, with great opportunities to view wildlife, especially if you're willing to get off the main road. Some people think that they can see the whole park from the loop road, and they want to know when the animals will "come out." In all of my years visiting and exploring the trails—including some old trails that are no longer maintained or published—I know I haven't seen the entire park. But I've seen lots of animals, including mountain goats, bighorn sheep, deer, antelope, elk, moose, buffalo, and bears. In fact, one of the most amazing (and a little scary) moments was when we witnessed a herd of buffalo charging because they were being chased by a bear!

I've seen a lot of changes over the years. Some changes are cyclical, and you can definitely tell when there's money being spent on the parks and when there isn't. I've seen the infrastructure get run down and facilities closed, but then a few years later, things will be open and repaired again. Other changes reflect the development of new—and often better—policies. My mother has some pictures of Yellowstone from the 1960s where bears are being fed out of car windows. They had been allowed to feed out of the park's trash dumps since the nineteenth century, and this was considered a tourist attraction. It wasn't until the 1970s that Yellowstone implemented new policies that kept people from feeding the bears and required visitors to properly store and dispose of food in the park. Today they are very careful, and everything is recycled that can be. This both cuts down on waste in the park and generates a small amount of income.

Some trails that could once be driven are now closed to cars. I think there are more areas that are open for easy access, but more of the backcountry areas have been closed off to the general public. You have to have a permit to go into the backcountry, which makes sense. It keeps the casual person from going into areas that they really shouldn't be in, and it makes sure the park rangers know where people are in case anything happens. I also like the fact they get updates from rangers in the backcountry, so when I check in before a hike, I get some additional information about what's going on in that area. Of course, some of these trails are closed during parts of the year as well, based on the condition of the trail or on the wildlife in that area. For example, I know that the Pelican Creek Trail is closed to hikers during the bears' mating season to prevent any interference or disruption of mating patterns. I think they've also done a good job at keeping these trails in good condition. On one of my last trips, we actually met one of the backcountry rangers on a trail and hiked with him for a while. He told us that he now spends a couple months of the year in the backcountry to do maintenance.

I appreciate the ability to go into the backcountry. I am most interested in getting "off the beaten path," hiking, and experiencing the quiet of nature. That's just me and my personality; I have to find my own way. However, there are places for everyone in the park; you just have to know where to go. At the big, easily accessible camping sites, you'll find lots of people and the big, luxury RVs. At the more primitive, remote sites, you'll find just a handful of hard-core campers. At the major entry points and scenic spots, you'll find tour buses unloading people from all over the world, but get a mile off the main road on a hiking trail, and you might be the only one out there.

—*Kim*

includes strict nature reserves and wilderness areas. These areas are typically considered to be the most ecologically fragile, and therefore activities within them are the most restricted. The strict nature reserves are generally limited to scientific study (e.g., Snares Island Nature Reserve, New Zealand); wilderness areas preserve largely uninhabited and unmodified lands but may be managed to allow some visitation (e.g., Red Rock–Secret Mountain Wilderness, United States). Category II consists of national parks, which are perhaps the most commonly recognized protected areas. These are typically areas with unique natural and/or scenic qualities that are intended to preserve natural heritage and may be managed for scientific, educational, and/or recreational use (e.g., Galápagos National Park, Ecuador).

Category III is designated for natural monuments, which are intended to conserve specific features that have unique natural or cultural value (e.g., Victoria Falls, Zimbabwe and Zambia). Category IV includes habitat and species management areas protected to prevent loss of biodiversity directly or indirectly due to the loss of habitat (e.g., Haleji Lake Wildlife Sanctuary, Pakistan). Category V comprises protected landscapes and/or seascapes and is intended to maintain the quality of human-environment interactions in that landscape that often take place in the form of tourism and recreation (e.g., Logarska Dolina Landscape Park, Slovenia). Finally, Category VI, managed resource protection areas, represents the least amount of restrictions. These areas need to be managed to allow for multiple uses that might combine sustainable resource harvesting with recreation activities (e.g., Tamshiyacu-Tahuayo Communal Reserve, Peru).

Each of these potential benefits—improvement, maintenance, and preservation—is just that: potential. Concerted efforts must be undertaken to recognize the value of the physical resources for tourism and to ensure the existence of a high-quality environment for tourism. Although this may be considered a necessary prerequisite for tourism, these efforts require knowledge, planning, and financial resources that destinations don't always have. Thus, it is important to carefully consider what efforts are being undertaken at a destination and how they weigh against the negative effects—or environmental costs—of tourism.

# Environmental Costs of Tourism

The majority of research on the environmental effects of tourism has focused on costs, as the interactions between tourists and the environments of the places they visit are far more likely to have negative consequences. This includes resource consumption, pollution, and possibly even landscape destruction.

## RESOURCE CONSUMPTION

Tourism—particularly large-scale mass tourism—can place a heavy demand on local resources. These demands are likely to be in competition with other local economic activities and/or residential uses. In many cases, tourism as an economic activity is given priority, which means that these resources will be unavailable for other uses. In the worst-case scenario, the high demand for resources from tourism activities depletes that resource, not only to the detriment of future tourism but to the detriment of all activities undertaken in that environment. This can include land, construction resources, water, fuel, and/or power supplies, among others.

Land is a resource that is needed for tourism infrastructure, which can be extensive, including airports, roads, accommodation facilities, entertainment venues, and more. While this extent of infrastructure may not necessarily be a prerequisite for tourism, it accompanies tourism development and facilitates tourism activities. As a result, local people may be displaced and other economic activities supplanted in prime tourism development land. Competition for land between tourism and local uses is typically most intense in small island destinations, such as those in the Caribbean or the South Pacific, where land is a scarce resource. This is something that may be taken for granted by the tourists who visit that destination and do not consider how that land was used before tourism or how it might otherwise be used. Yet, as an economic activity, tourism must create enough jobs to compensate for the lost agricultural jobs. These jobs must provide sufficient wages for local people to purchase from external suppliers the food that they need to support their families to compensate for the loss of the food they once produced for themselves.

Additionally, various types of construction resources are consumed in the development of tourism infrastructure. Local lumber resources may be used in hotel/resort construction. As such, this resource is no longer available for local construction or other uses (e.g., as a source of fuel). Sand may be mined from beaches to make concrete, for building construction, or for construction of roads and airport runways. In both cases, trees and sand may additionally have the potential to serve as a tourism resource. If they are removed from the environment to be used as a construction resource, this also means that they will no longer contribute to the tourism base.

Water is another resource that is used in high quantities in tourism. The accommodation sector accounts for some of the greatest water demands at tourism destinations. Water may be used on the hotel/resort property in decorative fountains and to maintain green vegetation and flower gardens, even at destinations that have a dry climate. Likewise, water may be used in swimming pools and spa facilities. Guests account for a proportion of accommodations' water usage. Western tourists, in particular, have reportedly high water uses with baths, long showers, and in some case multiple showers per day. Guest services also constitute a source of water consumption. This includes kitchen and restaurant facilities but is primarily accounted for with laundry facilities, as the guests' sheets and towels are typically washed daily. In addition, tourism attractions and activities utilize varying quantities of water resources, including water parks, golf courses, botanical gardens, and ski resorts that rely on snowmakers. Again, given the economic importance of tourism, these activities may receive priority access to water resources. This means that less water will be available for other economic activities, such as agriculture or industry, as well as local residential uses.

The situation is similar for local fuel and/or energy resources. Accommodations and tourism attractions may require high electricity consumption to power their operations. This can put a strain on the destination's electricity-generating capacity. To prevent shortages that would affect tourists and tourism activities, thereby creating dissatisfaction with the destination experience, power may be cut to local business and/or residential customers at peak times.

In cases where tourism is already developed, local resources may be exploited for tourists' consumption. Economically, a high demand for locally made souvenirs would be considered a positive. However, to meet this demand, local residents may mine coral to make craft items and jewelry or remove bamboo forests to make boxes, baskets, and mats, and so on.

## POLLUTION

Although tourism is described as a "smokeless industry," it can either contribute to or directly result in all types of pollution at both the local and global scales. Water and air pollution are considered the most severe problems, but other types of pollution—such as noise or visual pollution—can also be a concern for tourism destinations.

Because so many tourism activities are located in coastal areas or on lakes and rivers, water pollution is one of the most significant types of pollution associated with tourism. Untreated sewage is typically the largest source of water pollution from tourism. This is generally attributed to the fact that many international destinations around the world have either no sewage treatment and therefore discharge the sewage directly into the water supply, or an inadequate system and only a portion of sewage gets treated. Tourism growth may take place at a faster rate than infrastructure growth; consequently, existing systems cannot keep up with the seasonal increases in population. Cruise ships also constitute a significant source of tourism-related water pollution. Again, sewage is the main source but others include fuel leakages and the illegal dumping of solid waste and chemicals from onboard activities. Other sources include fuels from recreational boats, chemical fertilizers, herbicides or pesticides used on resort properties and golf courses that leach into the groundwater or run off into water supplies, and even lotions and oils on the skin of tourists swimming in the water.

As discussed earlier, poor-quality water can increase the risk of waterborne diseases for both the local and tourist populations. Likewise, water pollution can contaminate the food supply. More than just an aesthetic detraction, it can also have a negative impact on the tourism resources for the destination. For example, the discharge of untreated sewage into water causes eutrophication, which is a process of nutrient enrichment. This stimulates algae growth which can be unattractive, have an unpleasant odor, and cause ecosystem damage, such as the suffocation of coral reefs.

Air pollution is the type that currently receives the greatest attention due to the issue of global climate change (see box 10.3). However, air pollution may also be a localized problem with distinct consequences for destinations. In particular, one of the fundamental components of tourism is travel, which is dependent on the transportation that is available based on present technology. Where there is a dense concentration of vehicles for tourism, vehicle exhaust contributes to poor air quality. Interestingly, urban areas may be less likely to see a direct correlation between tourism and air pollution. These areas may already experience high numbers of vehicles, and they may have higher restrictions on cars (e.g., emission controls) and traffic (e.g., taxes or permits for vehicles in inner-city zones or traffic-free zones). In addition, there may be strong incentives for tourists to use public transportation systems, such as buses or trains, to get around in urban destinations (e.g., limited parking areas, high parking fees, or confusing traffic patterns). In contrast, places like the U.S. National Parks have experienced increasing problems with pollution during high seasons. Tourists need personal cars to reach and get around at these destinations. In recent years, new policies have been put into place to limit traffic congestion in the parks. Visitors may be required to park in designated areas and use buses for transport within the park. Moreover, parks such as Yosemite have replaced traditional diesel buses with lower emission biodiesel and hybrid buses.

Even when air pollution is not the direct result of tourism, it can have a negative impact on destinations. Air pollution adversely affects the health and quality of life of local residents. Similarly, tourists, particularly those with preexisting respiratory conditions such as allergies, asthma, or emphysema, can be affected by short-term exposure to environments with poor air quality. In addition, air pollution can adversely affect the quality of tourism resources. For example, air pollution has been cited as one of the greatest threats to ancient archaeological sites, such as the Parthenon in Athens, Greece. Related to air pollution, acid rain has the potential to damage forest resources, as has occurred in Germany's well-known Black Forest region.

Noise pollution takes place in areas with a dense concentration of tourism facilities and infrastructure, such as airports, roads, or entertainment districts. This type of pollution can generate annoyance and dissatisfaction among tourists. Tourists who are looking for relaxation, peace, and quiet will be frustrated with their experience if the destination is populated by large numbers of families with loud and boisterous children or young adults having loud parties late into the night. Of course, this issue may be avoided by thorough research resulting in an appropriate choice of destination and/or resort in the pre-trip stage. Likewise, tourists visiting natural and/or sacred sites where a reverence for the environment is expected will be unhappy with the levels of noise from excessive numbers of tourists, air or road traffic, and others. As with air pollution, this has been a growing problem in some of the popular U.S. National Parks. For example, noise levels have risen as a result of the increase in air traffic for scenic

# Box 10.3.  In-Depth: Climate Change Mitigation in Tourism

The relationship between global climate change and tourism has been gaining attention in recent years. This has become a key issue because the tourism industry is considered to be highly sensitive to the effects of climate change, as was discussed in chapter 6. Yet, it is recognized among researchers and stakeholders that a two-way relationship exists. According to the secretary general of the United Nations World Tourism Organization (UNWTO), "Tourism has become both the victim and the vector of climate change. Our sector has to reduce its emissions; it also has to adapt."[1] In other words, the tourism industry both affects and is affected by climate change.

A joint report produced by the UNWTO and the United Nations Environment Programme (UNEP) estimated that, as of 2005, the tourism industry was responsible for approximately 5 percent of the world's total greenhouse gas emissions. Thus, tourism is a smaller contributor to the problem than heavy industry, but it is a contributor nonetheless. Approximately three-fourths of these emissions come from transportation to, from, and at the destination. Although the proportion of emissions is divided relatively evenly between air transport and auto transport (40 percent and 32 percent, respectively), air transport accounts for a much smaller proportion of tourist trips (approximately 17 percent). The next largest source of emissions is accommodations, with approximately 21 percent (figure 10.3). Considering the phenomenal growth in the global tourism industry, tourism-related greenhouse gas emissions are projected to increase 152 percent between 2005 and 2035 if no mitigation measures are taken.[2]

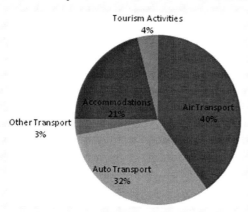

Figure 10.3.  **Transport, and air transport in particular, accounts for the largest proportion of greenhouse gas emissions from tourism. Thus, this sector of the tourism industry is often the primary target of climate change mitigation policies. However, as the industry encourages longer tourist stays at a destination to reduce the carbon footprint per tourist day, the accommodation sector's share of emissions could potentially increase.**

**Climate change mitigation** is defined as the technological, economic, and sociocultural changes that can lead to reductions in greenhouse gas emissions. Although one solution to reducing energy consumption and greenhouse gas emissions is to reduce travel, this is clearly unrealistic in the modern world. Thus, four mitigation strategies have been proposed for reducing greenhouse gas emissions from tourism: reducing energy consumption (e.g., increasing the use of mass transport over private cars; installing hotel key-card systems to ensure that lights, appliances, and in-room air conditioning units are not running when the guests are not in the room), improving energy efficiency (e.g., using hybrid or electric vehicles, relying less on air conditioning in buildings that utilize natural ventilation patterns), increasing the use of renewable energy (e.g., using

*(continued)*

---

## Box 10.3.  *(continued)*

biofuels in vehicles, using solar water-heating systems), and offsetting carbon emissions through the development of renewable energy projects or the planting of trees to act as carbon sinks (e.g., fees paid by tourists based on the amount of emissions incurred during travel, or investment made by tourism businesses to offset the emissions incurred by their operations). This last strategy—offsetting emissions—is the most controversial, and critics have argued that it provides wealthy tourists with a means of easing their guilt without actually having to change their behavior.

Because the tourism industry is international in nature, includes both public and private sector interests, and encompasses a range of different types of businesses and services, efforts to coordinate and regulate mitigation efforts are and will continue to be difficult. Moreover, the implementation of these mitigation strategies requires a financial investment that may be beyond the means of local tourism stakeholders. Yet, because the tourism industry is perhaps more vulnerable to the effects of climate change than other industries, many feel that it is vital to take a leading role in making changes. As such, there has been a precedent set by some tourism industry associations and entrepreneurs who have voluntarily adopted mitigation strategies and attempted to educate tourists about climate change.

*Discussion topic*: Find an example of a tourism venture that has implemented one or more of the climate change mitigation strategies. Identify what actions have been taken and discuss the potential benefits of these actions.

## Notes

1. United Nations World Tourism Organization, "Tourism Will Contribute to Solutions for Global Climate Change and Poverty Challenges," March 8, 2007, accessed February 22, 2011, http://www.unwto.org/newsroom/Releases/2007/march/globa_climate.htm.

2. Scott, Daniel, Bas Amelung, Suzanne Becken, Jean-Paul Ceron, Ghislan Dubois, Stefan Gössling, Paul Peeters, and Murray C. Simpson, *Climate Change and Tourism: Responding to Global Challenges, Summary* (Madrid: World Tourism Organization and United Nations Environment Programme, 2007), accessed February 22, 2011, http://www.unwto.org/climate/support/en/pdf/summary_davos_e.pdf, 14 and 18.

---

flights over the Grand Canyon. Noise pollution from tourism can also adversely affect local residents. For these people, the noise generated from tourism may be more than an annoyance; it may contribute to a general decline in their quality of life or contribute to serious physiological and psychological health concerns.

Visual pollution results in a decline in the aesthetic quality of an environment. This may occur when landscapes are changed by tourism development. The construction of tourism infrastructure may be considered visual pollution if it seems out of place in that particular environment. This can refer to the location of a hotel on an otherwise undeveloped beach or a ski lift or ski slope on an otherwise forested mountainside. Visual pollution may also occur as landscapes are degraded by tourist activities. One of the most commonly cited examples is the trash generated on mountain treks in remote destinations such as the Andes or the Himalayas. Early tourists and tour guides in these areas were not always careful about the waste that was produced

**Figure 10.4. For many, this hotel in Port El Kantaoui, Tunisia, constitutes a form of visual pollution. In contrast with the simple blue-and-white color scheme that characterizes classic Tunisian architecture, this hotel has accessorized its property with garish plastic neon palm trees and cacti. (Source: Velvet Nelson)**

during the course of the trip. As it was left behind, it became an unexpected source of visual pollution for future generations of tourists expecting a more pristine environment. Awareness of this issue has led to cleanup efforts and stricter regulations of how waste is disposed of on such excursions. Finally, visual pollution can also result from tourism facilities that have been constructed without consideration for local environments, materials, and architectural styles (figure 10.4).

## LANDSCAPE DESTRUCTION

The various costs of tourism development and tourist activities can ultimately contribute to, or result in, the destruction of landscapes. In addition to changing the fundamental nature and appearance of the landscape, this can contribute to further environmental problems such as disruption of habitats, fragmentation of ecosystems, and reductions in biodiversity.

Much of the world's tourism development has taken place in coastal areas. There are several unique and specialized ecosystems in these areas—including sand dunes, coastal wetlands and mangroves, and coral reefs—all of which have been threatened by tourism development. Each of these ecosystems has a high level of biodiversity and helps protect the coastal land area from erosion and the potentially damaging effects of storm waves and tidal surges. However, sand dunes have been leveled and wetlands drained for beachfront hotel/resort development. This can lead to problems with erosion and beach loss, as well as an increased amount of silt in coastal waters, which will smother coral reefs. At the same time, tourists themselves may trample dunes and damage coral by touching it, standing on it, or taking pieces as souvenirs. Similarly, the nature of the land may be lost to the construction of tourism infrastructure and facilities. In a forested environment, this contributes to local and global problems associated with deforestation, ranging from increased erosion to increased carbon dioxide in the atmosphere.

Finally, these environmental impacts can destroy habitat and disrupt the species that inhabit them. The destruction of an ecosystem can contribute to a loss of biodiversity, while the destruction of parts of the landscape may fragment the wider habitat and affect species' migration patterns. At the same time, the encroachment of tourism activities into these ecosystems may bring species into closer contact with people, both tourists and tourism industry workers. This can affect eating and/or breeding patterns.

# Factors in Environmental Effects

As with the other effects, there are some clear examples of how tourism directly affects the environment. This is particularly applicable when tourism activities are developed in environments where few or only small-scale human activities otherwise occur. For example, the development of a ski resort in an undeveloped area involves considerable changes to the landscape: the removal of trees and boulders, the recontouring of the landscape to create runs, and the construction of roads, lifts, accommodation facilities, and more. This development alone—without considering the potential effects of operation—may contribute to or result in deforestation, habitat destruction, loss of biodiversity, destabilization of the slope, erosion, an increased risk of landslides and avalanches, and visual pollution. Yet, in many cases, it may be difficult to separate what effects directly result from tourism and what would have occurred as a result of residential and industrial activities undertaken by the local population. This is particularly the case when tourism activities occur in already densely populated, highly urbanized, and/or industrialized areas. These destinations may experience problems with water or air pollution, yet tourism's contribution may be indistinguishable from that of other local industries.

The specific environmental effects of tourism at a destination, and the extent of these effects, will likely vary widely. The factors that may determine these effects can include the quantity of tourists that visit the destination, the carrying capacity of the destination, the seasonality of tourism, the type of destination, the level of infrastructure, local environmental policies and regulations, and the nature of the environment at the destination.

For example, as with social effects, it is often assumed that the larger the quantity of tourists, the greater the environmental effects. This can be true when the number of tourists visiting that destination within a relatively short period of time exceeds its carrying capacity. Carrying capacity is a widely used concept in environmental geography, as well as related fields such as biology, to indicate the size of a species or population that an environment can support and sustain. Adapted and applied in studies of tourism, carrying capacity refers to the number of tourists a destination or attraction can support and sustain. This helps the destination/attraction to understand its ability to withstand tourist use. Likewise, the destination must recognize that if the carrying capacity is exceeded, it is likely to result in varying degrees of damage which can lead to diminished tourist satisfaction.

For the purposes of tourism, the carrying capacity concept has been used in different ways. Physical, environmental, and perceptual carrying capacity are three forms of the concept that are particularly useful in the geography of tourism. **Physical carrying capacity** is a somewhat literal interpretation of the concept in that it refers to the limits of a particular space. This may include things like the number of cars that a tourist site's parking area will hold or the actual number of people that the site can reasonably contain. As such, it is fairly straightforward and allows explicit restrictions to be put in place. **Environmental carrying capacity** refers to the extent of tourism that can take place at a site before its environment experiences negative effects. This can be more difficult to understand because it may not be based simply on the number of tourists but also on the type and accumulation of tourism activities. **Perceptual carrying capacity** refers to the extent of tourism that can take place at a site before tourist dissatisfaction occurs. This carrying capacity will be reached when tourists decide that a site is too crowded and choose to go elsewhere. Perceptual carrying capacity can also be difficult to determine because the perceived level of crowding is primarily based on individual preferences but also cultural conventions (figure 10.5).

Clearly the relationship between the number of tourists and environmental effects is not always simple. The tourism season can also be a factor in the nature and extent of effects. Large quantities of tourists during the high season may put extreme amounts of pressure on local resources. If the environmental carrying capacity is greatly exceeded during this time, it may cause irreversible damage from which the environment of the destination will not be able to recover. Provided the damage is not irreversible, however, most destinations have a low or off season during which the site will receive few visitors. This may provide enough time for the environment to recover.

Similarly, the type of destination and the level of infrastructure will also play a role in what environmental effects may occur. For example, mass tourism is associated with higher quantities of tourists; thus, the potential for negative environmental effects may be multiplied in comparison with small-scale niche tourism. Indeed, some of the long-standing, popular Mediterranean mass tourism destinations have experienced some of the worst environmental effects of tourism. Rimini, Italy, has experienced severe problems with water pollution from the discharge of untreated wastewater and air pollution from traffic congestion, both of which are particularly bad during the high tourist season. Yet, other well-planned and developed mass tourism destinations may have the infrastructure in place to handle such quantities of tourists and strict regulations to control negative impacts.

In contrast, when a new and/or developing destination starts to receive more than just a few drifters, the infrastructure simply may not be in place yet to handle these numbers, even though they are still small compared to large-scale mass destinations. Moreover, even small numbers of tourists can have a negative impact on the destination's environment. For example, hikers in backcountry areas can cause considerable damage

**Figure 10.5.  Visitors to Wannian Monastery looking for a serene experience at a Buddhist temple surrounded by nature on this sacred mountain in China may be dissatisfied due to the level of noise and crowds at the site. (Source: Velvet Nelson)**

when they stray from prescribed paths, leave ruts or scars, disturb wildlife, pick plants, fell trees for firewood, light campfires carelessly, or improperly dispose of their waste.

The nature of the environment at the destination can also determine the extent of effects from tourism. Fragile ecosystems, such as mountains, rain forests, or coral reefs, may be more vulnerable than others in that they are less able to withstand human use and recover from overuse. Likewise, historic and prehistoric sites are also vulnerable and need to be highly regulated to ensure that they are not adversely affected by increased exhaust from car traffic, wear and tear from foot traffic, dust and debris deposits, and careless or malicious behavior (e.g., vandalism and theft). Each of these environments has lower **tourism carrying capacities**. In some cases, the benefits of tourism may be negated when more of the visitor entrance fees must go toward combating the problems generated by tourism rather than restoring and/or preserving additional sites.

# Knowledge and Education

Education—of tourists, tourism industry workers, and local residents at a tourism destination—is often one of the simplest and easiest-to-implement means of preventing the negative environmental effects of tourism. In the case of tourists, ignorant and careless behavior can have a direct impact on the environment of the places they visit. Yet, tourists have little connection to these environments, and given the short-term nature of their experiences in these environments, they may not see the consequences of their behavior. For example, some tourists feel that they are paying for the services that a hotel or resort provides. Thus, they will use the facilities as they see fit—whether it is having their linens laundered on a daily basis or leaving the room's lights, air conditioning, and/or appliances on when they are not in the room—without considering the implications of their wasteful resource consumption. Tourists may give little attention to how they dispose of their waste without considering that it may alter the eating habits of local wildlife, cause some species to fall ill or die, or attract predators. While only a small subset of tourists travel specifically for educational purposes, the potential nonetheless exists for tourists to learn about the places they visit and to understand the consequences of their actions at that place.

Tourism industry workers play an important role in the implementation of mitigation strategies. A destination may have good intentions in devising a code of conduct or a sustainable development policy; however, these strategies will fail if tourism industry workers are not properly informed of it and do not understand its rationale. For example, most tourists have been made aware of water consumption issues use by hotel placards informing them of the destination's water resources and requesting that guests elect to reuse their linens. Many are willing to support this policy on the basis that they would not change their linens daily at home. However, it is too often the case that tourists find that their linens have been replaced by the housekeeping staff regardless of their decision. Similarly, tourists may be requested to separate their trash into designated bins for recycling, only to see staff dumping the bins together as waste. These tourists may become frustrated with this lack of follow-through and therefore ignore such requests in the future.

Finally, local residents must also understand the pertinent environmental issues of the destination and the strategies that are being undertaken to maintain its resources. Again, the best efforts of tourism stakeholders to develop activities with minimal environmental costs can be undermined by unsustainable activities undertaken by the local population. For example, the destination may seek to establish policies to conserve its resources—say sand or trees. However, if people in the local community have a basic need for these resources, or if they have little direct stake in tourism but can profit from the extraction of these resources, they will use them. This, of course, erodes the basis for tourism at the destination and contributes to a decline in the environmental quality and general quality of life in that place.

# Conclusion

Environmental geography is a vital component in the geography of tourism, as it represents the intersection of people and environment. Although there are certainly exceptions, much of tourism involves some type of interaction between tourists and the environments of the places that they visit. As with all human-environment interactions, this will have an impact on the environment. While these impacts are more likely to have negative consequences, concerted efforts can be made by stakeholders at all scales (i.e., locally, nationally, and globally) to maximize the benefits that tourism can have for the environment at the destination and to minimize the costs.

# Key Terms

- climate change mitigation
- environmental carrying capacity
- environmental geography
- perceptual carrying capacity
- physical carrying capacity
- protected area
- tourism carrying capacity

# Notes

1. Visit Baltimore, "An Inner Harbor Timeline," accessed February 16, 2011, http://baltimore.org/misc/uploads/meetingplannerspdf/Inner_Harbor_Timeline.pdf.
2. The Wilds, "The Wilds," accessed February 16, 2011, http://www.thewilds.org/.
3. Makasutu Culture Forest—The Gambia, "History," accessed February 19, 2011, http://www.makasutu.com/index.php.
4. Kalemani Jo Mulongoy and Stuart Chape, "Protected Areas and Biodiversity: An Overview of Key Issues," United Nations Environment Programme, accessed February 19, 2011, http://development.unep-wcmc.org/protected_areas/pdf/protected_areas_bioreport.pdf.

# Sources

Castree, Noel, David Demeritt, and Diana Liverman. "Introduction: Making Sense of Environmental Geography." In *A Companion to Environmental Geography*, edited by Noel Castree, David Demeritt, Diana Liverman, and Bruce Rhoads, 1–16. Malden, MA: Blackwell, 2009.
Holden, Andrew. *Environment and Tourism*. 2nd ed. London: Routledge, 2008.
Nelson, Velvet. "Investigating Energy Issues in Dominica's Accommodations." *Tourism and Hospitality Research* 10 (2010): 345–58.
———. "Promoting Energy Strategies on Eco Certified Accommodation Websites." *Journal of Ecotourism* 9, no. 3 (2010): 187–200.
Williams, Stephen. *Tourism Geography*. London: Routledge, 1998.

# Part IV

# THE GEOGRAPHY OF SPACE, PLACE, AND TOURISM

Destinations are the places of tourism. Just the idea of them is enough to captivate our imagination and create a demand for our experience of them. We formulate an idea in our minds of what we think it will be like and then, if we can, we try to turn these daydreams into reality. Given this opportunity, there are many factors that will shape our trip—from the way the destination is organized to the ways we choose to experience it. As tourists, we would never conceptualize this in geographic terms. However, as geographers, we know that basic concepts, like space and place, can help us better understand the various patterns of the world, including those of tourism.

Geography is described as a spatial science. The concept of space is used to study the organization of various phenomena across the earth's surface. The geography of tourism allows us to explore the distinct spatial patterns of tourism at different geographic scales. Geography is also described as the study of places. The concept of place is used as a means of understanding the character of parts of the earth's surface as well as the ways in which people think about and interact with them. Adapted for the geography of tourism, we can use place as a tool to help us understand the character of tourism destinations, the ways in which people think about those destinations, and the ways in which they interact with the destinations they visit.

Earlier in the book, we used the topical branches of geography to help us better understand the context of and key issues in tourism. In this final section, we will use fundamental concepts in geography to explore tourism as a geographic phenomenon. Chapter 11 examines the creation and evolution of distinct spatial patterns at tourism destinations. Chapter 12 discusses tourism representations of place, in which ideas and expectations are created about places before they are visited. Finally, chapter 13 considers the ways in which tourists experience the places they visit.

# The Organization, Development, and Management of Space in Tourism

Tourism does not occur evenly across space, whether we are considering the distribution of tourism destinations at the global scale or a destination's activities at the local scale. However, the spatial perspective isn't just important in helping us understand patterns of tourism. It plays a vital role in helping stakeholders make informed decisions regarding the planning, development, organization, and management of tourism to maximize all those benefits and minimize the costs discussed in the previous section. While these issues may seem as though they would be best approached from a business perspective, the geographic perspective has been incredibly influential in developing concepts and strategies to ensure the best possible interactions between tourists and the places they visit. In fact, some of the most important contributions to our understanding of tourism have been made by geographers.

This chapter uses geography's spatial perspective to examine the organization, development, and management of tourism destinations. These factors play an important role in determining the nature of a destination, the type of tourists that will visit, and the experiences they will have there. In particular, we will examine the division of space at a destination and patterns of movement within the destination as a key spatial pattern. In addition, this chapter discusses some spatial management strategies that may be applied at destinations to maximize the economic, social, and environmental benefits of tourism and minimize its costs, to ensure long-term sustainability.

## The Organization of Space in Tourism

Tourism destinations are organized in different ways depending on the nature of the destination and its attractions. In one of the most important analyses of tourism as a social phenomenon, Dean MacCannell drew upon work in sociology to describe this organization.[1] In particular, he starts with sociologist Erving Goffman's structural division of social settings. Goffman's theory suggests that places have front regions and back regions. Front regions are those that are open to and intended for outsiders. This is the part of a place that is carefully constructed to present a certain image to outsiders, and it's where these outsiders interact with the insiders who function as hosts or service providers. Back regions are those that are reserved for insiders. This is the part of the place that facilitates insiders' daily activities; it's where they can be themselves rather than putting on a show or providing a service. Because the back region is generally closed to outsiders, this helps maintain the illusions presented to outsiders in the front. In his work, MacCannell extends this structural division into a continuum of stages from front to back and applies it to the context of tourism. This continuum is a useful tool in helping us appreciate the complex organization of space in tourism destinations.

The first stage of this continuum is a true **front region**; it is the space that has been entirely constructed for the purpose of tourism. This includes all-inclusive tourist resorts and theme parks. These sites have little, if any, relation to the character of the larger place in which they are situated. For example, one of the Busch Gardens amusement parks is referred to as Busch Gardens Europe. This does not reflect its location—which is, in fact, Williamsburg, Virginia—but rather describes the park's European theme. This, of course, differs substantially from the other offerings of Colonial Williamsburg as a tourism destination. The people tourists encounter in these front regions are either also tourists, and therefore other outsiders, or employees doing a job. In the case of Busch Gardens, this ranges from the ticket taker to the "German barmaid" serving food and drinks at one of the park's restaurants and the Irish dancers performing regular shows.

The second stage is also a front region designed for tourists, but it is has been decorated in a style intended to be reminiscent of a back region in that place. These areas are not likely to be mistaken for a back region; however, they aren't intended to be. The Wimbledon Tennis Club in Las Vegas, Nevada, might make use of the name of the famous professional tennis tournament and perhaps even decorate their facilities with championship merchandise. Yet, no one will ever confuse this site with the All England Lawn Tennis and Croquet Club in Wimbledon, near London, England.

The third stage is still a front region, but it is a simulation of a back region. In contrast with the second stage, areas in this stage may be intended to convince visitors that they are, in fact, visiting a back region. While many working dude ranches offer the opportunity to participate in a cattle drive, interest in such experiences has given rise to tourist ranches. These ranches may exist within the same setting as the working ranches, which contributes to the appearance of authenticity, but it is a romanticized—and most likely sanitized—version of ranch life that is re-created for visitors to experience. These outsiders may not be aware of the difference between the actual and simulated experiences, either due to the provider's attention to detail or simply their own lack of knowledge.

In some cases, it may be difficult to distinguish the third stage from the fourth stage. As a front region, space in the third stage is still constructed for the purpose of tourism. In contrast, the fourth stage is a back region open to outsiders. As such, it was not explicitly constructed for tourism, but it has been altered, to varying degrees, to accommodate tourism. Thus, working ranches would fall into this category. Likewise, this would include other types of working farms or factories that are open to visitors or conduct tours. For example, vineyards and breweries are primarily intended to produce wine and beer for sale, and these places conduct their normal business on a daily basis. Yet, at the same time, many are open to the public, at least on certain days or at specific times, to see the process and to sample the product.

The fifth stage is nearer to a true back region, but it is not completely closed to outsiders. Under various circumstances, outsiders may be allowed the occasional glance into these spaces. As a result, they might be "cleaned up" or modified a bit. While the home environment is typically a true back region described by the final stage, there are cases in tourism in which outsiders may be permitted into residents' homes, again with varying degrees of accommodation. In some destinations with a poorly developed tourism infrastructure, there may be a lack of formal restaurants; therefore, tourists may take meals in residents' homes. Although this is typically done on an informal basis, there are some examples of destinations that recognize this practice and have legal regulations for such in-home "restaurants" (e.g., Cuba's *paladares*). Similarly, home stays and couch-surfing are intended to provide opportunities for tourists to meet local people and get an idea of what their life is like by staying in their homes. While residents who provide these services are unlikely to have the formalized arrangements for guests that might be found at bed-and-breakfasts, they will have to make some minor accommodations for their occasional guests.

The final stage, the sixth stage, is the true **back region**. This is the space that is not intended for, or expected to receive, outsiders. Such areas may be so far off of the typical tourist path at the destination that most tourists won't find themselves there. They may not be of interest to tourists, or, in some cases, tourists may be prohibited from visiting them. Because tourists visiting the destination are generally not present here, the nature of the space and insiders' patterns of behavior remain largely unchanged. With the exception of the cases described above, the home environment is typically a true back region. Even if an individual or a family lives in a destination region and works in the tourism industry, their home would provide a sort of refuge, a space of their own that need only meet their own expectations and allows them to do what they choose. Some cultural institutions place restrictions on social outsiders (i.e., foreign citizens or nonbelievers), such as dictating times they can be present, the services they can observe, and the attire they must wear. In some cases, these places may be closed entirely to outsiders. For example, although the Islamic holy city of Mecca is one of Saudi Arabia's most popular tourism destinations, non-Muslims are prohibited.

This discussion of stages is part of a larger debate about the nature of the tourism experience. As we have already seen, the "tourist" is commonly generalized as and criticized for being someone who travels to another place without really experiencing it. In other words, the tourist's experiences are primarily concentrated in the first stages of the continuum—those that represent front regions. The parts of a place he or she experiences are staged for the benefit of tourists and do not reflect the lived character of the place. As such, they are criticized as inauthentic. Indeed, some tourists are content with these experiences, as their primary motivation for travel may be to escape their normal environment as opposed to experiencing a new place. However, we know there are different types of tourists, and they have varying degrees of interest in experiencing the character of the place they are visiting.

Organized mass tourists will be those who are most content to experience only the front regions of a place, those that are designed for and cater to tourists. These tourists might travel to and stay at a popular all-inclusive chain resort on one of the well-developed islands of Hawaii, such as Oahu or Maui (stage 1). Individual mass tourists and explorers may experience more regions of the destination. They might stay at a resort on one of the islands (stage 1) but perhaps also eat at a Polynesian-themed restaurant (stage 2), attend a luau (stage 3), tour a pineapple plantation (stage 4), or rent a car and enjoy lunch at a local picnic grounds (stage 5). Drifters will choose a destination based on their desire to experience back regions. Thus, they might choose one of the least frequented islands of Hawaii, such as Molokai, or perhaps look even farther afield to the less developed islands of the South Pacific (figures 11.1 and 11.2).

This type of organization allows the interests and demands of different tourists to be met. At the same time, it may allow that place to better maintain its character. To attract all but the drifters, some adaptations must be made at the destination. At the least, this includes the development of a basic tourism infrastructure that will allow tourists to reach the destination, stay in facilities with the expected features and level of service, and participate in the activities that they want. However, niche destinations may be able to incorporate these adaptations into existing space that will fall into the middle stages of the spectrum without having to create any wholly artificial front regions. Mass destinations may choose to spatially concentrate this infrastructure into tourist zones that are entirely front regions, while the surrounding areas can be kept as back regions that continue to serve local functions.

# Spatial Organization and Movement

Patterns of movement vary widely in tourism. We have already seen that movement can encompass the entire experience stage (e.g., cruises or road trips). There are also cases in tourism where little movement occurs during the experience stage. This is common at S destinations with all-inclusive resorts; there is little perceived reason or incentive for tourists to leave these resorts, as all of the desired amenities are available on-site. This can also be the case at destinations where tourists feel unsafe. In high crime areas, tourists may be advised against leaving the hotel or resort unnecessarily. However, movement will be a part of most tourists' experience of a destination. These spatial patterns will depend on the organization of the destination, the nature of attractions, and the type of tourism, as well as the type of tourist and their level of comfort with the destination.

Some destinations, especially those that were planned and explicitly designed as tourism destinations, are compact in nature. The majority of accommodations, attractions, and other tourism services are spatially concentrated in a central tourism district (CTD). This makes it easy for tourists to comfortably move around the destination and limits their need to travel outside of the tourist zone. However, other destinations, such as major cities where attractions are scattered throughout the urban area and tourist districts may be established in multiple neighborhoods, are much more complicated. Tourists' range of movement will be much greater, as they seek to visit each of the attractions. Drifters and explorers might choose to navigate this widespread

**Figures 11.1 and 11.2.** While organized mass tourists travel to the Hawaiian Islands every year to enjoy the front regions of lavish resorts in a beautiful setting (top), there are also ample opportunities for explorers and drifters to get "off the beaten path" and experience the unique back regions (bottom). (Sources: Patricia Burnette and Kim Sinkhorn)

# Box 11.1.  Experience: The Back Regions of Russia

My major is Russian history. As part of my university curriculum, I had the opportunity to do a semester study abroad at the Russian State University for the Humanities in Moscow. I spent most of my time in the city and occasionally took day trips to some of the small towns nearby. I took classes on the Russian language and worked on a project called Cities in Transition that took me north to St. Petersburg and south to Volgograd. On both of these trips, I went on my own. It really gave me the opportunity to see more of Russia and also to put my language skills to the test.

The trip to St. Petersburg took place over a long weekend. It wasn't exactly a normal trip. Before I left, I glanced at a map but didn't bring it with me. I didn't make any reservations. I bought a train ticket on Thursday night, arrived on Friday morning, and just started walking. I have a pretty good sense of direction, and I went with my instincts. I didn't use the tourist information office because I wasn't interested in the "tourist" offerings, things like river cruises. I wanted to try to blend in and do more local things. I found an area that looked like there would be some hostels and used what language I knew to ask a few people for directions to find one. I spent most of my time walking around, visiting sites such as the Peter and Paul Fortress, the Hermitage, and even the mall. This used to be a state mall with each storefront offering a different state-issued product to meet peoples' basic needs; now it is filled with high-end international name brand products from Nike to Gucci.

I didn't need a map to see what I wanted, and because I wasn't tied to a preplanned itinerary, I was able to experience some things I hadn't expected. One of my roommates at the hostel was Russian. He was actually from St. Petersburg, but he was staying in the hostel during this time when he didn't have a place to live. We talked a bit, and one night he took me out for a local event. There are hundreds of drawbridges over the river system all over the city, and for a five-hour-long period in the middle of the night, they are opened in succession. It's quite a sight to see the bridges up and the boats streaming through at once, and it's something that people go out to watch (figure 11.3).

**Figure 11.3.  Watching the nighttime bridge opening in St. Petersburg, Russia, is a popular activity shared by locals and visitors. (Source: Isaac Watson)**

When I went to Volgograd, I had a holiday with five days off from classes. For this trip, I did a bit more research and planning before I left. Because Volgograd doesn't get as much tourist traffic, and almost no international tourists, there weren't any hostels. I ended up staying in a fairly nice hotel that only had a handful of people staying there, all of whom were Russian. It was dark by the time I arrived, so I decided to stay close for the night and eat at the hotel's restaurant until I could get my bearings the next day. Restaurants in Russia can be very expensive. When you're at home, you're often better off to cook on your own. As a college student on a budget, when I was traveling I tried to stick to the cheaper kiosks, small fast food restaurants, or bar-restaurants. But this restaurant turned out to be a great experience, as I spent the better part of the night talking with the server, who had lived in New York for a while, and the bartender. They even offered to let me try an absinthe—the Russian way—on the employee discount.

Volgograd is a smaller city, and my trip here was probably the best, most authentic experience of my entire stay in Russia. I visited sites such as Mamayev Kurgan, a memorial at the site of a World War II battle that is considered one of the bloodiest battles in the world. I was the only foreign visitor. I really had to rely on my Russian skills, but this earned me one of the best compliments I could have imagined: in Volgograd, a woman asked me for directions. I had to explain to her that I was just a visitor, so I couldn't tell her where she needed to go. She was surprised and told me how good my Russian was.

On the twenty-hour train trip home, I shared a coupe with a family who had a young daughter. They had brought their dinner with them to eat on the train, mostly traditional items like bread, chicken, vegetables, et cetera. I had brought a granola bar. They were very welcoming, and it's custom to share what you have, which goes back to the hard times they've experienced over the years. They insisted I eat with them and wouldn't let me take just one thing. When we weren't sleeping, we spent most of the trip talking about everything from the differences between Russia and the United States to life in general. The parents didn't speak English, so I used my Russian. The daughter was just starting to learn English at her elementary school, so she knew some words. The parents would quiz her on what she knew and ask me if she was right. For a while, she was using her parents' cell phone, with its Russian-English dictionary, to "cheat." Finally, they took it away from her to see how much she really knew. When they asked her a word that she had no idea about, she looked to me for help. At that moment, I didn't feel like a stranger or a foreigner but a family friend.

—*Isaac*

area on foot or by public transit systems, while mass tourists may be more comfortable with specialized tourism transport services (e.g., hop-on hop-off sightseeing buses).

Similarly, the nature of the destination's attractions will shape patterns of movement. As discussed in chapter 3, top-tier attractions exert a tremendous pull force. Tourists will make a point to visit these attractions, even if they have to travel out of their way to do so. Because secondary attractions exert less of a pull force, tourists will make decisions and prioritize which attractions they want to see most. To maximize the experience, those that are more expensive, difficult, or time consuming to reach may be dropped from the itinerary in favor of those that are more easily accessible. Tertiary attractions are the most substitutable. Because tourists do not have a strong motivation to visit these attractions, they may only choose those that can be reached most easily and cheaply, or possibly even en route to another, higher-level attraction.

Some tourists' movement may be limited to the area immediately surrounding the accommodation due to the tourism product. For example, tourists traveling to participate in a specific event or activity may have limited time to generally explore the destination. Conference or congress tourists may have a desire to experience more of the destination while they're there. However, because the majority of their time is spent in meetings, they may only have free time in the evenings or a day before or after the event. Most find that it's simply not worth the cost of renting a car and paying to keep it parked, often in premium space and pricey downtown lots or garages. As a result, they are most likely to visit attractions, shop, and go to restaurants or nightclubs that can be reached relatively easily from the hotel and/or conference site either by walking or taking taxis.

The extent of movement will also vary with the type of tourist. The most adventurous explorers and drifters may place few restrictions on their own movement because they are willing to do whatever it takes to have the experience they want, be it renting a car or using public transportation. Mass tourists may feel more uncertain about themselves in a new place and about the destination; therefore, they may initially choose to stick to places in the CTD near their hotel. As they become more comfortable, they may begin to travel farther and beyond the destination's front regions.

In addition, there are other factors that have the potential to shape patterns of movement. For example, aging populations often face declining personal mobility. This not only plays a role in what places they have the opportunity to experience but also in how they experience them. Some seniors may still be interested in traveling to new places, but due to health conditions, they may not be physically able to experience the destination in certain ways. As a result, they might need to take a coach tour of the destination instead of a walking tour, even though they will not be able to experience the sights, sounds, and smells of place as viscerally. Likewise, persons with disabilities face various constraints to their experience of place. Tourists' ethnicity may also present a constraint to patterns of movement. This is particularly the case when they are traveling in a place where they are not part of the majority population and there are visible "markers" that would identify them as outsiders (e.g., appearance or pattern of dress). Because they are uncomfortable receiving undue attention, or because they fear potential harassment or crime, they will adjust their travel accordingly. Similarly, female travelers, especially those traveling alone, may also be subject to both physical/logistical and perceptual constraints. This will be discussed in greater depth in chapter 13.

# Developing and Managing Destinations

Good planning and management are essential in minimizing the negative and maximizing the positive effects of tourism discussed in part III. Many strategies, borrowed from the topical branches of geography and other fields, have been adapted and proposed as means of developing the spaces of tourism in ways that will achieve this goal. Among others, some of these include construction regulations, land management, codes of conduct, and sustainable development.

# Box 11.2.   In-Depth: Enclave Tourism

**Enclave tourism** refers to geographically isolated and spatially concentrated tourism facilities and activities. We tend to associate enclave tourism with large-scale, all-inclusive resorts catering to the S tourism market. Indeed, the Dominican Republic—the Caribbean's largest destination—is often cited as a primary example of enclave tourism, where foreign tourists spend their entire vacation inside the walls of a resort compound. In fact, these resorts have been described as "concentration camps of leisure."[1] However, enclave tourism can be associated with other tourism products as well. These facilities can be located in remote rural areas based on different, primarily physical, resources.

Enclave tourism most commonly emerges in less developed countries that are using tourism as an economic development strategy. The almost exclusively foreign-owned facilities may develop as a function of constraints in the local infrastructure. Small, poor, rural communities will not have the extent of infrastructure—whether it is good-quality roads, reliable sources of power, or access to clean water—that is necessary to provide the base for tourism. A multinational company may come in and develop what they need within a specific geographic area. These self-contained spaces are separate and closed off from any existing communities in the area. This creates a form of spatial segregation. Local people will not receive the benefits of the newly developed infrastructure, and they will no longer have access to any resources that exist in that area. The company will also typically import food, equipment, and even personnel; therefore, economic leakages are high, and the local people receive few benefits from the newly developed industry. As a result, they may come to resent, and possibly even undermine, tourism. In addition, the resort will have standardized facilities and appearance that has little relation to the wider characteristics of the place in which it is situated.

These places are almost exclusively visited by foreign tourists. Enclave tourism typically reflects a package purchase, where visitors pay a single fee for everything from transportation to accommodation, meals, drinks, sightseeing excursions, and more. This fee is paid up-front to an agent located in the tourists' country of origin. For mass tourists, this is considered an attractive option because it is easy. The agent has already done the research, negotiation, and logistical arrangements of the trip. For certain demographics of tourists, such as families with small children or senior citizens, it may also be considered attractive because it reduces or eliminates any potential hassles associated with patterns of movement at the destination. For example, the package may include dedicated transportation from the airport to the resort so that tourists won't have to deal with things like navigating unfamiliar roads, negotiating with potentially unscrupulous drivers, physically managing luggage, and so on.

Especially in the case of less developed nations, enclave tourism can present an attractive option for foreign tourists who have a demand for certain places but doubts or concerns about the actual experience. These enclaves are predicated on providing the expected level of quality in accommodations in otherwise materially poor areas and assurances that standards of sanitation and hygiene are at the level tourists demand. They provide reliable transportation services to/from the resort and activities outside of the resort, as well as whatever security is deemed necessary to ensure that tourists are safe, even in potentially volatile environments.

The S tourism enclave resorts are designed to be autonomous; nearly all of the facilities and/or services that tourists might desire are included in the initial price paid and can be obtained on site. Tourists visiting these resorts have little need or incentive to leave. They see little of the wider destination that they have traveled to, and there is little interaction with local people. Moreover, little additional money is spent at the destination and virtually none

*(continued)*

## Box 11.2.   *(continued)*

of it outside the resort. However, enclave tourism based on other products, such as nature tourism, will experience a slightly different variation on this pattern. These tourists will leave a clearly demarcated spatial area to have the intended experience, such as wildlife viewing, but the structure of the package keeps them isolated from the place nonetheless.

For example, the Okavango Delta in Botswana is one of the country's most important tourism destinations, as it is recognized as a wetland and wildlife habitat of international significance. There are approximately 122,000 people living in this area, which receives an average of 50,000 foreign tourists a year. This number has been growing in recent years as the Delta has come to be known as one of the world's new and exotic destinations. Yet, the tourism infrastructure remains poorly developed in Botswana. Thus, a form of enclave tourism was developed to meet the specific demands of international tourism without developing a comprehensive tourism infrastructure. These tourists arrive in the country's primate city (the city that is larger than all others in the country, usually in less developed countries) and are transported by the tour company directly to their resort. The tourists have virtually no interaction with the local population.

The majority of the resorts and tour companies operating in the Delta are foreign owned, and few of the goods and/or services used by these companies are obtained from the local population. Poverty levels among this population have been high, and it has only increased since tourism has come to the area. These people were not included in decisions about tourism, and they have received few benefits from the industry. Moreover, they no longer have access to certain areas, and they feel increasingly disconnected from the place. Given these factors, the local population has come to resent both foreign tourists and the tourism industry. According to one study, "interviews with community leaders and household representatives in the Okavango indicate that there is a general assumption that the Delta has been taken from them by government and given to foreign tour operators. . . . They believe that their resources have been usurped from them by foreign tourism investors."[2]

## Notes

1. Alastair Reid, "Reflections: Waiting for Columbus," *New Yorker*, February 24, 1992, 75.
2. Joseph E. Mbaiwa, "Enclave Tourism and Its Socio-Economic Impacts in the Okavango Delta, Botswana," *Tourism Management* 26 (2005), 163.

## Sources

Anderson, Wineaster. "Enclave Tourism and Its Socio-Economic Impact in Emerging Destinations." *Anatolia—An International Journal of Tourism and Hospitality Research* 22, no. 3 (2011): 361–77.
Ceballos-Lascuráin, Héctor. *Tourism, Ecotourism, and Protected Areas*. Gland, Switzerland: IUCN Publication, 1996.

Construction regulations may be used to limit the extent or to shape the character of tourism development. For example, regulations on many island destinations around the world mandate that buildings must be no taller than or even shorter than the height of surrounding vegetation, typically palm trees (figure 11.4). This typically equates to two or three stories. This type of regulation seeks to restrict the potential negative impacts of mass tourism development. Essentially, it prevents the development of the high-rise megaresorts that dominate the coastal landscape of many popular S destinations. This effectively places limits on the numbers of tourists in that space, as well as the amount of resources used and waste generated

**Figure 11.4.  This luxury resort in Barbados was constructed with only two stories. Being lower than the surrounding palm trees, these buildings blend into the environment instead of dominating it like other resorts' high-rise beachfront buildings. (Source: Velvet Nelson)**

by those tourists. Similarly, development companies may be required to submit architectural designs for tourism infrastructure to ensure that it doesn't conflict with local styles and become a source of visual pollution.

**Spatial zoning** is a land management strategy that designates permissible uses of an area based on its resources and/or character. In tourism, zoning determines what tourism activities may be undertaken where. Typically, governmental regulatory agencies identify the resources within particular areas of a destination, as well as the demand for tourism opportunities in those areas. Then, officials determine which areas have the most appropriate resources to allow those activities. Each zone permits an increasing amount of human activity. This includes primary conservation areas with strictly controlled access, natural areas with minimal facilities, and recreation areas with the greatest access and opportunities for hiking, fishing, camping, picnicking, and more.

Zoning may be used to either spatially concentrate tourists or disperse them. **Preferred sites** are typically planned locations that attract visitors through advertisements and promotions; they have facilities like parking lots, restrooms, refreshments, picnic areas, designated paths, and/or information and interpretation centers. These sites spatially concentrate general visitors to ensure that their needs are met and to limit the effects of tourism to one particular area that is designed to handle it. The experience of these places may be enough for many visitors who don't feel the need to venture into other zones with less infrastructure and more fragile ecosystems (figure 11.5). In con-

**Figure 11.5. Managed natural areas may provide limited facilities for activities such as camping, such as this space in Acadia National Park, Maine. This prevents users from environmentally destructive behavior as they attempt to create their own spaces. However, the majority of users will look for camping alternatives outside of the park that have more amenities such as bathrooms, showers, grills, refreshment stands, convenience stores, recreation areas, and more. (Source: Kim Sinkhorn)**

trast, tools like planned scenic drives or tourist routes may be used to disperse tourists. These routes take people away from pressure points and spread them out over a wider area so as to not exceed the carrying capacity in one particular place.

Entry restrictions, pricing policies, and/or guiding may also be used to shape patterns of tourism within certain zones. General visitors may not be permitted in certain zones or only with guides. For example, Galápagos National Park is a highly attractive tourism destination but one that has a distinct need for controlling both tourist numbers and behavior. The park has an adult foreign tourist entrance fee of US$100, and all visitors are required to travel with a certified guide. Not only does this promote a high-quality visitor experience with interpretation of the islands' natural features, but it also ensures that park rules and regulations are enforced.

Similarly, **codes of conduct** have been proposed by governmental agencies, nongovernmental organizations (NGOs), tourism industry associations, and even entrepreneurs to help mitigate the negative effects of tourism. These codes may be targeted at any number of tourism stakeholders including the industry, the local community, and tourists themselves to inform patterns of behavior for the purpose of minimizing the negative effects of tourism. Codes of conduct have limitations in that they are seen as broad principles rather than specific policies. Their adoption is voluntary rather than mandated, and there is little means of monitoring practices to ensure that the codes are being upheld.

In one example, the well-known environmental NGO World Wildlife Federation (WWF) developed a set of codes specifically to minimize the negative environmental effects of tourism in the Mediterranean destination region. The overarching categories of their code of conduct for tourists include (1) support integration between environmental conservation and tourism development; (2) support the conservation of biodiversity; (3) use natural resources in a sustainable way; (4) minimize your environmental impact; (5) respect local cultures; (6) respect historic sites; (7) local communities should benefit from tourism; (8) choose a reputable tour operator involved in environmental protection with trained, professional staff; (9) make your trip an opportunity to learn about the Mediterranean; and (10) comply with regulations. Correspondingly, the categories for their code of conduct for the tourism industry (defined as tour operators, hotels and airlines) include (1) support integration between environmental conservation and tourism development; (2) support the conservation of biodiversity; (3) use natural resources in a sustainable way; (4) minimize consumption, waste, and pollution; (5) consider local cultures and attitudes; (6) respect historic sites; (7) provide benefits to local communities; (8) educate and train staff to support sustainable tourism; (9) ensure that tourism is educational; and (10) comply with regulations.[2]

The final concept that will be discussed here is sustainable development. Although this concept has a long history among conservation movements, its modern usage is credited to the 1987 *Report of the World Commission on Environment and Development: Our Common Future*, widely known as the Brundtland Report. The report defined **sustainable development** as "development that meets the needs of the present without compromising the ability of future generations to meet their own needs."[3] While this is the most commonly referenced definition, it is far from universally accepted. The idea has been criticized for its vagueness, and it is often interpreted in many different ways by various governmental agencies, NGOs, business interests, and researchers. Some of the strictest interpretations seek to limit most forms of development on the basis that sustainability and development are mutually exclusive. Other interpretations take a far more relaxed stance and seek to allow all but the most destructive forms of development. Moreover, the critics of sustainable development argue that it is merely an idea that lacks practical applications that would guide "sustainable" uses of the environment.

Even as the debate about the concept continues, sustainability and sustainable development have been used in a wide variety of contexts, including tourism. Applied to tourism, the Brundtland definition would indicate that sustainable tourism development would allow for the demands of present tourists to be met without eroding the tourism base that would reduce or prevent tourism in the future. In essence, tourism development needs to be sustainable development because it is highly dependent on the resources on which tourism is based. Some interpretations of **sustainable tourism** correspond with the concept of niche or alternative tourism because these forms of tourism are typically presented as an alternative to large-scale organized mass tourism. However, poorly planned and/or managed niche tourism can be highly unsustainable. At the same time, equating sustainable tourism with niche tourism implies that mass tourism cannot be undertaken sustainably.

Because sustainable tourism is not a tourism product—like those discussed in chapter 3—but rather an approach to tourism, it has the potential to be extended to all forms of tourism. In fact, it may be argued that it is particularly important for sustainable practices to be implemented at mass tourism destinations because of the potential for negative consequences to be magnified by the large scale at which tourism takes place. As with sustainable development in general, however, it is difficult to apply concepts of sustainable tourism. Similar to other concepts, such as codes of conduct, various public and private sector interests have proposed principles for sustainable tourism. Yet, there continues to be a distinct need for specific, place-based guidelines for these goals to be of practical use in tourism development.

# The Evolution of Destinations

The **tourist area life cycle** (TALC) model, sometimes also referred to as the resort life cycle, has been one of the most influential concepts throughout studies of tourism. This model was proposed over thirty years ago by a geographer, Richard Butler.[4] Ever since, it has been widely discussed and applied to cases of tourism development around the world. Butler has argued that there was (and perhaps still is) a need to challenge the prevailing ideal that once a place was established as a tourist destination, interest in and visits to it would be maintained indefinitely.[5] In reality, few destinations can remain unchanged over time. Tourism is a dynamic industry. Transportation innovations have increased the accessibility of places around the world, and new destinations are developing all the time. With greater freedom to explore new, different, and unknown destinations, modern tourists have less place loyalty. A destination that doesn't respond to market trends will be perceived as outdated and unfashionable. Consequently, it will lose competitiveness in this highly competitive industry.

As he was a geographer, Butler's initial idea focused on the spatial implications of growth and development of tourism destinations. Using concepts such as carrying capacity, he argued that there are limits to growth. A destination that doesn't manage its tourism resources in light of the demands being placed on it will experience a decline in quality. This leads to a corresponding decline in the quality of tourists' experience and ultimately a decline in tourist visits. The TALC model provides a means of thinking about the development and evolution of destinations over the course of a series of stages. It describes changes in the character of the destination as well as in the types of tourists visiting and the nature of the effects from tourism there.

The first stage in the model is exploration. In this stage, tourists begin to be attracted to the destination for its inherent physical and/or human resources. Therefore, the primary attractions are most likely to be natural or human (not originally intended for tourism). The first tourists to "discover" the destination are typically adventurous, most likely categorized at the drifter end of the spectrum. With only a small number of tourists, the effects of tourism—positive or negative—are generally minimal. Given both the undeveloped nature of the destination and the type of tourists visiting in this stage, however, there is often a high level of interaction between tourists and local people.

The second stage is involvement. Following the arrival of the first tourists, local people begin to recognize the demand for tourism and develop new facilities. Subsequently, the public sector may offer some support, such as infrastructure development. The new stakeholders may begin to advertise the destination to encourage visits. Consequently, the destination experiences an increase in tourist numbers, more of whom would be characterized as explorers, and characteristics of the tourism industry in that place, such as season, become clearer. In this stage, the destination may experience some of the positive economic, social, and environmental effects of tourism.

The third stage is development. The number of tourists continues to increase, and more development occurs. Control over the tourism industry begins to pass from small business owners and local offices to a national governmental agency and large-scale, possibly even multinational, companies. With this continued development, individual mass tourists may begin to arrive. In this stage, the destination begins to experience many changes and an increase in the negative effects of tourism. For example, leakages will likely increase, tensions may build between locals and outsiders, and the overuse of resources may become apparent.

The fourth stage is consolidation. The tourism industry has become firmly established in that place, and the destination has become characterized by major multinational chain hotels and restaurants. A distinct CTD has emerged with a dense concentration of infrastructure and activities. However, many of the earliest facilities have become dated and may need to be upgraded. Tourism is the main economic contributor at the destination. With organized mass tourists visiting the destination, numbers are at a high, but the rate of increase begins to slow. In order to attract new markets, the destination may undertake widespread promotional campaigns.

The fifth stage is stagnation. The original natural and/or human attractions have been replaced by human-designed and artificial attractions. Consequently, the tourist area becomes divorced from the character of the place in which it is situated. The infrastructure has continued to deteriorate, and it experiences greater economic, social, and/or environmental consequences from the tourism industry. Although it is well known, it suffers from a poor reputation. The peak in tourism has been reached, and thus major promotion efforts must be undertaken. In addition, substantial discounts may need to be offered to maintain visitor numbers; however, cheap vacation packages will attract a new demographic of tourist that will further discourage earlier generations of tourists from returning.

The sixth stage can consist of decline, stabilization, or rejuvenation, depending on the decisions of destination stakeholders. If no action is taken, the tourist area will enter a period of decline. It may be immediate and drastic or slow and prolonged, but tourists will move on to other, newer destinations. The area will receive a smaller number of tourists from a more limited geographic area for weekend or daytrips. However, if minor adjustments are made and/or efforts are undertaken to better protect tourism resources, the tourist area may stabilize or perhaps see a limited amount of growth. If significant redevelopment projects are undertaken, the area can rejuvenate. This will involve investment in new facilities or upgrading existing ones. It may also involve creating new (human-designed) attractions, finding new ways to utilize previously untapped natural or human (not designed) attractions, and/or trying to attract new markets. If successful, this will create a new wave of growth.

TALC was created to be a general model of the tourism process. While it was intended to be applicable to destinations in various contexts around the world, not all will progress through the stages in the same way. The model has been criticized as being descriptive in nature, meaning that it is most useful in describing the process of development after it has occurred. Indeed, it can be difficult to identify and analyze the stages of a destination's development as it is taking place. Nonetheless, it can be predictive in the sense that it identifies what will happen if destinations are not appropriately planned, developed, and managed from the beginning. Although the concept of sustainable development had not been established when this model was proposed, the two are very closely related. As with sustainable development, TALC requires the acceptance of limits to development and necessitates a long-term perspective to minimize the negative effects of tourism.

# Conclusion

Space is a fundamental concept in geography, and the spatial perspective offers valuable insight into patterns of tourism at destinations around the world. The spatial organization of a destination can play an extraordinarily important role in shaping the ways tourists experience that place (see chapter 13). Moreover, the spatial perspective provides an important basis for destination management strategies to maximize the benefits and minimize the costs of tourism identified in part III. These strategies are vital in maintaining the destination and, crucially, its reputation (see chapter 12). Ultimately, this will extend the destination's "life."

# Box 11.3.  Case Study: Atlantic City's Extended Life Cycle

Since it was first proposed, the TALC model has been applied in the context of destinations around the world. For example, the evolution of many of the first resorts (such as spas) to develop in Britain in the nineteenth century (see chapter 4) has been examined through the life cycle. Likewise, early American resorts could also be considered in this way. One of the most interesting, if perhaps extreme, examples has been the case of Atlantic City. This destination progressed through the stages of the life cycle and even appeared to have reached the end with decline. However, stakeholders were able to turn the final stage around, successfully rejuvenate the destination, and extend its life.

Atlantic City dates back to the mid-nineteenth century. By this time, there was an increasing demand for tourism experiences in the United States, and several resorts had already been developed. However, the location of these resorts was highly dependent on the available transportation and accessibility by water or overland carriage routes. The development of rail lines dramatically re-created patterns of tourism. Investors in the nation's growing rail infrastructure also became influential resort developers, as was the case for Atlantic City. A group of investors identified a demand for tourism from the large and growing cities, such as Philadelphia, and a site with resources for tourism development—a white sand beach, clean ocean water, and fresh air. Then, a rail line was constructed to link Philadelphia with the selected site. This new line was the shortest all-rail route from the city to the coast, which gave Atlantic City a distinct advantage over other coastal resorts.

Atlantic City was created to be a tourist resort based on the successful model of other early American resorts. It was located on a sparsely populated island with few economic activities. It was developed based on a combination of the natural attraction of the coast and the human-designed attractions, with a host of brand new hotel, restaurant, and entertainment facilities. Initially, the only available mode of transport to reach the destination was rail, which meant that tourists primarily walked at the destination. As such, the destination was highly spatially concentrated and oriented around pedestrian walkways. With the rapid development of infrastructure, stakeholders also worked to create a reputation for the destination. Although it was primarily a middle-class resort, it was promoted as a fashionable place that would be visited by the social elite. The resort continued to grow and reached a period of peak popularity in the early 1900s. During this time, it was widely known and boasted reputations such as "The Queen of the Jersey Shore" and "The World's Playground."

Beginning in the years following World War I, the destination began to experience a series of changes. It was becoming easier and cheaper for more of the lower socioeconomic classes to make daytrips to the resort. As more of these tourists arrived at the destination, new, cheap entertainments began to cater to their tastes. Families and the upper socioeconomic classes considered this vulgar. With increased mobility and the development of ever more destinations, many of these tourists looked elsewhere. As this market declined, little new investment was made in high-end facilities. In addition, rail services were eventually reduced, and more people were traveling by car. Yet, the destination was not designed for automobile traffic. There was limited space for parking, and given the physical location, it was unable to expand to accommodate this new development. More tourists chose to stay elsewhere and simply drive in for the day. As a result, they spent little money in the city.

*(continued)*

## Box 11.3.   *(continued)*

Atlantic City entered a period of stagnation, where the infrastructure deteriorated and the physical resources were degraded and polluted. Then, it finally entered decline with reduced visitor numbers. Given high vacancy rates, capacities were reduced as older hotels were demolished. With rising levels of unemployment—20 percent on average—residents who had the ability to look for new opportunities elsewhere did, and the city lost a quarter of its population. The remaining population typically consisted of minorities and the elderly; in some neighborhoods, as much as 80 percent of the population was over the age of 65. Poverty levels averaged nearly 10 percent for the county, with some of the hardest-hit areas seeing figures as high as 46 percent. The economy, social conditions, and the environment reached dismal conditions.

By the 1960s, Atlantic City desperately needed revitalization. Casino gambling was proposed as a last-ditch effort for what many considered to be a hopeless situation. While it was a highly contested issue, in 1976 New Jersey became only the second state to legalize gambling. It was hoped that the casino hotel industry would bring new capital to the resort, generate tax revenues for the state, create jobs, attract new tourists, revitalize the economy, and create a base for urban redevelopment. However, in two years' time, the city had only one casino license application. It appeared that other companies were waiting to see if the experiment would be successful. In an analysis of the resort's life cycle in 1978, geographer Charles Stansfield wrote, "Gambling may fail to be the universal panacea which its champions asserted it would offer."[1]

Yet, within fourteen years, twelve casinos accounting for a $5.3 billion investment had been developed. Whereas Atlantic City had once been seen as a summer destination, gambling increased visits year-round. This significantly reduced seasonal employment variations. An estimated fifty thousand jobs were created in the casinos and another fifty thousand in related industries. Income levels increased, and additional redevelopment efforts were undertaken. For a short time in the 1990s, Atlantic City reached a new high and was ranked as the country's most popular destination based on tourist visits. Receiving over 30 million visitors, it outstripped Las Vegas and Orlando. Over the past decade, several failed development projects and economic recession have indicated that the resort has entered another period of stagnation and uncertainty. Nonetheless, the redevelopment of Atlantic City has been considered one of the most successful examples of rejuvenation that few resorts could replicate.

*Discussion topic*: Why do you think gambling was such a successful rejuvenation strategy for Atlantic City? Do you think that other destinations would experience similar levels of success?

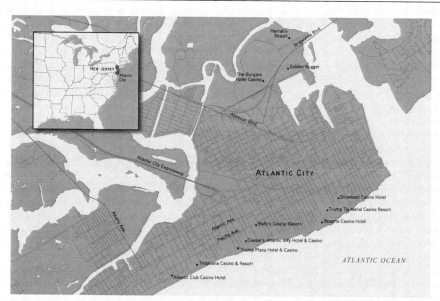

**Map 11.1.   Atlantic City, New Jersey. The success of this rejuvenated destination has primarily been based on casino development. (Source: XNR Productions)**

# Note

1. Charles Stansfield, "Atlantic City and the Resort Cycle: Background to the Legalization of Gambling," *Annals of Tourism Research* 5, no. 2 (1978): 250.

# Sources

Braunlich, Carl G. "Lessons from the Atlantic City Casino Experience." *Journal of Travel Research* 34 (1996): 46–56.

Butler, Richard. "The Tourist Area Life Cycle in the Twenty-First Century." In *A Companion to Tourism*, edited by Alan A. Lew, C. Michael Hall, and Allan M. Williams, 159–69. Malden, MA: Blackwell, 2004.

Stansfield, Charles. "The Rejuvenation of Atlantic City: The Resort Cycle Recycles." In *The Tourism Area Life Cycle*, vol. 1, *Applications and Modifications*, edited by Richard W. Butler, 287–305. Clevedon, UK: Channel View Publications, 2006.

# Key Terms

- back region
- code of conduct
- enclave tourism
- front region
- preferred sites

- spatial zoning
- sustainable development
- sustainable tourism
- tourist area life cycle

# Notes

1. Dean MacCannell, *The Tourist: A New Theory of the Leisure Class* (New York: Schocken Books, 1976; reprinted with foreword by Lucy R. Lippard, Berkeley: University of California Press, 1999).

2. Simone Borelli and Stefania Minestrini, "WWF Mediterranean Programme," accessed February 24, 2011, http://www.monachus-guardian.org/library/medpro01.pdf.

3. World Commission on Environment and Development, *Our Common Future*, accessed February 24, 2011, http://www.un-documents.net/wced-ocf.htm.

4. R. W. Butler, "The Concept of a Tourist Area Cycle Evolution: Implications for Management of Resources," *Canadian Geographer* 24, no. 1 (1980).

5. Richard Butler, "The Resort Cycle Two Decades On," in *Tourism in the 21st Century: Lessons from Experience*, edited by Bill Faulkner, Gianna Moscardo, and Eric Laws (London: Continuum, 2000), 288.

# Sources

Butler, R. W. "The Concept of a Tourist Area Cycle Evolution: Implications for Management of Resources." *Canadian Geographer* 24, no. 1 (1980): 5–12.

Butler, Richard. "The Resort Cycle Two Decades On." In *Tourism in the 21st Century: Lessons from Experience*, edited by Bill Faulkner, Gianna Moscardo, and Eric Laws, 284–299. London: Continuum, 2000.

———. "The Tourist Area Life Cycle in the Twenty-First Century." In *A Companion to Tourism*, edited by Alan A. Lew, C. Michael Hall, and Allan M. Williams, 159–169. Malden, MA: Blackwell, 2004.

Dove, Jane. *Access to Geography: Tourism and Recreation*. London: Hodder & Stoughton, 2004.

Lew, Alan, and Bob McKercher. "Modeling Tourist Movements: A Local Destination Analysis." *Annals of Tourism Research* 33 (2006): 403–23.

MacCannell, Dean. "Staged Authenticity: Arrangements of Social Space in Tourist Settings." *American Journal of Sociology* 79, no. 3 (1973): 589–603.

———. *The Tourist: A New Theory of the Leisure Class*. New York: Schocken Books, 1976. Reprinted with foreword by Lucy R. Lippard. Berkeley: University of California Press, 1999.

CHAPTER 12

# Tourism Representations of Place

"Beautiful beaches," "Spectacular sunsets," "Majestic mountains," "Fragrant flowers," "Colorful costumes"—clichéd though they are, these are frequently used tourism terminology to evoke vivid images of places in our minds. These ideas and images play an important role in shaping both our demand for and our experience of tourism destinations. In tourism studies, these issues are frequently approached from a marketing perspective. However, as places are the product to be sold in tourism, the geography of tourism is an equally relevant framework.

Place is a way of understanding the world. It refers to the parts of the earth that have been given meaning. These meanings come from a variety of sources. For example, they can be a product of the cultural preferences and values of a particular group of people at a specific point in time. In the historical geography of tourism (chapter 4), we saw that early generations of tourists perceived mountains as dark and dangerous places, to be feared and avoided if possible. Yet, as pervasive and enduring as the meanings associated with places can be, they do change over time. In this case, ideas about mountainous environments were gradually revised, partially as a result of technological advances that made travel in these places easier and safer. Equally as important, however, was the popularization of new aesthetic concepts, such as the sublime, that allowed people to appreciate these places in different ways. As such, media representations can be extraordinarily important in shaping the meanings associated with places. While these meanings are often created indirectly through media (e.g., popular literature or film), they may also be explicitly produced through the practice of place promotion.

In this chapter, we will examine the representation of places. This describes the ways places are summarized and portrayed to an audience that then creates ideas and images about those places. This has implications for our discussion of the geography of tourism, as these ideas and images factor into tourists' decisions to visit a place and shape their expectations for their experiences there. The first part of the chapter introduces concepts associated with the representation of places in tourism, while the second part provides a brief discussion of the types of media that contribute to our ideas about places and our expectations for tourism experiences in those places.

243

Finally, the chapter concludes by examining some of the consequences of representations of place in tourism.

# Representations of Place and Place Promotion

Our understanding of places to which we have never been is shaped by the ways they are represented through media. The proliferation of media allows more places to be "experienced" than ever before. In fact, there are few parts of the world that we have not been exposed to in one form or another and therefore have an impression of what we think that place is like. Yet, representations cannot replace direct experience. It may be easy to take these representations at face value as accurate portrayals of reality, especially visual representations such as photographs and videos. However, as vivid as these images may be, they are nonetheless partial and selective. The audience becomes a passive observer who sees only what someone else has chosen.

One of the most prominent scholars on the geography of place, Edward Relph, criticized media representations of place, particularly advertising and promotion. He argued that these representations create superficial ideas of places based on simplified, recognizable, perhaps even exaggerated concepts that may be readily accepted by an external audience; they do little to convey the sense of place that can only be obtained through direct experience.[1] Yet, representations of place are recognized to be extraordinarily important in tourism. As put by tourism scholar Dean MacCannell, "Usually, the first contact a sightseer has with a sight is not the sight itself but with some representation thereof."[2]

Not all representations of place are innocent or incidental. Some are deliberately created with specific meanings to "sell" a place to potential tourists. Tourism is a highly competitive global industry; therefore, the success of modern tourism destinations depends on the creation and promotion of clear and ultimately distinctive ideas. **Place promotion** is the deliberate use of marketing tools to communicate specific and selective ideas and images about a place to a target audience for the purpose of shaping perceptions of that place and ultimately influencing decisions. It is a form of advertising and can be deceptive. Because place promotion draws selectively upon the real nature of places and presents only those elements that will appeal to the target market segment, there may be many different representations of a destination. Each representation will highlight a different aspect of the destination, draw upon a different theme, and utilize different images to attract specific types of tourists.

Not all destinations use place promotion in the same way. For many of the world's largest tourism destinations—such as France, the United States, or Australia—there is little need to promote the destination as a whole. Ideas about these places already abound in representations, and there is a preexisting suppressed demand (i.e., many people already believe they want to visit these places if/when they have the opportunity). It may be more important that these destinations promote specific regions or places, as tourists are likely to only visit a part of the country during their trip. This can help provide more detailed information about the unique resources and experiences available in different places. In contrast, place promotion is especially important for those destinations about which little is known, those that might have a less-than-favorable reputation, or those that are perceived to be similar to other destinations. In these cases, place promotion becomes the primary means of shaping what is known and perceived to be important about the destination.

Poorly known destinations—often new or remote destinations—are perhaps the easiest to promote. Essentially, potential tourists have few ideas about these places to begin with, and therefore there is greater leverage for creativity in crafting promotional strategies that will shape tourists' ideas about a place. In contrast, destinations that have a negative image are the hardest to promote. Deserved or not, a poor reputation in the minds of potential tourists can be extraordinarily hard to overcome. A poor reputation may be based on serious past or present issues or events in the country or region of the country, including conflicts, political upheaval, acts of terrorism, human rights violations and/or atrocities, problems associated with the drug trade, crimes against tourists, and so on. Likewise, a poor reputation may be based on the destination's tourism industry, such as a poorly developed infrastructure, an unfriendly or hostile local population, and even an overdevelopment of tourism in which mass commercialization supplants the local character of the place or the sheer volume of tourists overwhelms the experience of place. Some destinations attempt to ignore the issue entirely in the creation of a new identity, while others choose to address it head-on in their promotions to show that it has been resolved.

Destinations perceived to be similar to others present a challenge for place promotion, but this problem can be more easily overcome. The Caribbean is one such example. People often see the islands of the region as a collective, and the fact that they have at times acted cooperatively to strengthen their position on the global market contributes to this perception. However, this becomes a problem when potential tourists think one island is the same as another. This not only affects the choice of specific destination but may also serve to discourage these tourists from returning and visiting another island because they think they have already had the "Caribbean experience." Consequently, each island tries to create and promote a distinctive place identity that plays up the resources that make them unique. Grenada has drawn upon its long-standing agricultural industry that produces nutmeg, ginger, and cinnamon to identify itself as "the spice isle." Trinidad is known for hosting the biggest annual party in the region: its Carnival. One of the islands containing two countries—Dutch St. Maarten and French St. Martin—capitalizes on the idea of two destinations in one with the slogan "twice the vacation, twice the fun."

Destination slogans or "taglines" such as these are used to condense the idea of the place represented to tourists into a short, memorable phrase. While these might be easily dismissed as superficial marketing ploys, they play a role in the promotion of a place identity. In fact, the ideas conveyed in a slogan can be so important that they may become controversial. For example, in 1991, the newly created country of Slovenia was relatively unknown and needed to create a place identity for the purpose of stimulating tourism. Not only did Slovenia need to create a positive place identity for itself, but the country also needed to distance itself from the violence of the independence wars among the other Yugoslav states. As such, Slovenia adopted the slogan "The sunny side of the Alps" to capitalize on both the country's physical resources for tourism—particularly the

# Box 12.1.  Case Study: The Re-Creation of Croatia's Tourism Industry

Croatia's long Adriatic coast has an extensive history of tourism, from the development of fashionable seaside resorts in the mid-nineteenth century to the rise of mass 3S tourism in the mid-twentieth. During the late Yugoslav era, Croatia was inundated with over 10 million tourists a year, primarily from the other countries of Europe. However, the industry was devastated by the outbreak of war following Croatia's declaration of independence in 1991.

Despite any lingering effects of travel advisories and a "war-torn" image, the Croatian tourism industry made a complete recovery in ten years' time. By 2005, the number of international tourist arrivals once again reached 10 million. In the following year, *National Geographic Adventure Magazine* named Croatia "Destination of the Year." This exceptional recovery is at least partially attributable to a strategic and aggressive postwar promotional campaign to re-create the country's international image and identity. Given Croatia's legacy of tourism, the first step was to recapture the European market. Already familiar with the destination, these tourists just needed to be reassured that security had been restored and the quality of the tourism product had not been diminished.

The second step was to target new markets. This required creating distance from the Eastern European and Balkans regions, which were considered backward and unstable; this was achieved by disengaging from conflict and emphasizing historical connections and similarities to the countries of Western Europe. These efforts were aided by poor geographic literacy and a poor understanding of the Yugoslav conflicts in much of the world. Specifically, the Mediterranean became the focal point of the country's place promotion. Not only have Croatia's tourism offerings long been concentrated along the coast, but the Mediterranean is considered a "known quantity" with positive connotations. Based on this, the Croatian National Tourist Board created the tourism slogan "The Mediterranean As It Once Was."

*Discussion topic*: What are the strengths and weaknesses of "The Mediterranean As It Once Was" as a slogan for place promotion?

*Tourism on the web*: Croatian National Tourist Board, "Croatia," at http://croatia.hr/en-GB/Homepage

**Figure 12.1. The seaside town of Opatija in Croatia's Istrian Peninsula was once a popular tourist resort for the nobility in the Austro-Hungarian Empire. This is part of the legacy that the country draws on in its tourism industry today. (Source: Renata Grbac Žiković)**

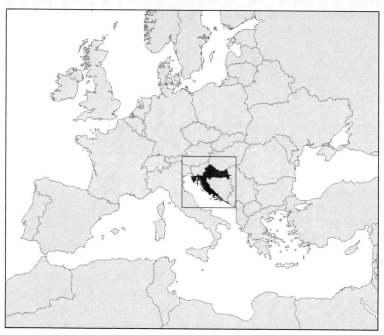

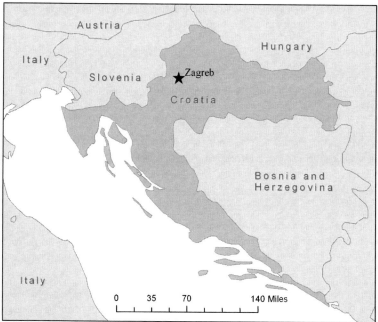

**Map 12.1. Croatia. This European destination promotes itself as "the Mediterranean as it once was." (Source: Gang Gong)**

# Sources

Hall, Derek. "Brand Development, Tourism, and National Identity: The Re-Imaging of Former Yugoslavia." *Brand Management* 9 (2002): 323–34.

Rivera, Lauren A. "Managing 'Spoiled' National Identity: War, Tourism, and Memory in Croatia." *American Sociological Review* 73 (2008): 613–34.

attractive destinations in the Julian Alps—and the preexisting positive tourism imagery associated with the larger Alpine region. However, Italy objected to this slogan and the perceived implication that, as Slovenia's neighbor, it was not physically and/or meta-phorically "sunny." Consequently, Slovenia was forced to abandon the slogan.

Additionally, tourism is an extremely visual phenomenon. Given the old adage "A picture is worth a thousand words," images are often considered the most impor-tant aspect of promotions. These representations are powerful in instantly creating an impression of a place in the viewer's mind. In fact, it has been argued that the image of a destination plays a key role in potential tourists' decision-making process.[3] Early tourism imagery included illustrations and black-and-white photographs; today it is dominated by vivid full-color photographs and video files. These images depict char-acteristics of the place, including attractive landscape vistas and iconic scenes, as well as tourists participating in activities and enjoying themselves there—such as relaxing on the beach, hiking in the forest, or dining at sunset.

There are some very obvious and standardized messages conveyed in place promo-tion (e.g., fun or relaxation), but there are also subtler messages embedded in them as well. A number of key themes are used to convey ideas about places, generate interest, and play upon potential tourist motivations for travel. These themes include excite-ment and adventure, tradition and timelessness, fantasy and romance, pristine and unspoiled, or exotic and different.

One of the most common tourism representations of place is an empty natural landscape—such as a deserted beach or an undisturbed forest—without people or evi-dence of people. This emphasizes the naturalness and authenticity of the destination; it implies an earlier time, when life was slower, simpler, and people had a closer con-nection to their environment. As such, it is targeted at tourists who live in places with the opposite character: namely, overcrowded urban areas with the fast pace of modern life. While this has typically been intended for the traditional major tourist-generating regions of northeastern North America and Northwestern Europe, it can now also apply to the emerging generating regions in parts of East and South Asia. Clearly, this plays upon the tourist inversions discussed in chapter 2 in terms of creating a sense of contrast with those places and activities that make up tourists' daily lives.

Moreover, this type of representation invites potential tourists to imagine them-selves in that place. The setting is provided and some suggestions might be made about what could be done there, but everything else is left open. This allows viewers to tap into their own dreams and desires and fill in what they want from the experience. This helps create a demand for the imagined experience and encourages tourists to visit that place for the purpose of turning fantasy into reality.

Representations clearly play an important role in shaping ideas about a destination and attracting visitors. Accordingly, destinations at all geographic scales are concerned with these issues. Tourism boards or convention and visitors' bureaus (e.g., Chicago Convention and Tourism Bureau) may be responsible for a local destination's image. Large destinations may have state- or regional-level agencies (e.g., Tourism Western Australia), while most countries now have some type of national tourism organization or association (e.g., Tourism Authority of Thailand). These organizations typically concentrate on creating a national tourism brand identity that can be promoted to an external or foreign audience, although there may be efforts to promote domestic tourism as well. In some cases, small and/or relatively similar destinations may work cooperatively through regional (supranational) tourism organizations to promote a specific destination region (e.g., Caribbean Tourism Organization, open to any country with a Caribbean coast; Walk My Alps, consisting of Austria, France, Germany, Italy, and Switzerland). The resources available for place promotion vary widely based on the size of the destination, level of overall economic development, and the extent to which tourism development is a priority.

# Types of Representations

As long as people have traveled, they have represented the places they experienced through written descriptions and visual illustrations. These representations have proliferated exponentially since those times, as all parts of the world have become more accessible, more people have had the opportunity to travel, and new forms of media have allowed us to vicariously experience places in a multitude of ways. Many of these representations have no overt connection to tourism and are not explicitly intended to encourage visitation to the place depicted. Yet, these representations must be considered alongside the less ambiguous promotional representations. Both have the potential to create distinct impressions of places in the minds of their audience, which factors into demand for travel as well as destination choice. Moreover, there may be an explicit relationship between popular media and place promotion. A film may highlight a place as a means of advertising, similar to product placement, or a place may draw upon popular literary, film, or even music references in its promotions.

## POPULAR MEDIA

Literature—including plays, poetry, and prose—was one of the earliest representations of other places to popular audiences. This medium has been credited with creating some of the powerful ideas of places discussed above. For example, far-off and exotic tropical islands frequently played an integral role in literature, not only providing the setting but also distinctly shaping the events of the story. William Shakespeare's *The Tempest* (early seventeenth century) was written at a time in which reports were coming back from parts of the world that were being "discovered," and his story contributed to the mythology of these places. Although it is unclear whether the setting for the play is an island off the coast of Africa or in the Caribbean, the specific location is less important than the idea of the place represented to audiences who would never have any direct experience with the tropical island environment. These ideas have persisted over time in works such as *Robinson Crusoe* (Daniel Defoe, 1719), *Treasure Island* (Robert Louis Stevenson, 1883), and *Lord of the Flies* (William Golding, 1954). Although these novels may not be read as widely as they were in the past, the stories and themes nonetheless remain familiar to us today. In fact, they are often updated and given modern twists, such as in Alex Garland's *The Beach* (1996).

Literature has also played a role in shaping ideas about distinct places, and consequently in creating a demand for experiences there. For example, the Lake Poets (i.e., William Wordsworth, Samuel Coleridge, and Robert Southey) played an instrumental role in popularizing England's Lake District during the time period in which domestic tourism was expanding. In particular, Wordsworth's poetry is considered to be intimately connected to the region. Having lived most of his life among the lakes, he was often inspired by the landscape, which was represented in his work. In one of his most well-known works, "I Wandered Lonely As a Cloud" (1804), he reflected on a sight he encountered along Ullswater Lake. The readers of such works often became interested in experiencing these places for themselves, and new developments in tourism at the time, such as the railroad, increasingly allowed them to do so. Similarly, in the American context, authors such as Washington Irving and James Fenimore Cooper helped popularize the Hudson River Valley. Also at a time in which tourism was developing in the region, stories such as Irving's "Rip Van Winkle" (1819) and Cooper's *Last of the Mohicans* (1826) described real places that their readers might know or be able to experience for themselves.

Literature continues to represent places and shape ideas of them. Indeed, many avid readers will argue that written descriptions constitute some of the most powerful conceptions of place because they work in concert with their imagination. However, the rise of visual media has, to some extent, superseded the importance of literature. While novels still represent places, it is often the film adaptations of those novels that reach the widest audience. That the visual is extraordinarily important is evidenced by the fact that new versions of such novels are produced with images from the film replacing the original cover art. In the example of Alex Garland's *The Beach* discussed above, the novel was a best seller in Europe but had relatively little impact on the American market. Yet, the story is widely known today among American audiences from the movie version starring Leonardo DiCaprio (2000). After more than a decade, the film continues to inspire tourism, and rather than seeking the places that might have inspired Garland to write the story, tourists have flocked to the place in which the movie was filmed (figure 12.2).

In addition to influencing the way we think about places, films may also encourage or discourage us from visiting these places for ourselves. This has become such an important representation that tourism promoters will often seek to capitalize on the publicity that films generate. For example, following the release of Baz Lurhman's film *Australia* (2008), the country's national and regional tourism associations began to use the film images of Australian actors Nicole Kidman and Hugh Jackman in their promotions.

In some cases, the place plays such an important role in the film that tourists seek to re-create the characters' experiences by visiting featured sites. For example, visitors to New York City often seek out iconic spots such Tiffany & Co., prominently featured in the classic *Breakfast at Tiffany's* (1961), or Katz's Deli, made famous by Meg Ryan's "I'll have what she's having" scene in *When Harry Met Sally* (1989). In other cases, epic films highlighting dramatic landscape scenery often create a demand for experiences in such places, even though tourists do not expect to replicate the experiences of the film. The *Lord of the Rings* trilogy, for example, stimulated a demand for

**Figure 12.2.   Maya Bay, on Thailand's Phi Phi Leh Island, served as one of the film locations for _The Beach_. Even the official tourism website for the province (Krabi Tourism, "Maya Bay, Krabi—Thailand," accessed May 25, 2011, http:// www.krabi-tourism.com/phiphi/maya-bay.htm) cites the "horde of day-trippers" who now flock to the once unknown beach. (Source: Wesley Mills.)**

tourism to New Zealand based on the unique natural landscapes that provided the setting for the action of the film.

Interestingly, movies can also create an interest in and demand for tourism in a place, even when the movie was not actually filmed at that location. For example, _The Last Samurai_ (2003) highlights attractive scenes from the Japanese countryside but was actually filmed in New Zealand. Parts of the first three _Pirates of the Caribbean_ movies were filmed on islands in the region and contributed to the already powerful imagery of the tropical island theme. Yet, the fourth installment was, in fact, not filmed in the region but in Hawaii. However, as with _The Tempest_, the actual location of the tropical island in the film becomes less important than the ideas created about the place, and the title of the series continues to promote the Caribbean regardless.

At the same time, an unflattering representation of a place in a film can change viewers' ideas of that place and convince them they have no desire to visit. Such movies often portray tourists getting caught up in a violent local conflict (e.g., _Beyond Rangoon_ [1995], in which an American tourist finds herself in the middle of Burma's 1988 uprising) or finding themselves—deservedly or not—stuck in the miserable conditions of a foreign prison (e.g., _Brokedown Palace_ [1999], in which a pair of young

American tourists are accused of drug smuggling and imprisoned in Thailand). In other examples, the stark portrayal of a place in a film might contrast with generally glorified representations of that place. For example, Paris is typically associated with romantic imagery of lovers walking down the historic boulevards or kissing on a bridge over the Seine. However, the action film *Taken* (2009) shows a much darker side of the city—and a much scarier idea of traveling abroad—when the young American tourists are kidnapped to be sold in the sex trade.

Serialized television shows can serve a similar purpose in creating ideas about general place types, such as the tropical island theme re-created in the fantasy series *Lost*, as well as specific places, such as New York City scenes featured in the rom-com series *Sex and the City*. While these shows may not be the primary motivation for tourists to visit that particular place, they still may shape patterns of tourism. In the case of Hawaii, regular viewers of *Lost* might visit show film locations, such as the beach containing the "wreckage" of Oceanic flight 815. In the case of New York City, viewers might seek the places frequented by *Sex and the City* girls, including the building shown as Carrie's apartment, the Jimmy Choo boutique, or Magnolia Bakery.

Finally, travel-themed television programs blur the boundaries between these types of popular media, the more specific travel-related media, and explicit place promotions. For example, Rick Steves' *Best of Europe* series highlights different aspects of destinations throughout the region and is essentially a visual representation of the type of information that is included in his tourist guidebooks. In addition, the Travel Channel hosts many programs that have become increasingly specialized to focus on certain components of destinations, such as food in Andrew Zimmern's *Bizarre Foods*. Although most shows are primarily intended for entertainment purposes, there may also be an instructive aspect in which prospective travelers to the featured destination might be able to use the programs to help them plan their own trip.

Representations of place in any of these media have the potential to create a demand for tourism. However, much of the audience for these media will not have the opportunity to visit the places represented and will therefore only experience them vicariously through representations. As such, this will contribute to the creation of suppressed demand (see chapter 2).

## TRAVEL LITERATURE

Few written records have been preserved from the earliest eras of travel; however, starting with the Age of Exploration in the Elizabethan Era, explorers and adventurers kept logs and journals of their journeys, some of which were later published. This practice continued with the next wave of scientific travelers. In fact, their "authority" was often contingent upon their published accounts of the places they visited. The primary purpose of published travel journals was to convey information and descriptions about the new places being explored. One of the most well-known examples of this type of account is Charles Darwin's *The Voyage of the Beagle: Journal of Researches into the Natural History and Geology of the Countries Visited During the Voyage of H.M.S. Beagle Round the World* (1839). In this text, Darwin described the geography, geology, biology, and anthropology of the places that he visited, including Brazil, the Galápagos Islands, New Zealand, Madagascar, and St. Helena.

As travel and tourism continued to evolve, a new type of text also evolved, with elements of other genres. Travel literature might include the "objective" descriptions of earlier scientific accounts, as well as stories reminiscent of the adventure novels discussed above, and the advice found in the tourist guidebooks that also emerged in the early nineteenth century. Travelogues became a popular genre of English-language literature at this time, particularly in England but also in the United States.

Some of the first examples of travel literature came from established authors of both fiction and nonfiction, including the likes of James Fenimore Cooper, Charles Dickens, Henry James, Robert Louis Stevenson, and Mark Twain. The well-known writers of this period had the time and the means to travel when both were still scarce for much of the population. They also had connections with publishing houses and were household names that would generate interest in and ultimately sell their books. Such writers sought out new places to experience and were among the first tourists to visit these places. Still intended to be informative about other places, these books were also clearly written to be entertaining. They helped fulfill readers' sense of adventure and satisfy their curiosity about places they might not have the opportunity to visit themselves.

Yet, these narratives were also extraordinarily influential in generating new attitudes toward travel. The written accounts of early tourists' journeys were one of the first ways in which the majority of the population was exposed to the idea of travel for pleasure, which helped tourism to come to be seen as a normal activity. As tourism began to open up to a wider market, these written accounts of what other places were like encouraged travel. Although not strictly intended to be promotional, they had the power to influence what destinations tourists chose, what activities they participated in, and what expectations they had for their experiences.

For example, during the prolific career of Anthony Trollope, one of the Victorian Era's most recognized English novelists, he also wrote travel narratives based on his experiences across the Americas, Australia and New Zealand, Africa, and Iceland. He described the places he encountered and his experiences—good and bad—with these places. His personal writing style gave readers the impression he was speaking directly to them as they planned a (real or imagined) trip of their own. In *Central & South America with the West Indies* (1858), Trollope wrote the following about hiking in the Blue Mountains of Jamaica to view the sunrise: "As for the true ascent—the nasty, damp, dirty, slippery, boot-destroying, shin-breaking, veritable mountain! Let me recommend my friends to let it alone."[4] After publication, this work was frequently cited in other books on the region. In particular, one of the early published travel guides, *The Pocket Guide to the West Indies* (1910), cited Trollope's narrative as one of the "volumes which, in the opinion of the writer, should prove most useful and interesting to those contemplating a visit to the West Indies."[5]

With this precedent, the new generations of tourists who traveled for pleasure also wrote letters, kept journals, and made sketches over the course of their journey, for their own record as well as for the purpose of publishing their own travel narrative. As a result, these books were increasingly written by tourists for other tourists. Because the places visited were becoming more familiar to readers, there was less need for these writers to provide the same extent of detailed descriptive information. Instead, they gave greater emphasis to their *experience* of place. As writers highlighted the specific sights they saw and provided advice based on what they did, potential tourists could essentially follow the itineraries that had been laid out by those who went before them.

At the same time, publishing companies began to produce explicit guidebooks to cater to the burgeoning tourist market. At the forefront of this industry, Thomas Cook began to put together a guidebook for his expeditions to describe the places that would be encountered and the sights seen during the course of the journey. On this side of the Atlantic, Gideon Minor Davison has been credited with producing the first American guidebook. It described a specific route—termed the "fashionable tour"— that Davison intended readers to follow. One of the unique characteristics of this new book, however, was that it was small and cheaply printed. As such, it was intended to be portable for the duration of the trip and disposable after the trip was completed.[6]

By the late nineteenth century, magazines were publishing not only special articles by travel writers but also dedicated travel columns that also provided advice to potential tourists. For example, the British women's magazine *Queen* was one of the first to make "The Tourist" a featured column. As travel was just starting to become more accessible to women, many were uncertain about what to expect from their first experience, especially in foreign countries. The column offered practical advice on travel arrangements, suitable accommodations, expected patterns of dress, and etiquette, among other topics. This was intended to give women the confidence to travel and the ability to experience new places with pleasure rather than fear or anxiety.[7]

The lines between this travel literature and early place promotion began to blur as some of the first tourism industry stakeholders began to "sponsor" writers. Railroad or steamship companies would hire writers to undertake trips or provide them with complimentary trips using their services, which the tourists would then write about. For example, in the preface to the travel narrative *Back to Sunny Seas* (1905), Frank Bullen wrote:

> But I want to make it perfectly clear that I was the guest of the great Royal Mail Steam Packet Company, whose hospitality to me was more generous and farther-reaching than I could ever have dreamed of receiving. Yet I would like to make it clear too, if possible, that I have subdued my natural bias in favour of the Company, so that I have written only what I believe to be literally and exactly true.[8]

These companies were interested in creating and maintaining demand for their services. To some extent, that also meant creating and maintaining a demand for experiences in the places that they served. As the tourism industry continued to grow and destinations began to compete for tourists, they, too, began to offer incentives for authors to visit and write about their places.

Travel writing has continued to evolve, with new trends in both tourism and media. As a genre of literature, travel writing has experienced a marked decline since its rise to popularity in the nineteenth century. Of course, this may at least partially be attributed to the same reasons literature in general has experienced declining readership. Nonetheless, narratives of travel continue to comprise a small section in most bookstores, typically alongside the now more prolific guidebooks. These stories are still written by established authors, such as V. S. Naipaul, recipient of the Nobel Prize for Literature (e.g., *A Turn in the South*, 1989), and recently by other well-known personalities as well, such as chef and Travel Channel host Anthony Bourdain (e.g., *No Reservations: Around the World on an Empty Stomach*, 2007). As in the past, these individuals are more likely to have the flexibility and the means to undertake the extensive trips to unusual places that become the subject of such books. In fact, some of the most widely known travel writing today is based on the type of extended stays in a place that stretch the limits of the definition of tourism, such as *A Year in Provence* (Peter Mayle, 1989) or *Under the Tuscan Sun: At Home in Italy* (Frances Mayes, 1996). The primary function of these books is entertainment; the instructive function of these books has all but disappeared, as few readers would have the ability or the interest to replicate the writers' experiences.

The more typical experience of modern tourism does not lend itself as well to travel writing. The majority of tourists travel to prominent destinations visited by thousands if not millions of other tourists each year. Although more people are able to participate in tourism than ever before, their trips are of a far shorter duration than earlier generations of tourists. Americans, for example, receive an average of two weeks' vacation time per year, and few take a single trip for that duration. Given the extent of information about the places visited and the compressed time frame, modern tourists have fewer opportunities for extensive noteworthy experiences. No one writes letters to family and friends back home during these trips; few tourists even send postcards, which notoriously arrive well after the tourists' return. Instead, with increased access to the Internet, even at many foreign destinations, some tourists choose to transmit a few of their experiences or pictures in the far more ephemeral e-mail or post on a social networking site.

Yet, today's amateur writers are nonetheless able to find an outlet for the stories of their travels on the web. With the proliferation of blogs on every subject imaginable, travel blogs have become a popular option for individuals to share their experiences. This can be seen on any general blog hosting site as well as the specialized TravelBlog, which in January 2012 boasted over 200,000 members and an average of 100 new members a day.[9] While many of these are intended to keep family and friends up-to-date on the traveler's activities, they are publicly available (figure 12.3). As a result, these sites are often encountered through keyword searches and therefore become part of the representations of a place that make up a potential tourist's pre-trip information search.

Guidebooks, which appear to be one source that has experienced relatively few changes, continue to be an extraordinarily popular source of information for tourists. Most destinations are now covered—at least within a region—while some of the most popular destinations have a tremendous selection of guides from companies such as Baedeker's, Fodor's, Frommer's, Insight Guides, Lonely Planet, Michelin Green Guides, Rick Steves, and Rough Guides. Although these companies also maintain some online content for pre-trip planning, websites have not replaced the books themselves. That guidebooks are still used as a portable reference during the course of a trip is easily seen at any major destination.

**Figure 12.3. Florinda Klevisser created this blog to keep her friends and family updated during the course of a three-month-long trip. Upon her return home, she used this blog as a basis for writing a travel narrative, published in her native Italian, called *Viaggia Con Me*. (Source: Florinda Klevisser)**

## PLACE PROMOTION

At least initially, tourism stakeholders relied on travelers' written accounts and word of mouth to promote both places and the services that would allow people to get to those places. Throughout much of the nineteenth century, rail companies in Britain did relatively little to advertise their services or the places they served. However, their American counterparts more quickly realized the value of generating tourism for the purpose of creating a steady market for the places they served. These companies, and later the British ones, produced abundant information and advertised in newspapers and magazines.

Both of these patterns were perpetuated in the twentieth century. Travel service companies—also including airlines by this time—and national/regional tourism organizations continued to produce pamphlets, brochures, and magazines to highlight the specific attractions of the destination(s). These materials could be distributed to potential tourists by mail (through targeted marketing or by request) or through travel agencies. In addition, these stakeholders continued to adapt to new forms of media by using television advertisements as well. To some extent, television advertising is still used, often by specific destinations or resorts. For example, starting in 2009, the California Travel and Tourism Commission began to run a series of "Life in California" television ads featuring a host of celebrities ranging from Jason Mraz to Kim Kardashian, David Beckham, and Betty White.

In today's world, the Internet has become the most important medium for place promotion. Although Internet access is still not evenly distributed around the world, the areas that continue to have the least access are the poorest places, which export relatively few tourists. For the major tourist-generating regions, the Internet has quickly become the way in which the majority of people learn about a destination, book their travel arrangements, and form expectations for their experiences. It is sometimes argued that electronic media will not entirely replace print media for this purpose, and some types of information will continue to be made available at the point of consumption (e.g., the destination). It is still typically necessary for tourists to have access to printed information during the course of the trip; yet, the dramatic rise of smartphones and other portable electronic devices with Internet capabilities, e-reader functions, and apps for just about everything may ultimately change this in the future.

The destination website, typically produced by national tourism organizations, has become a particularly important source for place promotion. This has largely superseded the role of destination magazines or brochures in raising awareness, providing information, and creating a demand for tourism to that place. Websites are considered to be more accessible than print media in that they have the potential to reach a much wider audience. They are also more flexible since they have the ability to provide a greater quantity of information and more options for the viewer to customize the information to his or her interests. Websites offer a greater quantity and variety of media, including more images as well as sound and video files. In addition, the Internet now also hosts sites for specific hotels and resorts (e.g., Sandals.com), tour packages (e.g., VikingRiverCruises.com), various types of tourism experiences (e.g., SkyAdventures.travel), travel booking sites (e.g., Expedia.com or Vayama.com), and travel review sites (e.g., TripAdvisor.com or VirtualTourist.com).

# Consequences of Representing Places in Tourism

Representations of place can be extraordinarily powerful, and they can have distinct if not always intended consequences. These are not accurate portrayals of reality but partial and selective ideas about places. Typically intended for an external audience, place promotion is sometimes criticized for creating superficial ideas about a place that have little to do with reality or the meanings that place has for the people who live there. Tourism promotions naturally represent places as something to be experienced and enjoyed by tourists. As such, aspects of the place, including its people, may be objectified as they are essentially turned into an attraction for tourists. The idea of place as playground discounts the daily activities, lifestyles, and livelihood patterns of local people. Moreover, place promotions that represent places without people or nontourist activities can reinforce the segregation of local people and tourists. For example, the destination may prevent residents from undertaking activities in a place to ensure that the "natural" condition of the site that is used to attract tourists is maintained for their pleasure.

# Box 12.2. In-Depth: The Cycle of Expectation in Caribbean Tourism Representations

Today, any reference to the Caribbean is likely to conjure up certain images: bright sunny skies, clear turquoise waters, soft white sands, and lush green palm trees gently swaying in the breeze. This is the ubiquitous imagery that populates the place promotions across the region's island destinations. Yet, these images associated with the modern tourism industry are hardly new. In fact, they have a long history that can be traced back to an earlier era of tourism in the region and the representations of the islands produced by the first generations of tourists.

As the Caribbean was one of the first colonial regions in the era of Western European colonialism, explorers, scientists, and plantation owners had long produced information about the region. However, it was not until the end of the Napoleonic Wars in 1815 that the Caribbean came to be seen as a potential tourism destination. At this time, the region was relatively free from conflict, largely devoid of a hostile native population, and increasingly accessible by transatlantic steamship routes. Many of the first tourists to the islands made sketches of the scenes they saw and kept journals of the experiences they had. Then, as tourism continued to increase, subsequent tourists relied on the accounts of those who had gone before them. They prepared for a journey by reading the available literature and even took these books along for reference. Thus, they already had an idea in their mind of the places they were going to see before they arrived. For the most part, they found that their own experiences lived up to their expectations, and they perpetuated these ideas in their own travel narratives.

Ultimately a circular relationship evolved between representations of place and experiences of place: representations created preconceived ideas and images of the places to be visited; experiences in places tested those preconceptions. Because tourists generally felt that the experience lived up to their expectations, these ideas and images were reaffirmed and perpetuated through successive generations of tourists. As a result, traces of the past may be seen in modern representations of tourism in the Caribbean. Certainly the nature of these representations has changed over time, but the legacy is nonetheless clearly seen. For example, in 1869, English historian and novelist Charles Kingsley wrote of Dominica, "The whole island, from peak to shore, seems some glorious jewel—an emerald with tints of sapphire and topaz, hanging between blue sea and white surf below, and blue sky and white cloud above."[1] In 2002, the Caribbean Tourism Organization's annual publication described St. Lucia as "a brilliant green jewel in the blue Caribbean . . . from the Pitons' majestic twin peaks rising above the southeast coast, to Mt. Gimie—the island's highest point—to its miles of pristine beach. . . ."[2] Although early visual representations were charcoal sketches, pen-and-ink drawings, or black-and-white photographs, similar scenes are depicted in glossy color photographs of today (figures 12.4 and 12.5).

*Discussion topic*: Why do you think the same ideas and images are as effective in place promotion today as they were in the past?

## Notes

1. Charles Kingsley, *At Last: A Christmas in the West Indies* (New York: Harper & Brothers Publishers, 1871), 57.
2. Caribbean Tourism Organization, *Caribbean Vacation Planner* (Coral Gables, FL: Gold Book, 2002), 53.

## Source

Nelson, Velvet. "Traces of the Past: The Cycle of Expectation in Caribbean Tourism Representations." *Journal of Tourism and Cultural Change* 5 (2007): 1–16.

**Figures 12.4 and 12.5.** The waterfall is one of the most common features in tourism representations of landscapes, as shown in this image from 1887 (left). Cascading through the center of the image, the waterfall is surrounded by jungle-like vegetation. The water collects in a pool at the bottom with large rocks in the foreground, and the people positioned at this pool marvel at the scene. Scenes highlighted in tourism promotions often feature images such as this (right). (Sources: James A. Froude, *The English in the West Indies or the Bow of Ulysses* [London: Longmans, Green and Co., 1909], 72, and Velvet Nelson)

Place promotion must maintain a balance between tapping into generalized ideas of place and creating a sense of distinction among other destinations. Because some destinations appeal to the same tourist motivations as others, promotions from places around the world draw upon the same themes. However, these places then run the risk of becoming "placeless." **Placelessness** is described as a loss of identity, in which one place looks and feels like other places, often as a result of the superficial, stereotypical images circulated by the media.[10] As tourism destinations, these places essentially have the same experiences to offer. For example, the idea of a tropical island paradise is clearly important in tourism representations, but the stereotypical imagery associated with it can, in fact, describe places in many different parts of the world. In their search for a destination, potential tourists may seek this *type* of place, where they believe they will have the experience they desire, rather than a specific place. As such, a destination needs to be able to attract potential tourists' interest with these themes but also provide them with a reason to choose it over other destinations that may appeal to the same motivations or desires.

Perhaps most important, the representations in place promotion must maintain a balance between presenting the characteristics of a destination that are most likely to attract tourists and creating realistic expectations for the experiences they would have at the destination. The ideas and images created for promotional purposes are often simplified and generalized, and not all aspects of the destination will fit that mold. To some extent, destinations can mitigate the potential for conflict between expectations and reality by the way in which tourism is developed. In many destinations, the tourism infrastructure channels tourists into certain places that are most likely to fit the idea of the destination presented to them before they arrive. Likewise, they are kept away from those parts of a place that don't fit the image, such as an inner-city slum adjacent to a fashionable metropolitan district, a section of clear-cut forest near popular hiking trails, or a landfill just a few miles from a pristine beach. Because of this geographic separation, tourists' expectations for a place are often met or even exceeded.

However, if tourists encounter a reality that is vastly different from their expectations, they are likely to leave dissatisfied. Consequently, in the post-trip part of the tourism process, they will return home to tell friends and family about their experiences, submit posts to review sites, or even blog. This negative reporting can be hard for a destination to overcome. People are frequently skeptical of advertising; thus, even though promotional images and literature show one thing, the reports of someone who has been there can prove to be more powerful.

# Conclusion

Place is one of the key concepts in geography, and it is equally important in the geography of tourism. Tourism is an inherently place-based geographic phenomenon. Yet, we must first understand the ways in which people think about places before we can begin to examine ways in which people interact with and experience places through tourism. Our most concrete ideas about places come from firsthand experience, but we also have ideas about all kinds of places we've never been. In a sense, we "experience" these places through representations. These representations can be

---

## Box 12.3.    Experience: Disappointed Expectations

We live in the northern part of the country. By March, we're pretty much fed up with winter and ready for a change. I am a professional tennis instructor, and after teaching inside for months, I look forward to the opportunity to experience some nice weather and play outside. My wife is a teacher, and she looks forward to her spring break from classes. One year, when my wife and I were looking for someplace warm to go on a nice—but reasonable—week-long vacation, I came across an ad on my national association's website. A pro was promoting his resort by offering discounts to other pros (and, presumably, their families and clients). This place was described as a "golf and tennis resort" in San Antonio, Texas. Of course, I imagined what I think anyone would of a golf and tennis resort: a beautiful, spacious, quiet property with nice facilities and well-manicured grounds; high-quality, comfortable—if not luxurious!—accommodations; lots of activities and guest services, and more. I checked out the resort's website. Everything sounded good, and the pictures looked nice. I assumed that the weather in Texas at that time of year would be a marked improvement over what we would be experiencing. I went ahead and made the reservation, and, for the next couple of months, we anticipated our trip.

Come March, the reality of what we found was disappointing to say the least. It turns out that the "resort" was located not in the *vicinity* of San Antonio but in the city itself on a busy commercial street. The place itself was very old and run-down. I distinctly remember the carpets throughout the property being stained and threadbare, and the rooms were no better than those of a cheap motel. The golf course turned out to be a 9-hole par 3, with no evidence of recent maintenance. The tennis courts were equally neglected, with ragged nets and a faded, cracked playing surface. The tennis pro who had made the promotional offer was long gone by that time, and there was no organized program. To top it all off, the weather that week was cold and dreary, and it rained often.

My wife, good soldier that she is, never complained about any of these poor conditions, or her disappointed expectations. We still managed to have a good time exploring San Antonio; however, we'll always remember that "resort," but not for the right reasons. I learned my lesson, though, and since then, I have been much more careful about researching the places that we choose to go on vacation.

*—Tom*

---

extraordinarily powerful in shaping our perceptions of places, which plays a role in determining whether or not we wish to visit that place for ourselves. In recognition of this, destinations around the world have now also taken an active role in trying to represent their place in specific ways that will attract tourists. However, the impact of representations does not end with the destination-decision-making process. The ideas of places created by representations also shape the way we experience places, which will be examined in the final chapter.

# Key Terms

- placelessness
- place promotion

# Notes

1. Edward Relph, *Place and Placelessness* (London: Pion, 1976), 58.
2. Dean MacCannell, *The Tourist: A New Theory of the Leisure Class* (New York: Schocken Books, 1976; reprinted with foreword by Lucy R. Lippard; Berkeley: University of California Press, 1999), 110. Citations refer to the California edition.
3. Kelly J. MacKay and Daniel R. Fesenmaier, "Pictorial Element of Destination in Image Formation," *Annals of Tourism Research* 24, no. 3 (1997), 538.
4. Anthony Trollope, *The West Indies and the Spanish Main*, 4th ed. (London: Dawsons of Pall Mall, 1968), 50.
5. Algernon E. Aspinall, *The Pocket Guide to the West Indies*, 2nd ed. (London: Duckworth & Co., 1910), 42–43.
6. Richard H. Gassan, *The Birth of American Tourism: New York, the Hudson Valley, and American Culture, 1790–1830* (Amherst: University of Massachusetts Press, 2008), 73–75.
7. Jill Steward, "'How and Where to Go': The Role of Travel Journalism in Britain and the Evolution of Foreign Travel, 1840–1914," in *Histories of Tourism: Representation, Identity, and Conflict*, ed. John Walton (Clevedon, UK: Channel View Publications, 2005), 44–45.
8. Frank T. Bullen, *Back to Sunny Seas* (London: Smith, Elder & Co., 1905), vii.
9. TravelBlog, "Free Online Travel Diary," accessed January 3, 2012, http://www.travelblog.org/about.html.
10. Relph, *Place and Placelessness*, 90.

# Sources

Gassan, Richard H. *The Birth of American Tourism: New York, the Hudson Valley, and American Culture, 1790–1830*. Amherst: University of Massachusetts Press, 2008.

Hall, Derek. "Brand Development, Tourism, and National Identity: The Re-Imaging of Former Yugoslavia," *Brand Management* 9 (2002): 323–34.

Morgan, Nigel. "Problematizing Place Promotion." In *A Companion to Tourism*, edited by Alan A. Lew, C. Michael Hall, and Allan M. Williams, 173–83. Malden, MA: Blackwell, 2004.

Relph, Edward. *Place and Placelessness*. London: Pion Limited, 1976.

Simmons, Jack. "Railways, Hotels, and Tourism in Great Britain, 1839–1914." *Journal of Contemporary History* 19 (1984): 201–22.

Steward, Jill. "'How and Where to Go': The Role of Travel Journalism in Britain and the Evolution of Foreign Travel, 1840–1914." In *Histories of Tourism: Representation, Identity, and Conflict*, edited by John Walton, 39–54. Clevedon, UK: Channel View Publications, 2005.

Suvantola, Jaakko. *Tourist's Experience of Place*. Aldershot, UK: Ashgate, 2002.

Urry, John. *Consuming Places*. London: Routledge, 1995.

Williams, Stephen. *Tourism Geography*. London: Routledge, 1998.

# CHAPTER 13

# Experiences of Place in Tourism

While media representations play a crucial role in the creation of place meanings, these meanings can also be individual. This will be shaped by overarching cultural conventions, personal preferences, and perhaps most importantly, direct experiences with places. Although place is an important topic in geography, studies in the geography of tourism have been criticized for giving the experience of place in the context of tourism relatively little attention.[1] This is primarily due to the fact that the human geography tradition has focused more on the meanings that come from experiences in places that are most familiar. However, the potential to draw upon this tradition in the geography of tourism to explore the experience of other places is clear.

Places are complex entities, and they become even more complex with the development of tourism. The character of a place may be changed as a result of tourism, and it may become more stratified as some areas of the place embrace the influx of outsiders while others remain reserved for locals. Likewise, the meanings associated with a place may be changed and new layers of meaning added, based on the experiences of outsiders in addition to those of insiders. This chapter further examines the relationship between place and tourism; in particular, how tourism shapes the character of places and how tourists experience the places they visit.

## Places and Tourism

In the previous chapter, we saw how important representations of places are in shaping the ways in which people think about tourism destinations. While these representations are selective in the images that are offered to potential tourists, they must have some basis in the character of the place; otherwise, the destination runs the risk of tourist dissatisfaction when the experience does not match up with expectations. As such, the character of a place is important in attracting and maintaining tourism. Yet, the unique character of a place may ultimately be affected by tourism.

One of the most influential works on the geography of place has been Edward Relph's *Place and Placelessness* (1976). In this work, Relph defines a geography of places that are unique and full of meaning; these places create a world that is rich and varied. He contrasts this with a placeless geography. Non-places have few characteristics that situate them in their location or distinguish one from another, and they lack meanings beyond certain stereotypical ideas. Thus, in a placeless geography, the character of the setting is devoid of significant or unique features, and people don't recognize that places are different. Consequently, placelessness involves both a look and feel of sameness.

For example, the tropical beach has been described as one such non-place. These beaches feature the same, typically stereotyped characteristics (e.g., sunny skies, palm trees, white sands, clear waters, possibly even umbrellas and lounge chairs), regardless of their actual location in the tropical world. In fact, even when such a place is visited, there may be few readily apparent features that would distinguish it from other, similar places or indicate the wider character of the place in which it is situated. These beaches are loaded with superficial meanings, such as fun, relaxation, and escape, but they often lack the depth of meaning associated with places that are unique (figure 13.1).

Relph is particularly critical of tourism and argues that it plays an integral role in creating placelessness: "Tourism is an homogenizing influence and its effects everywhere seem to be the same—the destruction of the local and regional landscape that very often initiated tourism, and its replacement by conventional tourist architecture and synthetic landscapes and pseudo-places."[2] In other words, tourism destinations are prone to becoming non-places. This is often attributed to the standardization of

**Figure 13.1.   Is there anything about this scene that might give you a clue as to where it is? (Source: Tom Nelson)**

# Box 13.1.  Case Study: China's Deliberate Creation of Placeless Tourism Destinations

Hallstatt is a small, lakeside Austrian town in the Salzkammergut Lake District. The area has a long history of human settlement based on the presence of salt, which has been mined over three thousand years, since the Middle Bronze Age. Hallstatt became the type site for the predominant pattern of life characterizing much of Central Europe during the Early Iron Age, now referred to as the Hallstatt Culture. The modern town has origins that date back to the medieval period, although much of the architecture is characterized by the late Baroque style after a fire destroyed part of the town in 1750. Today, the picturesque town set against a dramatic Alpine landscape has less than 1,000 inhabitants but receives some 800,000 tourists each year. UNESCO has designated Hallstatt and the greater Salzkammergut region a World Heritage Site based on its natural beauty and its great human heritage, as well as the integrity with which it has been preserved over the years.

And soon it can be seen in China.

In mid-2011, China Minmetals Corporation began construction on what is intended to be an exact replica of Hallstatt in Guangdong Province, near Hong Kong. The decision to re-create a European town in China may not be as surprising as it initially sounds. Chengdu's British Town was modeled after Dorchester, England, and the "Shanghai One City, Nine Towns" plan has already seen the development of a Nordic Town, Holland Town, Thames Town, and German Town intended to represent "typical" towns from the respective European countries. Moreover, Austria's Hallstatt has been a popular destination among Asian tourists. The new town is designed to serve as a tourism destination for the middle-class Chinese market and European expatriates living in China.

The architectural aspects of the town are to be replicated down to the last detail, and it is intended that the shops will offer some traditional products, including Austrian crystal and other souvenirs that might be bought by tourists in the original town. However, it will be difficult to replicate Hallstatt's unique geographic setting. Although an artificial lake will be created, the hilly, subtropical region can little compare to the Alpine climate and landscape of the original. Additionally, the replication will necessarily lack the rich history of Hallstatt and the meanings that have accrued to the place over the years. Representatives of the Catholic Church, in particular, have expressed serious concerns about the traditional village church being stripped of the functions that it serves in its community and instead merely providing an aesthetic focal point in a tourist attraction.

Responses from the Hallstatt community have varied. Some residents and officials are flattered by the imitation, and the local tourist board suggests that the new town will serve as an advertisement for and possible inducement to visit the original. Others have questioned the legality of replicating a town and UNESCO World Heritage Site without permission, although there appears to be no legal precedent against it. In the media, the idea has been widely condemned. In one commentary after the news of this development broke, AOL Travel contributor Andrew Burmon criticized the plan for its blatant Disneyfication. He writes, "Chinese tourists apparently like visiting Western-style towns denuded of their history and context. A similar thing could be said, I suppose, of people who go to Epcot Center, but Epcot seems much more innocent, presenting tamed ideas of different countries rather than simulations of specific places."[1] Also in response, CNN's foreign affairs host Fareed Zakaria blogs: "What I would love to find in China is a beautiful replica of a traditional Chinese village, but these have become almost impossible to find nowadays."[2]

(continued)

## Box 13.1. *(continued)*

*Discussion topic*: As a tourist, are the meanings of a place important to you? Would you visit a destination such as China's Hallstatt replication? Why or why not?

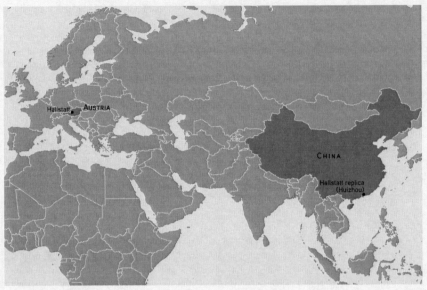

**Map 13.1.   Hallstatt—the old (Austria) and the new (China). (Source: XNR Productions)**

# Notes

1. Andrew Burmon, "Hallstatt, an Austrian Hamlet in Communist China," AOL Travel, June 17, 2011, accessed July 5, 2011, http://news.travel.aol.com/2011/06/17/hallstatt-an-austrian-hamlet-in-communist-china/.

2. Fareed Zakaria, "China Replicating Western Towns," *CNN Global Public Square Blogs*, June 21, 2011, accessed July 5, 2011, http://globalpublicsquare.blogs.cnn.com/2011/06/21/china-replicating-western-cities/.

# Source

United Nations Educational, Scientific, and Cultural Organization. "Hallstatt-Dachstein/Salzkammergut Cultural Landscape." Accessed July 5, 2011. http://whc.unesco.org/en/list/806.

mass tourism. Mass tourism destinations are typically characterized by multinational companies that build resorts and restaurants in the same style and offer the same services regardless of location. These multinational companies reflect the demands of organized mass tourists that the places they visit—even if they are foreign places—have at least certain elements of home that are familiar and comfortable. To maintain tourism, destination stakeholders seek to meet these demands. However, in the process, this fundamentally changes the character of that place, at least within certain areas (i.e., the tourist zone). Thus, there may be a certain sameness to mass tourism destinations in many parts of the world.

Another variation of placelessness refers to places that are artificial, contrived, and have little relationship to the history and/or reality of the places in which they are situated. Again citing tourism as a crucial contributing influence, Relph describes this as a process of "Disneyfication" in which the synthetic world of the theme park has begun to affect the character and development of other places.[3] Indeed, scholars have applied this concept to various places around the world, including existing places that have been subject to Disneyfication, such as New Orleans or Cornwall, as well as places that have been developed in this way, such as Las Vegas or Cancún.

Although there is certainly some truth in the relationship between tourism and placelessness (both non-places and Disneyfied places), this type of blanket criticism of tourism is not entirely justified. There is a tremendous variety in tourism, and not all tourists are looking for a standardized experience. Tourists at the opposite end of the spectrum—the explorers and drifters—specifically avoid such destinations and instead seek out new and different places to experience. Although tourism will inevitably bring changes to these destinations, these changes can be made conscientiously to avoid destroying the character of that place.

In addition, the perceived homogenization of places in the modern world has stimulated a process of localization. In other words, in the face of standardization as a result of global processes, including tourism, some places have attempted to reassert local interests, traditions, and distinctiveness. This helps reinforce, and in some cases re-create, a unique sense of identity and character for places that might otherwise be lost. While this process of localization may be initiated by local people to protect their heritage, it also has the distinct advantage of giving that place a competitive advantage among tourists (or place consumers) who are looking for a unique experience of place.

# Sense of Place

**Sense of place** refers to the association with and emotional attachment to places based on the meanings given to those places. It is one of the ways in which we are connected to the world and therefore an integral part of the human experience.[4] A sense of place is developed by experience in and a relationship with a place. In particular, geographer Yi-Fu Tuan has argued that "sense of place is rarely acquired in passing. To know a place well requires long residence and deep involvement."[5] Thus, the places of our everyday lives are those that hold the most meaning for us and therefore are the ones to which we are most attached. As such, these are the places, relationships, and meanings that geographers have been most interested in. Nonetheless, sense of place can contribute to our understanding of the geography of tourism.

For example, the relationship with and feelings we have toward the places of our everyday lives can play a role in the demand for tourism. In addition to feelings of affection and attachment, the familiarity of these places can generate feelings of complacency or even hostility if we begin to perceive that we are tied to or imprisoned there. Even though we know that these are the places to which we'll always return, we may still feel the need for a temporary change of place. Tourism provides us with this opportunity.

The sense of place that we have for "our" places is instinctive and unconscious. In fact, it is something that we think little about. However, developing a sense of place can also be a conscious act. Although tourists will not develop a sense of a place equal to an insider's, they nonetheless have the potential to gain insight into a place if they are willing to be open-minded and sensitive to its nuances.[6] Taken a step farther, tourism becomes the means of experiencing new places and places in new ways. Unfamiliar places are experienced differently than familiar ones. While we take certain aspects of a familiar place for granted, everything in a new place is different and unknown. We may have a greater sense of curiosity and excitement. Activities that seem mundane in our daily lives—driving from one place to another, taking a walk up the street, going to the store, finding something to eat—can suddenly turn into an adventure. As we have the potential to encounter new things, we tend to observe more carefully. We typically have a greater sense of security in the places that we consider our own; thus, to varying degrees based on the context, we may even be challenged to pay more attention to our surroundings in a new place to find what we need or to keep ourselves safe.

Because of widespread representations of places in today's world, there are few places for which we have no preconceptions or expectations. The meanings these places hold may be abstract and are most likely based on stereotypes. However, with every experience we have in places, we build upon these preconceived ideas. Over the course of a trip, we create more nuanced, personal meanings of place that constitute a type of sense of place.

Finally, experiences in new places often cause us to reflect on our experiences in those places most familiar to us, those that constitute the setting of our daily lives. In some cases, the sudden absence of those aspects of a place that we take for granted may prompt us to appreciate them more upon our return, at least for a little while. We may find that there are aspects of a place we would rather see changed, to be more like that of a place visited. In essence, experiences in other places may cause us to refine our sense of place.

# Experience of Place

There are countless factors that can affect tourists' experience, ranging from poor infrastructure to the presence of pests. Perhaps one of the greatest factors that have a distinct impact on tourists' experiences is the weather conditions of a place at the time of a trip. Nothing is likely to ruin a tourist's experience more than unexpected and undesirable weather conditions that prevent them from seeing or doing the things they had planned (see box 6.1). While it may be an unusual—perhaps even unprecedented—occurrence for that place, it's the only experience tourists have with that place. Of course, other factors may be unrelated to the place but will affect the tourists' experience of it nonetheless. For example, tourists who are sick during their vacation may not be able to participate in certain activities, and they are likely to enter into their experiences with far less enthusiasm than they would have otherwise.

Interactions with the people at a destination can play an important role in tourists' experience of that place. In a new place, we may not know where to go, how to act, or whom to trust. Tourists are often wary of being taken advantage of or cheated—in some cases, rightly so. Tourists may have little knowledge of how much things should cost or the way things work; consequently, they are at the mercy of tourism stakeholders and local people to deal with them fairly. Encounters with local people who are honest and friendly, or those who go out of their way to help strangers, can have an extraordinarily positive impact on tourists' experience. Conversely, encounters with even a few people at the destination who are dishonest, unhelpful, hostile, or harassing can ultimately shape the way tourists forever think about that place.

Personal factors, such as previous experiences and personality, play a role in the way an individual experiences a place. We approach experiences with different attitudes. Some tourists feel apprehension, anxiety, or even fear, perhaps from the very moment they leave home, at the unknown of experiencing a new place. This is most often the case among tourists who have had little experience with new and especially different places. However, this should lessen with time spent in the new place, as the tourist becomes more familiar and comfortable with the circumstances. In contrast, other tourists may experience a sense of euphoria at being in a place where everything is novel. This, too, can lessen with time as the novelty of the experience begins to wear off.

Tourists have different logistical options for experiencing a destination. The following sections discuss guided tours and independent travel as two options and how each shapes the experience of place.

## GUIDED TOURS

Guided tours present one option for tourists to experience a destination. There is an endless variety of experiences that range from a complete package trip to a day-long excursion as one part of a larger trip, from a group with dozens of participants to a one-on-one experience. Tourists might choose this experience for a number of different reasons, reflecting the type of tourist, the desired tourism product, the choice of destination, or the motivations for the trip. Essentially, guided tours can serve different purposes and provide different types of experiences of place.

For example, organized mass tourists are often interested in the convenience of a package tour such as the "European Dream" eight-day coach tour spanning London, Amsterdam, Paris, Lucerne, Milan, Venice, and Rome. The itinerary is preplanned (e.g., what places to visit and for how long), and all of the logistical arrangements have already been made (e.g., how to travel, where to stay, where to eat). This creates a "worry-free" holiday for tourists who don't have the time or interest in planning a trip and don't want any surprises. These tours may be considered suitable for relatively inexperienced travelers who are anxious about traveling in an unfamiliar, especially foreign, destination where they may not know the customs or speak the language.

Although these tours are tremendously popular, they are commonly criticized for minimizing the experience of place. There is little need to come to the destination with any knowledge of the place, as all arrangements have already been made and guides provide necessary information along the way. With a set itinerary, there is little opportunity for exploration and interaction with the place or its people. The spontaneity of the tourism experience is eliminated, and tourists are reduced to passive observers of place through the windows of a climate-controlled bus.

In comparison, individual mass tourists are likely to visit the same, or similar, destinations as their organized counterparts (e.g., London or Rome); however, they are likely to outline their own itineraries and/or make their own travel arrangements. This will require more research and planning in the pre-trip stage. At the destination, they may choose to do a combination of the guided tour and independent travel for their experience; for example, they might take a day tour or sightseeing bus to get information about the place and to see the highlighted attractions before exploring a bit more on their own.

Guided tours may also be used to facilitate certain types of special-interest tourism, such as those that require specific skills. For example, tourists may be interested in participating in an activity at the destination—such as rock climbing, scuba diving, or horseback riding—but have little previous experience with that activity. As such, a tour provides them with instruction, necessary equipment, and a guide to help them along the way and ensure their safety. Likewise, special-interest tourism may require in-depth local knowledge. Tourists interested in bird watching, wildlife photography, hunting, or fishing may require a local guide who will know when and where they will have the greatest opportunities for these activities.

Finally, guided tours may be necessary to allow tourists to visit places they would not otherwise know about or have access to (i.e., MacCannell's back region stages). This can include places not generally made known to outsiders, such as an unmarked hiking trail, or those not open to outsiders except on a tour because of logistical or safety reasons (e.g., the subterranean passages of the Seattle Underground). Some destinations impose such specific regulations on tourists that a guide is necessary to ensure that proper procedures are followed; some of the strictest controlled destinations actually require that tourists travel with a guide. This is the case in places like Tibet and Bhutan. Thus, while the types of tourists who visit these "off the beaten track" destinations are fairly adventurous explorers and drifters looking for a unique experience, they must travel in a different manner than they would normally.

The existence of tour guides dates back to the earliest eras of tourism. Tour guides played a particularly important role in the Grand Tour era, before the tourism industry and infrastructure were developed. With little in the way of guidebook information, maps, signs, or other features that facilitate tourism, outsiders were dependent on guides. On one hand, the guides would literally guide tourists in places that were unfamiliar, inaccessible to outsiders, and in which they would be met with suspicion or hostility by the local population. On the other hand, these guides would metaphorically guide tourists in the process of personal development that was intended to accompany an experience such as the Grand Tour.[7]

Modern tour guides continue to serve a variety of functions (figure 13.2). In addition to taking care of logistical arrangements, guides are generally responsible for the safety and well-being of tourists during the course of the trip. At the same time, they are responsible for ensuring that tourists are familiar with and abide by local customs and policies. This is particularly the case in places where guides are required. For example, if a tourist does something in Tibet that is prohibited by the Chinese government (e.g., staying to travel independently after the tour or engaging in political activism), the tour guide and/or the travel agency that arranged the tour will be punished for the offense.

**Figure 13.2. This tour guide in St. Kitts transported his tour participants to a local hiking trail, provided information about the area's flora and fauna, and told stories about exploring the forest as a child growing up on the island. (Source: Tom Nelson)**

Tour guides are expected to have a good knowledge of the places visited. While some tour itineraries are preplanned, others are flexible, and it is up to the guide to determine the course of the trip/excursion to reflect the interests of tour participants. The guide may be expected to find routes that will yield the best opportunities to encounter desired points of interest. This is particularly applicable on special interest tours where those points are moving targets (e.g., wildlife). In addition, guides must be able to convey their knowledge of a place to participants. This must be done in a way that is easily understood by visitors, which may require translating or interpreting things that might seem strange or unusual to outsiders. Yet, guides must also balance providing information about places and entertaining tourists on holiday (for a humorous take on this topic, see the 2009 film *My Life in Ruins*).

Tour guides may be required to have certain skill sets, such as fluency in multiple languages, and also some knowledge of the tourists' culture to understand what their interests are, what type of experience they want, and how to best represent the places visited. Some tourists may want information about the places, while others may be more interested in myths or personal stories. In some cases, tourists may not want any interpretation at all; the guide is simply intended to facilitate travel and highlight sights to be seen and/or photographed. Guides must be flexible and accommodating to meet the needs of tour participants as they arise.

Tour guides can have a highly important role to play in tourists' experiences of a place. They constitute another form of representation; they represent local peoples and places to tourists. As such, they have tremendous power in determining what is important and will be seen—and, conversely, what won't—and shaping what tourists think about those places and their experiences. Guides are considered an essential interface between tourists and the destination. However, they are not entirely autonomous; they may be required to represent the aspects and stories of the place that are officially sanctioned. In other words, they may be limited by what places the government will allow guides to take tourists and what topics they can discuss.

Tourists place a great deal of trust in their guides to be honest, give them accurate information, and generally deal with them fairly. Of course, this is not always the case. Guides may fabricate information, advise them to purchase inauthentic souvenirs, or require them to pay additional "fees" that line their pockets or those of their acquaintances. However, tour companies depend on their reputation, and the Internet has become a powerful forum for dissatisfied customers to spread the word about any problems they had with a tour. Moreover, because tour guides play such an important role in representing the destination, governments frequently implement regulations and/or require licenses for tour guides. Nonetheless, unlicensed guides operating in the informal sector of the economy are common in many destinations around the world, and experiences with them vary widely.

## INDEPENDENT TRAVEL

Many tourists—particularly explorers and drifters—prefer to experience a place on their own. Just as organized package tours are criticized for minimizing tourists' experience of place, independent explorations are often considered to provide the greatest opportunities for tourists to develop a sense of place. Of course, a deeper experience of a place does not necessarily translate into a positive one, and there can be both advantages and disadvantages of going it alone at the destination.

Those who prefer independent travel typically value the flexibility to set their own itinerary. Based on their interests and priorities, they can choose what places they want to visit and what sights to see. These may be primary attractions, but one of the advantages of independent travel is the ability to get off the traditional tourist track and experience more of the place than the front regions. For example, tourists come en masse to visit Piazza dei Miracoli, the main tourist complex in Pisa, Italy, featuring the famous Leaning Tower. This is a well-known primary attraction and one that all kinds of tourists to Tuscany are likely to see. However, those on a guided tour will likely only experience this part of Pisa, while those traveling independently have the potential to explore other parts of the historic city if they choose.

Likewise, tourists who travel independently are not bound by a strict schedule, unless they set it for themselves. They have the flexibility to linger at a site that they find enjoyable or interesting without feeling rushed, and conversely, they are free to move on to the next attraction if they decide they have done all they wanted in that place. Consequently, tourists can feel that they had the fullest experience of a place with little perceived wasted time (e.g., waiting at rendezvous points).

To some extent, those who travel by personal vehicle may be subject to the same criticisms as those who travel by tour bus: that their only experience of other places is from a distance and in passing. However, personal vehicles can be used as a means of getting *to* a destination but not the primary means of *experiencing* it. Independent travelers may choose to walk or use public transportation at the destination, which will provide opportunities for interactions with local people, access to back regions, and insight into the lived experience of the place.

This more flexible style of travel allows for greater spontaneity in the experience of place. Independent travel does not always go as planned; in fact, it frequently does not. Yet, for many tourists, their most memorable and rewarding experiences of a place are those that were stumbled upon by accident in the course of exploring—and in some cases, getting lost—on their own. These are the experiences where they met interesting local people, found a great restaurant, saw places they never would have encountered otherwise, and observed or participated in a unique local event.

Of course, not all unexpected experiences are pleasant ones. For many tourists, the prospect of traveling without a guide and the prospect of facing the unexpected alone are great sources of stress. Tour participants benefit from operators who scout out the best attractions, accommodations, or restaurants. Tourists who plan their own trips, on the other hand, must make selections from their best guess based on whatever information is available, and not always with positive results (see box 12.3).

Similarly, tour participants benefit from dedicated transportation that takes them directly to points of interest. In contrast, those who rely on public transportation may be frustrated by restrictive schedules and an inability to get to tourist sites not served by transportation systems. Independent tourists also run the risk of getting lost. For some, this is an adventure and creates opportunities, but for others, it is a source of stress. These tourists face the potential frustration of not reaching the desired attractions as well as the potential anxiety of finding themselves in undesirable, possibly unsafe, locations.

Independent tourists may not always have access to the same extent of information about the places and attractions visited. Sites have varying degrees of information available to independent tourists. Some highly developed sites have self-guided audio tours, guidebooks, and/or well-annotated displays; however, many sites present little information or use only the local language. Moreover, this information is typically limited to basic facts without providing the level of detail or richer stories that a good tour guide might have to offer.

Finally, tour guides act as a middleman between tourists and local people. These guides should speak the local language and understand local customs and therefore be able to help tourists navigate foreign destinations. Even the most conscientious tourists who try to familiarize themselves with the local culture and speak some basic words of the language can run into problems with miscommunication and misunderstanding when they have to manage various situations on their own. The stress, frustration, and/or dissatisfaction that arise from any of these aspects of a trip can affect tourists' attitudes toward the place and their experience of it.

## SOLO INDEPENDENT FEMALE TRAVEL

Although it is recognized that tourists are not a single, homogenous group that will experience places in the same ways, tourism research has not always given these differences much consideration. However, supported by developments in feminist geography, more attention has recently been given to the factors that cause women to experience places differently than men. This is exemplified by the attitudes toward and patterns of solo independent travel (i.e., traveling without a companion or an organized tour group).

Although there are examples of female travelers throughout history, travel has generally been seen as the province of men. Throughout the early eras of tourism, only a small percentage of women had the time, money, and social standing to be able to travel, and very few traveled alone. The prevailing sociocultural attitude was that it was inappropriate for respectable women to travel extensively and simply unacceptable for them to travel by themselves. Those who did were viewed by society as eccentric at best; at worst, they faced a ruined reputation.

Opportunities for women in the more developed Western countries to travel gradually increased over the course of the twentieth century. More women entered the workforce (i.e., the public sphere), became more financially independent, and to some extent, experienced less social pressure to start a family at a relatively young age. The number of women traveling now is nearly equal to that of men, and an increasing number of women are choosing solo independent travel. Yet, attitudes toward women traveling—especially abroad and alone—remain somewhat antiquated.

For the most part within modern societies, the idea that a woman traveling alone is absolutely unacceptable no longer applies; however, these societies continue to per-

## Box 13.2.  Experience: Same Place, Difference Experiences

I have had two very different experiences of Europe. After I got my first job out of college and had a little bit of extra money, I wanted to travel. I was single and hadn't traveled much before, so I joined a group tour that my parents were organizing through American Express. These were whirlwind multicountry trips, where we covered a lot of territory and hit most of the major attractions but didn't spend long in any one place. I ended up going on three of these kinds of trips. Everything was arranged for us, from transportation (the transatlantic flight and tour bus) to meals (at the hotel or tourist restaurants). There were some afternoons where we had some time to do our own thing, but, for the most part, we had a schedule and we stuck to it. After I got married, my husband and I started traveling on our own. Now, he does all of the planning for our trips (so I still don't have to do any of that myself!). We only visit one country at a time, and we choose one central location to use as a base for our excursions. We usually use the rail system to visit other parts of the country or sometimes local buses. Sometimes we'll plan out an itinerary ahead of time, but we're certainly flexible based on whatever circumstances arise once we get there.

On our trip to Switzerland, we used Zürich as our base. We had a pretty good guidebook and from its recommendations, we made a half-day trip to visit the Rheinfall. We took the early train out of the city, about twenty-five minutes, to the first stop below the falls. There was nothing there but a little path that took us down to the river where we were able to hike up to the top of the falls. We walked through the café there, which was obviously a tourist trap with kitschy souvenirs, and discovered (with some amusement) that they were charging people to go to the viewing platform that we had just walked by. We didn't stop but continued on into the town. We walked around a bit there, ate our picnic lunch, and continued along the river until we got to the next stop where we could catch a train back to Zürich.

Just recently, I found a copy of a travel journal that a friend had written from the first group tour I went on. I was amazed to discover that I had actually been to the Rheinfall on this trip. It seems that the tour bus stopped at the café at the top of the falls, and we were given about a half hour to go to the bathroom, get a coffee or snack, and maybe buy a souvenir from the shop. I have absolutely no recollection of this. It's not that I didn't have a good experience on this trip—I did. I think my lack of memory is more a function of the type of trip it was. We visited a lot of places in a very short period of time. In fact, one of the frequent complaints in my friend's journal is that we didn't have enough time at destinations such as this.

Today, I prefer to travel independently rather than with a group. But, having done both, I know that each has its advantages and disadvantages. As with this example, I like being able to spend as long as I want in a place and have a memorable experience of it. I like having the opportunity to interact with people in the places we go, whether it's on the trains, in the markets, or at an off-the-beaten path pub. However, you do have to be a little adventuresome. I don't know if I would have had the confidence to do some of the things we've done if it weren't for my husband. There have been times when I thought we would never find our way or that we would miss the last train back, but it always works out.

*—Rachel*

petuate ideas about female vulnerability. The prospect of negotiating an unfamiliar place can be scary for anyone, especially those who have little previous travel experience. Getting lost, facing language barriers, and dealing with cultural misunderstandings are fears that are common to many travelers. Women often admit their doubts about traveling alone and not having anyone to rely on but themselves. These fears are magnified by tourism industry guidelines for female travelers (e.g., dos and don'ts lists or security warnings), news and word-of-mouth stories (e.g., tourists being drugged, raped, or kidnapped), and concerns from family and friends. After announcing their intentions to travel alone, women are frequently subject to reactions that may range from surprise (e.g., "Are you sure that's safe?") to disapproval (e.g., "I don't think that's a good idea.") and even outrage (e.g., "How could you think of doing something like that?"). These reactions may be well intentioned, as they reflect a concern for the woman's well-being, but they also perpetuate the perception that women are vulnerable and thus solo independent travel is unwise.

Perceptions of acceptable behavior for women and toward women vary widely around the world. Consequently, solo independent female tourists may be judged by the sociocultural norms of the destination and subject to the reactions of local people. In some places, the idea of a woman traveling alone may still be unacceptable. When traveling to other culture regions, women often report feeling conspicuous, receiving unwanted attention, sensing hostility, experiencing some form of harassment, and feeling insecure or unsafe. In particular, women traveling without a male companion may be viewed as sexually available. For example, in some culturally conservative destinations, it may be unusual for a woman to appear in public unaccompanied, and those who do—including foreign tourists—will be thought of as prostitutes. In destinations that have received some female sex tourists, all foreign women may be perceived to be looking for that sort of relationship and approached accordingly.

All of these factors affect women's travel patterns and the ways they experience other places. They affect whether or not a woman decides to travel alone; if she does travel, they affect where she goes. She may choose to visit destinations that are closer to home, within her own country, or within similar culture regions where she is less likely to stand out. She may also consider her choice of destinations more carefully than a man, considering its reputation for safety and treatment of women. Likewise, these concerns affect where she stays at the destination, including the neighborhood in which an accommodation is located and the level of security it affords.

These factors affect the places she visits at the destination and the type of activities she participates in. She may feel safest within a certain part of the destination, perhaps the front region where there are other people (especially other tourists) that make her feel less noticeable and less of a target. Some types of places are perceived to be less safe than others (e.g., large urban areas with high crime rates or remote, isolated forested areas) and may be avoided. Certain "masculinized" places may also be avoided by solo independent female tourists. For example, in some cultures, the café is a male-dominated space. If a woman enters that space, she is immediately the target of attention, and she may feel her presence is unwanted. In addition, time of day plays a role; a woman might feel comfortable in a particular place during the day, when it is well lit and populated by other women and children, but less comfortable at night when she might be more likely subjected to harassment. As a result, she may choose to stay in or close to her accommodation at night.

In addition, a woman may make other sorts of adjustments during a trip in an effort to minimize the risk of encountering problems while traveling alone. She may modify her patterns of behavior to be more in line with what is acceptable for women in that place, such as talking softly or lowering her eyes. She may change her patterns of dress to fit local norms (e.g., covering her hair in conservative Muslim countries), to be more conservative (e.g., longer skirts or pants, longer sleeves, or higher necklines) so that she attracts less unwanted attention and/or incorrect assumptions, or simply to be more similar to local women and therefore less conspicuous. She may wear a band on her ring finger to give the impression that, although she is not traveling with a man, she is not "available."

Given real and perceived security issues, a woman may feel that it is her responsibility to not put herself in unsafe places or dangerous situations. Consequently, she has to be constantly aware of her surroundings. This can increase the level of stress associated with travel, which can generate frustration because she is unable to relax and enjoy the experience. Moreover, she may feel that she has an incomplete experience of place because there are certain areas of the destination where she isn't comfortable going, typically back regions where she would be conspicuous. Likewise, there may be certain activities that she would like to participate in but doesn't feel like she can.

These constraints play a real role in shaping women's travel patterns. Not all women will approach travel and experience destinations in the same ways. For some women, these issues may generate suppressed demand. Many women will acknowledge that places at home can also be unsafe, and the experiences faced by solo independent female travelers can also happen to single women at home. However, for women in their home environment, harassment usually occurs in isolated incidents over a long period of time, rather than being compounded during a week-long vacation. Moreover, women at home typically understand the situation and know how to best respond, whereas this is not always the case in foreign environments, which can be extremely unsettling and/or distressing. Yet, many women travel alone. It may be a matter of not giving in to fears or becoming a victim of social pressure. It may be that the rewards of travel outweigh the risks. Many female tourists find that solo independent travel is empowering and fulfilling, as they gain confidence in themselves and a sense of accomplishment for overcoming constraints.

# Consumption of Places

As we saw in the last chapter, images are a tremendously important component of tourism representations that are intended to stimulate viewers' imaginations so that they will visualize themselves at the destination. This sort of daydream generates a demand for the actual experience, or consumption, of place. As a fundamentally place-based activity, places are the primary object of consumption in tourism, which is typically visual (i.e., sightseeing). In fact, tourism is often defined by the act of tourists traveling to other places to see new things.

Sociologist John Urry has described this process of visual consumption as the tourist gaze. In particular, Urry distinguishes between two types of the tourist gaze: romantic and collective. The **romantic tourist gaze** is a private or personal experience, where the tourist can gaze in peace and feel as though he or she formed a connection with that place. This is typically undertaken in natural tourist sites (e.g., scenic vistas) and spiritual places (e.g., religious temples). Tourists who prefer the romantic gaze consider this the only way to experience such places; consequently, they may think the experience is "ruined" by the presence of others or the perceived inappropriate behavior of others given the character of the site (e.g., loud talking or laughing). In contrast, the **collective tourist gaze** depends on the presence of people. This occurs in public places that are at least partially characterized by the people found there. For example, the main square or plaza in a major metropolitan area may be a tourist attraction, not just for the architecture of the buildings that define the space, but also for the extent—and cacophony—of life there.[8]

Whether tourists seek a romantic or a collective gaze, the places chosen must have something distinctive from other places, particularly the places from which tourists are coming. Some places are so different than anywhere else that they automatically attract the gaze. For example, many people feel that Venice is unique and, despite detractions (e.g., hostile local attitudes, high prices, overcrowding), it is ultimately a sight worth seeing (figure 13.4). However, for many destinations, tourist offices must establish that their place has something worthy of being gazed upon. This may be a matter of selecting and promoting a particular characteristic or feature of that place. Trim is a small but attractive traditional town in County Meath, Ireland, with one distinctive characteristic worth visiting: Trim Castle. This restored twelfth-century castle is not only the largest Norman Castle in Europe but also one of the locations for the 1995 film *Braveheart*. In other cases, the object of the gaze must be created. In one of the most notable examples, the aging London Bridge was sold to a real estate developer who reconstructed it in Lake Havasu City, Arizona, for the purpose of bringing tourists to the little-known town.

While efforts to highlight a place (or part of a place) as "worthy" of the tourist gaze often takes place in the form of media representations, it can also be done onsite. Tour guides or self-guided-tour information identifies the sights to be seen. Most blatantly, signs literally identify the places or objects that should be gazed upon and direct tourists to them. Of course, this signposting is necessary, to some extent, to help tourists reach the sights to be consumed. Moreover, this may help destinations concentrate tourists in specific areas (e.g., the preferred sites identified in chapter 11) and steer them away from other areas that might not match up with their expectations. However, someone must decide what is significant or interesting, which may or may not be what tourists would actually choose to see.

In addition to the criticisms of tourism discussed above, Edward Relph argues that this practice of identifying and highlighting those things worth seeing for tourists creates an inauthentic sense of place. Tourists who accept this professionally prepackaged portrayal may think they have a sense of that place. Yet, this isn't a deep association with and emotional attachment to place but a partial, selective, and superficial impression of a place that is not even based on their own explorations, findings, and assessments.[9]

# Box 13.3.   In-Depth: When the Romantic Gaze Becomes a Collective One

From media representations, we are all well familiar with iconic, awe-inspiring scenes such as Half Dome, Machu Picchu, Stonehenge, Victoria Falls, Angkor Wat, or the Great Wall of China. Some are purely spectacular natural environments; others combine tremendous human heritage with a dramatic setting. Still others are mystical in ways we can't always explain. When presented with these images, we can't help but imagine ourselves there, taking in the gaze. With few if any people present in these images, we can picture ourselves standing alone and appreciating the scene the way we want to and having a semi-spiritual experience of these exceptional places—in other words, the romantic gaze.

Yet, the experience of these places has become decidedly collective as millions of tourists visit every year. Countless cars, RVs, and tour buses create traffic congestion and smog and require extensive parking facilities located near the site or viewing area for convenience. Both tour groups and independent tourists may roam the site and accumulate in key spots. The concentration of tourists brings hawkers selling a range of products, as well as pickpockets and hustlers looking for opportunities. This mass of people affects the physical quality of the site by trampling paths, accumulating waste, increasing noise levels, and leaving graffiti or vandalizing property. This detracts not only from the view but also the sensory experience of the gaze and the relationship that the tourist has with the object of the gaze (figure 13.3).

**Figure 13.3.   We normally see photographs of Stonehenge without people, and it is easy to imagine that our experience will be characterized by the romantic gaze. However, this is the scene we are far more likely to encounter today. (Source: Lori Rose)**

*(continued)*

## Box 13.3.  *(continued)*

As places such as these become victims of their own popularity, the much-anticipated romantic gaze is fundamentally changed to a collective one. There are, of course, places sought specifically for the collective gaze. However, when a tourist is expecting a romantic gaze but gets a collective one instead, he or she is likely to be frustrated and dissatisfied. For the sites that have a distinct hold on our imagination, countless tourists will still visit, even though they know that the experience isn't likely to live up to their expectations. Yet, other tourists will avoid popular sites in favor of others that may be considered secondary or tertiary attractions but continue to offer the more personal experience of the romantic gaze.

*Discussion topic*: How can a destination or attraction work to maintain the romantic gaze?

For most tourists, it isn't just about seeing the sights; it's also about recording them. In a recent study on tourism and photography, scholars Mike Robinson and David Picard argue, "To be a tourist, it would seem, involves taking photographs. Whilst photography is clearly not the exclusive preserve of tourists, it is nonetheless one of the markers of *being* a tourist."[10] Tourists have long sought to "capture" the scene and bring it home with them as evidence of having been there and a tool to remember the experience. In the earliest eras of tourism, tourists would sketch the places

**Figure 13.4.  Despite imitations in places like Las Vegas and Macau, there is no substitute for the character, the history, and ultimately the spectacle that is Venice, such as this typical scene of the Grand Canal from the Rialto Bridge. (Source: Velvet Nelson)**

visited or purchase paintings and replicas of famous sites. This practice became even more firmly embedded in tourism with the development of small, portable, easy-to-use personal cameras. While the camera has, to some extent, become a symbol of "the tourist"—with all its negative connotations—most tourists are nonetheless willing to endure potential derision to be able to record the places they visit as well as themselves in those places. Tourist photographs and video recordings comprise another type of representation for the destination, as they are shown to family, friends, and potentially wider audiences on the Internet.

This desire to record can ultimately shape the ways tourists experience the destination. The itineraries of both package and self-guided tours are often structured around stops at locations that have been predetermined to offer the best photographic opportunities. Thus, the first and perhaps the only thing tourists do at these locations is to take a picture. These tourists may not even be aware of what they are taking pictures of or why. At well-known destinations, tourists commonly look for the sights they have seen countless times before in media representations, places like the Eiffel Tower, the Sydney Opera House, or the Christ the Redeemer statue, so they can capture it for themselves. In fact, tourists are often so focused on this objective that they lose the opportunity to explore the character of places for themselves and miss other sites and scenes that are equally or more interesting. While such tourists have visual evidence of the places they visit, they don't really see or experience them through their other senses. They are, in a sense, merely "collecting" places (figure 13.5).

**Figure 13.5.   A part of the modern tourism industry involves directing tourists to sights to be photographed. For example, this tour group has stopped at a key vantage point in Zagreb, Croatia, and the tourist in the front of the image is taking a picture of the iconic Church of St. Mark's. (Source: Velvet Nelson)**

# Conclusion

Tourist experiences have been considered the realm of related fields in tourism studies, such as psychology and sociology; geography has had generally little to contribute. Yet, as a fundamentally place-based activity, there is much potential for cross-fertilization between the geography of tourism and the geography of place. Just as representations of place are an extraordinarily important part of tourism, so is the experience of places. Yet, we must always remember, as John Urry wrote in *The Tourist Gaze*, "There is no universal experience that is true for all tourists at all times."[11]

# Key Terms

- collective tourist gaze
- romantic tourist gaze
- sense of place

# Notes

1. Jaakko Suvantola, *Tourist's Experience of Place* (Aldershot, UK: Ashgate, 2002).
2. Edward Relph, *Place and Placelessness* (London: Pion, 1976), 93.
3. Relph, *Place and Placelessness*, 95.
4. Relph, *Place and Placelessness*; Edward Relph, "Sense of Place," in *Ten Geographic Ideas That Changed the World*, ed. Susan Hanson (New Brunswick, NJ: Rutgers University Press, 1997).
5. Yi-Fu Tuan, "Place: An Experiential Perspective," *Geographical Review* 65 (1975): 164.
6. Relph, *Place and Placelessness,* 142; Relph, "Sense of Place," 208.
7. Erik Cohen, "The Tourist Guide: The Origins, Structure, and Dynamics of a Role," *Annals of Tourism Research* 12 (1985): 5–8.
8. John Urry, *The Tourist Gaze* (London: Sage, 1990); John Urry, *Consuming Places* (London: Routledge, 1995), 131.
9. Relph, *Place and Placelessness*.
10. Mike Robinson and David Picard, "Moments, Magic, and Memories: Photographic Tourists, Tourist Photographs, and Making Worlds," in *The Framed World: Tourism, Tourists, and Photography*, ed. Mike Robinson and David Picard (Farnham, UK: Ashgate, 2009), 1.
11. Urry, *The Tourist Gaze*, 1.

# Sources

Ap, John, and Kevin K. F. Wong. "Case Study on Tour Guiding: Professionalism, Issues, and Problems," *Tourism Management* 22 (2001): 551–63.
Cresswell, Tim. *Place: A Short Introduction*. Malden, MA: Blackwell, 2004.
Jordan, Fiona, and Heather Gibson. "'We're Not Stupid . . . But We'll Not Stay Home Either': Experiences of Solo Women Travelers." *Tourism Review International* 9 (2005): 195–211.

MacCannell, Dean. *The Tourist: A New Theory of the Leisure Class*. New York: Schocken Books, 1976. Reprinted with foreword by Lucy R. Lippard. Berkeley: University of California Press, 1999.

McNamara, Karen Elizabeth, and Bruce Prideaux. "A Typology of Solo Independent Women Travellers." *International Journal of Tourism Research* 12 (2010): 253–64.

Moir, James. "Seeing the Sites: Tourism as Perceptual Experience." In *Tourism and Visual Culture*, vol. 1, *Theories and Concepts*, edited by Peter M. Burns, Cathy Palmer, and Jo-Anne Lester, 165–69. Oxfordshire, UK: CABI, 2010.

Relph, Edward. *Place and Placelessness*. London: Pion, 1976.

———. "Sense of Place." In *Ten Geographic Ideas That Changed the World*, edited by Susan Hanson, 205–26. New Brunswick, NJ: Rutgers University Press, 1997.

Robinson, Mike, and David Picard. "Moments, Magic, and Memories: Photographic Tourists, Tourist Photographs, and Making Worlds." In *The Framed World: Tourism, Tourists, and Photography*, edited by Mike Robinson and David Picard, 1–38. Farnham, UK: Ashgate, 2009.

Suvantola, Jaakko. *Tourist's Experience of Place*. Aldershot, UK: Ashgate, 2002.

Tuan, Yi-Fu. "Place: An Experiential Perspective." *Geographical Review* 65 (1975): 151–65.

Urry, John. *Consuming Places*. London: Routledge, 1995.

———. *The Tourist Gaze*. London: Sage, 1990.

Williams, Stephen. *Tourism Geography*. London: Routledge, 1998.

Wilson, Erica, and Donna E. Little. "A 'Relative Escape'? The Impact of Constraints on Women Who Travel Solo." *Tourism Review International* 9 (2005): 155–75.

———. "The Solo Female Travel Experience: Exploring the 'Geography of Women's Fear.'" *Current Issues in Tourism* 11, no. 2 (2008): 167–86.

# Glossary

**accessibility**. The relative ease with which one location may be reached from another

**acculturation**. The process of exchange that takes place when two groups of people come into contact over time

**affect**. To act on or produce a change in something

**back region**. The part of a destination that is not intended for, or is closed to, tourists

**beautiful**. An aesthetic landscape concept dating back to the eighteenth century, describing a landscape that is soft, smooth, and harmonious in appearance, the experience of which is reassuring and pleasurable

**biogeography**. The study of living things

**circular itinerary**. A trip in which tourists travel from home to multiple destinations before returning home

**climate change adaptation**. The technological, economic, and sociocultural changes that are intended to minimize the risks and capitalize on the opportunities created by climate change

**climate change mitigation**. The technological, economic, and sociocultural changes that can lead to reductions in greenhouse gas emissions

**climatology**. The study of climate

**code of conduct**. A set of voluntary principles intended to inform patterns of behavior among tourism stakeholders and tourists to minimize the negative environmental effects of tourism

**collective tourist gaze**. The visual consumption of public places that are characterized by the presence of other people

**commodification**. The transformation of something of intrinsic value into a product that can be packaged and sold for consumption

**complementarity**. The relationship between people who have a desire for certain travel experiences and the place that has the ability to satisfy that desire

**critical regional geography**. An evolution of traditional regional geography based on the idea that regions are "social constructions" that must be critically examined to understand the ways in which they are defined and the meanings with which they are associated

**cultural geography**. A broad topical branch in human geography that studies various issues pertaining to how societies make sense of, give meaning to, interact with, and shape space and place

**deferred demand**. Those people who wish to travel but do not because of a problem or barrier at the desired destination or in the tourism infrastructure

**demonstration effect**. Changes in attitudes, values, or patterns of behavior experienced by local people as a result of observing tourists

**direct economic effect**. The introduction of tourist dollars to the local economy

**discretionary income**. The money that is left over after taxes and all other necessary expenses have been taken care of

**distance decay**. Exponential decrease in demand for a product or service as the distance traveled to obtain that product or service increases

**domestic tourism**. Tourists traveling within their own country

**drifter**. A type of tourist that seeks out new tourism destinations, utilizes local infrastructure, and immerses himself or herself in the local culture

**economic development**. A process of change that creates the conditions for improvements in productivity and income of the population

**economic geography**. The study of the spatial patterns of economic activities, including locations, distributions, interactions, and outcomes

**ecotourism** (the International Ecotourism Society definition). Responsible travel to natural areas that conserves the environment and improves the well-being of local people

**effect**. Something that is produced by an agency or cause; a result or a consequence

**effective demand**. Those people who wish to and have the opportunity to travel

**enclave tourism**. Geographically isolated and spatially concentrated tourism facilities and activities

**environmental carrying capacity**. The extent of tourism that can take place at a site before its environment experiences negative effects

**environmental geography**. A topical branch of geography that lies at the intersection of physical geography and human geography and is concerned with the ways in which the environment affects people and people affect the environment

**experience stage**. The primary stage of the tourism process, in which tourists participate in a variety of activities at a destination

**explorer**. A type of tourist that travels for more than pleasure or diversion, utilizes a combination of tourist and local infrastructure, and seeks interaction with local people

**front region**. The part of a destination that has been entirely constructed for the purpose of tourism

**geomorphology**. The study of landforms

**geotourism** (National Geographic Society definition). Tourism that sustains or enhances the geographical character of a place, including its environment, culture, aesthetics, heritage, and the well-being of its residents

**globalization**. The increasing interconnectedness of the world

**historical geography**. The study of the geography and geographic conditions of past periods and the processes of change that have taken place over time to better understand the geography of the present

**hub-and-spoke itinerary**. A trip in which tourists travel from home to a destination and use that destination as a base from which to visit other destinations

**human geography**. One of the two main subdivisions of geography, which focuses on the study of the patterns of human occupation of the earth

**hydrology**. The study of water

**inbound tourism**. Tourists traveling to a place of destination

**indirect economic effect**. The second round of spending, in which recipients of tourist dollars pay the expenses of and reinvest in their tourism business

**individual mass tourist**. A type of tourist that travels for pleasure and seeks experiences different from those that may be obtained at home without straying too far from his or her comfort zone

**induced economic effect**. An additional round of spending after the recipients of tourist dollars pay the government, employees, suppliers, etc.; money spent by these new recipients for their own purposes

**interchange**. A node within a transportation network

**international tourism**. Tourists traveling to another country

**last chance tourism**. A recent trend in tourism in which tourists seek environments that are experiencing fundamental changes and might ultimately "disappear"

**leakages**. The portion of the income from tourism that does not get reinvested in the local economy; occurs with each round of spending

**leisure time**. The free time left over after necessary activities have been completed, in which an individual may do what he or she chooses

**lingua franca**. A language used for the purpose of communication between people speaking different languages

**linkages**. The connections formed between tourism and other local economic sectors that can support tourism and help provide the goods and services demanded by tourists

**mass tourism**. The production of standardized experiences made available to large numbers of tourists at a low cost

**meteorology**. The study of weather

**movement stage**. The stage of the tourism process in which tourists use some form of transportation to reach the destination and to return home; may be a means to an end or a part of the experience stage

**multiplier effect**. A ratio of the additional income generated by the indirect and induced economic effects from the re-spending of tourist dollars in the local economy

**niche tourism**. The production of specialized experiences for relatively small markets based on a particular resource at the destination or a specific tourism product

**no demand**. Those people who do not travel and do not wish to travel

**organized mass tourist**. A type of tourist that travels purely for diversion, in which place is less important than experience, and is entirely dependent on the tourism infrastructure

**outbound tourism**. Tourists traveling from their home environment

**perceptual carrying capacity**. The extent of tourism that can take place at a site before tourist dissatisfaction occurs

**physical carrying capacity**. The limits of a particular space, such as the number of tourists a site can contain

**physical geography**. One of the two main subdivisions of geography, which focuses on the study of the earth's physical systems

**picturesque**. An aesthetic landscape concept dating back to the eighteenth century, describing a landscape that has a rough, varied, or irregular quality that gives it an interesting character for observation and illustration in painting

**picturesque tourism**. A type of tourism popular in the late eighteenth and early nineteenth centuries, which dictated what types of places to visit and how to experience these places based on a set of predetermined criteria

**place**. A unit of the earth's surface that has meaning based on the physical and human features of that location

**placelessness**. A loss of identity where one place looks and feels like other places, often as a result of the superficial, stereotypical images circulated by the media

**place promotion**. The deliberate use of marketing tools to communicate both specific and selective ideas and images about a particular place to a desired audience for the purpose of shaping perceptions of that place and ultimately influencing decisions

**point-to-point itinerary**. A trip in which tourists travel from home to a destination and back

**political geography**. The study of the ways states relate to each other in a globalized world

**post-trip stage**. The final stage in the tourism process after the tourists return home, in which they relive their trip through memories, pictures, and souvenirs

**potential demand**. Those people who wish to travel and will do so when their circumstances change

**preferred sites**. Planned locations that have sufficient tourist facilities to spatially concentrate visitors, thereby limiting the environmental effects of tourism to a particular area

**pre-trip stage**. The first stage in the tourism process, in which potential tourists evaluate their travel options, make decisions, and complete all arrangements for a trip

**pro-poor tourism** (Pro-Poor Tourism Partnership definition). Tourism that results in increased net benefits for poor people and ensures that tourism growth contributes to poverty reduction

**protected area** (Convention on Biological Diversity definition). A geographically defined area which is designated or regulated and managed to achieve specific conservation objectives

**pull factor**. Something in the destination environment that attracts people to visit that place over another

**push factor**. Something in the home environment that impels people to leave temporarily and travel somewhere else

**region**. A unit of the earth's surface that is distinguished from other areas by certain characteristics

**regional geography**. An approach in geography that studies the varied geographic characteristics of a region

**relative location**. The position of a place in relation to other places

**romantic**. An aesthetic landscape concept dating back to the nineteenth century, describing a landscape that is wild and untouched by humans, immersion in which can help refresh the mind, body, and soul

**romantic tourism**. A type of tourism popular in the nineteenth century that encouraged people to immerse themselves in nature, particularly through walking, hiking, or roving

**romantic tourist gaze**. A private, personal experience in which tourists feel they form a connection with a place through the visual consumption of that place

**rural geography**. The study of contemporary rural landscapes, societies, and economies

**scale**. The size of the area studied

**sense of place**. The association with and emotional attachment to places

**social geography**. The topical branch of geography concerned with the relationships between society and space, such as space as a setting for social interaction or the ways in which spaces are shaped by these interactions

**space**. Locations on the earth's surface

**spatial distribution**. The organization of various phenomena on the earth's surface

**spatial zoning**. A land management strategy that designates permissible uses of an area based on its resources and/or character—i.e., what tourism activities may be undertaken where

**sublime**. An aesthetic landscape concept dating back to the eighteenth century, describing a landscape that is rugged, vast, or dark, the experience of which may be frightening and thrilling

**suppressed demand**. Those people who wish to travel but do not

**sustainable development** (World Commission on Environment and Development definition). Development that meets the needs of the present without compromising the ability of future generations to meet their own needs

**sustainable tourism**. An approach to tourism recognizing that the demands of present tourists must be met without eroding the tourism base and thus reducing or preventing tourism in the future

**terminal**. A node where transport flows begin and end

**topical geography**. An approach in geography that studies a particular geographic topic in various place or regional contexts

**tourism** (United Nations World Tourism Organization definition). The activities of persons traveling to and staying in places outside of their usual environment for not more than one consecutive year for leisure, business, and other purposes

**tourism attractions**. Aspects of places that are of interest to tourists and can include things to be seen, activities to be done, or experiences to be had

**tourism carrying capacity**. Refers to the number of tourists a destination or attraction can support and sustain

**tourism demand**. The total number of persons who travel, or wish to travel, to use tourist facilities and services at places away from their places of work and residence

**tourism itinerary**. The planned route or journey for a trip

**tourism products**. The increasingly specialized types of experiences provided in the supply of tourism

**tourism resource**. A component of the destination's physical or cultural environment that has the potential to facilitate tourism or provide the basis for a tourism attraction

**tourism resource audit**. A tool that can be used by destination stakeholders to systematically identify, classify, and assess all of those features of a place that will impact the supply of tourism

**tourism stakeholders**. The various individuals and/or organizations that have an interest in tourism

**tourism supply**. The aggregate of all businesses that directly provide goods or services to facilitate business, pleasure, and leisure activities away from the home environment

**tourist area life cycle**. A model proposed to explain the process of development and evolution of tourism destinations over six stages, including exploration, involvement, development, consolidation, stagnation, and an undetermined post-stagnation stage

**tourist dollars**. The money that tourists bring with them and spend at the destination on lodging, food, souvenirs, excursions, and other activities or services

**tourist-generating regions**. The source areas or origins for tourists

**tourist inversions**. The theory that the experience that a tourist seeks in his or her temporary escape is one of contrasts and involves a shift in attitudes or patterns of behavior away from the norm to a temporary opposite

**tourist-receiving regions**. The destination areas for tourists

**tourist typology**. An organizational framework to identify categories of tourists based on motivations, behavior, demographic characteristics, or other variables

**transport geography**. The topical branch of geography concerned with the movement of goods and people from one place to another, including the spatial patterns of this movement and the geographic factors that allow or constrain it

**transportation mode**. The means of movement or type of transportation; generally air, surface or water

**transportation network**. The spatial structure and organization of the infrastructure that supports, and to some extent determines, patterns of movement

**transportation node**. An access point on a transportation network

**travel account**. The difference between the income that the destination country receives from tourism and the expenditures of that country's citizens when they travel abroad

**urban geography**. The study of the relationships between or patterns within cities and metropolitan areas

# Bibliography

Aitchison, Cara, Nicola E. MacLeod, and Stephen J. Shaw. *Leisure and Tourism Landscapes: Social and Cultural Geographies.* London: Routledge, 2000.

Albalate, Daniel, and Germà Bel. "Tourism and Urban Public Transport: Holding Demand Pressure under Supply Constraints." *Tourism Management* 31 (2010): 425–33.

Amsterdam Tourist Board. "Amsterdam Metropolitan Area." Accessed February 1, 2012. http://www.iamsterdam.com/en/visiting/amsterdam-metropolitan-area.

Anderson, Wineaster. "Enclave Tourism and Its Socio-Economic Impact in Emerging Destinations." *Anatolia—An International Journal of Tourism and Hospitality Research* 22, no. 3 (2011): 361–77.

Andrews, Hazel. "Feeling at Home: Embodying Britishness in a Spanish Charter Tourists Resort." *Tourist Studies* 5, no. 3 (2005): 247–66.

Andrews, Malcolm. *The Search for the Picturesque: Landscape Aesthetics and Tourism in Britain, 1760–1880.* Stanford, CA: Stanford University Press, 1989.

Ap, John, and Kevin K. F. Wong. "Case Study on Tour Guiding: Professionalism, Issues, and Problems." *Tourism Management* 22 (2001): 551–63.

"Arenal Volcano Costa Rica." Accessed October 29, 2011. http://www.arenal.net/.

Ashley, Caroline, Charlotte Boyd, and Harold Goodwin. "Pro-Poor Tourism: Putting Poverty at the Heart of the Tourism Agenda." *Natural Resource Perspectives* 51 (2000): 1–6.

Ashley, Caroline, Dilys Roe, and Harold Goodwin. "Pro-Poor Strategies: Making Tourism Work for the Poor." *Pro-Poor Tourism Report* 1 (2001).

Aspinall, Algernon E. *The Pocket Guide to the West Indies.* 2nd ed. London: Duckworth & Co., 1910.

Association of American Geographers. "Washington, D.C.: Building Partnerships for Geography." May 2010. Accessed December 1, 2012. http://www.aag.org/galleries/meridian-files/201005Meridian.pdf.

Awwad, Ramadan A., T. N. Olsthoorn, Y. Zhou, Stefan Uhlenbrook, and Ebel Smidt. "Optimum Pumping-Injection System for Saline Groundwater Desalination in Sharm El Sheikh." *WaterMill Working Paper Series* 11 (2008). Accessed October 26, 2011. http://www.unesco-ihe.org/WaterMill-Working-Paper-Series/Working-Paper-Series.

Bagchi-Sen, Sharmistha, and Helen Lawton Smith. "Introduction: The Past, Present, and Future of Economic Geography." In *Economic Geography: Past, Present, and Future*, edited by Sharmistha Bagchi-Sen and Helen Lawton Smith, 1–8. London: Routledge, 2006.

Barbados Tourism Authority. "Perfect Weather." Accessed February 4, 2011. http://www
.visitbarbados.org/perfect-weather.

Baum, Tom. "Images of Tourism Past and Present." *International Journal of Contemporary Hospitality Management* 8, no. 4 (1996): 25–30.

Beckerson, John, and John K. Walton. "Selling Air: Marketing the Intangible at British Resorts." In *Histories of Tourism: Representation, Identity, and Conflict*, edited by John Walton, 55–68. Clevedon, UK: Channel View Publications, 2005.

Berghoff, Hartmut, and Barbara Korte. "Britain and the Making of Modern Tourism: An Interdisciplinary Approach." In *The Making of Modern Tourism: The Cultural History of the British Experience, 1600–2000*, edited by Hartmut Berghoff, Barbara Korte, Ralf Schneider, and Christopher Harvie, 1–20. Houndmills, UK: Palgrave Macmillan, 2000.

Bermingham, Ann. *Landscape and Ideology: The English Rustic Tradition, 1740–1860*. Berkeley: University of California Press, 1986.

Blacksell, Mark. *Political Geography*. London: Routledge, 2006.

Boniface, Brian, and Chris Cooper. *Worldwide Destinations: The Geography of Travel and Tourism*. 4th ed. Amsterdam: Elsevier Butterworth Heinemann, 2005.

Borelli, Simone, and Stefania Minestrini. "WWF Mediterranean Programme." Accessed February 24, 2011. http://www.monachus-guardian.org/library/medpro01.pdf.

Braunlich, Carl G. "Lessons from the Atlantic City Casino Experience." *Journal of Travel Research* 34 (1996): 46–56.

Bullen, Frank T. *Back to Sunny Seas*. London: Smith, Elder & Co., 1905.

Burmon, Andrew. "Hallstatt, an Austrian Hamlet in Communist China." AOL Travel. June 17, 2011. Accessed July 5, 2011. http://news.travel.aol.com/2011/06/17/hallstatt-an-austrian -hamlet-in-communist-china/.

Burnford, Angela. "Honduras, National Geographic Announce 'Geotourism' Partnership." *National Geographic News*, October 24, 2004. Accessed February 1, 2011. http://news .nationalgeographic.com/news/2004/10/1025_041025_travelwatch.html.

Butler, R. W. "The Concept of a Tourist Area Cycle Evolution: Implications for Management of Resources." *Canadian Geographer* 24, no. 1 (1980): 5–12.

Butler, Richard. "The Resort Cycle Two Decades On." In *Tourism in the 21st Century: Lessons from Experience*, edited by Bill Faulkner, Gianna Moscardo, and Eric Laws, 284–99. London: Continuum, 2000.

———. "The Tourist Area Life Cycle in the Twenty-First Century." In *A Companion to Tourism*, edited by Alan A. Lew, C. Michael Hall, and Allan M. Williams, 159–69. Malden, MA: Blackwell, 2004.

Buzzard, James. *The Beaten Track: European Tourism, Literature, and the Ways to Culture, 1800–1918*. Oxford: Clarendon Press, 1993.

Caribbean Tourism Organization. "2009 Country Statistics and Analysis [Barbados]." Accessed February 4, 2011. http://www.onecaribbean.org/content/files/Strep1.pdf.

———."About Us." Accessed October 24, 2010. http://www.onecaribbean.org/aboutus/.

———. *Caribbean Vacation Planner*. Coral Gables, FL: Gold Book, 2002.

Carnival Corporation. "Cruise to Nowhere." Accessed November 6, 2010. http://www.carnival .com/cruise-to/cruise-to-nowhere.aspx.

Castree, Noel, David Demeritt, and Diana Liverman. "Introduction: Making Sense of Environmental Geography." In *A Companion to Environmental Geography*, edited by Noel Castree, David Demeritt, Diana Liverman, and Bruce Rhoads, 1–16. Malden, MA: Blackwell, 2009.

Ceballos-Lascuráin, Héctor. *Tourism, Ecotourism, and Protected Areas*. Gland, Switzerland: IUCN Publication, 1996.

Central West Virginia Regional Airport Authority. "Yeager Airport History." Accessed October 29, 2011. http://yeagerairport.com/about.html.

Chang, T. C., and Shirlena Huang. "Urban Tourism: Between the Global and the Local." In *A Companion to Tourism*, edited by Alan A. Lew, C. Michael Hall, and Allan M. Williams, 223–34. Malden, MA: Blackwell, 2004.

Christopherson, Robert W. *Geosystems: An Introduction to Physical Geography.* 7th ed. Upper Saddle River, NJ: Pearson Prentice Hall, 2009.

Chu, Petra ten-Doesschate. *Nineteenth-Century European Art.* New York: Abrams, 2003.

Cohen, Erik. "Authenticity and Commoditization in Tourism." *Annals of Tourism Research* 15 (1988): 371–86.

———. "The Tourist Guide: The Origins, Structure, and Dynamics of a Role." *Annals of Tourism Research* 12 (1985): 5–29.

Cohen-Hattab, Kobi, and Yossi Katz. "The Attraction of Palestine: Tourism in the Years 1850–1948." *Journal of Historical Geography* 27, no. 2 (2001): 166–77.

Crang, Mike. *Cultural Geography.* London: Routledge, 1998.

Cresswell, Tim. *Place: A Short Introduction.* Malden, MA: Blackwell, 2004.

Davie, Tim. *Fundamentals of Hydrology.* 2nd ed. London: Routledge, 2002.

De Freitas, C. R. "Tourism Climatology: Evaluating Environmental Information for Decision Making and Business Planning in the Recreation and Tourism Sector." *International Journal of Biometeorology* 48 (2003): 45–54.

Del Casino, Vincent J. *Social Geography: A Critical Introduction.* Malden, MA: Blackwell, 2009.

Diab, Atef M. "Bacteriological Studies on the Potability, Efficacy, and EIA of Desalination Operations at Sharm El-Sheikh Region, Egypt." *Egyptian Journal of Biology* 3 (2001): 59–65.

Dickinson, Janet E., and Derek Robbins. "Representations of Tourism Transport Problems in a Rural Destination." *Tourism Management* 29 (2008): 1110–1121.

Dominica Hotel and Tourism Association. *Destination Dominica.* North Miami, FL: Ulrich Communications Corporation, 2003.

Dove, Jane. *Access to Geography: Tourism and Recreation.* London: Hodder & Stoughton, 2004.

Duncan, James, Nuala C. Jackson, and Richard H. Schein. "Introduction." In *A Companion to Cultural Geography*, edited by James Duncan, Nuala C. Jackson, and Richard H. Schein, 1–9. Malden, MA: Blackwell, 2004.

Duval, David Timothy. *Tourism and Transport: Modes, Networks, and Flows.* Clevedon, UK: Channel View Publications, 2007.

Fair Trade in Tourism South Africa. "Welcome to Fair Trade in Tourism South Africa." Accessed January 15, 2012. http://www.fairtourismsa.org.za/index.html.

Fédération Internationale de Football Association. "Lessons from 2006." July 9, 2010. Accessed November 23, 2010. http://www.fifa.com/worldcup/archive/southafrica2010/news/newsid=1270860/index.html.

Feifer, Maxine. *Tourism in History: From Imperial Rome to the Present.* New York: Stein and Day, 1986.

Fennell, David A. *Ecotourism.* 3rd ed. London: Routledge, 2008.

Froude, James A. *The English in the West Indies or the Bow of Ulysses.* London: Longmans, Green and Co., 1909.

Ganley, Elaine, and Bouazza Ben Bouazza. "Tunisia Riots: Tourists Evacuated As Protests Continue." *Huffington Post*, January 14, 2011. Accessed February 4, 2012. http://www.huffingtonpost.com/2011/01/14/tunisia-riots-tourists-ev_n_809118.html.

Gassan, Richard H. *The Birth of American Tourism: New York, the Hudson Valley, and American Culture, 1790–1830.* Amherst: University of Massachusetts Press, 2008.

Gibson, Chris. "Locating Geographies of Tourism." *Progress in Human Geography* 32, no. 3 (2008): 407–22.

Gilbert, Anne. "The New Regional Geography in English- and French-Speaking Countries." *Progress in Human Geography* 12 (1988): 208–28.

Godfrey, Kerry, and Jackie Clarke. *The Tourism Development Handbook: A Practical Approach to Planning and Marketing.* London: Cassell, 2000.

Goeldner, Charles R., and J. R. Brent Ritchie. *Tourism: Principles, Practices, Philosophies.* 9th ed. Hoboken, NJ: Wiley, 2006.

Goh, Carey. "Exploring Impact of Climate on Tourism Demand." *Annals of Tourism Research* 39, no. 4 (2012): 1859–1883.

Gómez Martín, María Belén. "Weather, Climate, and Tourism: A Geographical Perspective." *Annals of Tourism Research* 32, no. 3 (2005): 571–91.

Graburn, Nelson. "The Anthropology of Tourism." *Annals of Tourism Research* 10 (1983): 9–33.

Gregory, Derek. "Scripting Egypt: Orientalism and the Cultures of Travel." In *Writes of Passage: Reading Travel Writing,* edited by James Duncan and Derek Gregory, 114–50. London: Routledge, 1999.

Gregory, Derek, Ron Johnston, and Geraldine Pratt. *Dictionary of Human Geography.* 5th ed. Hoboken, NJ: Wiley-Blackwell, 2009.

Gunn, Clare A., with Turgut Var. *Tourism Planning: Basics, Concepts, Cases.* 4th ed. New York: Routledge, 2002.

Hall, Derek. "Brand Development, Tourism, and National Identity: The Re-Imaging of Former Yugoslavia." *Brand Management* 9 (2002): 323–34.

Hall, Derek R. "Conceptualising Tourism Transport: Inequality and Externality Issues." *Journal of Transport Geography* 7 (1999): 181–88.

Hall, Michael C., and Alan Lew. *Understanding and Managing Tourism Impacts: An Integrated Approach.* New York: Routledge, 2009.

Hanson, Susan. "Thinking Back, Thinking Ahead: Some Questions for Economic Geographers." In *Economic Geography: Past, Present, and Future,* edited by Sharmistha Bagchi-Sen and Helen Lawton Smith, 25–33. London: Routledge, 2006.

Henderson, Joan. "Transport and Tourism Destination Development: An Indonesian Perspective." *Tourism and Hospitality Research* 9, no. 3 (2009): 199–208.

Higgins-Desbiolles, Freya. "More Than an 'Industry': The Forgotten Power of Tourism as a Social Force." *Tourism Management* 27 (2006): 1192–1208.

Holden, Andrew. *Environment and Tourism.* 2nd ed. London: Routledge, 2008.

Horner, Susan, and John Swarbrooke. *International Cases in Tourism Management.* Burlington, MA: Elsevier Butterworth-Heinemann, 2004.

Hyundai Motor Manufacturing Alabama. "HMMA Employment." Accessed March 31, 2011. http://www.hmmausa.com/jobshmma/hmma-employment/.

Ioannides, Dimitri. "The Economic Geography of the Tourist Industry: Ten Years of Progress in Research and an Agenda for the Future." *Tourism Geographies* 8 (2006): 76–86.

———. "Strengthening the Ties between Tourism and Economic Geography: A Theoretical Agenda." *Professional Geographer* 47 (1995): 49–60.

Ioannides, Dimitri, and Keith G. Debbage. "Introduction: Exploring the Economic Geography and Tourism Nexus." In *The Economic Geography of the Tourist Industry,* edited by Dimitri Ioannides and Keith G. Debbage, 1–13. London: Routledge, 1998.

Islas Travel Guides. "Welcome to Magaluf." Accessed February 8, 2011. http://www.majorca-mallorca.co.uk/magaluf.htm.

Ivanovic, Milena. *Cultural Tourism.* Cape Town: Juta, 2008.

Ives, Joseph C. *Report upon the Colorado River of the West; Explored in 1857 and 1858*. Washington, DC: Government Printing Office, 1861.

Jordan, Fiona, and Heather Gibson. "'We're Not Stupid . . . But We'll Not Stay Home Either': Experiences of Solo Women Travelers." *Tourism Review International* 9 (2005): 195–211.

Kaplan, Dave, James Wheeler, and Steven Holloway. *Urban Geography*. 2nd ed. Hoboken, NJ: Wiley, 2009.

Keeling, David J. "Transportation Geography: New Directions on Well-Worn Trails." *Progress in Human Geography* 31 (2007): 217–25.

Kentucky Derby. "2011 Kentucky Derby." Accessed November 23, 2010. http://www.kentucky derby.info/.

Kershaw, Steve. *Oceanography: An Earth Science Perspective*. Cheltenham, UK: Stanley Thornes, 2000.

Kevan, Simon. "Quests for Cures: A History of Tourism for Climate and Health." *International Journal of Biometeorology* 37 (1993): 113–24.

Khadaroo, Jameel, and Boopen Seetanah. "The Role of Transport Infrastructure in International Tourism Development: A Gravity Model Approach." *Tourism Management* 29 (2008): 831–40.

Kingsley, Charles. *At Last: A Christmas in the West Indies*. New York: Harper & Brothers Publishers, 1871.

Korte, Barbara. *English Travel Writing from Pilgrimages to Postcolonial Explorations*, translated by Catherine Matthias. Houndmills, UK: Macmillan, 2000.

Koshar, Rudy. "'What Ought to Be Seen': Tourists' Guidebooks and National Identities in Modern Germany and Europe." *Journal of Contemporary History* 33 (1998): 323–40.

Krabi Tourism. "Maya Bay, Krabi—Thailand." Accessed May 25, 2011. http://www.krabi -tourism.com/phiphi/maya-bay.htm.

Lanegran, David A., and Salvatore J. Natoli. *Guidelines for Geographic Education in the Elementary and Secondary Schools*. Washington, DC: Association of American Geographers, 1984.

Lemelin, Raynald Harvey, Emma Stewart, and Jackie Dawson. "An Introduction to Last Chance Tourism." In *Last Chance Tourism: Adapting Tourism Opportunities in a Changing World*, edited by Raynald Harvey Lemelin, Jackie Dawson, and Emma J. Stewart, 3–9. London, Routledge, 2012.

Lew, Alan. "Tourism Is NOT the World's Largest Industry—So Stop Saying It Is!" *Tourism Place Blog*, May 1, 2008. Accessed February 4, 2011. http://tourismplace.blogspot.com/2008/04/ tourism-is-not-worlds-largest-industry.html.

Lew, Alan, and Bob McKercher. "Modeling Tourist Movements: A Local Destination Analysis." *Annals of Tourism Research* 33 (2006): 403–23.

Light, Duncan. "'Facing the Future': Tourism and Identity-Building in Post-Socialist Romania." *Political Geography* 20 (2001): 1053–1074.

Löfgren, Orvar. *On Holiday: A History of Vacationing*. Berkeley: University of California Press, 1999.

Lomine, Loykie. "Tourism in Augustan Society (44 BC–AD 69)." In *Histories of Tourism: Representation, Identity, and Conflict*, edited by John Walton, 69–87. Clevedon, UK: Channel View Publications, 2005.

Lumsdon, Les, and Stephen J. Page. "Progress in Transport and Tourism Research: Reformulating the Transport-Tourism Interface and Future Research Agendas." In *Tourism and Transport: Issues and Agenda for the New Millennium*, edited by Les Lumsdon and Stephen J. Page, 1–28. Amsterdam: Elsevier, 2004.

MacCannell, Dean. "Staged Authenticity: Arrangements of Social Space in Tourist Settings." *American Journal of Sociology* 79, no. 3 (1973): 589–603.

———. *The Tourist: A New Theory of the Leisure Class*. New York: Schocken Books, 1976. Reprinted with foreword by Lucy R. Lippard. Berkeley: University of California Press, 1999.

MacKay, Kelly J., and Daniel R. Fesenmaier. "Pictorial Element of Destination in Image Formation." *Annals of Tourism Research* 24, no. 3 (1997): 537–65.

MacLeod, Nicola. "Cultural Tourism: Aspects of Authenticity and Commodification." In *Cultural Tourism in a Changing World: Politics, Participation, and (Re)presentation*, edited by Melanie K. Smith and Mike Robinson, 177–190. Clevedon, UK: Channel View Publications, 2006.

Makasutu Culture Forest—The Gambia. "History." Accessed February 19, 2011. http://www .makasutu.com/index.php.

Manwa, Haretsebe A. "Is Zimbabwe Ready to Venture into the Cultural Tourism Market?" *Development Southern Africa* 24, no. 3 (2007): 465–74.

Martin, Geoffrey J. *All Possible Worlds: A History of Geographical Ideas*. New York: Oxford University Press, 2005.

Mathieson, Alister, and Geoffrey Wall. *Tourism: Economic, Physical, and Social Impacts*. London: Longman, 1982.

Mbaiwa, Joseph E. "Enclave Tourism and Its Socio-Economic Impacts in the Okavango Delta, Botswana." *Tourism Management* 26 (2005): 157–72.

McElroy, Jerome L., and Courtney E. Parry. "The Characteristics of Small Island Tourist Economies." *Tourism and Hospitality Research* 10, no. 4 (2010): 315–28.

McGill, Kevin. "Jindal: BP Funding Millions for Oil Spill Recovery." Associated Press, November 1, 2010. Accessed November 4, 2010. http://www.businessweek.com/ap/financialnews/ D9J7J43G1.htm.

McKercher, Bob, and Hilary du Cros. *Cultural Tourism: The Partnership between Tourism and Cultural Heritage Management*. New York: Haworth Hospitality Press, 2002.

McKercher, Bob, and Alan A. Lew. "Tourist Flows and the Spatial Distribution of Tourists." In *A Companion to Tourism*, edited by Alan A. Lew, C. Michael Hall, and Allan M. Williams, 36–48. Malden, MA: Blackwell, 2004.

McKnight, Tom, and Darrel Hess. *Physical Geography: A Landscape Appreciation*. Upper Saddle River, NJ: Prentice Hall, 2000.

McNamara, Karen Elizabeth, and Bruce Prideaux. "A Typology of Solo Independent Women Travellers." *International Journal of Tourism Research* 12 (2010): 253–64.

Meethan, Kevin. *Tourism in Global Society: Place, Culture, Consumption*. Houndmills, UK: Palgrave, 2001.

Moir, James. "Seeing the Sites: Tourism as Perceptual Experience." In *Tourism and Visual Culture*, vol. 1, *Theories and Concepts*, edited by Peter M. Burns, Cathy Palmer, and Jo-Anne Lester, 165–69. Oxfordshire, UK: CABI, 2010.

Morgan, Nigel. "Problematizing Place Promotion." In *A Companion to Tourism*, edited by Alan A. Lew, C. Michael Hall, and Allan M. Williams, 173–83. Malden, MA: Blackwell, 2004.

Moscardo, Gianna, Philip Pearce, Alastair Morrison, David Green, and Joseph T. O'Leary. "Developing a Typology for Understanding Visiting Friends and Relatives Markets." *Journal of Travel Research* 38, no. 3 (2000): 251–59.

Mulongoy, Kalemani Jo, and Stuart Chape. "Protected Areas and Biodiversity: An Overview of Key Issues." United Nations Environment Programme. Accessed February 19, 2011. http:// development.unep-wcmc.org/protected_areas/pdf/protected_areas_bioreport.pdf.

National Geographic Education Foundation. "Survey Results: U.S. Young Adults Are Lagging." Accessed August 22, 2011. http://www.nationalgeographic.com/geosurvey/highlights.html.

National Geographic Society. "The Geotourism Charter." Accessed February 1, 2011. http:// travel.nationalgeographic.com/travel/sustainable/pdf/geotourism_charter_template.pdf.

National Park Service. "Grand Canyon Trip Planner." Accessed October 26, 2011. http://www.nps.gov/grca/parknews/upload/trip-planner-grca.pdf.

Nelson, Velvet. "The Construction of Slovenia as a European Tourism Destination in Guide-books." *Geoforum* 43 (2012): 1099–1107.

———. "Investigating Energy Issues in Dominica's Accommodations." *Tourism and Hospitality Research* 10 (2010): 345–58.

———. "Promoting Energy Strategies on Eco Certified Accommodation Websites." *Journal of Ecotourism* 9, no. 3 (2010): 187–200.

———. "'R.I.P. Nature Island': The Threat of a Proposed Oil Refinery on Dominica's Identity." *Social & Cultural Geography* 11, no. 8 (2010): 903–19.

———. "Traces of the Past: The Cycle of Expectation in Caribbean Tourism Representations." *Journal of Tourism and Cultural Change* 5 (2007): 1–16.

New Mexico Tourism Department. "North-Central Region." Accessed February 1, 2012. http://newmexico.org/explore/regions/northcentral.php.

Ohio Sauerkraut Festival. "Festival History." Accessed November 23, 2010. http://www.sauerkrautfestival.com/.

Okey, Robin. "Central Europe/Eastern Europe: Behind the Definitions." *Past & Present* 137 (1992): 102–33.

Oktoberfest. "The Oktoberfest Is Over!" Accessed November 23, 2010. http://www.oktoberfest.de/en/article/About+the+Oktoberfest/About+the+Oktoberfest/The+Oktoberfest+is+over!/2205/.

Oppermann, Martin. "Sex Tourism." *Annals of Tourism Research* 26, no. 2 (1999): 251–66.

Page, Stephen. "Transport and Tourism." In *A Companion to Tourism*, edited by Alan A. Lew, C. Michael Hall, and Allan M. Williams, 146–58. Malden, MA: Blackwell, 2004.

———. *Transport and Tourism: Global Perspectives*. 2nd ed. Harlow, UK: Pearson Prentice Hall, 2005.

Pain, Rachel, Michael Barke, Duncan Fuller, Jamie Gough, Robert MacFarlane, and Graham Mowl. *Introducing Social Geographies*. London: Arnold, 2001.

Prideaux, Bruce. "Links between Transport and Tourism—Past, Present, and Future." In *Tourism in the Twenty-First Century: Reflections on Experience*, edited by Bill Faulkner, Gianna Moscardo, and Eric Laws, 91–109. London: Continuum, 2001.

———. "The Role of the Transport System in Destination Development." *Tourism Management* 21 (2000): 53–63.

Priskin, Julianna. "Assessment of Natural Resources for Nature-Based Tourism: The Case of the Central Coast Region of Western Australia." *Tourism Management* 22, no. 6 (2001): 637–48.

Rayan, Magdy Abou, Berge Djebedjian, and Ibrahim Khaled. "Water Supply and Demand and a Desalination Option for Sinai, Egypt." *Desalination* 136 (2001): 73–81.

Reid, Alastair. "Reflections: Waiting for Columbus." *New Yorker*, February 24, 1992, 57–75.

Reilly, Jennifer, Peter Williams, and Wolfgang Haider. "Moving towards More Eco-Efficient Tourist Transportation to a Resort Destination: The Case of Whistler, British Columbia." *Research in Transportation Economics* 26 (2010): 66–73.

Relph, Edward. *Place and Placelessness*. London: Pion, 1976.

———. "Sense of Place." In *Ten Geographic Ideas That Changed the World*, edited by Susan Hanson, 205–26. New Brunswick, NJ: Rutgers University Press, 1997.

Rivera, Lauren A. "Managing 'Spoiled' National Identity: War, Tourism, and Memory in Croatia." *American Sociological Review* 73 (2008): 613–34.

Roach, John. "Young Americans Geographically Illiterate, Survey Suggests." *National Geographic News*, May 2, 2006. Accessed August 22, 2011. http://news.nationalgeographic.com/news/2006/05/0502_060502_geography.html.

Robinson, Mike, and David Picard. "Moments, Magic, and Memories: Photographic Tourists, Tourist Photographs, and Making Worlds." In *The Framed World: Tourism, Tourists, and Photography*, edited by Mike Robinson and David Picard, 1–38. Farnham, UK: Ashgate, 2009.

Rodrigue, Jean-Paul, Claude Comtois, and Brian Slack. *The Geography of Transport Systems*. 2nd ed. New York: Routledge, 2009. Accessed February 10, 2011. http://people.hofstra.edu/geotrans.

Roskill, Mark. *The Languages of Landscape*. University Park: The Pennsylvania State University Press, 1997.

Scott, Daniel, Bas Amelung, Suzanne Becken, Jean-Paul Ceron, Ghislan Dubois, Stefan Gössling, Paul Peeters, and Murray C. Simpson. *Climate Change and Tourism: Responding to Global Challenges, Summary*. Madrid: World Tourism Organization and United Nations Environment Programme, 2007. Accessed February 22, 2011. http://www.unwto.org/climate/support/en/pdf/summary_davos_e.pdf.

Seven Natural Wonders. "Grand Canyon." Accessed October 27, 2011. http://sevennaturalwonders.org/the-original/grand-canyon.

Shaffer, Marguerite. *See America First: Tourism and National Identity, 1880–1940*. Washington, DC: Smithsonian Institution Press, 2001.

Sharpley, Richard. "Tourism and the Countryside." In *A Companion to Tourism*, edited by Alan A. Lew, C. Michael Hall, and Allan M. Williams, 374–81. Malden, MA: Blackwell, 2004.

Shaw, Gareth, and Allan M. Williams. *Critical Issues in Tourism: A Geographical Perspective*. 2nd ed. Malden, MA: Blackwell, 2002.

Sheller, Mimi. *Consuming the Caribbean: From Arawaks to Zombies*. London: Routledge, 2003.

Shepherd, Robert. "Commodification, Culture, and Tourism." *Tourist Studies* 2, no. 2 (2002): 183–201.

Simmons, Jack. "Railways, Hotels, and Tourism in Great Britain, 1839–1914." *Journal of Contemporary History* 19 (1984): 201–22.

Smith, Melanie K. *Issues in Cultural Tourism Studies*. 2nd ed. London: Routledge, 2009.

Smith, Stephen L. J. "Defining Tourism: A Supply Side View." *Annals of Tourism Research* 15, no. 2 (1988): 179–90.

Stansfield, Charles. "Atlantic City and the Resort Cycle: Background to the Legalization of Gambling." *Annals of Tourism Research* 5, no. 2 (1978): 238–51.

———. "The Rejuvenation of Atlantic City: The Resort Cycle Recycles." In *The Tourism Area Life Cycle*, vol. 1, *Applications and Modifications*, edited by Richard W. Butler, 287–305. Clevedon, UK: Channel View Publications, 2006.

Steward, Jill. "'How and Where to Go': The Role of Travel Journalism in Britain and the Evolution of Foreign Travel, 1840–1914." In *Histories of Tourism: Representation, Identity, and Conflict*, edited by John Walton, 39–54. Clevedon, UK: Channel View Publications, 2005.

Suvantola, Jaakko. *Tourist's Experience of Place*. Aldershot, UK: Ashgate, 2002.

Swarbrooke, John. *The Development and Management of Visitor Attractions*. 2nd ed. Burlington, MA: Butterworth-Heinemann, 2002.

Swiss Travel System. "Switzerland by Train, Bus, and Boat." Accessed October 13, 2011. http://www.swisstravelsystem.com/en/.

Taylor, Peter J. "New Political Geographies: 'Twixt Places and Flows." In *The Student's Companion to Geography*, 2nd ed., edited by Alisdair Rogers and Heather A. Viles, 113–17. Malden, MA: Blackwell, 2003.

The International Ecotourism Society. "What Is Ecotourism?" Accessed November 20, 2010. http://www.ecotourism.org/what-is-ecotourism.

Thompson, Paul. "Blarney Stone 'Most Unhygienic Tourist Attraction in the World.'" *Daily Mail*, June 16, 2009. Accessed November 13, 2010. http://www.dailymail.co.uk/news/article-1193477/Blarney-Stone-unhygienic-tourist-attraction-world.html.

Torres, Rebecca. "Linkages between Tourism and Agriculture in Mexico." *Annals of Tourism Research* 30, no. 3 (2003): 546–66.

———. "Toward a Better Understanding of Tourism and Agriculture Linkages in the Yucatan: Tourist Food Consumption and Preferences." *Tourism Geographies* 4, no. 3 (2002): 282–306.

Torres, Rebecca, and Janet Henshall Momsen. "Challenges and Potential for Linking Tourism and Agriculture to Achieve Pro-Poor Tourism Objectives." *Progress in Development Studies* 4, no. 4 (2004): 294–318.

Torres, Rebecca Maria, and Janet D. Momsen. "Gringolandia: The Construction of a New Tourist Space in Mexico." *Annals of the Association of American Geographers* 95, no. 2 (2005): 314–35.

Torres, Rebecca Maria, and Velvet Nelson. "Identifying Types of Tourists for Better Planning and Development: A Case Study of Nuanced Market Segmentation in Cancún." *Applied Research in Economic Development* 5, no. 3 (2008): 12–24.

Tourism BC. "Vancouver Things to Do." Accessed February 1, 2012. http://www.hellobc.com/vancouver/things-to-do.aspx.

Tourism Ireland. "Shannon—Clare County." Accessed March 2, 2011. http://www.discoverireland.com/us/ireland-places-to-go/placefinder/s/shannon-clare/.

Tourism Toronto. "Places to Explore." Accessed February 1, 2012. http://www.seetorontonow.com/Visitor/Explore/City-Neighbourhoods.aspx.

Towner, John. "The Grand Tour: A Key Phase in the History of Tourism." *Annals of Tourism Research* 12 (1985): 297–333.

TravelBlog. "Free Online Travel Diary." Accessed January 3, 2012. http://www.travelblog.org/about.html.

Trollope, Anthony. *The West Indies and the Spanish Main*. 4th ed. London: Dawsons of Pall Mall, 1968.

Tuan, Yi-Fu. "Place: An Experiential Perspective." *Geographical Review* 65 (1975): 151–65.

Uncyclopedia. "Tourist—The Stereotype." Accessed October 12, 2010. http://uncyclopedia.wikia.com/wiki/Tourist_-_the_stereotype.

United Nations Educational, Scientific, and Cultural Organization. "The Criteria for Selection." Accessed September 10, 2011. http://whc.unesco.org/en/criteria/.

———. "Hallstatt-Dachstein/Salzkammergut Cultural Landscape." Accessed July 5, 2011. http://whc.unesco.org/en/list/806.

United Nations Office of the High Representative for the Least Developed Countries, Landlocked Developing Countries, and the Small Island Developing States. "Small Island Developing States." Accessed January 15, 2012. http://www.unohrlls.org/en/sids/43.

United Nations World Tourism Organization. "International Tourism 2010: Multi-Speed Recovery." January 17, 2011. Accessed January 27, 2011. http://85.62.13.114/media/news/en/press_det.php?id=7331&idioma=E.

———. "Tourism Will Contribute to Solutions for Global Climate Change and Poverty Challenges." March 8, 2007. Accessed February 22, 2011. http://www.unwto.org/newsroom/Releases/2007/march/globa_climate.htm.

———. *UNWTO Tourism Highlights 2011 Edition*. Madrid: World Tourism Organization, 2011. Accessed February 7, 2012. http://mkt.unwto.org/sites/all/files/docpdf/unwtohighlights11enlr_1.pdf.

———. *UNWTO Tourism Highlights 2012 Edition*. Madrid: World Tourism Organization, 2012. Accessed December 10, 2012. http://dtxtq4w60xqpw.cloudfront.net/sites/all/files/docpdf/unwtohighlights12enlr_1.pdf

———. *World Tourism Barometer* 8, no. 1 (2010). Accessed October 24, 2010. http://www.unwto.org/facts/eng/pdf/barometer/UNWTO_Barom10_1_en.pdf.

United States Census Bureau. "2010 Census Urban and Rural Classification and Urban Area Criteria." Accessed April 28, 2011. http://www.census.gov/geo/www/ua/2010urbanruralclass.html.

Urry, John. *Consuming Places*. London: Routledge, 1995.

———. *The Tourist Gaze*. London: Sage, 1990.

The Venetian Las Vegas. "Human Resources." Accessed March 31, 2011. http://www.venetian.com/Company-Information/Human-Resources.

Visit Baltimore. "An Inner Harbor Timeline." Accessed February 16, 2011. http://baltimore.org/misc/uploads/meetingplannerspdf/Inner_Harbor_Timeline.pdf.

Visit Scotland. "All about Scotland." Accessed October 20, 2011. http://www.visitscotland.com/guide/scotland-factfile/.

———. "Scottish Climate." Accessed October 20, 2011. http://www.visitscotland.com/guide/scotland-factfile/geography/climate/.

Walton, John K. "Prospects in Tourism History: Evolution, State of Play, and Future Development." *Tourism Management* 30 (2009): 783–93.

Wearing, Stephen. *Volunteer Tourism: Experiences That Make a Difference*. Wallingford, UK: CABI, 2001.

Weaver, David B. "Comprehensive and Minimalist Dimensions of Ecotourism." *Annals of Tourism Research* 32, no. 2 (2005): 439–55.

Whyte, Ian D. *Landscape and History since 1500*. London: Reaktion Books, 2002.

The Wilds. "The Wilds." Accessed February 16, 2011. http://www.thewilds.org/.

Williams, Stephen. *Tourism Geography*. London: Routledge, 1998.

Wilson, Erica, and Donna E. Little. "A 'Relative Escape'? The Impact of Constraints on Women Who Travel Solo." *Tourism Review International* 9 (2005): 155–75.

———. "The Solo Female Travel Experience: Exploring the 'Geography of Women's Fear.'" *Current Issues in Tourism* 11, no. 2 (2008): 167–86.

Wimbledon 2010 Official Website. "About Wimbledon." Accessed November 23, 2010. http://aeltc2010.wimbledon.org/en_GB/about/guide/club.html.

Woods, Michael. *Rural Geography*. London: Sage, 2005.

World Commission on Environment and Development. *Our Common Future*. Accessed February 24, 2011. http://www.un-documents.net/wced-ocf.htm.

World Tourism Organization. *Collection of Tourism Expenditure Statistics, Technical Manual No. 2*. Madrid: World Tourism Organization, 1995. Accessed January 22, 2011. http://pub.unwto.org/WebRoot/Store/Shops/Infoshop/Products/1034/1034-1.pdf.

Zakaria, Fareed. "China Replicating Western Towns." *CNN Global Public Square Blogs*. June 21, 2011. Accessed July 5, 2011. http://globalpublicsquare.blogs.cnn.com/2011/06/21/china-replicating-western-cities/.

# Index

# About the Author

**Velvet Nelson** received her BS in business administration from West Liberty University, her MA in geography with a concentration in rural development from East Carolina University, and her PhD in geography from Kent State University. She joined the Department of Geography and Geology at Sam Houston State University in Huntsville, Texas, in 2006 and was promoted to associate professor in 2012. She is a human geographer with interests in cultural geography and human-environment interactions, but her primary research focus has been on tourism. She has conducted archival research on historical patterns of tourism in the Caribbean, as well as fieldwork on islands such as Dominica, Grenada, and St. Vincent to examine current issues. In 2010, she received a Fulbright Fellowship to teach and conduct research in Slovenia. She has published her research in peer-reviewed journal articles and presented it at regional, national, and international conferences both within geography and in the interdisciplinary field of tourism studies. In addition, she strongly believes in direct experience through travel as a means of learning about new places. As such, she travels at every opportunity.